Empowering the People of God

CATHOLIC PRACTICE IN NORTH AMERICA

Empowering the People of God

CATHOLIC ACTION BEFORE AND
AFTER VATICAN II

Edited by Jeremy Bonner, Christopher D. Denny,
and Mary Beth Fraser Connolly

FORDHAM UNIVERSITY PRESS
New York   2014

Fordham University Press has no responsibility for the persistence
or accuracy of URLs for external or third-party Internet websites
referred to in this publication and does not guarantee that any
content on such websites is, or will remain, accurate or appropriate.

Fordham University Press also publishes its books in a variety of
electronic formats. Some content that appears in print may not be
available in electronic books.

Library of Congress Cataloging-in-Publication Data

Empowering the people of God : Catholic action before and after
    Vatican II / edited by Jeremy Bonner, Christopher D. Denny, and
    Mary Beth Fraser Connolly. — First edition.
        pages cm. — (Catholic practice in North America)
    Includes bibliographical references and index.
    ISBN 978-0-8232-5400-2 (cloth : alk. paper)
    1. Catholic Action—United States—History—20th century.
    I. Bonner, Jeremy, editor of compilation.
    BX2348.Z6E47 2014
    267'.18273—dc23

                                                    2013017376

Printed in the United States of America

16 15 14   5 4 3 2 1

First edition

To our mothers and our fathers, laypeople who bore witness.

Contents

Acknowledgments

Like all collaborative publications, this book stands at the endpoint of years of planning, evolution, and consensus in which many people and institutions had a part. Special thanks are due to the Sisters of Mercy of the former Chicago Regional Community (now West Midwest), and especially its archivist, Joella Cunnane, R.S.M.; the reference and circulation librarians of Purdue University North Central; the Lilly Fellows Program in Humanities and the Arts; St. John's University and Brendan Hickey for research support; the archival staff at the Jewish Theological Seminary in New York City and the Woodstock College Archives at Georgetown University in Washington, D.C.; Joseph Komonchak, professor emeritus at the Catholic University of America; and Fredric Nachbaur and Will Cerbone at Fordham University Press.

Empowering the People of God

Introduction

JEREMY BONNER, JEFFREY M. BURNS,
AND CHRISTOPHER D. DENNY

The early 1960s were a heady time for Catholic laypeople. Almost overnight, it seemed, the winds of change had begun to blow through the corridors of the Vatican, ruffling the feathers of its clerical doorkeepers, while at the same time conveying an assurance to lay leaders throughout the world that the shaping of the Church's future was in their hands. By the close of the decade, a very different vista loomed. "Good" Pope John XXIII had died too soon, and the "progressive" legacy of the Second Vatican Council was repudiated by his "conservative" successor, Paul VI. Such representations—no matter how one-sided—constitute the essence of the theory of an unfinished revolution that has dominated the rhetoric of those Catholic activists who came of age between 1930 and 1960. Nowhere was this sense of missed opportunities more pronounced than among the American veterans of the struggle for greater lay autonomy, but in no other nation had lay Catholics come so far in so short a period of time.

The history of American Catholicism in the United States during the nineteenth century is a history of immigrant communities. While only a minority of Catholic parishes was officially designated for a specific ethnic group, the ethos of the enclave permeated Catholic parochial life. Non-Catholic suspicion of the ultimate loyalties of Catholic immigrants served only to reinforce the separatist mentality fostered by Catholic organizations ranging from such fraternal societies as the Knights of Columbus and the Daughters of Isabella to immigrant aid associations. In the parish, the priest served as ultimate arbiter of parish life, while male and female members of the congregation participated in activities tailored to their gender. Lay leadership operated within clearly defined limits and presumed its inevitable subordination to those in ordained ministry, and the notion that laypeople might have some responsibility for oversight of a parish's mission was a dangerous Protestant innovation. In the early days of the American Church, it had resulted in what was later termed the lay-trusteeship crisis, and priests and bishops of the early twentieth century had no intention of tolerating its recurrence.

With the rise of a second generation of American Catholics, many of whom (male *and* female) were born in the United States, educated in public schools and, in many cases, recipients of a college education, it was inevitable that habits of deference to clerical authority would erode. Despite outbreaks of anti-Catholic paranoia, particularly during the Tribal Twenties, American Catholics increasingly found themselves acknowledged as loyal citizens of the republic. Coincidentally, the Great Depression inflicted a mortal wound on the hitherto impregnable ethnic enclave. As ethnic banks and insurance companies closed their doors and chain stores displaced neighborhood markets, so the character of Catholicism moved ever closer to ethnic homogeneity.

Accompanying this cultural shift was the New Deal–inspired unionization of unskilled laborers—many of them practicing Catholics—in the mid-Atlantic and Midwest. Not only did this give rise to such sectarian entities as the Association of Catholic Trade Unionists, but it also brought working-class Catholics into association with their non-Catholic counterparts and ultimately into positions of national leadership. From 1941 to 1960, American Catholicism further consolidated its acceptability in non-Catholic eyes both by its participation in the Second World War and its vocal anticommunism in subsequent decades. In a decade notable for the anti-Catholic broadsides of Paul Blanshard, Senator Joseph McCarthy's aggressive campaign against communism helped affirm the patriotic credentials of his coreligionists

It is in such a context that the rise of Catholic Action, first defined by Pope Pius XI in 1931 as "the participation of the laity in the apostolate of the hierarchy," must be understood. This papal assertion both confirmed and promoted the transformation of lay Catholic identity then underway in Europe and the United States, as movements such as the settlement-house movement and the Jeunesse Ouvrière Chrétienne (JOC, or Young Christian Worker Movement) of Canon Joseph Cardijn of Belgium began to alter laypeople's understanding of their role in the Church. Thirty-one years later, Pope John XXIII, in opening the Second Vatican Council, further enhanced the role of the laity by proclaiming the Church to be the "people of God." The Council's confirmation and promotion of the laity's new status within the Church marked the fulfillment of three decades of development that had followed Pius XI's embrace of Catholic Action.

In the United States, pressure from the secular world for Catholics to conform to "American"standards of behavior inevitably cast a shadow over the Catholic enclave. Catholic Action, imported to the United States during the 1930s, promoted an integrated Catholicity purged of its ethnic accretions, while the initially more peripheral liturgical movement based at St. John's University in Collegeville, Minnesota, but spread by sympathetic priests throughout the country, promoted forms of parish worship that emphasized congregational participation over contemplation. It would prove a short step from such participation in the liturgy to the development of a conviction that priests were not uniquely qualified to oversee the Catholic community at prayer.

The process of ecclesiological Americanization of lay Catholics between 1930 and 1960 was only accentuated by the changes within the Church hierarchy. From a loosely associated body of diocesan fiefs, the American Church was transformed into an increasingly centralized national church body surmounted by the National Catholic Welfare Conference (although the NCWC enjoyed no formal conciliar status) and such ancillary agencies as the National Catholic Rural Life Conference. The presence of such Catholic clergy as Monsignor John Ryan and Bishop Francis Haas in consultative roles within the apparatus of Franklin Roosevelt's New Deal served notice that the Church need not be apolitical in its attitudes. Moreover, if priests might be involved in the affairs of the world, then laypeople might be tempted to seek greater involvement in the affairs of the Church. National Church agencies were less and less staffed principally by priests and bishops, and an inevitable distancing, sometimes subtle and sometimes not, occurred between the episcopal hierarchy and such bodies as the Christian Family Movement, the National Council of Catholic Men, and the National Council of Catholic Women. These newer entities relegated clerical involvement to an advisory role and relied on educated, middle-class laypeople who now were considered to have the capacity to read contemporary theology and conduct adult Christian formation.

Following the Second World War, as Catholics participated in the postwar boom and took advantage of the G.I. Bill of Rights, an increasingly well-educated Catholic middle class (more Catholics attended high school and college than ever before) emerged, with women also enjoying the fruits of the expansion of Catholic higher education. Like other Americans, many Catholics began to abandon the inner cities for the promise of suburban life. The old ethnic working-class neighborhoods began to dissolve even as more diverse suburban parishes arose. The demographic shift from an immigrant, urban, working-class Church to an educated, suburban middle-class Church would prompt the development of an entirely new definition of lay responsibility.

If laymen came into their own during the 1940s and 1950s, their wives, sisters, and daughters were not far behind. Traditional Catholic practice had relegated laywomen to a separate sphere of parish life, with parochial organizations that reflected that fact. The embourgeoisement of the American Catholic milieu challenged this paradigm by creating an increasingly sophisticated body of Catholic laywomen who challenged the absolute nature of the complementarity of the sexes. Whether as individuals, such as Maisie Ward, or in groups, such as the Grail, Catholic laywomen asserted a radical notion of personhood that suggested a greater equality of the sexes, at least by prevailing standards. The very modus operandi of the Christian Family Movement, the poster child of lay Catholics during the 1950s, downplayed male headship of the family and emphasized the necessity of co-parenting by Catholic spouses. To be a Catholic and active in the world, a woman need no longer join a sisterhood or confine her sphere to hearth and home. There might still be limits on what one could apply from the tenets of secular feminism, but such attitudes were no longer absolutely forbidden. Similar sentiments were apparent among many of the female religious orders during the 1950s, most notably among the cadres of the Sister Formation Movement, which promoted greater education and enhanced leadership roles for women religious.

For many Catholic men and Catholic women, therefore, the announcement by Pope John XXIII of his intention to summon an ecumenical council served as confirmation of a process that they had been undergoing as individuals and congregations for twenty or thirty years. The Church in which they had been raised had largely shed its pariah status in the American civic landscape. The election in 1960 of a Catholic president who pledged not to allow the views of the Church's hierarchy to compromise his political judgment confirmed the full accommodation of

American Catholics to the modern world. As American bishops flocked to Rome to begin their deliberations, Catholic and secular journalists alike speculated on the characteristics of the future Church to which the Council would inevitably give rise.

Historiography of the Second Vatican Council has tended to oscillate between paradigms of renewal and revolution. On the one hand are those scholars who identify a fundamental continuity between Catholic tradition and the "renewal" promoted by the Council; on the other are those who view the Council as constituting a dramatic break (whether for good or ill) with the past. Their divergence is particularly noteworthy when it comes to consideration of conciliar pronouncements on the place of the laity in the life of the Church, to which the American episcopal contingent greatly contributed. Previously marginalized in the preconciliar Church, the American bishops succeeded in contextualizing their views in conciliar pronouncements ranging from liturgical renewal to religious freedom. Their interventions, widely reported in secular and religious media, conveyed the impression to many laypeople in their dioceses that essentially American values had come to inform how the Catholic Church related to the world. It is hardly surprising that expectations about lay participation would be dramatically raised in the mid-1960s only to be dashed by the close of the decade.

The Second Vatican Council coincided with several profound disruptions of the secular realm. The Council called for laypeople to act prophetically, even as the civil-rights movement gave them a prophetic cause. The Council promoted equality in the sight of God, even as the feminist movement urged women not to confine themselves to designated gender roles. The Council spoke of bishops and priests working with laypeople entrusted to their charge, even as radical student movements bemoaned the absence of real democracy even in nominally democratic systems. As the conciliar documents emerged, educated laypeople studied them, discussed their practical implications, and frequently imparted to them meanings that were sometimes far removed from those envisaged by the Council Fathers. Such phrases as "democracy and equality" and "participation and justice" were incorporated into the lingua franca of Catholic lay activists whose ecclesiology looked more and more Protestant in form. Then, like an earthquake, came Pope Paul VI's decision in 1968 not to publish the report of the Birth Control Commission and then to promulgate the encyclical

Humanae Vitae. The postconciliar atmosphere took on a political quality in which the American hierarchy found itself ranged against some of the most engaged of its priests and laypeople. In the wake of the encyclical, the laicization of disillusioned priests and religious would accelerate, and Catholic triumphalism gave way to a period of retrenchment. Never again would the Catholic hierarchy enjoy the same commitment from the laity as a whole that it had enjoyed over the previous century.

The present collection of essays provides a fresh look at the Catholic laity and its relationship with the hierarchy in the era immediately preceding the Second Vatican Council and in the turbulent era that followed. It demonstrates that the transformation of the laity was well under way before the Council, as various forms of Catholic Action then flourishing in the United States gave laymen and laywomen an ever-increasing role in the life of the Church. The essays explore a diverse assortment of manifestations of Catholic Action, ranging from genteel reform to radical activism, and an equally wide variety of locales, apostolates, and movements. The central theme that unites these essays is the growing confidence of the Catholic laity, which proclaimed a new understanding of the Church and the laity's role within it. The new understanding might best be summed up in Pope Pius XII's assurance to the laity: "You do not belong to the Church. You are the Church."

Catholic Action in the preconciliar era remains an underexamined area. Few studies have been undertaken that connect the developments in lay activism before the Council with the new understanding of laity that emerged following the Council. Catholic Action has often been presented in rather narrow terms, limited to movements such as the study clubs of the National Conferences of Catholic Men and Catholic Women, or the Legion of Decency's monitoring of the movie industry. At best, scholarship has highlighted the difference between official Catholic Action (approved by the hierarchy) and the specialized Catholic Action movements, such as the Christian Family Movement, that employed Cardinal Cardijn's observe-judge-act formula. The essays of this study demonstrate that preconciliar Catholic Action was neither narrow nor monolithic. Rather, it was noted for its breadth, richness, diversity, and dynamism.

As rich as Catholic Action was before the Council, lay activity in its immediate aftermath exploded and headed in directions not easily controlled by traditional authority. The post–Vatican II laity built on the accomplishments of the preconciliar Church but forged new roles and developed a new understanding of their role, an understanding that their forebears might have had difficulty comprehending. Their newfound confidence emboldened the laity to challenge Church authority in ways previously thought unthinkable. Even as lay Catholic Action flourished in the preconciliar Church, Pope Pius XI's earlier definition of Catholic Action implied a darker side. If laypeople were only now invited to participate in the "apostolate of the hierarchy," what in fact had been their role before? In the classic understanding, there was a fundamental distinction between the lay and the clerical states. The clergy were the "Church Teaching" and the laity was the "Church Taught." Laypeople were docilely to receive directions from the clergy and hierarchy and to follow their lead. For the most part, holiness was left to the religious professionals. The laity, in the now-familiar dictum, were to "pay, pray, and obey," and throughout the era we are examining there was an abiding mistrust of the laity. In San Francisco, William Issel notes that while Archbishop John J. Mitty pushed and supported lay Catholic Action, he appointed a clerical watchdog "so that the group would keep within the reservation." In the same vein, we may take note of Frank Sheed's quip that many priests "were more afraid of the laity than of the Communists," or observe in Mary Henold's study of the National Council of Catholic Women one priest's concern that there were too many chiefs and not enough Indians in the Church. Anecdotal, perhaps, but such reactions reflect a deep suspicion or mistrust of the laity that survived well after the Second Vatican Council affirmed the role of the laity. The great liturgical reformer Virgil Michel summed up the problem best: "Some day an 'official teacher' will have to [restate] the age-old doctrine that the lay folk are not merely trained dogs but true living members of the Church and in their way true Apostles of Christ."[1]

Preconciliar U.S. Catholics demonstrated a cohesiveness, assurance, and confidence born of a common worldview. Historian Philip Gleason has argued that the Catholic philosophical system known as "neoscholasticism" was the glue holding together what he calls an "organic Catholic culture" and that it provided the "ideology" for the preconcilar Church.[2] The context was understandable. Catholic identity was clear, and the world could be transformed to bring "all things to Christ." The evil forces attacking the Church and modern society were also clear: secularism, materialism, communism, anti-Catholicism—all reflecting an "anti-Christian civilization." Catholicism had the antidote. But Catholic culture was defined not just by what it was against. Catholics strove to realize and implement the idea of the Mystical Body of Christ, a concept that assured laypeople that they were integral parts of the most intimate reality of the Church and part of the Mystical Body of Christ. Secure in that knowledge, lay Catholics could confront the world and work to "restore all things in Christ."

For the most part, the Catholic laity acted in respectful collaboration with the hierarchy. If they thought of themselves as adjuncts to the hierarchy (as many bishops regarded them), they nevertheless took their role seriously, and in so doing they sowed the seeds for subsequent calls for the assumption of autonomy and responsibility that blossomed following the Council. The transformation of the laity dramatically affected the relationship between the laity and the clergy. As the laity's role expanded, the identity of clergy and hierarchy was also transformed. What was the clergy's role in light of the new lay assertiveness? The role of the bishop? What was the role of women? Of women religious? The Church found itself in unexplored territory. Complicating matters, the dynamism of the laity coincided with a burst of social activism in the larger culture during the 1960s, with the civil-rights, antiwar, and women's movements making "rights" language common in American parlance. To Catholic lay activists, inspired by the freedom born of the Council, the talk of rights made eminent sense. The once-docile laity of the preconciliar Church might now view the Church as "oppressor," as did many women in the 1970s. Challenges to authority on the basis of "rights" became regular occurrences. The new aggressiveness of progressive lay enthusiasts, who invoked the "Spirit of Vatican II," gave rise to a conservative backlash. Lay groups such as Catholics United for the Faith (CUF), who argued that such activists had "hijacked" the Council and that a brake was needed to restore the Council's true meaning, proliferated in the late 1960s and 1970s and laid the foundation for the present polarization of the Church.

The first five chapters of this book examine the preconciliar lay apostolate. The first is a study by Patrick Hayes of a rather genteel form of Catholic Action—the Catholic Club of the City of New York (CCCNY). The CCCNY represents Catholic Action in its broadest formulation, less an action movement than a gentlemen's club serving the professional, intellectual, social, and entertainment needs of well-to-do Catholics in New York. This is not to say that the Club did not encourage service. At the prompting of Cardinal Patrick Hayes, members of the Club worked diligently to promote and support the Cardinal's Catholic Charities initiatives. Furthermore, like many other Catholic Action groups, the Club reflected a moral conservatism that promoted "decent literature" and a more "moral public media." Cardinal Hayes thus articulated a new concept of lay action, for the Catholic Charities campaign was intended to "arouse the responsibility of the laity. The care of Catholic Charities . . . does not all rest with the clergy." Although the cardinal promoted greater lay responsibility, it was still largely under his guidance, and New York's Catholic laity remained adjuncts to the cardinal. Much of the importance of the essay is that it explores an element of the Catholic community that is often neglected—the Catholic upper class. Small though it may have been in this era, it made significant contributions to the Church.

Katharine Harmon's chapter, by contrast, captures the importance of the liturgical movement to Catholic Action. Indeed, the success of the liturgical movement depended upon the active participation of the laity in the liturgy. Laypeople took what they experienced in the liturgy into the world, prompting liturgical advocates such as Virgil Michel to assert that the liturgy was the basis of social regeneration. Even more surprisingly, lay women played a very important role in promoting the liturgical renewal.

Harmon examines the National Council of Catholic Women (NCCW), publisher Maisie Ward, and the American Grail Movement, each of which participated in the Liturgical Movement and helped promote the concept of the Mystical Body. In 1929, the NCCW sponsored a study-club program on the liturgy, to which the response of NCCW members was overwhelmingly positive, reflecting the enthusiasm of a "new generation" of young Catholic laywomen both for the liturgy and the possibilities of adult education. It was to such young Catholics that Maisie Ward, who with her husband Frank Sheed established the publishing house of Sheed and Ward, exposed the best of contemporary European Catholic theological thought. Once again, young Catholic laywomen revealed an intellectual hunger demanding to be met. By contrast, the Grail, which was perhaps the most significant women's apostolate in the preconciliar era, initially did not conceive of itself in such terms. The Grail trained young women to be "apostles" by emphasizing the centrality of the Eucharist to social action; immersion in the liturgical movement would lead to deeper involvement in Catholic Action. Harmon points out that the increased participation of women in the liturgical movement created new avenues for women and inspired a new understanding of Catholic womanhood that resulted in an increasing dissatisfaction with the traditional concept of what was acceptable for women within the Church. This tension was, for the most part, suppressed in the preconciliar Church but came to full flower after the Council.

William Issel's insightful chapter examines the impact of Catholic culture and lay Catholic Action on the public and political culture of San Francisco. With the assistance of layman Sylvester Andriano, Archbishop John Mitty promoted Catholic Action in San Francisco through the agency of the Catholic Men of San Francisco (organized in 1938). The Catholic Men did engage with traditional Catholic Action concerns such as indecent literature and vice, but its most significant contribution came in the articulation of Catholic social teaching in a manner that made a lasting impact on urban life and urban political culture. Future San Francisco mayors Jack Shelley and Joseph Alioto were both schooled in Catholic Action, which subsequently informed their style of political governance. Alioto clearly internalized Catholic Action principles in his promotion of a just moral economy grounded in a notion of the common good, just as Shelley's experience in the labor movement led him to emphasize Catholic labor theory. Issel contends that Catholic teaching on labor issues became part of the general San Francisco ethos, as Catholic Action themes resonated with the general public and directly influenced public discourse and policy. In sum, Catholic Action in San Francisco achieved one of its stated goals: the integration of Catholic thought with the non-Catholic world, an unprecedented synthesis.

Christopher Denny's chapter takes a new look at John Courtney Murray. Though best known for his novel interpretations of the American experience in light of the Church's teaching on Church and state, Murray also made a significant contribution to the theology of Catholic Action. In the course of reviewing Murray's early writings, which offer a theological justification for the role of lay Catholic Action in the transformation of society, Denny explores the changing nature of the Church in history and places Catholic Action "within a historical trajectory that demonstrates how the Church moved from a predominantly institutional conception of itself towards a self-definition of emancipated Catholic Christians acting for the greater good within a properly differentiated society."

Denny further argues that Murray "was not an activist but an educator" who sought an "intellectual grounding for the Catholic culture that the activist apostolates labored to create." Murray saw Catholic Action as a bridge between Church and society and rejected "seminary theology" as too ethereal and lacking in practical application for the real world. Catholic Action required a lived theology that the ordinary Catholic could take into the world. (In some ways, this might seem to presage the call for relevance that became central to the postconciliar Church). Significantly for Murray, Catholic Action "respected the distinction between the temporal and spiritual orders while simultaneously working to reform temporal society." Lay Catholics would play a pivotal role in the advent of the next stage of the Church and the transformation of society. While it is hard to demonstrate the extent of Murray's impact on Catholic Action, his reflections had a clear relevance to the lay activist of the 1940s and 1950s.

The final chapter dealing with traditional Catholic Action is Mary Elizabeth Brown's study of two post–Second World War Italian American Catholic Action groups, one in Boston and the other in Washington, D.C., both directed by the Scalabrinian Fathers, further reflecting the breadth of what was considered Catholic Action. As Brown notes, these groups were less about Catholic Action and more about "sustaining ethnic culture." Indeed, with their emphasis on social events and not social action, they were more extensions of the Italian national parish than Catholic Action. In many ways the clubs operated as poor-men's CCCNYs, but with a special ethnic dimension. While Brown argues that the clubs assisted the transformation of the immigrant community into an Italian American community, they seem to have done little to develop lay leadership and remained largely under the control of the clergy.

The second section of this book addresses the transformation of lay identity and the emergence of the concept of the People of God in the postconciliar Church. The Second Vatican Council's affirmation of the dignity of the lay vocation gave rise to an explosion of new possibilities for lay Catholics. Laymen and laywomen were increasingly considered autonomous, critical, independent agents, striving to find a place and a voice in a Church that had long undervalued their counsel and experience. New lay assertiveness often found itself in conflict with clerical authority, a conflict that dovetailed with the general questioning of authority so prevalent in the United States in the 1960s. Authority seemed to be under assault everywhere, and the frequently clumsy response of ecclesial and secular leaders only exacerbated the problem. "[If] as is true in every order today, authority is challenged," Cardinal John Dearden, archbishop of Detroit observed, "we must recognize the challenge for what it is. Most often it is not authority that is questioned, but the way in which authority is exercised. . . . If authority is to retain credibility, it must function in a manner different from that of the past." Bishops, clergy and laity all struggled with new notions of authority that involved such concepts as shared responsibility, collegiality, and adult responsibility. No longer were the dictates of bishop and clergy to go unchallenged, but how were such new notions of authority to come into being? What would the new structures look like?

Influencing the debate over authority was an equally central theme of the 1960s—the search for relevance and authenticity. Rejecting what they perceived as the conformity and hypocrisy of the 1950s, young Americans sought a more authentic way of being, a deeper sense of meaning in their lives, the "really real." Inspired by the Council, young Catholics shared in the era's search for meaning and relevance, but what did this mean in practical terms, and could it even be achieved within the Church? The questioning inspired both by the era and by the Council called into question many previously unchallenged verities of Church and society. The new Church was deeply influenced by the new laity, and the final six chapters of this book explore the reality of the new laity and their vision of the Church. They provide six rich case histories of these new developments, ranging from Chicago, Detroit and Pittsburgh to Oklahoma and Atlanta, and explore the attempt by the laity to implement the concept of the People of God at the national, diocesan, and local levels.

In her examination of the Extension Lay Volunteer Program (ELV), Elizabeth Duclos-Orsello not only captures the enthusiasm and promise of the 1960s in Church and society but also highlights two of the central themes of the postconciliar era—the search for relevance and the new possibilities available to women. Extension was a domestic missionary

program designed to assist the poorest parishes in some of the most neglected areas of the United States. The vast majority of the volunteers
were young Catholic laywomen who sought to serve Church and society
and whose enthusiasm and optimism the ELV sought to channel. While
initially setting out to serve the institutional needs of the Church, the
young volunteers found that their work also fulfilled their personal, spiritual, and professional needs. Operating as a Catholic alternative to the
Peace Corps, ELV addressed the 1960s' quest for relevance and authenticity, providing young women with an outlet for service to American society
and a means of applying Catholic social teaching in the world. Equally
important, ELV represented an alternative to the convent and sodality for
young Catholic women who wished to move out into the world to serve
Church and society. As Duclos-Orsello puts it, ELV offered a "new and
different way of being Catholic and female." That new way gave rise to a
newfound confidence that allowed young women to assert themselves
against authority figures within the Church.

Mary Beth Fraser Connolly, by contrast, engages the problem of lay
identity from the singular perspective of laicization of women religious,
whether by overt rejection of a formal commitment to the vowed religious
life or redefinition of the terms under which women religious exercised
their vocation. Focusing on those Sisters of Mercy of the Union engaged
in parochial education, Connolly identifies a yearning on the part of
women religious for inclusion in the life and work of the Church on equal
terms with the laity. In place of the 1950s wall of separation that separated them from laymen and laywomen of the parishes they served, many
Sisters of Mercy came to see their predominant role not as shapers of a
new generation of Catholics but as servants to the last, the least, and the
lost, of whatever color, ethnicity, or creed. The process of renewal within
their congregation merely accelerated a trend, toward individual autonomy among members of female religious, that had been brewing since the
mid-1950s. Absent the sacramental faculties of the priest, many sisters
increasingly viewed their vocation as little different from that of the committed layperson. In such fashion did the mission of Catholic Action com-
municate itself to a community that its founder would never have
imagined had need of it.

Mary Henold further develops the new understanding of women in the
postconciliar era with her examination of the National Conference of

Catholic Women (NCCW), the national Catholic organization for women overseen by the U.S. Bishops and derided by feminists as an "antifeminist" organization. Henold, however, demonstrates that during the mid-1960s, at least, the NCCW was open to the new possibilities for women and undertook a serious reevaluation of the traditional Catholic understanding of the role of women. Indeed, NCCW executive director Margaret Mealey set the tone in 1966 by challenging bishops and clergy who "are reluctant to let them [women] fly" and stressing the need to make the Church "relevant in the world." Henold suggests that "moderate and even conservative women [espoused] feminist ideas before the definition of 'feminist' hardened into something they could no longer support," most notably in respect to abortion and the Equal Rights Amendment.

Until the elevation of these issues, however, Catholic women were open to exploring the ideas of the women's movement in the light of Vatican II. Women were encouraged to look beyond home and parish, to "embrace . . . adult discipleship" and reject traditional subservience of women, but old habits proved hard to break. The deference of the preconciliar era persisted even as the new understanding of woman flourished. As the editor of the NCCW journal *Word* observed somewhat sardonically in 1968: "Isn't it amazing to realize that women, who . . . are teachers, lawyers, nurses, doctors, secretaries, and manage the great institution called home . . . become simpering idiots in their communication and understanding with the parish priest?" Be that as it may, the NCCW's new understanding of women often brought them into conflict with the Church authorities, and though they did not self-identify as feminists, they readily employed feminist language and concepts, at least until the early 1970s.

The problem of confronting authority was not limited to women and their newfound understanding of Church but pervaded almost all aspects of life during the 1960s. In his chapter, Jeremy Bonner assesses the attempt to adopt democratic structures at the parochial and diocesan levels in a Church unused to democratic structures. To democratize the Church required a major restructuring of power and authority, which in turn required a major revisioning and understanding of Church, interest in which was far from universal, particularly among those in authority. What, they asked, would democratizing mean for the authority of the priest and the bishop, and even for Church teaching? What would be the effect of acknowledging lay responsibility in and for the Church? What would the transfer of some power to the laity look like?

Bonner examines two bishops who, in varying degrees, embraced the new understanding of lay participation, Bishop John Wright of Pittsburgh and Bishop Victor Reed of Oklahoma City and Tulsa. Both encouraged parish councils and diocesan pastoral councils and both sought the transfer of real power to the laity. Their openness contrasted with a greater reticence on the part of some of their fellow bishops, who feared the loss of their authority. Nonetheless, laypeople increasingly reveled in their newfound status within the Church, however reluctantly granted, and while bishops and clergy imagined they were "sharing authority," the laity looked for real concessions. Bonner observes that while most of the Pittsburgh laity "acknowledged a sphere reserved solely for clerical adjudication, it was far smaller than many bishops and priests appeared to think." As a result, the brakes were applied to the transfer of power to the laity, and traditional authority reasserted itself. "Authority had reasserted itself," Bonner concludes somewhat dolefully, "and the expansive dreams of Catholic liberals were over." The experience of exercising authority and responsibility, however, gave rise to a more contentious laity that more readily questioned and even challenged Church authority, undercutting the clarity of hierarchical identity so valued in the preconciliar Church.

Samuel Thomas expands on this theme of redefined authority by examining the pronouncements of another prelate who sought to empower the laity, Cardinal John Dearden of Detroit, the first president of the National Conference of Catholic Bishops. Dearden advanced a vision, inspired by the Council, of a Church that was in the world and had to engage the world but was not "above" the world. Central to the new notion of engagement was the concept of the shared responsibility of laypeople. Dearden's commitment to decentralizing authority was evident in his archdiocesan synod of 1969 and in the controversial national Call to Action conference in 1976. He represented a new style of episcopal authority that took seriously the Council's admonition that clerical authority was a "ministry of service" to be exercised collegially. His personal gifts, especially useful in a time of transition, enabled him to be comfortable with "ambiguity" and "diversity," and he embodied the elusive "Spirit of Vatican II," allowing more participatory decision-making (perhaps also a reflection of the secular activists' call for participatory democracy in the United States).

Dearden espoused less clericalism and a gentle personalism that valued persons over institutions, and his vision of Church was rooted in the person of Jesus rather than in papal or magisterial teaching. Though he recognized the difficulty in realizing the new authority, he believed that it had to be attempted, and he was aware that the process was as important as the teaching. "I know if I want to win cooperation and the understanding of those with whom I am working, priests, religious and laymen," he insisted, "I must be prepared to participate with them in the process of moving toward the decisions that have to be made. It is a reality. . . . This is the process that is important to the life of the Church. In our own stumbling, bumbling way we are trying to reflect our understanding and faith of what it means to be a member of a Christian Community."

The dangers posed by the new style of authority are evident in the final chapter by Andrew Moore, which explores the experimental parish community of Christ Our Brother in Atlanta. Created to explore ministries that traditional parishes could not fully address, including ministries dedicated to social justice, ecumenism, and liturgical renewal, the experimental status of Christ Our Brother gave it greater leeway, but the community (and its pastor) quickly overstepped the archdiocese's vision of the project. Archbishop Paul Hallinan and his auxiliary bishop, Joseph Bernardin, had hoped to empower the laity as Archbishop Dearden had done but with "appropriate pastoral oversight and respect for Church authority." The experimental parish quickly spiraled out of control as the pastor and lay members of the community "substituted the authority of their own consciences and the democratic consensus of the community for the authority of the Archbishop and Church teaching." The result was almost constant conflict between the parish and diocesan leaders. The community and its pastor became increasingly critical of the Church, impatient with the speed with which they perceived change within the Church was being implemented, and disgusted by official timidity on social issues. Moore describes the pastor's behavior as "erratic" and even "heretical." Despite the open conflict with Church authority, the community argued that the parish should be maintained as a "safety valve" for Catholics discouraged by traditional parish life, but the intransigence of the pastor and the refusal of the community to defer to the diocesan authorities in any way resulted in its dissolution. Indeed, the pastor ultimately left the priesthood as well. The antinomian impulse in the parish represented a real and ongoing challenge as the Church tried to adapt to new modes of authority.

The essays in this book chart the development of lay Catholic identity from the preconciliar to the postconciliar era, from Catholic Action to the People of God. During the preconciliar era, laypeople assumed a new identity that respected their dignity and gifts, mobilizing them for leadership in the world rather than within the Church per se. They were now allowed to "participate in the apostolate of the hierarchy," and Catholic Action was not to be limited to clergy and religious. The result was an explosion of lay apostolates, charitable, liturgical, civic, intellectual, and even ethnic. The laity's newfound understanding of itself sowed the seeds for the frenzied activity that followed the Second Vatican Council. Inspired by the Council, the laity, embracing the concept of the People of God, increasingly demanded greater responsibility, autonomy, and power. Conscience became a watchword of the era, as did the search for relevance in and to the world. The newly invigorated laity sought to bring both a new Church and a new world into being. Their vision of an adult empowered laity conflicted with the preconceptions of a clergy and episcopacy that were less than enthused about relinquishing power. While exceptions such as Wright, Reed, and Dearden existed, their vision of lay empowerment could not hold the day.

Nonetheless, the central problems of authority and identity that plagued the postconciliar era had been engaged. How were new modes of authority to be implemented that respected the new lay identity? How was identity to be maintained as the authority of the Church began to splinter? How much authority could be surrendered to laypeople? How was the teaching authority of the Church to be maintained? None of these are easy questions, but one recent study suggests that they persist in the contemporary Church.[3] The new lay identity that has emerged will most likely never revert to the deference and docility of earlier days. For better or for worse, the Church has to engage an educated, reflective, questioning laity, intent on understanding the rationale behind Church teaching and actions and on being heard. It is our hope that the essays in this volume will contribute to a better understanding of why Catholic lay identity, both its self-understanding and its mission, have been transformed over the course of the last century.

Part I: Catholic Action

1   Catholic Action in the Archdiocese of New York

The Case of the Catholic Club of New York City

PATRICK J. HAYES

The roots of Catholic Action in the Archdiocese of New York are to be found in the long nineteenth century.[1] Though evident in some of the works of Pope Leo XIII and Pope Pius X, the parameters of Catholic Action are limned only in specific contexts. Because such early papal writings on the subject were intended largely for Italian audiences, there was no specific aspect of Catholic Action that took on a transalpine character or became universally binding, even among such lay-dominated initiatives as the European Jocist movement in the 1920s, which only gradually made a crossing to America in any significant way in the aftermath of the Second World War.[2] Catholic Action in its European incarnations did not affect American Catholic groups, except those, such as the Sons of Italy, which maintained deep ties to their mother country.[3] Such groups, however, were largely confined to immigrant aid; they did not have a broader vision of transforming society in and through Christ. Most papal directives, such as Pius X's *Il Fermo Proposito* (1905), were addressed to Italian bishops. Nevertheless, when it was printed in the *Acta Sanctae Sedis* in both Latin and Italian, a note prefixed to the Latin version suggested the encyclical's merits to Catholics everywhere.[4] Less astute observers could easily miss this, with the result that widespread understanding of the nature of Catholic Action was neither immediate nor absolute, leaving considerable room for novel and creative forms.

A peculiar difficulty in formulating a definition of Catholic Action is that it can be "used to designate both a concept and an organization of laity" or the place where laity work out "the church's actual engagement in the world and in politics."[5] Neither a philosophy nor a movement, let alone a particular instantiation of each, it was groping for clarification. That came in 1922 through Pope Pius XI's first encyclical, *Ubi Arcano Dei Consilio*, which directed the world's bishops:

Tell your faithful children of the laity that when, united with their pastors and their bishops, they participate in the works of the apostolate, both individual and social, the end purpose of which is to make Jesus Christ better known and better loved, then they are more than ever "a chosen generation, a kingly priesthood, a holy nation, a purchased people," of whom St. Peter spoke in such laudatory terms (I Peter 2:9). Then, too, they are more than ever united with Us and with Christ, and become great factors in bringing about world peace because they work for the restoration and spread of the Kingdom of Christ.[6]

In May 1923, less than six months after *Ubi Arcano*'s release, the pope continued to encourage Catholic Action:

There is no one who does not see of what advantage it is, not only for the life of religion and the good of the Church, but even for civic culture and the interests of human society. . . . Accordingly in the Encyclical [*Ubi Arcano*] we have mentioned we have said openly and clearly that this Catholic Action belongs without doubt to the pastoral ministry, on the one hand, and, on the other, to Christian life, so that whatsoever is done towards increasing or lessening it would seem to be done towards the guarding or violating of the rights of the Church and souls.[7]

The bonds between sacred pastors and the lay faithful were instrumental for the leavening effects of Catholic Action, though their relation was heavily weighted toward clerical leadership and lay obedience. Gradually, lay Catholics perceived that despite the privileged place still accorded the clergy, organized lay work in apostolic fields of endeavor now enjoyed a new standing. So frequently did the pope return to this theme that by 1928 Catholic Action had acquired its now classic definition, easily internalized, and economically phrased: "Catholic Action has no other purpose than the participation of the laity in the apostolate of the hierarchy."[8]

Though Pope Pius XI would not formally endorse Catholic Action until 1931, with his encyclical *Non Abbiamo Bisogno* the tenets and practices of a host of groups that fell under its rubric were already well organized and under way. The postwar openness to forms of Catholic Action that could be adapted to local circumstances was manifested in the Archdiocese of New York, where a special kinship between the wider metropolis and those directly involved in Catholic Action dated back to at least 1809, when Jesuit Father Anthony Kohlmann instituted a subscription to benefit the city's poor and where, in 1817, Catholic laypeople incorporated, by act of the legislature, the New York Catholic Benevolent Society for orphaned children.[9]

In the popular mind, however, throughout much of the nineteenth century, Catholic contributions to social welfare were viewed as unwelcome intrusions into civic life and a drain on city finances. Only at the outset of the twentieth century were there pronounced advances in organized charitable works of social consequence. While the latter included such ventures as the early Catholic Worker houses, the Laymen's League for Retreats and Social Studies, and the launch of the Association of Catholic Trade Unionists (ACTU), the archdiocese itself proved an especially fertile field for a form of Catholic Action that was devoted to projects that complemented the ministries of the hierarchy through the shared expenditure of time, talent, and treasure.[10] Each of these organizations was concerned in some way with the laborer and his spiritual dignity, but there were other social strata that were also engaged. In this chapter, I offer a portrait of a relationship between Archbishop (later Cardinal) Patrick Joseph Hayes (no relation to this author) during his tenure as New York's chief pastor (1919–38), and the Catholic Club of the City of New York (CCCNY). Both of have been understudied, and their intersections provide an interesting instance of lay participation in the mission of the hierarchy.

The CCCNY and New York's Archbishops

Both Hayes and the CCCNY grew up together. The cardinal was born on the Lower East Side, on the fringes of the infamous Five Points, on November 20, 1867, while the original incarnation of the CCCNY was the St. Xavier Alumni Sodality, established at 15th Street in Manhattan, in 1863.[11] By 1871 it had added to its spiritual responsibilities a concern with providing continuing education to alumni of St. Francis Xavier College. Under the guidance of Father Patrick Dealy, S.J., who later became president of St. John's College at Rose Hill, the sodality opened its ranks to non-alumni and became known as the Xavier Union, under whose name it was chartered by the State of New York. On January 1, 1888, the name of the Xavier Union was changed to the Catholic Club of the City of New York. According to its constitution and bylaws for 1891:

Its purposes [sic], further, to promote the study of good books, and to foster a taste for the sciences and art; but it intends more especially to exert itself in awakening and keeping alive an interest in Catholic history and literature. While pursuing these ends, it has in view to give its members every desirable means for proper recreation, both of mind and of body. Thus, by guarding youth against the temptations of youth itself, and by withdrawing it from the no less insidious than dangerous associations of a city, the Club hopes to encourage educated young men to the proper use of both mind and body, and to make them ambitious to be and to do good, that they may exert upon society that influence which is a duty.[12]

From its inception CCCNY's Committee on Catholic interests arranged all Club activities relating to the faith, including cooperative endeavors with the archbishop. In 1889, a group of some of the city's wealthiest Catholics settled on the site of a new clubhouse. In 1892, a new building was erected at 120 59th Street—what is today 122 Central Park South—at a cost of nearly a quarter of a million dollars. The Club's five stories were exquisitely appointed, as befitting the best of New York City's social clubs, though it was smaller in scale than the Metropolitan or Knickerbocker Clubs a few short blocks away. Built in the Italian Renaissance style, it contained a suite of parlors for billiards, cards, smoking, and dining—the ladies having their own tearoom. The main stairwell was constructed of English oak, and in the upper floors were stately mantelpieces that supplied an air of solidity and understated elegance. Wall hangings included tapestries in velour from various parts of Europe and a portrait of George Washington by Gilbert Stuart. After 1909, the basement had a bowling alley lit by tungsten lamps, while the second floor contained a ballroom. On floors 4 and 5 were bachelor apartments. The third floor was marked by an imposing library that boasted some fifty thousand volumes at its zenith.[13] Throughout the year, tournaments in bowling, bridge, and billiards, together with music, lectures, and evening smokers or "bachelors' dances" occupied members, often in conjunction with the old Xavier Alumni Sodality. In addition, the U.S. Catholic Historical Society presented its annual lecture at the Club.

Woolen baron Charles V. Fornes, who devoted thousands of dollars of his money to the provision of furnishings, art, and books, was the CCCNY's president at the time of its opening on Central Park South. It was this prominent New Yorker—chairman of the New York board of aldermen, trustee or director of several corporations, and future congressman from New York (1907–13)—who in 1890 first approached Archbishop Michael Corrigan about the laity's plan to erect the club house, thereby beginning a long and harmonious relationship between the CCCNY and the archbishops of New York. After Corrigan's death in 1902, Fornes commented: "I shall never forget the radiance of his countenance as he spoke, in his memorable gentle tones, of his cordial approval of the club's enterprise, and of his continued interest in its behalf. Gently he rested his hand on my arm, saying, 'Yes, it is time that the social work of the Church should be represented by a central home of art, literature, and science.'"[14] The link between lay action and the need for a cultured approach to social problems was something befitting Catholic New York. And though Corrigan's approbation of the cause was given in a whisper, the message reverberated loudly in Fornes's encomium and, more importantly, in the deeds of his fellows.

Thus began a very different kind of Catholic Action—one that served both the spiritual aspirations of its members and their intellectual formation, all for the sake of putting the whole man into service for Church and society. These Catholic leaders were largely self-made, dedicating themselves to assuming positions in New York society largely off limits to their parents in the nineteenth century, while showing their fealty to their Church in the process. Unlike the Jocists, for instance, among whom Catholic leaders were cultivated and trained, the elites of the Catholic Club came as ready and able assistants who needed little coaxing from the hierarchy. Unlike the Jocists, the CCCNY did not seek to strip away social standing in an effort to Christianize the masses. Its members were the masses. In a city like New York, the goals for lifting up one's fellow man were different. No one needed to be convinced of the inherent dignity of the foreigner, for instance, because many in the Catholic Club were from families not long off the boat. The products of upstanding families, CCCNY men were well educated and moving into social circles that were both profitable and interested in spiritual comradeship outside the usual Sunday obligation. It is difficult to ascertain why applicants sought entrance and were willing to pay the fifty-dollar entrance fee, but surely one reason was to seek social advancement in the company of fellow believers—from whatever ethnic group or profession. They knew that cooperation could bring mutual benefit. The city was the place to cultivate that cooperation; the Club, its conduit.

As the city's Catholics rose in number throughout the long nineteenth century, there grew up a vast web of Catholic city employees who could be found at many levels within the postal union, shipping and conveyance trades, and in police and fire services; in short, they packed three vital sectors—communications, transportation (mostly logistics), and safety. Of course, Catholics were leaders in other professions during this period and these were, in the main, the CCCNY's members. They could be found at all levels of city government, real estate and contracting, mercantile concerns, insurance, banking, and at the bar. The New York judiciary, from the lower courts to the appellate divisions, contained many faithful Catholics, dozens of whom were members of the Catholic Club. The Catholic nouveau riche gathered to enjoy a smoke or a game of cards, but it was also a place for serious men to find solutions to New York City's social problems. In August 1922, with the popular media increasingly devoid of moral content, Club members heard the concerns of John S. Sumner, the secretary of the New York Society for the Suppression of Vice and successor in that office to the late Anthony Comstock. Sumner's topic was a proposed voluntary submission of book manuscripts for review, and his talk was followed by remarks from Judge Alfred Talley and Father Daniel Quinn, S.J., no doubt on the legal and canonical measures affecting the printing of books.[15] As New York was the center for many of the nation's publishing concerns, the expression of opinion of well-placed Catholics served to introduce into the publishing world wholesome motivations that went beyond mere profit. More than a decade earlier, in an effort to give the city a shining example of Catholic literary prowess, and in an effort to demonstrate its civic involvement with a tangible public display, the Club had erected a large bronze bust of Orestes Brownson on Riverside Drive (and now resting at Fordham's Rose Hill campus in the Bronx).[16]

Gradually, the administrative bodies of the Club extended their programmatic efforts to influence national politics as well. In February 1926, the National Council of Catholic Men enlisted the CCCNY in a protest movement against the Curtis-Reed Bill, then pending before Congress, which would establish a federal Department of Education.[17] Many Catholics were fearful that a move toward federalizing education would squeeze out parochial schools from the educational landscape or otherwise impinge on the rights of parents to decide the type of education provided for their children.

Members of the Club were also kept informed about international affairs. In March 1926, its regular monthly meeting of the membership passed resolutions denouncing atrocities against Catholics, especially priests and nuns, in Mexico. Two members, Judge Talley and Judge Morgan O'Brien, personally visited with Secretary of State Frank Billings Kellogg, on behalf of the CCCNY, to register the membership's disgust at "the incalculable dangers that would exist to this Country from the establishment of bolshevism in such near proximity to us."[18] Both men petitioned that the resolutions passed by the CCCNY be submitted to Secretary Kellogg through Congressman John J. Boylan, representative of the Fifteenth Congressional District of New York, and a Club member. In order to broaden the reach of the Club's policy interests, members were eventually authorized to speak on questions of the day before Catholic men's clubs such as parish Holy Name Societies or in Knights of Columbus meetings.[19] Wives of Club members were also informed about current international problems, as when the April 1926 meeting of the New York Archdiocesan Council of Catholic Women hosted Monsignor Pace of The Catholic University of America, who gave a discourse "The Papacy and International Relations."[20]

In addition to being a social club, the CCCNY was a teaching tool and cultural venue. At least once every month a prominent authority would lecture on a subject of general interest. In 1923, members heard Dominican priest Bede Jarrett speak on "The Voice of the Church in Modern Problems" and Commonweal founder Michael Williams lecture on "the intellectual expression of Catholicism."[21] Often, when a speaker represented a branch of the armed services and spoke on some aspect of the national defense, an unusually large number of CCCNY members would attend. In 1924 civic officials would address audiences on such topics as "Aerial Warfare and Modern International Law" (Captain Elbridge Colby of the United States Air Force) and "The Evils of Pistols and Narcotic Drugs" (William G. McAdoo, the city's chief magistrate).[22] They could also hear discourses on Dante or Louis Pasteur or Joyce Kilmer.

At other times, the Club served as social entertainment for members' families, with Punch and Judy shows for children or "mind reading and memory tests" for young adults—all of which served to solidify family life in a Catholic context.[23] New movements or organizations within the American Church were brought to the attention of the members through such representatives as Bishop Francis C. Kelley, who spoke before the Club in March 1923, on the Catholic Church Extension Society of America, and John LaFarge, S.J., who spoke about the Cardinal Gibbons Institute, under the title "The Catholic Church as the Hope of the Negro."[24] In April 1924, the CCCNY brought Father John A. Ryan, the director of the Social Action Department of the National Catholic Welfare Conference to speak on "The Church and Radical Social Movements."

Every year, Club members were invited to participate in the Catholic Summer School of America on Lake Champlain. They often filled the "New York" cabin, but the Summer School was a presence at the CCCNY as well, periodically offering extension courses for the membership or supplying authorities from their speakers' bureau. Well into the 1920s and 1930s the Club was the conduit for retreats and other spiritual practices, such as those conducted at Mount Manresa, the Jesuit retreat house on Staten Island, or the annual Communion breakfasts that took place at St. Patrick's Cathedral, with hundreds enjoying breakfast following Mass in the Club house.[25] While no single Catholic group could claim to be all-encompassing, the Club could be held up as a locus of lay Catholic action in faith formation and in citizenship, educational, cultural, social, and charitable events.

The CCCNY was the source not only for immediate organization of Catholics throughout the archdiocese for projects that served the Church's charitable needs but also for political and social agendas affecting millions in the metropolitan area. In 1910 the Club's members were instructed by Archbishop John Farley to cable Rome to protest against that city's Mayor Ernesto Nathan. Addressing an audience of 1,000 CCCNY members, Farley called attention to Nathan's recent effrontery to the Holy Father by celebrating, on September 20, the fortieth anniversary of the day on which the Papal States came to an end.[26] In the process of renewing American Catholic filial sentiment toward the pope, Farley mobilized elite Catholic New York to escalate its disdain for the secular Italian regime.

Political questions of the day continued to be a perennial subject among the CCCNY membership into the tenure of Farley's successor, Archbishop Patrick Hayes. Together, they would partner in a truly transformational moment for Church and society through the Club's organization, with Hayes as honorary chairman, from the outset of his tenure. The

Club's leadership formed a "Special Membership Committee," which promoted the ends of the Club by drawing in devoted Catholics who were well situated to become a kind of leaven in society. Within months of his ascent to the See of New York, Hayes had for this committee a membership list of nearly three hundred men, augmenting the Club's general roster—the crème de la crème of Catholic New York. In early 1923, the number grew to five hundred, thanks in part to a letter from Hayes circulated to all the pastors in the archdiocese to commend membership in the CCCNY to worthy parishioners.

The CCCNY and the Cardinal of Charities

Hayes loved the Catholic Club and it, in turn, enjoyed him. He was the first Catholic bishop in the history of the diocese who was actually born in New York City, though his own membership in the CCCNY preceded his episcopacy. According to the register for the Xavier Union, the Rt. Rev. Monsignor Patrick J. Hayes, D.D., resident of Madison Avenue, New York City, became a member of the Catholic Club on January 10, 1911. At the time Hayes was chancellor of the archdiocese and rector of Cathedral College, the archdiocesan minor seminary. He was an honorary member, as were most clergy, who were excused from paying the fifty-dollar entrance fee, and was the 3,977th member to join since 1871. It must have been a momentous occasion for Hayes to record his name, which was immediately followed by that of United States Supreme Court Chief Justice Edward Douglass White.

Both gentlemen joined an illustrious group that included Father Thomas Lawrason Riggs, Washington, D.C. (December 13, 1910); Right Reverend Monsignor John Edwards, the Archdiocesan Vicar General (June 16, 1909); His Eminence Michael Cardinal Logue, Armagh, Primate of Ireland (June 9, 1908); Major General Thomas H. Barry, USN, Washington, DC (June 9, 1908); and Jacob L. Riis, 430 West 116th Street, New York City (April 9, 1907; resigned January 20, 1909), among others. They joined men like John D. Crimmins (building and railroad magnate), Nicholas F. Brady (CEO of Consolidated Edison), Thomas Fortune Ryan, and Judge Victor Dowling, as well as two mayors, William Gaynor and William R. Grace, and Governor Al Smith.[27] Several of these men contributed thousands of dollars over the years, served on various committees, or contributed rare books and art from their private collections. Crimmins, for instance, donated the Gilbert Stuart portrait of George Washington.

As a member of Cardinal Farley's curia, Hayes was often at the Club for functions, and his presence there afforded him ample time to build relationships with prominent laity. When the Club honored Joseph Frey, president of the German Catholic Central-Verein of New York, Hayes wrote to Farley and pronounced the evening a "great event." Crediting Club president Michael Mulqueen ("a wonder") for its organization, Hayes noted that "the gathering was very large and representative. While there was a pleasant strain of humor and fun, the serious note was dominant, especially on the lay apostolate. . . . Honoring Mr. Frey is a most beneficial stimulant to German Catholic life."[28] Mulqueen would grow in Hayes's estimation and, first as bishop and later as archbishop, Hayes would eventually celebrate the wedding of two of Mulqueen's daughters in the Cathedral.[29] The close ties that Hayes cultivated with the lay leaders of the Club would prove mutually satisfactory, as they ensured cooperation on projects of benefit to Church and society.

Hayes was a direct beneficiary of the CCCNY's generosity. At a Friendship Dinner given in his honor, during which he was welcomed as the archdiocese's latest bishop auxiliary, Hayes was feted not only by members of the CCCNY but, at their invitation, by many non-Catholic leaders as well.[30] CCCNY member Judge Alton B. Parker presided. A committee of a number of New Yorkers was enlisted to arrange the testimonial, including (future U.S. Senator) Royal S. Copeland, M.D.; Judge Victor J. Dowling; Michael J. Drummond, commissioner of the New York City Department of Public Charities; mining magnate John Hays Hammond (known as the man with the Midas touch); Adolph Lewisohn (investment banker and philanthropist); Thomas Mulry (head of the St. Vincent de Paul Supreme Conference and president of the Emigrant Savings Bank); Judge Morgan J. O'Brien; William Church Osborn (an anticorruption advocate and philanthropist; Herman Ridder, editor of the *Neue Staats-Zeitung*; investment bankers Simon Rothschild and Jacob H. Schiff; department-store mogul Louis Stern, and others.

About one hundred guests attended, including Governor Martin Glynn; the cardinal; Monsignor John J. Dunn, vicar for the Propagation of the Faith; Father Malick J. Fitzpatrick, head of the Mt. Loreto Home on

Staten Island; Monsignor Michael Lavelle, rector of the cathedral; Constantine J. MacGuire, M.D.; Monsignor Joseph Mooney, vicar general; Michael Mulqueen, attorney, and, curiously, Mayor John Purroy Mitchel, who was proving himself to be less than friendly toward the archdiocesan curia. In the next two years, Mitchel's investigation of the Catholic Charities would involve blind accusations, tapping of the chancery phones, and indictments of public officials who overreached in pursuit of financial accountability. Still, this was a moment not just to acknowledge the new bishop but to praise the ideals of the city. New York City's comptroller, William Prendergast, with whose office Hayes had tangled, from 1910 to 1912, over inquiries into the Catholic Charities' finances, noted that "the great charm of New York City, to my mind, is not only that it is the most cosmopolitan in its character but that it is a broad, liberal and tolerant city. . . . The best measure of its broadness and its tolerance is shown by the fact that on this occasion men of all religions, of all professions, and I may say, of all shades of public thought, have come together to do honor to you, Bishop Hayes."[31] Hayes then rose and put the laurels on the city itself:

> I glory in the fact that I am a New Yorker. . . . You have greatly embarrassed me by all the kindnesses that you have poured out upon me, but at the same time I realize that you are doing it not alone for me but for another purpose. That purpose is that we might all be cemented together, united here in this great City of New York, in order that every force, that every power that makes for good, shall come together in working out the mission and destiny of our City. Our City is a wonderful City. Sometimes, however, I almost think it is not part of the United States, when I hear the criticisms that have been hurled against it, when I hear men who might have better sense, charge it with being un-American, just because it is the harbor, the refuge of so many peoples, of so many nations, of so many different creeds and types. There are those beyond our borders who think they are American and that we are on foreign soil. And yet here, within the gates of our City, we have a problem, we have a mission, and all should unite together in working it out. . . . It will be my constant aim as a Catholic bishop, to do all in my power to fill up the valleys and bring down the hills, so that the chasm can be crossed and the obstacles removed, to the end that we may be a united people.[32]

Of all of the characteristics about himself that he cherished "as a real treasure," Hayes's American citizenship, he found, was a most solicitous expression of authentic humanity. It transcended all the other social distinctions and opened the way for the greatest possible pastoral outreach and care.

> Citizenship, to my mind, is the fruit and the flower, rather than the root and the branch, of our civic life. Citizenship to me does not mean that it confers much upon myself . . . [and yet] I have hallowed it, I have sanctified it, ennobled and inspired it, by my sacred calling; and there is nothing in my vocation, there is nothing writ down in the books which guide my footsteps and dictate my calling—there is nothing writ there against that citizenship. . . . And, oh, I say to the city of New York that, at least within our gates, we must meet the problem of dealing with the people, who come unto us, people from other soils and other lands who come across the seas, that the tent of the pilgrim might be turned into the home of the citizen, and that the staff of the wanderer might be turned into the plough of the man of toil. . . . There is a solemn principle, and it is this: that things apparently separate and distinct are really inseparable when you come to examine them.[33]

Hayes brought the house to its feet with some concluding lines that would serve as a touchstone for his reign as archbishop. With the din of modernism in the background—with all its attendant perils to the Church and the world—Hayes alerted his audience to the kind of persona he wanted to project and the kind of Church he wished to represent:

> If I stand for anything it is for this: that I do not, nor does my Church stand for the fancy of the hour, the folly of the moment, or the fad of the day. It stands for something abiding. And if we appear aloof when something new is proposed, it is not because we are opposed to progress, but we would like to be sure before we put our foot forward. We stand for things of that kind. We stand for what is permanent.[34]

Unity in the city and in the nation would be a recurrent theme for Hayes during his service as bishop ordinary of the Military Archdiocese— essentially placing him in charge of the largest diocese in the world—at the time of America's involvement in the First World War. Assisting Hayes in the responsibility of ministering to America's Catholic servicemen was the CCCNY, which itself supplied some two hundred of its members for the war effort, and which opened its apartments to those involved in war work, especially visiting chaplains passing through New York and in need of lodgings close to the episcopal residence.[35] CCCNY members also helped to organize a fund drive for war work on behalf of the American bishops, who, with the Knights of Columbus, sought lay assistance to supply chaplains and recreational facilities for soldiers. The archdiocese alone raised over five million dollars, largely through Hayes's efforts and in association with the CCCNY, particularly Club member Adrian Iselin, who served as chairman of the drive, and John Agar ("the Catholic of Wall Street"), who served as treasurer.[36] By war's end, there were some 1,300 members of the CCCNY, with over half drawn from Manhattan and the Bronx. In the final months of 1918, as Cardinal Farley's health declined, Hayes remained in New York to govern the archdiocese, and when Farley died in September 1918, Hayes was appointed his successor. Once again, the CCCNY had assumed a leading role in diocesan affairs.

Since all of the trustees of St. Patrick's Cathedral were members of the CCCNY, as were most of the heads of Catholic service organizations in the archdiocese, Hayes's familiarity with the Club allowed for seamless continuity in the governance of the See of New York. He was assured of the relative stability of its day-to-day operations and was consequently able to devote himself to the work of helping to organize the National Catholic War Council (NCWC)—a duty that fell to Hayes, as one of four bishops assigned the job—which he continued throughout 1918.[37]

Hayes's work on behalf of the NCWC ended when he resigned to take over as archbishop. On Thursday, May 8, 1919, less than two months after his installation, Hayes was solemnly invested with the pallium at St. Patrick's Cathedral. Apostolic delegate Archbishop John Bonzano officiated, and all of the Knights of St. Gregory who attended the archbishops were members of the CCCNY. That night Hayes celebrated with a reception in his honor at the Catholic Club.[38] There Hayes gave the CCCNY its mission in somewhat less prosaic terms than he had employed five years earlier:

> The Catholic Club, like other associations, has pledged to me its loyalty and its support, and I want to say here, publicly, that I accept the pledge. I love the Catholic Club, and you may be sure that I am thinking what kind of a project I am going to give to the Catholic Club. The

easiest thing you can do for me is to bring me in Three Million Dollars next October, for charity and reconstruction, and the only way you can improve on that is to make it Five Million Dollars.[39]

The figure was half in jest, but Hayes quickly realized the potency of his remark. The Club's Committee on Catholic Interests—comprised of Catholic New Yorkers who set the Club's agenda on subjects touching faith and action—immediately began to ruminate on fulfilling their prelate's wish.

The Inauguration of the Catholic Charities Campaign

In keeping with the general pressure for reform of Catholic charitable work along more scientific lines, the new archbishop of New York saw a need to understand better the myriad programs of social service operating within diocesan boundaries.[40] At the retreat of archdiocesan priests in the summer of 1919, Hayes announced the appointment of Father Robert F. Keegan as secretary for charities and proposed a massive reorganization plan for the Catholic charities of the diocese, whose aim was consolidation and the elimination of all duplication of services. On September 1, a plan was formally launched to conduct a comprehensive survey of every parish and every charity operating within the archdiocese. This plan had been developed by Hayes and Keegan, in association with Dr. John A. Lapp, an NCWC staffer. It enlisted the services of Father (and future bishop) Bryan J. McEntegart and Father James McCahill, who were joined by Mr. John P. Bramer and Miss M. B. Wise, with support from forty lay assistants.[41] When the Catholic Charities office was formally established at Grand Central Palace (at 47th Street and Lexington Avenue), Keegan served as overall secretary for charities; McEntegart would go on to oversee the Charities' office for children's services; McCahill would oversee the office of social activities (mostly recreational and youth-oriented programs); and Bramer would oversee the office for family relief.

The survey was intended to acquire information in five critical areas: relief work, children's welfare, health, protective work, and social action. In January 1920, Hayes spoke before the New York branch of the Catholic Federation of the United States and made an appeal for one hundred participants to be recruited in the work of war reconstruction. Although that never materialized (in part because of its calculated impracticality), in the audience was the New York chapter's president, Joseph H. Fargis, a CCCNY member who would later be asked to serve in a more formal capacity in the revamping of the archdiocesan Associated Catholic Charities.[42] Fargis helped organize on the parish level, but the real control of the effort was to be made by key clergy, handpicked by Hayes, and other members of the CCCNY.

By February 15, 1920, the group had submitted its two-thousand-page report to Hayes.[43] In the first week of March the archbishop called together priests from every one of the three hundred parishes in the archdiocese to tell them of his intention to organize the "Archbishop's Committee of the Laity"—an army of some twenty thousand permanent members that would help to enroll Catholics across the archdiocese in the inaugural Catholic Charities campaign.[44] Sixteen districts, each captained by a senior pastor and a cluster of zealous laypeople (women and men), would implement a twofold educational and financial campaign to assist in the work of the Church's charities. Catholics would be given information on the scope of the work of charities within the archdiocese in the hope of enlisting them to pledge what they could to offset standing expenses.

Hayes directed that the charities would continue their own fundraising independently of the campaign and would not be diminished in any way. The funds raised through the campaign would instead augment existing programs and assist in improving their outcomes, with the express purpose of increasing the work of charity for the good of souls everywhere. While Hayes was the president of the Committee of the Laity, its chairman was the archdiocesan attorney, George J. Gillespie, a CCCNY member of long standing. Its executive committee included many other CCCNY members, including John G. Agar, Nicholas F. Brady (as well as Mrs. Brady), Judge H. Bourke Cockran, Joseph H. Fargis, Thomas F. Farrell (who would go on to lead the National Conference of Catholic Charities), Francis P. Garvin, Joseph P. Grace (heir to the Grace shipping fortune), attorney William D. Guthrie, candy manufacturer Henry Heide, philanthropist George McDonald, Judge Morgan J. O'Brien, and banker Myles J. Tierney, president of the New York Catholic Protectory. Their campaign would run from April 18 to April 25.

Interestingly, Hayes issued his Easter pastoral, at the center of which he placed the Catholic Charities campaign, with an exhortation that is a corollary to the standard definition of Catholic Action. In his opening paragraph he maintained that the recent survey of the archdiocese's parishes and charities "has opened our eyes to the supreme urgency of reaching out the ministry of the clergy to a fuller sense of the pastoral office, in union with the apostolate of the laity whose willing hands and loving hearts are always open to the needy and neglected children of Christ."[45] At the CCCNY, the Committee on Catholic Interests was kept well informed about the progress of the campaign, and on March 15, 1920, the committee met and, Alfred J. Talley (soon to become Judge Talley) was instructed to write to Hayes that the committee "regards the work which is about to proceed under your direction as one which will mark an epoch in the progress of the Church."[46] As a mark of their commitment, the committee's members supplied the archbishop with the first donation, of one thousand dollars. Such a gesture undoubtedly bolstered Hayes's confidence and led to his ambitious call that one hundred thousand of New York's Catholics be contacted. At a kickoff dinner for representatives of each of the archdiocese's parishes, Hayes told those assembled that the Charities campaign was meant to "arouse the responsibility of the laity. The care of Catholic charities . . . does not all rest with the clergy."[47] Scores of workers in each parish took to the streets in a house-to-house effort to locate their Catholic neighbors and educate them about the goals and wants of the charitable services of their Church. A short motion picture was also developed to encourage participation. From an anticipated one hundred thousand Catholics, it was hoped that pledges of at least $500,000 each year could be secured to supplement existing charitable services.

The returns from the first week's pledge drive far exceeded expectations. The participation level was twice as high as anticipated, and pledges were three times higher. Within three years, Hayes could report that in consolidating the efforts of archdiocesan Catholic Charities, 233,000 Catholics pledged approximately $2.6 million over a three-year period. "The average yearly contribution from each person," he explained, "was not much over three dollars, payable at the convenience of the donor. The important thing—and this cannot be urged too strongly—was the creation and maintenance of the organization."[48] Applying the excess funding was easy. Among his first directives was the establishment of the Cathedral High School for girls and the creation of the Catholic Immigrant Auxiliary, today the Department of Refugee Resettlement of Catholic Charities

Community Services.[49] Without any non-Catholic assistance during this campaign, the Church in New York had demonstrated that it could stand on its own and for its own, on a platform underpinned by an essential unity of purpose and a near universal approbation of the principle that organized charity was fundamental to Catholic identity, even in the receipt of the widow's mite. Such a paradigm set it apart from other cities, even Dublin, where Catholic Action was hardly on the radar of either Church or society.[50] It also showed how such a massive organizational effort could be orchestrated in tandem with lay leadership, supplied—at least in its upper tier—by the CCCNY.

The CCCNY and Collaboration with the Hierarchy

The vitality of the CCCNY during the early years of Archbishop Hayes's tenure was a blessing for the whole Church in New York. This was not lost on the archbishop, who took the occasion of the Club's golden jubilee, November 17, 1921, to again wax eloquent about his relationship to the CCCNY:

> I cannot look out on such a body of laymen as constitute the membership of the Catholic Club without a feeling of joy. The Catholic Club has been the symbol, the sign and the token of loyalty throughout its entire history, a history of fifty years of intense loyalty to the Church and loyalty to the country. In all its fifty years there has been no deviation in your loyalty to your shepherds. You have been Catholic in every sense, and, therefore, I am here as your archbishop, with trials and vexations, with questions to be decided that are larger than armaments or taxation, and I say to you that it is a very gratifying thing for me to feel that there is such an organization as the Catholic Club. . . . Remember, I say to you, you have a mission. This is perhaps the only club of its kind here, in the city of New York. I appeal to you to take more seriously to heart your duty and your mission as laymen. . . . I tell you, gentlemen, you have before you a wonderful opportunity for service to your God and country. . . . I am going to leave here feeling that the future of the Catholic Club is secure, and that it will be the agency of such service as has been seldom seen in this diocese or in the world, and I know that every one of you will be more than ever consecrated to the high ideals of the club.[51]

Following on Hayes's remarks was an interesting and prophetic statement by former CCCNY president Percy J. King, head of the United States
Catholic Historical Society. King took a long view of the future direction of
the Club. It would not do to keep the Club house in its present state; the way
should be cleared for modernization of the building as well as of its programmatic offerings. "This beautiful home was built nearly thirty years ago
when club life was much more simple than it is to-day. It was beautifully
and substantially erected, and is an enduring monument to the faith and
courage of its founders, but no one can doubt that if built to-day the plans
would be entirely different. It is as obsolete as the brownstone era that has
long since passed from view." King wished the CCCNY would, rather than
ride a dinosaur into the coming age, provide the kind of amenities found in
more residential clubs, with facilities that provided for recreation, assembly,
and dining, with enough space "to work with freedom and celerity."

King called for more than just physical adjustments, however:

> With a splendid home and a large and loyal membership of old and
> young, we could then enter upon what I believe to be the club's special
> function, the coordination of the Catholic cultural aims of New York
> laity—to bring together by receptions, meetings, dinners, and discus-
> sions the Catholic art, literary, economic, and educational life of our
> city; to recognize the Catholic writer, the Catholic actor, the Catholic
> sculptor, the Catholic painter and the Catholic educator; to make this
> the clearing house of the Catholic intellectual activities of the metrop-
> olis, with ample funds to encourage by exhibitions, productions, con-
> certs, readings, prizes, art, craftsmanship, books, drama, and music;
> to bring these people to know each other and to know us, not by name
> but actually; to afford an opportunity for a forum for the discussion by
> eminent men of questions affecting Catholics and Catholicism; to open
> our house for dinner or reception to all visiting eminent Catholics,
> laymen or prelates; to be a living object to all the people of the city of
> the patriotism, standing, loyalty, culture and accomplishment of their
> fellow citizens, the Catholics of New York.[52]

All of this, of course, took money. Membership in the Club was increasing year by year, and, with the assistance of the archbishop, it was
sure to be something that most Catholics of standing would want to join.
But in the years preceding the economic calamities of 1929, membership

alone could not sustain the grand visions entertained by such men as King. What is so apparent in hindsight did not seem to bother anyone at the time. It was an age where prosperity seemed limitless. Why should anyone expect that New York's Catholic power elite should diminish or their capacities and reputation suffer? In unison with their bishop, they seemed on a flight to progress without end. When he became a cardinal in 1924, the CCCNY began a tradition of honoring Hayes each year with a "Cardinal's Day" dinner, April 30—the date of his homecoming after receiving the red hat.[53] They accompanied him in great numbers to the Chicago Eucharistic Congress of 1926, where several CCCNY members were part of his official entourage, and helped to sponsor the Pullman coaches of the "Cardinal's Train" for the journey to Chicago.

Throughout the 1920s, the Club supported its archbishop against the calumnies of anti-Catholic bigots, especially when uttered by public offi-cials.[54] This included a series of condemnations and editorials by CCCNY members who attacked the "cultured despisers" of Governor Al Smith in his quest for the presidency in 1924. Martin Conboy, the Club president that year, wrote an irenic tract for the Club's *Bulletin*, supplying members with thoughtful replies to those who called into question Smith's creden-tials because he was Catholic.[55] Conboy, also a member of the Committee on Catholic Interests for many years, organized the draft in New York City during the First World War and was later appointed U.S. Attorney for New York, where he had the dubious distinction of arguing, in the court of appeals, the case of the United States government against Random House, the publisher of James Joyce's *Ulysses*, the gravamen being that it was unlawful to import pornography.

Hayes often drew from the members' individual expertise, especially in the drafting of complex legal language in briefs and other official docu-ments submitted to the City and State of New York. So beneficial was the advice of the Club's members that Hayes consulted freely with them on topics of concern to the hierarchy, including various drafts of the Ameri-can bishops' pastoral letter on Mexico, which Hayes wrote in conjunction with attorney William D. Guthrie, who provided a commentary on the Mexican constitution.[56] The previous year, Guthrie, a Columbia law pro-fessor and CCCNY member, successfully argued the Supreme Court case *Pierce v. Society of Sisters*, which upheld the rights of parochial schools nationwide.[57] The case had been the subject of much discussion among

Catholics, and Guthrie must have gained confidence from fellow Club members, who had gone on record, in late January 1923, through its Committee on Catholic Interests, to "pledge their unwavering moral and material support to all who are threatened with deprivation of the exercise of . . . natural rights, and are resolved especially to sustain and uphold the Bishops and clergy of the Catholic Church in defending the parochial schools from all such attacks."[58] While much of the legal work was done at the Cardinal's residence, the laymen involved often took counsel with one another before and after their meetings with Hayes at the Catholic Club—making it a powerhouse in its own right.[59]

1929: The Death Knell for the CCCNY

With so much activity, little attention was likely given to the Club's own financial status, but when the curse of October 1929 set in motion the loss or ruin of so many personal fortunes, the Club suffered along with the rest of the nation. On King's earlier advice, the CCCNY had pursued an ambitious refurbishment program that was as lavish as it was ill timed. In 1927, it had appropriated $200,000 for the cleaning and repair of the library books alone and sought $400,000 from the Emigrant Industrial Savings Bank in a second mortgage on the property.[60] By 1931 the Club was deeply indebted to the archbishopric of New York, which had supplied short-term loans in order to make interest payments the Club could not meet. Attorneys were retained.[61] George Gillespie, the cardinal's lawyer and a Club member himself, calculated the grand sum of $63,460 owed to the Archbishopric. The Club's leadership, especially its president, Judge Carroll Hayes, was caught without the means to pay. Not even the sale of the building and all its contents could meet what was owed. If the Club managed to sell all its holdings at top dollar—unlikely, given the economic climate—it still would have an anticipated shortfall of over $80,000, and the Emigrant Bank knew it.

Already in February 1929, the Club's financial obligations had become difficult to maintain, so its leadership was obliged to ask the archdiocese to obtain on its behalf a loan in the amount of $69,000. The loan was made at a discounted rate, though the principal and interest were to be paid by the Club, the last payments to be made in November 1929. With the collapse of the markets, the Club's note was called in, but no payments were made through the spring of 1931, when Gillespie gave the Club notice. The Club's officers continued to borrow tens of thousands to pay its expenses, but very little was ever paid on the principal of the original 1929 loan.

The National City Bank, on whose terms the loan was made, gave Cardinal Hayes a deadline to pay the loan, then standing at $59,000, which was to come due on November 12, 1931. Although Hayes's chancellor, Monsignor (later Cardinal) James F. McIntyre, wrote Gillespie on November 4, 1931, there is no record of a reply. This was an unusual lacuna in the Hayes papers, since everyone knew the pain that this incident caused him and that he followed developments with considerable interest. Perhaps McIntyre either wished to spare him or, given his own previous prowess on Wall Street, decided to pursue the matter himself. On November 12, McIntyre wrote the bank, asking that the note be renewed again for six months and that the charge and credit of the note's payment be made through the "Special Account" of the archbishopric of New York. When May 1932 rolled around, McIntyre again requested a further renewal by the National City Bank. In November 1932, Hayes personally wrote to the bank to ask for another renewal. In each instance the interest was charged (albeit at discount) to the archbishop's account.

Thousands of dollars from Hayes's "Special Account" were used to service the interest, and before long the Emigrant Industrial Savings Bank, which housed this account, began to get nervous. Emigrant Savings Bank president Walter H. Bennett wrote to Gillespie: "As you know, we have frequently discussed with you as the legal representative of His Eminence, the Cardinal, the affairs of the Catholic Club and have kept you advised of the various plans we have tried to work out for the assistance of the Club culminating in our request to Mr. Hayes on February 2nd to be prepared to turn over a deed of the premises at 120 West 59th Street to a party designated by the Cardinal within a period of thirty days."[62]

Bennett seemed indulgent: "We outlined to you our reasons for making this suggestion and as we understand you felt that we were doing our utmost to prevent any unfavorable comment or publicity in the matter and to make it possible for a new club to be formed to continue to carry on all of the best traditions of the old Catholic Club and, in addition, to create a new center for Catholic action in the City of New York." Never-theless, Bennett saw the CCCNY's board acting without consultation of creditors as the final straw. At a CCCNY board meeting in February 1933, the members had voted in favor of a lien on the Club's furnishings and fixtures in favor of the archbishop, without giving prior notice to Ben-nett's bank. "In view of all the circumstances and of the two years during which we have had nothing but promises and no constructive action on the part of the Club to meet its obligations," wrote Bennett, "we feel that this final delay is not justified and that if the Club is not prepared to turn over a deed to a nominee of the Cardinal, as agreed upon, within the thirty day period, we shall proceed at once to foreclosure."[63]

Doubtless Judge Hayes was feeling the heat and called an emergency meeting of the CCCNY board in early March. In the coming days he was forced to report to the entire membership the following grim figures and gloomy prognosis:

The income of the Club from all sources, and its expenses, less depre-ciation, for the years 1929, 1930, 1931, and 1932 are set forth as shown in the accompanying table. In addition to the mortgage of $400,000 on the real property, the Club owes the Archbishopric of New York $59,000, and accrued interest, and on notes to the National City Bank, which notes are guaranteed by the Archbishopric of New York, $38,000. On the request of the attorney for His Eminence, a chattel mortgage on all of the personal property of the Club has been given to His Eminence, Patrick Cardinal Hayes, as Archbishop of New York. If the members of the Club were by voluntary assessment to raise a sum of money large enough to pay the outstanding interest and taxes now due, it would be necessary within a year to have another voluntary as-sessment because the income of the Club is not sufficient to pay for its operation. The decision to submit to the members of the Club a resolu-tion to turn over a deed of the property of the Club to the mortgagee, or to His Eminence as Archbishop of New York, or his designee, was arrived at only after many conferences with the officials of the Emi-grant Savings Bank, the attorney for the Cardinal and His Eminence himself. The giving of the deed has the approval of the Cardinal. The Catholic Club will continue its existence for the present at 120 Central Park South. A plan for its future continuance will be submitted to the members within a short time.[64]

	1929	1930	1931	1932
Income	$97,470.98	$91,279.15	$76,171.46	$49,945.84
Expense	$109,292.91	$109,117.45	$108,923.11	$86,761.17
Deficit	$11,821.93	$17,838.30	$32,751.65	$36,851.33

Meanwhile, Gillespie received from Judge Hayes, the Club president, a letter dated March 20, 1933. Hayes wondered whether the cardinal thought the Club ought to be kept alive. It was a ridiculous letter. It acknowledged that Judge Dowling had already submitted his resignation and that other members, perhaps too ashamed, were jumping ship by the score. It was obvious that the Club was in default and could not meet its obligations and, worse still, that the threat to the credit of the Archdiocese with local and national banks was something that could no longer be tolerated. If the See of New York could be seen as a risk, no diocese in the country would be able to borrow from any bank. Resuscitation of the CCCNY was the farthest thing from Gillespie's mind, and he no doubt communicated his reservations verbally to the cardinal.

The board met on April 17, 1933, in the presence of Gillespie, who attended at the request of Carroll Hayes. The purpose of the meeting was to determine the disposition of the furnishing, artwork, and library. A protest was lodged by Carroll Hayes against a group calling itself the Centre Association for Catholics, which was then in possession of the building and held the keys to the rooms. The group was excluding the Catholic Club from accessing its own Club files and records on the third floor. After this protest, all of the real property was voted to go to the cardinal, who could do with it as he pleased (provided he could get at it). Rather than risk any further embarrassment or ill will, Hayes himself paid the note in full in May 1933, and the contents of the Club and all the real property that once constituted the Club house were liquidated to pay its mortgage.[65] Without a Club house, was there a Club?

The Club's leaders had a genuine interest in maintaining an organization, if only for spiritual purposes. It was the death of the Club's chaplain, Monsignor William Guinan, in May 1933 that supplied a pretext for Judge Hayes to make an urgent plea to the cardinal to appoint a successor.[66] The Club president used the occasion to request that His Eminence speak a word of encouragement about a new Club plan then being entertained in rooms it rented at the Waldorf-Astoria.[67] The cardinal set the whole matter aside and retreated to his country estate in Sullivan County for the remainder of the summer. But on October 14, Carroll Hayes, along with W. Grey Leslie and Gillespie, met the cardinal at his residence and broached the subject in person. The Club was not dead yet. Writing a few days later to Hayes's secretary, Leslie noted that

> His Eminence the Cardinal clearly indicated to us his wish that the Catholic Club ought to be continued, and agreed to send us a letter expressing such a wish, using the occasion of the appointment of a new Spiritual Director, and the reorganization of the Club, for that purpose. His Eminence also agreed to leave the actual and precise evaluation of the Club's Library and the Works of Art, including the Gilbert Stuart Portrait of George Washington, in abeyance, or until some later time when an evaluation might more truly reflect their worth. His Eminence also agreed to take up the Club's note for $38,000 with the National City Bank, which the Cardinal guaranteed, or to pay the interest on its renewal on November 14, 1933. His Eminence also agreed that an effort should be made immediately, to induce those members of the Catholic Club who have an equity in the approximate sum of $15,000 which represents the Government's Refund of Tax on Dues, to waive their claim, and to make payment of this sum or a part of it to the Cardinal as partial liquidation of the advances to the Club under a previous administration. His Eminence expressed a desire to see the Catholic Club represented at various functions. His Eminence agreed to ask Msgr. [William E.] Cashin to act as Spiritual Director of the Catholic Club, its traditions and usefulness, its potential value as a nucleus for Catholic Gentlemen and an Agency for Catholic Action.[68]

For all this balderdash, the Club assembled at the Waldorf for a dinner in Hayes's honor on January 16, 1934, though he was not in good spirits. It was hard to be cheery at a sumptuous meal when the Depression was affecting so many adversely. The Club served one last useful purpose for the archdiocese when it opened its doors at the hotel for a reception tendered to Cardinal Eugenio Pacelli on November 4, 1936, on the occasion of the secretary of state's visit to America. By then, Hayes had gone above and beyond in coming to the Club's rescue, and it was apparent to all that the Club as such should be shuttered. When it collapsed, the Club was disposed to give all its furniture and fixtures and works of art to Hayes. The portrait of George Washington was to be stored at the seminary. (It never arrived.) Everything else was sold.[69] What remains a mystery through the whole affair is the virtual disappearance of the fifty-thousand-volume library. There are no records of the sale or donation of these books—an oddity given that many of them had exceedingly high value. It may be that individual members, seeing the writing on the wall, pilfered the collection with abandon. Throughout the 1920s, the Club printed in its bulletin a near-monthly request for members to return books that they "borrowed." But there was little accounting, and the "best Catholic library in New York" soon faded from memory.

Though it continued to exist on paper until 1964, the CCCNY was never the same after the economic crash of 1929. With its luster fading, and the archdiocesan charities in full swing, there was a gradual decrease in the need for a Catholic club. It became easily supplanted by more grass-roots or broad-based activities, such as labor schools or alumni associations. Still, Catholics in New York's professional class have recently sought to revivify the old impulses found in the CCCNY. Today there is a group of promising young Catholics who comprise the junior board of the Catholic Charities of the Archdiocese of New York. They have as their aim the support of the hierarchy in the accomplishment of the Church's social mission and seek to do their part in financing projects and lending time and talent to their completion. In many respects they mirror the ideals of the former CCCNY, though they go on with the work of Christ without benefit of a physical space to call their own. Like the Catholic Club, the junior board envisions a new form of Catholic Action for these times, in this place.

2 The Liturgical Movement and Catholic Action

Women Living the Liturgical Life in the Lay Apostolate

KATHARINE E. HARMON

At the first National Liturgical Week, held at the Cathedral of the Holy Name in Chicago in October 1940, a lively discussion followed Dom Roger Schoenbechler's presentation, "The Priesthood of the Laity and Catholic Action." Paul McGuire, popular lay lecturer and coeditor of *Restoring All Things: A Guide to Catholic Action* (1938), came to the floor:

> It seems to me that this conference might very well be a turning point in the history of this country, that we might very well see here a beginning to awaken the Catholics of this country to their full responsibility as members of the Mystical Body. The apostolateship is a dynamic something that grows . . . something that goes into the world to make the world Christ's, and gives the sense of a dynamic Church reaching out to make the world Christ's, to conquer it for Him. That can only derive from the full Christian community life, from the full spiritual life.[1]

For McGuire, the "doing" of Catholic Action needed the theological basis of "being" the "Mystical Body," a formation that would take place in the "vital force" of the "liturgical Mass." As McGuire stressed:

> If we have people seized with the knowledge [of Christ] and charged with the graces [of the Mass], growing and strengthening their unity which is in Christ, we can begin to grow a new social order. We can defend ourselves in this desocialized world, this world of loneliness, against anybody, any totalitarian dictator power which comes along and sends people marching together because of the loneliness of man.[2]

Lighting upon this charging of social action with social prayer, Bernice Strasser, of Milwaukee, next came to the floor:

> I wish we had this fire and this eagerness and this zeal in our pulpits on Sunday. If this detailed explanation of the liturgical life of the

sacraments and of the Mass could be given in our pulpits with the fire and eagerness and the zeal with which it has been given to us today, I am sure we could enkindle the same fire in our Catholic laity. I am sure it is there. But they are very complacent. You can't love a thing unless you know about it. . . . If we knew of God and of His greatness and sanctity and love, we would certainly want to do something for Him. It wouldn't be just a "Give me," it would be a complete subjection of ourselves. I don't know how else to go on, but I am just worked up so.[3]

With her keen and candid response, Miss Strasser rightly touched a central nerve for the coinciding hopes of liturgical renewal and social regeneration: "If we knew" the true meaning of the liturgy, we would not simply go to Mass to receive our dollops of grace; "if we knew," we would enter the liturgy seeking a transformation of self, a realization of the Mystical Body of Christ, and a touchstone for Christian responsibility in confronting the world.

Miss Strasser's evaluation of the intersection of social regeneration and the Mass in 1940 followed nearly two decades of increasing convergence between these two important and interconnected initiatives for American Roman Catholicism: the liturgical movement and Catholic Action. While the liturgical movement is often considered as one realization of Catholic Action, or, interestingly, described as a priest-led movement, such descriptions are not sufficiently nuanced. The liturgical movement was, on the contrary, a distinct phenomenon, but fascinatingly pervasive in that retrieval of liturgical participation was viewed by some as the most commonly shared characteristic among popular Catholic lay movements in the mid-twentieth century.[4] Neither was the liturgical movement the project of Benedictines alone. The liturgical movement would not have existed were it not for an extraordinary number of laywomen and laymen who made the movement come alive, participating in dialogue Masses, joining liturgical study clubs, praying the Divine Office, and, if they were parents, teaching the liturgy to their children. As the witness of McGuire and Strasser suggests, laymen and laywomen alike lived and breathed at the heart of the movement and contributed to its central meetings.

In particular, when the story of Catholic Action is told, not only its informer, the liturgical movement, is missed, but so too are the astonishing number of laywomen who were at the center of the liturgical movement, driving it forward in terms consonant with Catholic Action.

Laywomen took up the charge of becoming the Mystical Body of Christ, and their study, prayer, and activity, grounded in the liturgical movement, became a springboard for the broader work of Catholic Action. Attending to the work and experiences of laywomen who identified as participants in both the aims of the liturgical movement and in Catholic Action affords a unique vision into the aims and methods of both movements for initiative, education, and identity among lay Catholics. At the same time, focusing on laywomen also recognizes some inherent tensions for Catholics during this period. The liturgical movement asked the faithful to question traditions of private prayer and to consider the value of public worship experiences, while Catholic Action asked questions with regard to who among the faithful might provide leadership, prompting a largely anonymous body of laypeople to take on public roles of leadership. Likewise, modern Catholic women also faced new questions, particularly as they decided whether to embrace or ignore expectations about their private and public activities, as the ground for women's vocations and roles in the mid-twentieth century shifted.[5]

In order to describe how the liturgical movement and the aims of Catholic Action were realized in the lives and experiences of laywomen, this chapter will begin by providing a more descriptive framework for the intersection of Catholic Action and the liturgical movement, looking more closely at their historical and social context in the early twentieth century in the United States. Following this premise, three different situations will be considered in which women's work in the lay apostolate lived at the crossroads of the liturgical movement and Catholic Action. First, the case of the National Catholic Council of Women, whose members elected to study "the liturgy" in 1929, provides an example of a group that both was under an ecclesial umbrella explicitly identified as living out Catholic Action and was peopled and presided over by laywomen. A second example may be found in the career of the editor, writer, publisher, and lecturer Maisie Ward (1889–1975), best known for her role in the publishing company Sheed and Ward. Involved in the Catholic Evidence Guild, a national organization consonant with Catholic Action, Ward developed her own vocation as copublisher of one of the earliest Catholic publishing companies in the United States. Through her writing and lecturing and her work as a publisher, she promoted the liturgical movement and Catholic Action and was a respected authority on both subjects. Finally, the

American Grail movement, a completely lay-led organization, was described by its contemporaries as the ultimate realization of Catholic Action and the liturgical life. Central to the Grail's mission was the formation of young women in liturgical prayer and practice so that they might be better suited for their lives as Catholic women in the world. Together, these instances of mid-twentieth-century American Catholicism demonstrate how interconnected the goals of the liturgical movement and those of Catholic Action were for American Catholics and, particularly, how laywomen in the United States took up the charge to live the liturgical life as an active and committed lay apostolate.

The Crossroads of the Liturgical Movement and Catholic Action

As American Roman Catholics entered the new and challenging modern world of the 1920s, Catholic Action inspired these members of the lay apostolate to realize their potential to effect social change as members of the one body of Christ. At the same time, a resurging interest in the central Catholic actions, the liturgical experiences of the Mass and of daily prayer, prompted Catholic laity and religious alike to explore how formation in this one body of Christ might pour a truly Christian spirit into the world and prompt true social change. As a leading liturgical advocate, Virgil Michel, O.S.B. (1888–1938), of St. John's Abbey in Collegeville, Minnesota, would summarize: "Pius X tells us that the liturgy is the indispensable source of the true Christian spirit. Pius XI says that the true Christian spirit is indispensable for social regeneration. Hence the conclusion: The liturgy is the indispensable basis of Christian social regeneration."[6] One could draw "all things to Christ," the central message of Catholic Action, only by committing the self to Christ in the heart of Catholic life, the sacrifice of the Mass.

The relationship between social action and social worship was clear and cogent for liturgical advocates in the early to mid-twentieth century. Liturgical worship was a profoundly social event; nothing about the liturgy, from contemplation of its texts to participation in its action, invited the horrors of modern "individualism" and "subjectivism." As a leading liturgical pioneer, Rev. William Busch (1883–1971) would stress, just as personal piety might be formative for personal action, the "antecedent to social action" was social piety.[7] It was clear to Busch, and to others, that the *liturgy*—public worship, a "renewal-of-being" in Christ—was the school for all Catholic Action. Likewise, many Catholic Action groups explicitly looked to the liturgy as a fundamental textbook for formation in the life of Christ, finding the pattern for "observe, judge, act" in the "lex orandi, lex credendi, lex agendi."[8] The liturgy, then, was the room in which Catholics who desired to take up the call of Catholic Action and exercise their faith in the world would be fed and formed in Christ as Christ's living Body.[9]

On the one hand, both the liturgical movement and Catholic Action experienced significant evolution between their beginnings in the 1920s and the beginning of the Second Vatican Council, a watershed mark for both liturgical practice and lay Catholic activities.[10] But, between their beginnings in the American context and the denouement of the Second Vatican Council, the deepest change for either Catholic worship or Catholic Action was, in fact, the rift between them. Following the Second Vatican Council, an untimely split between "social justice" initiatives and "liturgical" renewal blurred the connection of the liturgical life and social regeneration that so many saw as inherently connected in the preconciliar era.[11] The aim of this chapter, however, is to draw attention not to their unraveling but rather to the tightly woven connection between Catholic Action and the wider initiatives of the liturgical movement.

While acknowledging the roots of the liturgical movement in nineteenth-century study and practice in European monasteries, liturgical historians generally agree that the liturgical movement began in the United States in 1926, with the first issue of its central journal, *Orate Fratres* (later, *Worship*), published by the monks of St. John's in Collegeville.[12] When the liturgical movement launched, it entered into an already robust landscape of organizations promoting Catholic Action, including Catholic intellectual life, Catholic arts, and institutional structures that ranged from hospitals to schools to charitable organizations. Laymen and laywomen alike were encouraged to assume the responsibilities of an active life of faith, not only by fulfilling Catholic "obligations" but by promoting Catholic activities and spirituality in the world through Catholic Action, as Pius XI (1857–1939) had articulated in his encyclical *Ubi Arcano* (On the Peace of Christ, 1922). Yet, in this atmosphere of heightened attention to the laity, an increasing number of Catholics began to identify an internal disconnect between the prayer life of the faithful and the official prayer of their Church, and an external disconnect between the official prayer of the Church and its surrounding society and culture. As early as 1903, Pius X (1835–1914) acknowledged this tension in his motu proprio *Tra le sollecitudini* (On Sacred Music), where he reminded Catholics that an "active Catholic faith" had its foundation in communal liturgy. He urged the faithful to actively participate in and develop an informed understanding of the liturgy, especially the meaning of the Eucharist; doing so would connect the people more deeply to the prayer of the Church, form them in the Christian life, and inspire them to transform the world around them. Responding to the need for social regeneration and the lack of connection experienced by many of the faithful in their worship, liturgical pioneers developed a series of strategies for promoting liturgical participation and involvement. These included the promotion of education and catechesis for all, and an emphasis on the social implications of liturgical worship, ranging from outreach to community, nation, and world to the cultivation of family life in the domestic Church. Not surprisingly, these strategies went hand in hand with the work of Catholic Action.

Complementing the intersection of Catholic Action and liturgical renewal, the emerging theology of the Mystical Body of Christ provided a powerful theological description of how incorporation into the eucharistic body extended throughout the Church and prepared Catholics to act as Christ in the world. Significantly, the concept of the Mystical Body asked Catholics to radically rewrite their understanding of liturgical worship. Instead of a series of private individual acts of prayer during a liturgical event, public, corporate participation in worship developed communal identity as one Body in Christ.[13] Virgil Michel saw the Mystical Body as the theological lynchpin between liturgical worship and social regeneration and, in the conclusion of his essay, "The Liturgy the Basis of Social Regeneration" (1935), borrowed a leaf from an article which appeared in *New Blackfriars* to illustrate this connection:

> The Mystical Body . . . is the link between liturgy and sociology; and in proportion as men are brought to realize, through the liturgy, their position as members of that Body, will their actions in a social sphere be affected thereby. . . . A visible manifestation of incorporation into

Christ, a visible united action on the part of the members, cannot fail to revive and foster in them a determination to carry their Christ-life into the social and economic sphere.[14]

The social and spiritual experiences of the liturgy sacramentally formed the faithful into this one body and prepared its members for action in the world.[15]

Furthermore, emphasis on the Mystical Body found practical ground with a resurging advocacy for frequent Communion, inviting the faithful to "center" their Catholicism on sacramental participation in the Eucharist. The campaign for frequent Communion, as advocated by Pius X in *Sacra Tridentina*, "On Frequent and Daily Communion" (1905), dovetailed with the liturgical movement's efforts for active and conscious participation not only in presence *during* the ritual of the Mass, but in comprehension and action *within* it.[16] In the following decades, advocates of the liturgical movement would push this renewed eucharistic participation to its theological, ritual, and social implications; certainly, the door was open for Catholics to participate more actively in the liturgy as soon as bans on eucharistic participation were adjusted. And so Catholics of the 1920s had learned that they exercised their faith by sacramentally partaking in the Eucharist instead of relying solely on devotions. With the call to Catholic Action, they likewise heard that laypeople might exercise their own volition in social matters by taking leadership roles instead of relying on their priests and the religious. In both cases, an emphasis on initiative and action invited Catholics to engage their faith in socially oriented ways; this emphasis would be evident in the frequency with which Catholics sought to connect their apostolic activity to Catholic liturgical worship and not simply to devotionalism.[17]

As Catholic Action matured and expanded through the 1930s, the close relationship between liturgy and Catholic Action was even more readily identified. A talk given during a Catholic Action week in Dubuque, Iowa, in 1935 stressed that "true Catholic Action must spring from the social, official, and universal worship of the Church, and particularly from the Eucharistic Sacrifice which forms its climax. Catholic Action must emanate from the altar and must lead back to the altar."[18] As both the liturgical movement and Catholic Action developed, liturgical pioneers and advocates stressed the importance of the relationship between a renewed prayer life, fed by active participation by the body of the lay faithful, and its implications for the action of this rejuvenated and informed Mystical Body in the world. The connection of prayer and action would be realized in a variety of social initiatives, including the Catholic Worker, the Christian Family Movement, and the National Catholic Rural Life Movement. As liturgical writer William Boyd would summarize, "The liturgy and Catholic Action are thus respectively the mystical body at prayer and sacrifice and the mystical body in action upon the world. *Each of these functions requires the other.*"[19] This dynamic understanding of Church life and liturgical participation stood in stark contrast to the prevailing understanding of liturgy, which had emphasized the external forms of worship and quiet contemplation on the part of the laity.

On the other hand, the most significant distinction between "mainstream" Catholic Action and the liturgical movement had to do with organization and location. Formal Catholic Action was overseen by Church hierarchy, with its various units, such as the National Council of Catholic Women and the National Council of Catholic Men, serving as conduits for conveying the Church's teaching to laypersons. Any given parish, at the encouragement of its local bishop, might become a location for programs of organized Catholic Action. While Catholic Action groups may have had more national possibilities, the liturgical movement, by contrast, excited little involvement on the part of the episcopal hierarchy at large but grew and developed through the interested involvement of laypersons, priests, and religious on a case-by-case basis, with a significant number concentrated in the Midwest. The gravitational pull of religious houses, including St. John's Abbey in Minnesota, St. Meinrad's Archabbey in southern Indiana, the motherhouse of the Dominican Sisters in Adrian, Michigan, and Conception Abbey in Conception, Missouri, undoubtedly gave some reason for the movement's great success in the middle part of the United States. Yet as liturgical historian Keith Pecklers, S.J., suggests, the unique cultural situation of the Midwest, heavily populated by those who had inherited German liturgical traditions and lay initiative, also lent to the movement's success.[20] Locations where immigrant populations, particularly descendants of the immigrant Irish, had arrived with little expectation for liturgical participation were less likely to embrace the initiatives of the liturgical movement.[21] Certainly parishes on coasts East and West had a certain amount of liturgical gravitas, including some examples located in Boston, Massachusetts, New York City, and Sunny-side, Washington. However, the liturgical movement was generally suc-cessful where an already extant Catholic population had the intellectual infrastructure to access, process, and put into action initiatives of the liturgical movement. This "infrastructure" might be present in the re-sources of a nearby academic or religious community, in laypersons who had experience and contacts with other members of the liturgical move-ment, or among priests in parishes and among religious sisters in schools, who brought the practices promoted by the liturgical movement to the hands, voices, and hearts of the faithful. In any case, any measure of the success of the liturgical movement depended on how well its aims of social regeneration, active participation, and liturgical sensitivity were known, desired, cultivated, and embraced by lay Catholics.

The Responsible Answer of Catholic Women, the NCCW

In the first part of the twentieth century, the Catholic Church enjoyed an increasingly coordinated network of social charities and agencies. Lay Catholic women, once prohibited by rules of modesty and expectations of domestically defined women's roles, began to exercise greater social lead-ership and freedom as they joined their Protestant sisters in parallel ef-forts to implement social and economic reforms inspired by the Progressive movement. No longer limited to parish-based activities or "ladies' auxiliaries" to men's organizations, Catholic women began estab-lishing their own national organizations, albeit often under the auspices of episcopal oversight. One of the most significant groups of organized Catholic women explicitly affiliated with Catholic Action was the Na-tional Council of Catholic Women (hereafter NCCW). Greatly interested in strategies for promoting a Catholic life, the newly minted NCCW saw the promotion of the liturgy being propelled by the liturgical movement as prime material for its apostolate and, at its ninth annual convention in 1929, NCCW members voted that every local Catholic Women's club would study the liturgy during that year. As NCCW president Mary G. Hawks declared, women had a special responsibility to "make Christ known" but could do so effectively only by knowing "the mind of the Church." Taking up the charge of Catholic Action, Hawks described this responsibility as a "work of apologetics—the apologetics of example."[22]

She continued: "If indeed, our activities as Catholics must 'make Christ known,' we must act as Christ would act. How can we hope to do this? . . . Now, the only way we have of knowing a person's mind is to study his words and his actions. The official language and actions of the Church are called the Liturgy."[23] The NCCW thus identified the study of the liturgy as a natural resource for "learning" how to unite women's lives with the papal initiative of Catholic Action. Liturgical study more deeply conveyed the meaning and significance of liturgical prayer and the eucharistic sacrifice and would serve as fuel, or food, for the women's work of converting the world. A faithful woman, educated in the liturgy, the primordial language of her faith, would be a formidable force with which rampart secularism and decadent movie starlets would have to reckon.

By 1929 the NCCW already had established precedent for study paired with action. Presiding over the NCCW's seventh annual convention in 1927, its national president, Mrs. Arthur F. Mullen, described the NCCW as seeking, since its establishment in 1921, to be the responsible answer of Catholic women to the needs of the world:

> We came not as of ourselves but in response to a call from our leaders in the Church, a call to service for God, for country, for humanity. A great national program was presented to us, a program which demanded faith, idealism, devotion. That progress had and still has but one end in view—the restoration of the reign of Christ the King. It proposes a great spiritual campaign, a campaigning which requires intelligent thought, definite action, but material resources as well, if it is to be affective.[24]

When NCCW members took up the banner of liturgy in 1929, they were already practiced at organizing study clubs, even though the topics of the early 1920s were more specifically social or moral and made no reference to the liturgy as a source for inspiration.[25]

Following the decision of the NCCW to study the liturgy (much to the delight of Virgil Michel, who included a news brief in the December 1929 *Orate Fratres*), the NCCW issued instructions in its *Monthly Message to Affiliated Organizations* describing the object of study and available resources.[26] Topics addressed as potential for study included the purpose of Advent—the objective being union with Christ through participation in the life of the Church—and a comparison of the "Incarnation or Christmas" cycle with the "Redemption or Easter" cycle.[27] The *Monthly Message* included, aside from focus on the liturgical year, more general outlines for study of the Mass and of Catholic Action, including an outline for women who had already used the earlier study-club outline on the Mass or were familiar with the missal, and an alternate version for beginners. The subject of the Mass was accompanied by questions on how to evaluate the meaning of ritual actions, questions about characteristics of the ministers, and encouragement to use liturgical texts as starting points for discussion, particularly with regard to Catholic Action.[28] Another resource, an outline under the title "The Mass and Catholic Action," assigned for the seventh Sunday after Pentecost, asked readers to consider the introit for that day, "Be joyful, all the world." The introit was followed by questions regarding how different elements of the Mass related to the theme and, second, how this theme, that all the world be joyful, related to Catholic Action.[29]

Evaluating the success of such ventures to connect the liturgy and Catholic Action, the NCCW *Monthly Message to Affiliated Organizations* issued in September 1930 reported: "A wide correspondence with the National Headquarters showing interest in the Liturgy; and giving evidence of earnest study on the part of certain groups. At the present time of the NCWC [National Catholic Welfare Conference] Study club outlines those pertaining to the Liturgy have the widest distribution."[30] Such evidence, as the article "Liturgy, Living with Mother Church" concluded, indicated that the NCCW was accomplishing its goal, set at its ninth annual convention, of widespread study of the liturgy. Continuing, the *Monthly Message* article praised the "Benedictine Fathers" who had supported Catholic women with a supply of resources and pamphlets, and urged all women to procure a missal and to use it during the study of and attendance at Mass. The article also encouraged Catholics to *assist at* rather than *attend* Mass, reminding readers that any local diocesan paper "no doubt carries three helpful features sent out weekly by the NCWC Press Service: Sunday's Liturgy, Masses for the Week, Catholic Customs and Symbols."[31] Strengthening networks of Catholic media, including diocesan newspapers, bolstered Catholic identity for liturgical devotees and Catholic Action initiatives alike.

Interest on the part of the NCCW in studying the liturgy was reaffirmed at its twelfth annual convention, held in Charleston, South Carolina, in

October 1932. At this meeting, time was set apart for those interested in the liturgy as well as for those interested in studies of social life, education, and missionary activities. For example, according to Miriam Marks of the "Parish Federation," who attended the convention and reported to *Orate Fratres*, the study-club programs conducted by the NCCW were effective:

> To be vitalizing, the subject for study must be of general interest. As the central act of Catholic worship is the sacrifice of the Mass—which Christ left to all men—a study of it makes a widespread appeal. Through study groups, understanding and appreciation of the Mass are increased; as we learn more of its infinite meaning, we are incited to express actively our devotions to our Savior. A greater unity or purpose is created when all organizations are simultaneously experiencing this spiritual growth.[32]

Information received from the secretaries of local organizations of Catholic women suggests that an "appreciable number" chose to become "intimately acquainted" with the Mass and the liturgy through the use of the Liturgical Press Study Club outline, *The Eucharistic Sacrifice* (1933). To demonstrate the widespread interest in liturgical renewal in America, *Orate Fratres* listed communications received from such diverse locations as Butte and Great Falls, Montana; Albert Lea and Faribault, Minnesota; Milwaukee; Belleville, Illinois; San Francisco; Austin, Texas; Rochester, New York; and the Hawaiian Islands.[33] Within the Diocese of Great Falls, Montana, the first convention of the Great Falls Diocesan Council of Catholic Women determined that "within each parish was established an altar society, with a sub-committee on the sanctuary, and at least one study club studying the Mass."[34] Frequent correspondence concerning study clubs, whether or not they were under the auspices of the NCCW or other organized national women's groups, suggests that the women who made the effort to write in to *Orate Fratres*, at least, acknowledged that study of the liturgy had helped them in their understanding and love of the liturgy. As Agnes M. Marceron of Washington, D.C., reported in 1933, this love of the liturgy had been instilled in numerous members of such groups, inspiring them to purchase missals.[35] Encouraging the use of missals, and thus active participation and comprehension, was central to the early decades of the liturgical movement.[36]

Unlike some other structures or initiatives of the liturgical movement, the NCCW's approach to the liturgy and Catholic Action had a distinctly apologetic character. The call to learn the liturgy so as to become active, spiritually informed members of the lay apostolate frequently was accompanied by the goal "to make converts." One interest of the liturgical movement was the creation of a liturgical life within the home, which, of course, was often the domain of women. Families were encouraged to pray together, attend Mass together, and, in the home, to develop practices in tune with the liturgical year or to establish a routine of home devotions, such as the dedication of a corner for a table with crucifix, candles, or other religious objects.[37] Such training in the liturgy, liturgical devotees argued, would form the family to Christ. The NCCW advocated a similar tactic but expressed sentiments unmatched by their mainstream liturgical movement peers. Mrs. John Bell Hood wrote in the *Monthly Message* of 1937 regarding the construction of shrines in the Catholic home:

> The little shrine in the home has worked wonders for others; it will work wonders for you. Mention may be made of FIVE converts due to ONE shrine in ONE home. Can you—and you—and you refuse the opportunity to bring ONE soul back to Christ? If every family brought just one soul back to God—what a conquest! Is not this united Catholic Action, so desired by our Holy Father? So pleasing to God?[38]

While the mainstream liturgical movement did have an underpinning motive of reforming society with liturgy as the answer to modern evils, the number of "converts" that a liturgical lifestyle might produce, a goal emphasized by Mrs. Hood, was not usually the goal of liturgical reformers. Such quantifying of liturgical experiences was too similar to the devotional practices and mentality of the Mass as a means to an end, or mere "machinery" for getting Communion, as Maisie Ward would later recall—a mentality that the liturgical pioneers sought to change.[39] In any case, taking the liturgy into daily life became associated with a fierce construction of Catholic identity.

The number of study clubs that were organized during this period is impressive.[40] For example, within the city of Springfield, Illinois, as Mrs. D. M. Walsh, diocesan chair on study clubs for the NCCW in Springfield reported in 1933, a study club focusing on the aforementioned *The Eucharistic Sacrifice* had been formed in every parish. On a diocesan level, the Catholic Action Committee of Women of the Diocese of Wichita, Kansas, reported that eighty-three study clubs had completed a course on the externals of the Mass using *Altar and Sanctuary*.[41] Such study clubs proliferated, according to some women, because of the enthusiasm of young Catholic laywomen. Walsh reported that the pamphlets her NCCW group were using had become so widespread because of the "enthusiasm and advertizing of these young people," who had inspired "several groups of older ladies" to ask for help in getting started.[42] Likewise, the report of the Des Moines Diocesan Council of Catholic Women, appearing in the May 1933 issue of *Catholic Action*, declared that fostering the "interest of young women who will so soon be our leaders" was especially significant.[43]

As the American Catholic Church entered the 1930s, it seemed that the "new generation" of young Catholics demanded activity, a sentiment echoed by other organized women's groups engaged in Catholic Action, such as the Daughters of Isabella or the Catholic Daughters of America.[44] A growing middle-class populace with greater access to education, an increased acceptance of Catholics in American culture, and increasing social and educational opportunities for women enabled significant numbers of American Catholics to publicly claim and evangelize their faith in new ways.[45] In turn, Catholics (both men and women) who became involved in groups that studied the principles of the Catholic faith were inspired to recognize their membership in Christ's Mystical Body and to actively respond by taking part in the conversion of the world.[46]

The Catholic Intellectual Revival and Maisie Ward

The trend toward using adult education, study clubs, and pamphlets to inform and mobilize American Catholic laywomen was made possible through Catholic women's increasing prominence among the educated middle class. The demographic shift from immigrant poor to middle-class ascendency allowed Catholic women to critically evaluate their faith and participate in its expansion.[47] Meeting this social change was the Catholic intellectual revival, another aspect of the development of Catholic Action as it intersected with the liturgical movement. The condemnation of modernism in 1907 (Pius X, *Pascendi Dominici Gregis*, "On the Doctrine of the Modernists") led to narrowly prescribed limits on matters of doctrine, and afterward Catholic scholarship found its inspiration in the reappropriation of St. Thomas Aquinas.

The Thomistic revival provided a fresh approach for Catholic scholarship around the world, prompting Catholic scholars to move away from neo-scholasticism formed by the manual tradition that had defined Catholic teaching in the late nineteenth and early twentieth centuries. While neo-scholastic moral theologians had composed manuals guided by an abstract system of moral classification, the Thomistic revival called for a return to original sources, including a closer reading of Thomas and of scripture.[48] For Catholics, natural law served as a bridge between Catholic philosophy and the "Protestant" rationalism of the Enlightenment. The new Catholic intellectual scene enabled Catholic philosophers and theologians to concede, on the basis of natural reason and supernatural revelation, that all humans had unalienable rights and that the purpose of government was to protect these rights, offering a rationale for the inclusion of Catholics and, increasingly, lay Catholics in the early social-justice movements that blossomed in the late 1910s and 1920s.[49]

With the burgeoning influence of neo-Thomism and the new possibilities for Catholic philosophical and social thought, American Catholics became interested in the theological concept of the Mystical Body. Emphasized by Catholic Action sources and liturgical movement advocates alike, the Mystical Body became the touchstone for the laity's understanding of its ownership over the project of converting the world.[50] At the same time, the interwar period saw the establishment of dynamic and influential lay-controlled, lay-led organizations—including the Catholic Worker, the National Catholic Rural Life Conference, and the Christian Family Movement—that led members to live out the theology of the Mystical Body in the world. Supporting the educational and intellectual needs of such organizations was the publishing firm of Sheed and Ward, born in England and transported to America by its cofounders, Frank Sheed (1897–1981) and Maisie Ward. Ward herself, a Catholic laywoman, worked to foster an understanding and love of the Mystical Body of Christ in her fellow Catholics, helping them to learn from the richness of their faith and to live out their faith in action.

Born in 1889 in England, Ward was the child of prominent Catholic writers who cultivated a life of intellectualism and liturgical interest.[51] Through her father she became acquainted with leading figures of the

Oxford Movement, which sought to connect theological inquiry with liturgical renewal in the Church of England.[52] As in touch with the intellectual world as she was, however, entering the social world of advanced education, which expected that women be chaperoned and was not particularly interested in Catholic sensibilities, proved a difficult prospect. While a Catholic woman could not independently attend Oxford University lectures, she could, however, more easily join a growing core of lay Catholic apologists defending the faith in public open-air lectures. One of the most prominent organizations in England was a new, outdoor lecture circuit conducted under the auspices of the Catholic Evidence Guild. Launched in 1918 in the Diocese of Westminster, England, the Catholic Evidence Guild sought to counter inflammatory anti-Catholic speakers in London's Hyde Park. Ward joined the Catholic Evidence Guild only a year after its beginning.[53] Its speakers were volunteers, including teachers, typists, bus drivers, nurses, scientists, housemaids, and professors. Ward, who had no profession, quickly assumed a role as organizer and trainer of new recruits. While Ward had been more associated with the "upper class" in her family life, her exposure to the Guild introduced her to working-class and professional people and alerted her to their own spiritual acumen. She would later reflect that her association with the Guild allowed her to appreciate faithful theological reflection "in the minds of everyday laboring people who never have the opportunity to reflect upon the theology or spirituality that comes trickling down to them through the hierarchy and clergy."[54]

Ward felt that her responsibility as a Guild member was to make Catholic teachings come alive for her outdoor audiences. Confident in the ability of laypersons to effectively (and accurately) teach fellow Catholics, she was continually annoyed with clergy and hierarchy who were nervous about Catholic street preachers.[55] Finding a ready audience in the increasingly educated Catholic population of the United States, the Catholic Evidence Guild movement arrived in America by the early 1920s, with lectures taking place even in major venues such as Washington D.C., with women, in fact, outnumbering men on the lecture circuit.

In 1926, at age thirty-seven, Maisie Ward married fellow Guild member Frank Sheed, a young law student of Australian heritage, and continued to lecture in tandem with him on topics related to Catholic theology, history, and social action. As Ward noted, two children (Rosemary, born 1927, and Wilfrid, born 1930) and the firm of Sheed and Ward were results of their union.[56] At the time of the establishment of the Sheed and Ward Publishing Company (in London, in 1926), there was no Catholic publisher exclusively dedicated to Catholic materials or geared to an audience composed of clerical *and* laypersons. Sheed and Ward's opening was, according to one description, "a daring attempt to launch a Catholic publishing firm that did not sell rosaries, medals, and statues to balance its budget."[57] As Frank Sheed would explain, the firm aimed to serve Catholics by hitting them "just above the middle of a brow," which was, as Sheed noted, "not a congested area."[58] Ward served as vice president of the company, with responsibilities including the selection of manuscripts, editing, translating, cultivating authors, drawing up contracts, and occasionally dealing in financial matters.

In 1929, while Sheed and Ward continued to expand, Frank Sheed had an opportunity to go on a lecture tour in North America. Maisie Ward accompanied him, and she found the warmth and eagerness of their audiences at Catholic colleges, Communion breakfasts, and parish gatherings a refreshing change. For Ward, the American Catholic lecture scene was ripe with excitement: "an exchange of ideas, a meeting of minds, a friendly clash of personalities."[59] Experiences with American Catholics prompted Sheed and Ward to move their publishing headquarters to New York in 1933. While an expansion of one's business in the midst of the Depression was risky indeed, its move to America proved auspicious. The Catholic intellectual revival in England had reached a standstill, despite an outpouring of Catholic literature, as the relatively limited number of Catholics and the distinctive history of the Catholic Church in England prevented Catholic materials from reaching into the educational system or the popular press, likely venues through which the readership of believers could have been expanded. A limited audience, however, was not the case for American Catholics.[60] An American Catholic audience interested in study clubs and Catholic libraries and in asserting an emerging public identity primed the market for Catholic books, and for a publisher to serve it.[61] Sheed and Ward's entrance on the American scene further hastened the momentum of the Catholic intellectual revival, with the added kindling of Catholic Action and liturgical renewal fueling the fire.

Both in the witness of its directors and through its publications, Sheed and Ward Publishing served from the mid-1930s through the late 1950s as a key disseminator of the theology of the Mystical Body, a concept they had had first encountered in Robert Hugh Benson's *Christ in the Church* (1911).[62] The dynamism of this theology, implying human solidarity in Christ, not only in the institutional Church but throughout the world, was a powerful thread that intertwined the proponents of lay initiative within Catholic Action circles with the efforts of liturgical advocates in renewing the laity's liturgical experiences. Sheed and Ward almost singlehandedly began the process of exposing American Catholics to the best in the European theological tradition, marketing their books to religious and clerical readers as well as to laypersons.

Ward saw how the increasing initiative and responsibility placed on the Catholic laity by Catholic Action intersected with the liturgical movement. Reporting to *Orate Fratres* in 1949 regarding a recent conference in Northhamptonshire, England, that was concerned with "the modern problems of the apostolate," Ward claimed that there was "nothing of which Catholics are becoming more keenly aware today than their union with other Catholics all over the world in the Mystical Body of Christ."[63] A complex network of liturgical advocates, intellectual societies such as the Catholic Evidence Guild, and "a very ardent intensification of lay spirituality and of Catholic home life" were all needed to form a profound spiritual and liturgical life for the Catholic, and to "win the world to Christ."[64] Ward understood the lay apostolate as slowly gaining momentum, slowly understanding what the relation of Christ's Mystical Body to the outside world might be, and slowly realizing its own responsibility.

Importantly, Ward believed that the liturgical movement succeeded only where active participation was encouraged first by parish leaders and then embraced by the laity. Despite years of "Catholic education," clearly articulating the meaning of the Mass, the liturgy, or the Mystical Body was challenging for many.[65] As Ward observed of her own experience, by "nothing was the lack of a Catholic mind more manifest in my youth than in our attitude towards the Mass."[66] In her estimation, Catholics viewed the ritual of the Mass as mere machinery for producing Communion. For Ward, a changed attitude would not rest with education alone but hinged on a changed liturgical experience that facilitated active participation and comprehension:

> If it is our sacrifice we must know what is happening and take part in it. The words at the altar should be audible. What mass is being said

should be announced, especially if the Proper is not being read in the vernacular. If at all possible we should be able to *see*. For this, modern churches are far better than gothic, with their pillars; an altar at which the priest faces the people far better than one at which his back is turned to them. The dialogue has done more to make the mass understood than anything else in my lifetime; and wherever it is adopted it has swept away such nineteenth century practices as the rosary said aloud at mass, or (even more distressing) the novenas that prevailed in so many American churches—"For this relief much thanks."[67]

Liturgical education and liturgical practice had to be paired together. For even fundamental shifts in practice, such as Pius X's restoration of frequent Communion, were very slowly accepted. As Ward noted, though frequent Communion became increasingly common, it seldom took its proper place in the Mass.[68] For the fullness of sacramental participation in the Mystical Body of Christ to be realized, the laity would need not only to be encouraged to take Communion but to understand how the liturgical experience of the Mass provided a ritual framework for communicants. According to Ward, liturgical renewal would be realized only through the laity's active involvement and acceptance of it; in short, success in pastoral application was "one chief test of liturgical development."[69]

Yet pastoral success did not end with intelligent ritual participants. Ward understood lay participation in the liturgy as the foundation for lay participation in the world and the source for the Christian response in social action. Formation in the liturgy required laypersons to embrace it actively and to live as the Mystical Body rather than passively accept grace and sacraments:

It is no accident that the revival of the Liturgy goes hand in hand in the Church today with Catholic Worker and Interracial Movements . . . and like groups everywhere living in voluntary poverty as laymen and making the Mass and the divine Office the food of an intense Catholic life. For others whose life is on a lower place than these it is still the essential heart of the apostolate and gathers day by day the confused threads of scattered energies out of which must somehow be woven a pattern worthy of God. The early morning brings with it a peace wrought by this great prayer of the Mystical Body going on all over the earth. Even if one is too tired or too busy to be present at Mass it is possible to be united with the Church as she offers it, to read the prayers, to join the action which somewhere in the globe of the world is being accomplished every hour of the day and night.[70]

Ward, as did others of the liturgical movement, saw both "official" Catholic Action movements and completely lay-led movements as working toward one aim of social regeneration. Particularly in the earlier days of the liturgical movement, until the Second World War, liturgical movement devotees not infrequently observed that "most persons interested in the liturgical movement are also interested in helping the poor."[71] Any action in the world—if it served Christ—began in the ritual location where the great Mystical Body gathered together, heard the word of God, and united in the sacramental participation of the Eucharist.

Through her multifaceted and long career, Maisie Ward significantly developed the literary and theological tools of the liturgical movement, through both her work with her husband and their publishing business and through her work as a lecturer among American Catholics. Sheed and Ward also helped to launch other print media representing the views of the lay apostolate, such as *Integrity*, which joined the crisscrossing web of Catholic literature promoting a holistically Catholic lifestyle for the lay apostolate, grounded in the liturgy and reaching into social responsibility and action.[72] Ward's work as a member of the lay apostolate not only served both the liturgical movement and the wider world of Catholic Action but facilitated bringing these two movements into dialogue.

Forming Women in the Lay Apostolate, the American Grail Movement

From its beginning, the liturgical movement in America was defined by its practical character. Inspired by the social encyclicals of Leo XIII (1810–1903) (*Rerum Novarum*, On Capital and Labor, 1891) and Pius XI (*Quadragesimo Anno*, On Reconstruction of the Social Order, 1931), the liturgical movement had as its original driving impulse social regeneration, for which the eucharistic liturgy served as a fundamental source. The Mystical Body of Christ, assembled in and shaped by the liturgical celebration of the sacrament, would work in the world to radically alter destructive political, economic, and social patterns of injustice.[73] Through the innovation of publishers such as Maisie Ward and Frank Sheed, and the scores of library associations, booksellers, and study clubs who circulated their literature, American Catholics increasingly became acquainted with the social encyclicals and the concept of the Mystical Body. Liturgical writers made use of such resources to explain how the liturgy served as the most direct experience of the Mystical Body of Christ, while journals such as *Commonweal* and the liturgical movement's own *Orate Fratres* offered some of the first national forums for laypeople to speak about their Catholic faith.[74]

Again, burgeoning interests in lay initiative coincided with social circumstances in the mid-twentieth-century United States. On the heels of the prosperous 1920s, the Great Depression had plunged Catholic Action circles into an atmosphere of intense social need. In response, a number of significant groups emerged to meet this need, seeking to put into practice the doctrine of the Mystical Body of Christ, which provided a paradigm for the inherent dignity of each person in the Church as a member of a united, just society.[75] At the same time, with regard to the liturgy, Catholic prayer had been in a pattern that promoted individualistic piety for many years. The liturgical movement was just beginning to encourage people to break this mold, calling not only for corporate prayer, but for prayer that extended through time and space, involving the whole of life and asking that this life be attentive to the needs of the world. As liturgical leader William Busch wrote:

> Prayer not only implores and honors God, it also educates mankind. This is especially true of liturgical prayer. The liturgy well understood will show us the meaning of the Christian religion in all its scope. The *lex orandi* will help us to know the *lex credendi* and the *lex agendi*. We shall be conscious once more of our social solidarity in Christ. We shall see a transformation of social life, agricultural, industrial and political. If this is too much to hope for Christian nations, then the outlook of the modern world is dark indeed.[76]

The attempt to reestablish the necessary connection between liturgy, life, and social action recalled the maxim of Prosper of Aquitaine (ca. fifth century) that *ut legem credendi lex statuat supplicandi*, often shortened to *lex credendi, lex orandi*: the law of prayer grounds the law of belief. Twentieth-century liturgical reformers added *lex agendi* (later, *lex vivendi*) to this axiom, as they wished to articulate that the fruits of liturgical prayer and belief fed a more holistic life.

The American Grail movement, a final example of the leadership of laywomen in developing the liturgical life through the action of the lay apostolate, epitomizes the intersection of lex orandi, lex credendi, and lex agendi. As the liturgical movement continued to develop, and the atmosphere of Catholic Action found more adherents among lay Catholics as the Church progressed into the 1940s and 1950s, American laywomen continued to explore how one might integrate a Catholic liturgical lifestyle with all realms of living, from social responsibility to family life. Specifically designed as an experiential, spiritual, and educational program for young Roman Catholic women, the American Grail movement exemplified this desire to fully integrate practical matters of life with the practice of the liturgy.

The Grail movement, begun in Holland, was organized by Rev. Jacques van Ginneken (1877–1949) as a Catholic organization for young working women.[77] Though small at the start, the association of women, who eventually took the name "the Grail" (in reference to the medieval legend of King Arthur), grew to become a widely popular and international youth movement. In Holland alone, Grail events could draw thousands of young women participants.[78] With the rise of the Nazis, however, Catholic organizational power plummeted, as did the Grail. Two members, Lydwine van Kersbergen (1905–98) and Joan Overboss (1910–69), left Holland and immigrated to the United States in 1940 with the hope of reestablishing the Grail there. In the American context, first in Libertyville, Illinois, and later in Loveland, Ohio, the Grail community offered a distinctive opportunity for young women to experience a simpler way of life. The American Grail movement, in concert with the "back to the land" initiatives such as that supported by the National Catholic Rural Life Conference, sought to introduce young Catholic women to an alternative lifestyle: Rather than the busyness of the modern world in which they could produce nothing and control little, young women were invited to a life in which they could have great control over forming their own identities and friendships and could learn how to do good work by hand. At "Grailville," free from the pressures of lipstick and fashion magazines, young women took lessons in gardening, baking, and weaving and enjoyed recreation centered in conversation, singing, and dramatics. Praying as a community framed each day for them at Grailville. Such a program had two chief goals: First, it invited women to action in community, and, second, it grounded all activities in the communal prayer of the Church.

Unique to the Grail experience was its explicit intention for the advocacy and education of young Catholic women in the United States. On the one hand, identifying the specific role of women in advocating the liturgical life and effecting social change was not new. On the European scene, Odo Casel, O.S.B. (1886–1948), Aemiliana Löhr, O.S.B. (1892–1972), and Ildefons Herwegen, O.S.B. (1874–1946), among others, wrote, spoke, and led discussions about the specific role of women in liturgical and social renewal.[79] And, when the liturgical movement arrived in the United States, Michel continued this trend in several articles and presentations to Catholic women's groups, with his usual enthusiasm:

> We are thus in crying need of a renewal in Christ, of a return to a deeper understanding of the ideals of Christianity, of a fuller submission of the souls of men to the action of divine grace as enacted in the life of the Church of God. How is that to be brought about? What is one of the most powerful natural means of bringing souls of men into contact with these channels of grace, of disposing them towards this contact? The answer is WOMAN![80]

While Michel introduced this particular mode of considering Christian women during the early stages of the liturgical movement, an emphasis on the specific role of women in establishing a reformed society did not become a major emphasis in most American liturgical movement venues until after the Second World War.[81] In the latter half of the 1940s, attention shifted to the family as the basic unit for social reconstruction, as an increasing Catholic population began to people the middle class, enjoying greater national organization, increased access to education, and weakening ties to immigrant pasts.[82] In response to the Catholic faithful's shifting social location, members of the liturgical movement were prompted to produce resources and commentaries on the family's role in living the liturgical apostolate.[83] In particular, as the liturgical movement developed through the latter 1940s and into the 1950s, Catholic women were encouraged to adopt devotional practices, such as baking Easter bread or decorating an "Advent wreath," that were previously ethnically based and to recast such activities as authentic ways of expressing American Catholic identity through liturgically appropriate means. An increasingly "American-ized" Catholic population embraced a melting pot of liturgically oriented devotional practices, eschewed socialism and "atheistic Communism," and looked to the restoration of Catholic family life as a central remedy for society.[84]

This complex nexus of Catholic identity, of reclaiming control over individuals, homes, and communities from "modern secularism," and of promoting *liturgically based* devotional practices, found a unique realiza-tion in the American Grail. Through experiential programs, Grailville, or the "Grail School," became an oasis for young women, in which they might cultivate the values of organized Catholic Action and learn to love the prayer life for which liturgical movement leaders longed:

> The Grail Schools are intensive periods of formation for positive Chris-tian action. Their purpose is to prepare young women all over America as great-hearted *women*, radiant *Christians*, and generous *apostles* to enable them to meet the profound universal problems of our time and to contribute in their specific capacity as women, in an organized postulate under the leadership of the hierarchy, towards a Christian future.[85]

To this end, the earliest members of the Grail movement emphasized the charisms available to young women, particularly their potential for the domestic vocation, and taught that women and men had complementary roles. As Grailville evolved, it continually grappled with the concept of the Christian "Woman" and the role of woman in modern society.[86] After the Second Vatican Council, the Grail became less identifiably Catholic and more associated with women's movements and feminism. But, this place, specifically inviting women to enter into the liturgical apostolate, was seen as a unique way for women to enter into the work of Catholic Action and, in the liturgical movement, to join in the goal of restoring society.

When the Grail movement first arrived in the United States in 1940, the women came to the Archdiocese of Chicago at the invitation of Aux-iliary Bishop Bernard Sheil (1888–1969), where they set up their program at what would become known as Doddridge Farm. During their first Holy Week, in 1941, the Grail community held a retreat for about thirty young women, drawn from Catholic Action groups in Chicago, Milwaukee, Toledo, and New York. Under the direction of Fr. James Coffey (1908–2007), retreatants experienced the "full and solemn performance of the rites of Holy Week" through active participation in the rites and by taking part in "exercises and ceremonies" that reflected the liturgy.[87] As the week progressed, the women took part in a paschal meal on Holy Thursday, in Stations of the Cross on Good Friday, and in a renewal of baptismal vows individually on Holy Saturday. The event, as longtime Grail member Janet Kalven detailed in her report in *Orate Fratres* on the group's retreat, was not only a time of individual sharing in the life of God, but an experience of sharing in the Mystical Body. Some participants even expressed surprise that social prayer could be spiritually formative, as one young woman who attended the retreat described her experience: "I wouldn't have believed that other people could be a help instead of a distraction during a retreat."[88] The Grail approach introduced women to a communal experience of liturgical prayer, a contrast to customary devotional practices that were, even if publicly performed, still performed by the individual.

The Grail more consistently commanded the attention of the liturigcal movement pioneers through the advocacy of such individuals as Robert B. Heywood, professor at the University of Chicago. In his article "The Spirit of the Grail," which appeared in *Orate Fratres* (June 1941), Heywood described the American Grail movement as a distinct manifestation of the best of Catholic Action correlated to the liturgical movement. He was concerned that "Catholic Action" had come to refer to any response, from the Catholic Worker movement to the formation of baseball teams for Catholic boys' high schools. The heart of Catholic Action, however, was not "action by Catholics," but action that had *expansion of the kingdom of God* at its heart: "the participation of the layman in the apostolate."[89] That is to say, any apostolic action or social action should flow from an awareness of and a desire to express Christian (or Catholic) identity. Drawing on *Liturgy and Life* (1938) by Theodore Wesseling, O.S.B., Heywood noted that before "doing something" or "acting" was possible, one had to be concerned about "being," or identity. Likewise, "before you think of the liturgical movement, be liturgical yourself."[90] Catholic Action had to flow from the Christian life—a Christian life that, Heywood observed, was synonymous with the liturgical life and the Grail program.[91]

The work of the Grail School was broadly attentive to the Christian life. Girls from high schools, colleges, parish cells, Catholic Action groups, and workplaces attended Grail programs promoting an intensive "liturgical" lifestyle. For example, a course offered by the Ladies of the Grail in the summer of 1943 offered two-to-three-week courses entitled "The Role of Women in a Christian World Reconstruction," "Leadership Training and Work with Children," "The Liturgy and Plainchant of the Church," and "The Principles and Practices of Rural Living."[92] Virginia Bogdan of Rochester, New York, attended one such Grail training course and reported positively on her experience for the readers of Orate Fratres, enthusiastically relaying how the Grail women experienced leading liturgical teachers and Catholic writers. At the end of the course, Bogdan concluded, the women "came to see that the best possible training for the apostolate is a life lived in the wholehearted spirit of the liturgy."[93]

Certainly, as witnessed by Bogdan, accounts of the Grailville summer programs of the 1940s through the 1950s presented an outstanding roster of Catholic thinkers and writers, including leaders of the liturgical movement. The women who participated in the Grail experienced the central tools and methods being promoted by liturgical pioneers to facilitate lay participation, including the dialogue Mass (or Missa recitata), the Divine Office, the missal, and chant.[94] As the Grail became more established with its move to new facilities in Loveland, Ohio, in 1943–1944, permanent Grail members continued their summer programs and added to the volume of resources, in multiple forms of media, that they produced and sold. According to Kalven, as the Grail women discovered "ideas and activities which proved vivifying for the community at Grailville," they compiled them and shared them through programs and publications.[95] For example, the National Liturgical Week of 1948 used the theme "Restore the Sunday," which inspired the Grail to create a resource of the same title (Restore the Sunday, 1949), an apostolic program that provided articles, plans for six meetings and a final celebration, and practical suggestions for family activities. As historian Alden Brown notes, many of the Grail's published materials were intended to draw Catholics—particularly Catholic families—into the liturgical life of the Church by emphasizing and describing how feasts and seasons of the liturgical year could be enacted.[96] Restore the Sunday was the most developed project that the Grail produced, followed by a companion volume, Toward a Christian Sunday (1949), which drew on other texts—such as Florence Berger's (1905–83) Cooking for Christ (1949), a "liturgical" cookbook—that sought to facilitate women's initiative in taking the liturgical life into the home.[97] The Grail women identified true social regeneration as beginning with the smallest unit of society, the family, within which women had a powerful influence in forming their families in a truly Catholic lifestyle, from awareness of the liturgical year to rejection of secularized and commercialized holidays. Resources such as *Let Us Baptize Thanksgiving* (1949) and *New Life for New Year's Eve* (1950) suggested ways to Christianize secular holidays, while other booklets, such as *Promised in Christ* (1955) and *The Church Blessed Motherhood* (1957), spoke of ways to "solemnize events" surrounding the female life cycle, including engagement, marriage, and childbirth.[98]

Continuing the drive for Catholic laypeople's assumption of responsibility for reforming society and culture, van Kersbergen gave an address on the theological and cultural aspects of Sunday in Grailville at the 1949 Liturgical Week meeting, held in St. Louis. Drawing on her publication, *The Normal School of Sanctity for the Laity* (1949), she described the modern world's capture by secularism in every sphere of life. It was the responsibility of the laity, who, by their vocation, "are the builders of the family, . . . the owners, managers, workers, patrons, members of the institutions to be Christianized."[99] She described how the dynamism of the Holy Spirit had raised up "a new organ in the mystical body," the apostolate of the laity, to accomplish this re-Christianization of society. The call to the Christian was to form her life in this life of the Church:

> With the Sacrifice of the Mass as the center of each day and the Divine Office as the consecration of the hours, with the Sunday to sanctify the week, the cycle of fasts and feasts to hallow the year, and the sacraments to elevate the span of life from birth to death, we find the fundamental plan for our growth in Christ.[100]

The Grail's mission was to invite young women into this task, training them in the faith through active participation and ownership in the liturgy.

While the Grail encouraged domestic homemakers, they also trained women for international mission fields. By the 1950s, the Grail had become a national group, with centers in a number of American cities, a School of Missiology in Grailville (1950) and the Institute for Overseas Service in Brooklyn (1956).[101] Kalven reflected on the popularity of the Grail movement:

Every summer, carloads came from the cities to Grailville for weeklong or summerlong courses, some staying on for the full year. Grailville burst at its seams, all the barns becoming sleeping places, the dining rooms spilling over to the porch and lawns. As strange as the lay apostolate, the liturgical movement, social action were to most Catholics, the momentum was gaining on all fronts, a quiet revolution, for new life in the church.[102]

By 1962, when the Grail held its first national conference, an estimated fourteen thousand women had taken part in Grail programs.[103] After this point, the Grail entered its next phase, with growing ecumenical initiatives, inviting women from various religious backgrounds to be part of the Grail as well as becoming increasingly involved in the emerging feminist movement.[104] Yet during the "heyday of Catholic Action" and the most promising days of the liturgical movement, during the 1930s through the 1950s, the Grail flourished as a center for liturgically fed Catholic Action. Its message and its method were immensely appealing, fueled by and formative for American Catholic laywomen.

Conclusion: The Role of Women in Catholic Action and the Liturgical Movement

The increasing involvement and initiative expressed by laywomen during the middle decades of the twentieth century within the realms of both Catholic Action and the liturgical movement paired with shifting societal and cultural norms for women. Changing needs for labor accompanying the Great Depression and the Second World War were accompanied by shifting perceptions of women's roles as solely homebound wives and mothers. Not only did secular society advocate new roles for women (and supply the material technology to make household tasks easier), but wartime demands issued women the patriotic charge to take up labor of all kinds. Yet many Catholics viewed this increased pressure on American women to leave the domestic realm as threatening. Journals and popular magazines such as *Our Daily Messenger* and *Catholic Women's World* continued to advocate values that would support traditional roles of women as wives and mothers.

Other Catholics, however, saw the development of the rights of women as educated citizens and contributing workers to be coincident with

Catholic Action. These advocates believed that Catholic professionals, including the increasing number of graduates from women's colleges, might contribute to a society in a way that was informed and practical.[105] Certainly, Catholic Action, which stressed the importance of gearing up, educating, and involving the laity in a myriad of activities both private and public, included women as well. As for the liturgical movement activists, most women demonstrated a significant educational background and involvement in multiple arenas of activity and not exclusively as mothers and wives. In fact, up to the 1940s, many of the most involved female activists were single women, divorced women, or women who married in middle age. The freedom of mobility enjoyed by socially independent women characterized the liturgical movement during the late 1920s through the 1930s, with its emphasis on education and study of liturgical tools, such as Latin or Gregorian chant, and its radical social realizations, such as involvement in the Catholic Worker movement or confronting the "interracial problem."

In short, a curious tension exists between the "traditional" Catholic values of woman as wife and mother and the most active figures of the liturgical movement, who tended to defy these values as they took up the charge of Catholic Action. At the same time, though their lives may have implicitly demonstrated women's freedom and independence, most women who became involved with the liturgical movement did not speak of women's rights or women's right to activity in the Church or the world. Instead, women had a *duty* to act. An emphasis on "women's work" can be found more frequently in the pronouncements of women's organizations under ecclesial figures (e.g., the NCCW) and was also part of the ethos of the early Grail movement. In contrast, Maisie Ward, though she felt called—even duty-bound—to use her gifts to educate other lay Catholics, identified her profession and activity in the lay apostolate not as distinctly feminine, but as Christian. Ward's example resonates more freely with the mainstream advocates of the liturgical movement who identified themselves as *Christians* who were called to social action: They were called to be the Mystical Body of Christ in the world.[106] One was formed in the Mystical Body by participation in liturgical prayer, consciously and actively; this was not necessarily a feminine task. However, by the close of the 1930s, and particularly with the advent of the American Grail movement, an increasing number of liturgical pioneers sought to exemplify how women *as women* might specifically contribute to a holistic liturgical life, in which labor and lifestyle prepared young women or women who were mothers, wives, or in other familial roles to incorporate the liturgical life into their homes and to model this life for those around them.

The three examples used here, the NCCW, the work of Maisie Ward, and the American Grail, represent different ways in which women entered into the burgeoning landscape of the liturgical movement and Catholic Action. Though these women's "womanhood" shaped their involvement to varying degrees, their role as laywomen was essential. The American liturgical movement became a natural focus for laywomen who were interested in greater spiritual understanding, intellectual grasp, and active realization of their faith as Roman Catholics in any of the venues promoted by Catholic Action. In part, these women were inspired to adopt the liturgical movement as a natural response to the needs of modern American Roman Catholicism by papal inspiration (e.g., Pius X's motu proprio *Tra le sollecitudini*) and by the intellectual and theological trends of their time (e.g., the concept of the Mystical Body).[107] They were also driven by a concern for what was increasingly regarded as rampart secularism: the social evils of industrialism, capitalism, and the relative usury of modern society, which stripped the individual of freedom, creativity, pride in one's work—in short, of all the vitality of human life. Thus, those lay Catholic women (and men) already interested in reform— from social action to education to the arts—found the ethos of the liturgical movement and its theological underpinnings in the Mystical Body easy to integrate. In fact, the distinctiveness of the American liturgical movement is often identified by its integration with the American scene of social action, and the activity of the laity was essential for the movement to succeed.[108]

Living the liturgical life allowed the liturgy to permeate the veil of passivity that had long plagued Catholic sacramental life and to invite Catholics to enter the world. The liturgical movement prepared the lay apostolate for Catholic Action, and Catholic Action primed the lay apostolate for greater initiative, interest, and ownership over the Faith from the fringes of Catholic liturgical life to its core, the eucharistic sacrifice of the Mass. Far from its fringes, laywomen worked, prayed, and lived at the heart of this vibrant period of American Catholicism.

3 "The Priesthood of the Layman"

Catholic Action in the Archdiocese of San Francisco

WILLIAM ISSEL

"Catholic Action opens up a new world for the zeal of the faithful, a new world wherein they can share in the Apostolate of the Church and cooperate with their pastors and priests in spreading the Kingdom of Christ in individual souls, in families and in society." San Francisco attorney Sylvester Andriano's eager anticipation of a Catholicism revitalized by lay activism followed his return from Rome in September 1938. Cardinal Giuseppe Pizzardo had just approved the plans for Andriano's proposed Catholic Action men's organization, and Andriano shared his enthusiasm at an assembly of laity and clergy called by Archbishop John J. Mitty at St. Mary's Cathedral:

> *Dieu le vault*—God wills it, cried the crusaders of old with Pope Urban II and Peter the Hermit when it was a matter of rescuing the Holy Sepulchre and the Holy Places from the hands of the infidels. *Dieu le vault*—we can repeat today in unison with our pastors and priests in answer to the clarion call of our Holy Father and of our own Archbishop when it is a matter of rescuing individual souls, the home, the school, public morals and Christian civilization itself from the blight of the new paganism and the frightful chaos of Communism.[1]

This chapter recounts the story of the San Francisco Catholic Action "lay apostolate" centered on attorney Sylvester Andriano and a variety of other laymen and laywomen. The program operated with the unqualified backing and blessing of Archbishop John J. Mitty (archbishop from 1935 to 1961) and began when the Archdiocese of San Francisco occupied 16,856 square miles, a territory slightly larger than Denmark. More than 400,000 Catholics lived in the thirteen Bay Area counties of the archdiocese, from Santa Clara in the south to Mendocino in the north, which comprised 174 parishes served by 600 priests. Catholic leaders claimed that the sixty parishes of San Francisco embraced fully half of the city's population, but a census-bureau count made in 1936 put Catholics at 28 percent of the population and 68 percent of all church members.[2]

This San Francisco Catholic Action program took place in a city that was dramatically different from the multicultural metropolis familiar to international tourists today. During the 1930s and 1940s, Irish, German, and Italian immigrants, their children, and their grandchildren made up nearly two-thirds of a population, 94 percent of which was of white European background. Not all San Franciscans were Catholics, but Catholics were predominant in the blue-collar workforce, and they filled executive, midlevel, and lower-echelon positions in business, government, and the professions. Not all Catholics practiced their religion, but a sizeable number—a "critical mass"—of the city's Catholics took their faith seriously by attending Sunday Mass, providing financial support to their parish churches and the archdiocese, and participating in outdoor neighborhood and citywide religious ceremonies. The specific lay apostolate work associated with Catholic Action from the 1930s through the 1950s existed in a context of Catholic activism that first became a feature of San Francisco life during the 1890s.[3]

San Franciscans were alert to the encyclical letters of popes Leo XIII, Pius X, and Pius XI from the time that Pope Leo XIII (1810–1903) issued his encyclical *Rerum Novarum* (On Capital and Labor) in 1891. San Francisco labor activists eagerly claimed the moral authority contained in the pontiff's defense of private property, his condemnation of laissez-faire business practices, and his defense of the right of workers to organize labor unions. The Pacific Coast Laborers' Union dispatched a letter to the Vatican expressing "our pleasure and gratitude for the Encyclical. It comes to us like rays of the sun, dispelling the gloom of our despair." Archbishops Patrick Riordan and Edward Hanna aggressively and consistently promoted *Rerum Novarum,* as did the popular and influential priest Fr. Peter Yorke, labor leaders such as Michael Casey of the Teamsters union, Patrick McCarthy of the carpenters union (who served one term as city mayor), and leading businessmen and professionals such as Chamber of Commerce president Frederick Koster and Hearst Publications counselor John Francis Neylan. From the 1890s to the 1930s, Catholic activists in San Francisco critiqued laissez-faire business principles and practices and promoted unionization and the principle that workers be treated with dignity and respect. Unfettered capitalism merited opprobrium, not praise, in the city's Catholic political culture; Archbishop Hanna (1915–35) chaired several mediation boards and regularly counseled the city's unionists.[4]

Papal pronouncements set the parameters for early twentieth-century San Francisco Catholic activism beyond labor relations, beginning with an explicit call for "Catholic Action" by Pope Pius X (1835–1914) in his 1905 encyclical *Il Fermo Proposito* (On Catholic Action in Italy), which urged the Catholic laity to become actively engaged in what might be called applied Christianity. The message was straightforward: "Bands of Catholics [will] aim to unite all their forces in combating anti-Christian civilization by every just and lawful means." Pius XI (1857–1939) reiterated the call to revitalize Catholic religious practice and to convince Catholics to participate more actively *as Catholics* in public life when he issued two letters at a time when the victory of the Fascists over the Italian Communist Party and the organization of a Catholic political party challenged the papacy to provide guidance to its communicants both inside Italy and beyond.[5] In 1922, Pius XI issued *Ubi Arcano Dei Consilio* (On the Peace of Christ in the Kingdom of Christ) and reiterated Pius X's definition of Catholic Action. In 1925, in *Quas Primas* (On the Feast of Christ the King), the pope announced a new Catholic feast day to be held on the third Sunday of October, as "an excellent remedy for the plague that now infests society . . . the plague of anti-clericalism, its errors and impious activities." Filled with martial rhetoric, the encyclical chastised Catholics generally, not only those in Italy. Pius XI was displeased because Catholics showed "a certain slowness and timidity," and he noted that they "are reluctant to engage in conflict or oppose but a weak resistance." Catholics were told that "it behooves them ever to fight courageously under the banner of Christ their King" and that "then, fired with apostolic zeal, they would strive to win over to their Lord those hearts that are bitter and estranged from him, and would valiantly defend his rights."

Sylvester Andriano (1889–1963), a scholarly San Francisco attorney with a keen interest in Catholic theology, paid careful attention to the encyclicals issued by Pius XI. The Italian-born Andriano graduated from St. Mary's College of California in 1911 and became a naturalized citizen in 1915. He became active in the archdiocesan Young Men's Institute and cofounded the Italian Catholic newspaper *L'Unione*. From the time he was a student through the 1920s, he worked with Archbishop Hanna to revitalize Catholic religious practice among the city's Italian American residents. Andriano was impressed by the militant spirit of *Ubi Arcano Dei Consilio*. He responded eagerly to the pope's call for Catholics, including "that whole group of movements, organizations, and works so dear to Our fatherly heart which passes under the name of 'Catholic Action,'" to lead the way in restoring "the fundamental principles of Christianity" to a central place in world affairs "both in public and private life." In his enumeration of the activities particularly crucial for lay activism, the pope emphasized "the *holy battle* waged on so many fronts to vindicate for the family and the Church the natural and divinely given rights which they possess over education and the school."[6]

Sylvester Andriano and some 80,000 fellow Catholics turned out on October 5, 1924, to mark the anniversary of the founding of the Holy Name Society; they marched the length of Market Street, San Francisco's major downtown thoroughfare, in a demonstration against the Ku Klux Klan. Andriano also supported a variety of Catholic Action youth programs during the 1920s. Whether it was because he was responding directly to Pius XI's call for waging a "holy battle" on the educational front, or because he was compensating for the fact that he and his wife were childless, or perhaps for both reasons (the record is silent), Andriano became especially active in the "Little Italy" North Beach neighborhood Catholic youth programs and served as the chairman of the statewide Knights of Columbus Catholic education committee. St. Mary's College depended on him as a guest instructor in their "transition course" for members of the graduating class, where he suggested Catholic alternatives to "the curse of individualism."[7]

By the late 1920s Andriano and his friend and law client Angelo Rossi had both gained citywide influence by serving on the San Francisco board of supervisors. Rossi became mayor in 1931, and he sent Andriano to Europe as the city's delegate to an international conference. During his trip abroad, Andriano visited his brother, a Salesian priest, in Turin, where the Fascist regime's thugs were attacking the papal Catholic Action youth organizations. Twelve years later Sylvester Andriano recalled the significance of this visit to Italy: The pope was "stoutly defending Catholic Action against the unwarranted attacks of the Fascists and denouncing some of the teachings and practices of Fascism including the Fascist oath.

I became really interested in Catholic Action and upon my return to San Francisco undertook the study of it in earnest."[8]

Andriano especially concurred with *Non Abbiamo Bisogno*'s (On Catholic Action in Italy) robust criticism of the Fascist government's attempts to limit the scope and effectiveness of lay Catholic organizations, especially those of children and young adults. And the attorney cheered on Pius XI's reassertion of the legitimacy of the Church's attempts to shape moral education and to ensure Christian morality in public affairs. Andriano also supported how *Quadragesimo Anno* (On Reconstruction of the Social Order) reasserted the principles of Leo XIII's 1891 encyclical on labor and capital, *Rerum Novarum*, in which he urged Catholics worldwide to insist on a moral economy. Pius XI condemned what he considered utopian left-wing ideologies and social movements and materialist business practices backed by laissez-faire governments that ignored the general good of the community. He urged Catholics to take the lead in organizing new community institutions designed to foster cooperation among workers, business owners, and government officials, and he excoriated the notions that class conflict was natural, that irreconcilable differences separated working people and the business class, and that an overthrow of all existing things would accomplish paradise on earth for the workers of the world.[9]

Pius XI eventually compromised with the Fascist regime by downsizing his Catholic Action initiative into a diocesan endeavor.[10] That being the case, it seemed reasonable that in the United States, as in Italy, American laypersons could make Catholic Action programs a high-priority local option, provided their bishops approved. Pius XI had agreed to shrink Catholic Action by removing it from electoral politics and restricting its remaining activities to diocesan boundaries. But the pope issued no corresponding reduction in the theory of Catholic Action; the scope and limits of Catholic Action theory had in fact expanded with the Vatican's call, in the encyclical *Quadragesimo Anno* (1931), for "reconstruction" of the social order. What did this ambiguity portend for Catholics in the United States? Did the papal agreement regarding Catholic Action in Italy cause bishops, priests, and laymen and laywomen in the United States to reduce Catholic Action interest-group efforts in the fields of education, labor and capital, and anti-Communism and as well in areas that touched on other issues such as birth control and public morals?

American bishops responded by actually intensifying their efforts to create more effective diocesan Catholic Action work nationwide along the lines of the encyclicals of Pius XI. The coordinating agency for this work was the National Catholic Welfare Conference, an interest group that represented American bishops with headquarters in Washington, D.C., and its chairman during this period was Archbishop Hanna of San Francisco. It was in this context that Sylvester Andriano dedicated himself to Pope Pius XI's Catholic Action program and that Hanna's newly arrived coadjutor archbishop, John J. Mitty, called for a revitalization of Christian practice by means of a new Catholic Action initiative in San Francisco. Mitty's call demonstrated that he and Archbishop Hanna intended to increase, not reduce, faith-based public activism in the city. This decision set the stage for an aggressive assertion of Catholic Action by San Francisco lay activists.[11]

Archbishop John J. Mitty (1884–1961; served 1935–61) brought a spirited martial approach to his work when he arrived in San Francisco as coadjutor archbishop in 1932 after having served as bishop of Salt Lake City. A former battlefield chaplain who had participated in the Meuse-Argonne offensive in France during the First World War, Mitty's leadership style combined efficient administration of archdiocesan business affairs with zealous evangelism in connection with the message of the papal encyclicals. He chose as the official motto of his episcopal office the phrase "Mihi vivere Christus est" (To me, to live is Christ).[12]

Scarcely a year after the Vatican promulgated the two 1931 encyclicals, Archbishop Mitty issued his first invitation to laymen and laywomen to join a Catholic Action campaign in San Francisco. Meeting with members of the local branch of the National Council of Catholic Women on May 7, 1932, Mitty called for a broad campaign on several fronts. "Catholic Action," the archbishop reminded his audience, "has been preached to us in season and out of season" and it was time to move beyond rhetoric to practice.

Our aim [in this campaign] is to bring the ideals and principles of Christ into every phase of human life, into our own individual life, into family, social, economic, professional, political and national life. We are striving to advance the interests of Christ, to bring the spirit of Christ into our homes, our reception halls, our workshops, our offices,

our legislative assemblies. We have a duty to make a contribution of
Christian ideals and principles to the nation.

The "purpose and object" of lay organizations, Mitty stressed, "is not political. Neither as a Church nor an organization are we interested in any
political aim or any political party." However, "we cannot live as if we
were not part of the country," and we must "work unceasingly for both
Church and country, for both Cross and Flag."[13]

Four months later, Sylvester Andriano responded to Archbishop Mitty's Catholic Action call when he and his law partner William R. Lowery
established a San Francisco branch of a national program of the new
Catholic League for Social Justice. Andriano and Lowery called their organization the Academy of San Francisco, and Archbishops Hanna and
Mitty approved their new lay initiative in April 1933. The Academy operated out of Andriano and Lowery's office at 550 Montgomery Street, in
the heart of the city's financial district. In the first six months, it enrolled
three dozen members, including several judges, numerous attorneys and
physicians, and Gordon O'Neill, the editor of the archdiocesan newspaper, the Monitor. Each member pledged "to inform myself on Catholic
doctrine on Social Justice, to conform my life to its requirements, and to
do everything in my power, in my home and religious life, in my social
and business contacts, to promote its principles." Their object, they explained, was "to mobilize the combined strength of all these existing [San
Francisco Catholic devotional and social] societies to enable their members to answer the call of our Holy Father." The men were now part of a
network of Catholic Action lay activists in fifty-four dioceses, from New
York City to San Francisco. Sylvester Andriano agreed to chair the Committee on Catholic Education in California.[14]

The response of Andriano and his colleagues to the call for intensified
Catholic Action work attracted the attention of the pope's representative
in the United States, Apostolic Delegate Archbishop Amleto Giovanni
Cicognani, who praised San Francisco efforts "to prepare laymen for
Catholic Action. It is becoming urgently necessary," Cicognani wrote, "to
prepare laymen who under the guidance of the Bishops and priests will
speak for the Church. Students of our Universities and Colleges should
give special attention to the Social Question so that they may assume a
lay leadership which is truly Catholic and which will resourcefully make

popular Catholic principles. This is but complying with the wish of the Holy Father. It will make practical His Holiness' plan of Catholic Action."[15]

Attorney Roy A. Bronson advertised the work of the Academy in a letter sent to the pastors of every Catholic Church in San Francisco, urging them to provide "the Catholic laity with a program of Catholic action and an opportunity to exercise their full moral and civic duty in the reconstruction of our social and economic order in the Christian spirit of justice, charity, moderation and fortitude." In August the Academy announced its first project, a yearlong program of biweekly lectures devoted to "finding out the facts in connection with Education in our country and to test the value of these facts in the light of Catholic principles." When members assembled at the Hotel Cecil that fall and winter, they heard a variety of presentations analyzing education from the perspective of Catholic Action, including presentations by Sylvester Andriano praising "The Catholic Educational Program" in California and by Judge Robert McWilliams critiquing secular attempts "to nationalize the system of education in this country."[16]

Two weeks after the McWilliams lecture, the *Monitor* published a lengthy attack on the school-reform work of Columbia University professor John Dewey, a leading critic of Catholic natural-law philosophy who had repelled Catholic intellectuals by rejecting the concept of an absolute Deity while cynically acknowledging the utility of religion in society. Dewey was only the tip of the iceberg, according to the editorial "A Revolution by Professors," which warned against an insidious process underway throughout the nation: "Teachers in the American public schools are invited and urged to become agents of a revolution; which has as its objective the American brand of communism." Echoing Pope Leo XIII's condemnation of social democracy in 1901, the editorial warned against "a monopolistic State, governed by materialist university men. Our only hope is to make the Church felt in practical political and communal life."[17]

On March 3, just over a month after the *Monitor* urged its readers to make their presence felt in the city's public affairs, the union representing dockworkers on the Pacific Coast began a strike that lasted until the end of July. Catholic Action activists seized the opportunity provided by the strike to demonstrate they were a force to be reckoned with in San Francisco. Throughout the strike, Hanna, Mitty, and the *Monitor* spoke out against the laissez-faire position of the waterfront employers' association. And Sylvester Andriano, representing the new Catholic Academy in Mayor Angelo Rossi's Citizens Committee of 25, successfully argued against those committee members who urged Rossi to ask the state's governor to send troops to settle the strike. "I was the only member of that committee on the side of labor and vigorously opposed the almost unanimous attempt of the committee to terrorize and brow-beat Mayor Rossi into petitioning the Governor to call in the militia."[18]

On July 20, Francis J. Neylan, a Catholic attorney who represented the Hearst interests on the West Coast and was close to Archbishop Hanna, hosted a meeting of the waterfront employers at his Woodside home and reminded them of the damage to the city's business reputation should they continue their uncompromising stance. Neylan echoed the San Francisco Academy's argument that *Rerum Novarum* and *Quadragesimo Anno* mandated approval of the strike committee's major outstanding demand: a union hiring hall controlled by the International Longshoremen's Association. Archbishop Hanna's arbitration board continued its deliberations as the teamsters returned to their jobs on July 21, and nine days later Hanna announced an end to the strike after negotiating a compromise: a hiring hall jointly operated by the union and the employers.[19]

In the months following the waterfront and general strikes of 1934, Sylvester Andriano and Archbishop Mitty intensified their relationship and collaborated in building a Catholic Action lay apostolate in San Francisco more extensive than the San Francisco Academy that Andriano and Lowery had organized in 1933. On May 12, 1935, the archbishop and the attorney participated in the graduation exercises at St. Mary's College in Moraga. Mitty awarded the diplomas to the eighty-six graduates, and Andriano gave the commencement address, praising the accomplishments of the class of 1935 but bemoaning "the lapse of Catholic Action" in the curriculum of Catholic schools and colleges. He decried the absence of Catholic Action courses in the Catholic high schools and colleges in California, suggested the importance of not only learning the theory of Catholic Action but also "developing workers in the ranks," and urged his audience to make Catholic Action an integral part of their private and public lives.[20]

The collaboration between Andriano and Mitty reflected their experience in bringing Catholic values to bear on the settlement of the 1934 waterfront and general strikes, but it also stemmed from their desire to implement the Vatican's plan for Catholic Action, which was newly detailed in the *Manual of Catholic Action* by Monsignor Luigi Civardi. Written and published in Italian in 1933, the first English translation of Civardi's work appeared two years later; the translator, Jesuit priest C. C. Martindale, suggested that the term "lay apostolate" served as the best translation of the Italian *Azione Cattolica*. The official archdiocesan newspaper published an extensive summary of Civardi's description of the theory and practice of this "lay apostolate" work in a series of articles from February through April 1935, concluding with a discussion of education—"the Scholastic Field"—stressing that "the school is among the most efficacious instruments of ideal propaganda and education. This is so well understood by the enemies of Christ, that they have at all times and everywhere attempted to mould the school system to their false educational standards."[21]

After the St. Mary's commencement, Archbishop Mitty turned to Andriano again, this time for advice about "the condition of the Italians in California with regard to religion," and the attorney responded with a detailed analysis. Then, after a ten-page discussion of the Italian question, Andriano wrote:

> You will pardon me if I seem to digress from my subject to speak of Catholic Action. . . . If it be desired to develop a lay apostolate worthy of the name, resort must be had to Catholic Action properly so called. The study of the encyclicals on the teachings of the Church on various questions is both useful and necessary but it is not an end in itself and unless it culminates in action it is of no very great avail. How fitting it would be for San Francisco to take the lead in fostering Catholic Action among American cities.[22]

Worried that the archbishop might consider his unsolicited advice an expression of "ill-regulated zeal," Andriano asked him to "forgive me for it." But rather than criticize the layman for his enthusiasm, Mitty asked him to participate in an even more important occasion. After indicating that the Catholic school-board members unanimously recommended Andriano, the archbishop asked him to present the commencement address for the 1936 graduation ceremony of all seven San Francisco Catholic high schools and academies, some 750 graduates, at the city's Dreamland Auditorium. Mitty's satisfaction with Andriano's speech before an audience of nearly ten thousand in the Dreamland Auditorium moved the attorney to draft a "Plan for Catholic Action," which he shared with the archbishop in September.[23]

In early October, the archbishop confided to Fr. Thomas N. O'Kane, a professor at St. Joseph's College, the preparatory seminary of the archdiocese, that he was impressed with Andriano's proposal of having a limited group of laymen make a study of real Catholic Action. "Mr. Andriano has probably read everything that has been published on the subject and has the Catholic ideal of it, and he wants to get a dozen or more laymen imbued with the same principles, so that we can get real Catholic Action instead of some of the fool things that parade under the name. Mitty asked O'Kane to meet with Andriano and his colleagues as they developed their plans "so that the group would keep within the reservation."[24]

Andriano met with Fr. O'Kane in October and then began buttonholing fellow members of the San Francisco Academy and other Catholic Action enthusiasts who were likely to share his ambitious vision to build a more extensive "real Catholic Action" program. One of the first men he approached was James L. Hagerty, a philosophy professor at St. Mary's College. Hagerty had begun teaching at St. Mary's immediately after graduating from it with a bachelor's degree in 1919. He earned a master's degree in 1921 and commenced a career as a philosophy professor at St. Mary's, and in 1930 he began publishing a Catholic literary review, the *Moraga Quarterly*. Hagerty was a lifelong bachelor who sported a Clark Gable mustache, and students flocked to his popular classes. He mentored a number of students who would later become leading figures in Bay Area Catholic circles, and in November 1936 one of his protégés, Joseph L. Alioto (1916–98), a twenty-one-year-old senior from Little Italy who would later become mayor of San Francisco, addressed the Young Men's Institute on Catholic Action.[25]

Alioto's 1936 speech, "The Catholic Internationale," marked the degree to which the papal program of Catholic Action had already made an imprint on the public discourse of Catholic San Francisco. Alioto began with a rhetorical evocation of communism; since the Russian revolution, "like an enormous, hideous octopus it [communism] has reached out over the world with its black tentacles to engulf other lands within the darkness of its soulless philosophy."[26] Alioto ended his speech with an explicit endorsement of the Catholic Action strategy, noting that the "Catholic

Church in its scheme of organization into parishes and diocese affords the effective means whereby we may infiltrate the social organism. From the individual the Catholic Internationale must build itself upward to the family, to the parish, to the diocese, until it permeates the whole world with its rich and happy philosophy. Then shall the emptiness and the stupidity of Communism be exposed."[27] Alioto's speech focused specifically on communism, but its larger message about the importance of Catholic Action brought him to the attention of Archbishop Mitty, who called on him for service in a variety of diocesan activities in the years to come. The speech appeared in the winter issue of the *Moraga Quarterly*, which was fast becoming a vehicle for spreading the Catholic Action message under the editorial guidance of Professor Hagerty.

Hagerty soon became Sylvester Andriano's partner in the Catholic Action program, and scarcely a month after Alioto's speech at the Young Men's Institute, Andriano reported to the archbishop that several others had joined the planning process. They included William Lowery, from his law office; Harold McKinnon, from the law firm Bronson, Bronson; and McKinnon; Jack Casey, the San Francisco city engineer; physician Milton Lennon; public-school teacher Peter Conmy; and Santa Clara College professor Umberto Olivieri. From Little Italy came Armand Demartini, brother of one of the priests at Sts. Peter and Paul Church. Andriano also consulted with aging Catholic teamster-union officials Michael Casey and John P. McLaughlin, "with a view of selecting two young, active, Catholic-minded labor leaders to join the group." In January, after the holiday season, Andriano distributed copies of Civardi's *Manual of Catholic Action* to his associates, and they met for the first time on February 12, 1937.[28]

Most of the men who attended this first meeting continued to gather every other week during that year for focused discussions on how to move from the theory of Catholic Action to the practice. By the autumn of 1937, Andriano and Hagerty had met with the pastors of each of the sixty parishes in San Francisco to solicit support for the new citywide Catholic Action lay organization, and on December 22, 1937, Archbishop Mitty invited several dozen men from throughout the city for a meeting in the basement of St. Mary's Cathedral to discuss "uniting the parishes of San Francisco in a definite program of Catholic Action." In addition to representatives from the largest parishes, the invitees included police chief William J.

Quinn, high-ranking officers from important municipal-government departments, and executives from the largest and most prestigious business firms in the city. On the Feast of the Epiphany, January 6, 1938, two hundred fifty men gathered in the cathedral's basement and formally inaugurated the Catholic Men of San Francisco. Hagerty announced that "Confirmation is the Sacrament of Catholic Action, making men soldiers," and suggested that the assembled volunteers should regard themselves as part of the "priesthood of the layman."[29]

Mitty appointed Andriano and Hagerty to the positions of president and executive secretary of the new organization, and in March, Andriano traveled to Rome to secure official Vatican approval of the Catholic Action initiative in San Francisco. Pope Pius XI gave the group his blessing, and Cardinal Giuseppe Pizzardo, the chief assistant for Catholic Action in Italy, and Monsignor Luigi Civardi, author of the *Manual of Catholic Action*, assured the San Franciscan that his plan was a sound one. After his return from Rome, Andriano and Mrs. John Murray of the Archdiocesan Council of Catholic Women laid the plans for a massive outdoor rally on behalf of Catholic Action. And on Sunday afternoon, October 29, fifty thousand Bay Area Catholics filled Kezar Stadium in the city's Golden Gate Park to celebrate the Feast of Christ the King. Archbishop Mitty led a procession, carrying the Blessed Sacrament, and then gave a benediction from an ornate oversized altar on the fifty-yard line. The archbishop began his "Address on Catholic Action" by announcing, "We must first of all get a grasp upon what the Holy Father wants in Catholic Action. What is it all about? I like to sum it up in one phrase: That what the Holy Father wants you to do is to vitalize your religion, make it something really vital in your lives." Mitty criticized the notion that

> religion is not supposed to come out of that [certain limited] compartment and overflow into our being. We have a feeling of inferiority about religion, due to an historic situation where we were outnumbered. But there is no necessity for it today. Human life has been practically denuded of Christian principles. What the pope wants is to vitalize them. That is the meaning of Catholic Action—no more, no less. . . . In doing that we not only make a contribution to the progress of the Church, but we are making a substantial contribution to the welfare of our own land, a contribution to America which it badly needs; we are making a contribution to human civilization, until we

bring about a right balance between material and spiritual things, which are going topsy-turvy.[30]

When Cardinal Pizzardo approved the San Francisco Catholic Action program, one of his charges to the San Francisco activists was to participate in "the apostolate of education [in] Catholic schools," something that Andriano had actively pursued years before his Vatican meetings with the Cardinal. The attorney's speeches at St. Mary's College and at a variety of San Francisco Catholic high-school events, combined with Archbishop Mitty's own proselytizing, influenced teachers to use the model of the Catholic men's organization at their own (boys') institutions. Students at St. Mary's High School in Berkeley were the first to organize, creating a club, Knights of Catholic Action, at their own campus, followed by the Student Catholic Action Council, a Bay Area–wide group. The Council and an associated "Federation of Catholic High School Religious Organizations of the Archdiocese of San Francisco" published the newsletter *Student Catholic Action* and the *Students Handbook of Catholic Action*. The students based their work on Pope Pius XI's urging that "centers of Catholic Action should be formed in universities and in secondary schools," and their newsletter quoted Archbishop Amleto Cicognani, the Vatican's apostolic delegate to the United States, about the importance among Catholic youth of "unity of action, harmony of purpose, and union of minds." Because Catholic high-school students were segregated, with boys and girls attending separate institutions, the Federation hoped to use its publications "to help united Catholic girls and boys in our Catholic high schools to do the great things they can do TOGETHER for Christ and his Church."[31]

Catholic Action work with youth played an important role in the agendas of San Francisco's Catholic women's organizations as well as in the program of the Catholic Men of San Francisco. Catholic women in San Francisco had organized a Young Ladies' Institute (YLI) in 1887, and in 1920 they established the city's Archdiocesan Council of the NCCW. By 1936, the YLI claimed a membership of "11,000 strong" in the thirteen counties of the archdiocese, and they celebrated their golden jubilee the following year with a parade down Market Street, a program at the War Memorial Opera House, and a solemn pontifical mass at the cathedral. Archbishop Mitty had first announced his Catholic Action campaign in

1932, at a speech before the women of the NCCW. Now, addressing the YLI members at their fiftieth-anniversary banquet, he reminded them that they must "stand out as the right arm of the Church in your parishes . . . participating in the apostolate of Christ himself."[32]

While both of the local women's organizations participated in the Catholic Action crusade during the middle to late 1930s, the women of the NCCW were more active, possibly on account of the close working relationship between Archbishop Mitty and Agnes G. Regan. As a board member of the NCCW from the time of its organizational meeting in Washington, D.C., in 1920, and then as executive secretary shortly thereafter, Regan developed effective communications with all the United States bishops. But she was especially close to the San Francisco scene because she grew up in one of the city's most wealthy and prestigious Irish Catholic families. Her father was a banker who also served for a decade as the personal secretary to the city's first archbishop, Joseph S. Alemany; two of her three sisters became Catholic nuns (there were nine children in the family); she graduated from a Catholic grammar school and St. Rose High School; and she graduated from the San Francisco State Normal School (today's San Francisco State University) and taught in the San Francisco public schools for several decades, eventually serving as a member and president of the city's board of education. It was Archbishop Hanna who sent her as a delegate to the first meeting of the NCCW, and she kept close watch on San Francisco affairs from her office in the nation's capital all through the twenty-year tenure she enjoyed as executive secretary.[33]

Archbishop Mitty made no secret of his determination to increase the local influence of the women's groups, writing to one local activist, "You are aware of the fact of how interested I am in the development of the National Council of Catholic Women in this Archdiocese." Mitty appointed Father Eugene J. Shea, a priest assigned to the Catholic Charities office, to work with local Catholic women to implement the youth-oriented programs coordinated by the Washington, D.C., headquarters of the NCCW. Father Shea and Margaret McGuire, president of the archdiocesan council, organized a series of leadership conferences in the spring of 1937 designed to train "young women who would be interested and helpful in developing activities for girls of high school and college age." By the late summer of 1939, Father Shea had learned that "parish organizations

for high school girls are the most difficult to organize and yet most necessary since most of the public high school youngsters have only an elementary knowledge of their religion." All the more reason, then, for
participating in the NCCW's strategy of using radio broadcasts to reach
women who might be persuaded to join their local Catholic Action activities. Archbishop Mitty endorsed and publicized Agnes Regan's *A Call to
Youth* radio programs, which were broadcast on NBC over seventeen
weeks during the winter and spring each year from 1937 to 1940—"a leaders' training school for diocesan, deanery and parish youth chairmen,
youth leaders and youth officers throughout the country."[34]

In October 1936, Margaret McGuire answered Mitty's call "to develop
a program for girls." Her organization now had eleven councils and one
hundred fifty affiliated organizations that were operating in the archdiocese as "an official part of the Program of the Catholic Church in the
United States." "Every organization, parish and inter-parish, is a distinct
unit yet a very definite part of the great Catholic Federation. In this affiliation no individual organization loses its identity or autonomy. It continues to function for the purpose for which it was founded but through the
Federation it promotes a united Catholic Action on a wider scale." Mc-
Guire asked the archbishop to approve a plan to hold the 1939 national
conference of the NCCW in San Francisco, the meeting to coincide with
the Golden Gate International Exposition scheduled to be held on Treasure Island that year. Mitty endorsed the proposal, and the following May
he congratulated the NCCW women "for the work you are accomplishing.
I feel that with Catholic Action, with earnest effort, with self-sacrificing
zeal, we can begin to accomplish some of the things the Holy Father is
asking of the laity to do. We can help to bring the spirit of Christ into the
environment in which we live and where we function."[35]

On March 9, 1938, Margaret McGuire visited the chancery office and
reported that the city's tourist and convention bureau had donated $2,000
to help defray the expense of holding the NCCW's national convention in
San Francisco and that she had booked accommodations and meeting
rooms in the stately Fairmont Hotel high atop Nob Hill. Preparations for
the convention continued through the year, and by the following January,
Maude Fay Symington, president of the Marin County unit of the organization, reported on the progress for what promised to be "in every way an
exceptional convention; not only the first time the N.C.C.W. is meeting in

the West, but holding a convention during the great Golden Gate Exposition year. California, so very Catholic, must lead the World Council of Catholic women in its public avowal of united, triumphant, and militant Catholicism; a challenge to the subversive influences and anti-God activities saturating the entire world today." In May, Archbishop Mitty reiterated his alarm that "we are surrounded by an atmosphere of secularism and worldliness" and his determination to present "the Catholic point of view, in showing forth the Catholic principles and Catholic philosophy of life." "I really want you to realize," he continued, "the amount of dependence that I put upon lay cooperation. The clergy cannot do everything, and the bishop can accomplish only as his clergy and laymen and lay women are willing to do with him. . . . The problems of the future, the great things that confront us must be solved by the action of our laity, under the direction of the hierarchy."[36]

During the five-day conference in September 1939, at sessions held in the Fairmont Hotel and at a special Catholic Women's Day in the San Francisco Building at the Golden Gate Exposition grounds on Treasure Island, the importance of establishing Catholic standards of morality was a recurring theme. Hitler's troops had invaded Poland on the first day of the month, triggering declarations of war against Germany by England and its allies, and on September 9, the opening day of the conference, the Battle of the Bzura began, which would end ten days later with a German victory that foreshadowed the Polish defeat at the end of the month. During his speech on the last day of the conference, Sylvester Andriano spoke on the compelling importance of Christian morality in the face of such events, echoing Cardinal Pizzardo's insistence that Catholic Action included "the moral apostolate concerned with the defense of Christian morality wherever threatened." And so did Pope Pius XII insist when he spoke to the delegates who attended the annual congress of the International Union of Catholic Women's Leagues in Rome in April. The newly installed pontiff, who had taken up his duties on March 2, announced his intention to continue his predecessor's "all-embracing program" of "the training and preparation of the Catholic woman in her various fields of apostolate, for the Christian restoration of modern society." He reminded the delegates of "the golden rules outlined by the Pontiff of happy memory who was the great promoter of Catholic Action and who is still its invisible inspiration." And he exhorted Catholics to unify and work against "the absolute denial of invisible realities, of the noble moral values, and of every supernatural ideal."[37]

When Cardinal Pizzardo announced in mid-1938 that "Catholic Action is essentially an apostolate," he included in "the moral apostolate" work aimed at ensuring that the values communicated "in the press, over the radio, in the theater, motion pictures" were compatible with Christian teaching. In San Francisco, the Archdiocesan Council of Catholic Women took action in defense of "decent literature" by launching a "Clean Reading Campaign" focused on magazines for sale in public places. The city's efforts on this front were not unique, linked as they were to both international and national Catholic faith-based activism on behalf of the moral apostolate. In January 1938, Bishop John F. Noll of Fort Wayne, Indiana, published an article describing his city's League for Clean Reading. Noll was the publisher of a nationally distributed newspaper, *Our Sunday Visitor: The National Catholic Action Weekly*. He was also a National Catholic Welfare Conference (NCWC) official, and his article appeared in the NCWC's magazine *Catholic Action*. In February, Father William G. Butler, assigned by Archbishop Mitty as the official adviser to the city's Catholic women, suggested to Margaret McGuire and her colleagues that the Archdiocesan Council "work out a diocesan scheme" modeled on the Fort Wayne campaign. The Council's purpose was clear; it would "assist the law enforcement agencies of this jurisdiction to suppress literature and pictures" and "eliminate from magazine sales racks and tables publications which 1. Glorify crime and criminals; 2. Contain matter which is predominantly sexy; 3. Feature illicit love; 4. Print indecent or sexy pictures; and 5. Carry disreputable advertising."[38]

Archbishop Mitty asked Sylvester Andriano and James Hagerty to take action on this issue in concert with the Archdiocesan Council of Catholic Women, and they established a Committee on Indecent Literature. Members of the committee and volunteers then contacted the city's major news and magazine distributors, only to discover that "the profit motive is much stronger than any moral urge in all too many retail outlets to guarantee any success from such an approach." Another joint working group made a survey of "legislation on pornographic literature, of postal regulations, law enforcement, the honor system, direct censorship, and the boycott." Three months later, the committees reported that the laws were adequate and the postal regulations sufficient, "but law enforcement is impractical because of the laxity of some jurists and juries in returning convictions." And "the element of goodwill [on the part of vendors] is obviously lacking, thus reducing our means of attack to some sort of public boycott."[39]

The laymen and laywomen urged Archbishop Mitty to enlist the support of "the Protestant and Jewish church councils" as well as the assistance of city newspapers, city officials, and "all other groups who should be interested in decency." Mitty followed up in June with official instructions to the priests of every parish in the entire archdiocese to read his official letter condemning "magazines and other periodical literature which are detrimental to the morals of our people, and particularly to the morals of our growing boys and girls." On Sunday, June 12, the archbishop's letter was read at every Mass in all thirteen counties of the archdiocese, and it was repeated the next Sunday, June 19, after which, at every Mass, the congregations repeated the Clean Literature Pledge after the priests.[40]

Thousands of San Franciscans took the clean-reading pledge during the summer, some of whom presumably boycotted the purveyors of "pernicious literature" filled with "pagan manifestations" of "flagrant evil." But the Catholic Action activists in the clean-reading campaign were hampered in their efforts because, as Florentine Schage, one of the lay activists, complained to the assistant chancellor, they found "it very difficult to ask retailers to remove literature we consider objectionable when they have no list to use as a check." Archbishop Mitty had such a list, and he invited Miss Schage and several colleagues to pick up a copy at the chancery office. In November, Bishop Noll and his like-minded colleagues established the National Organization for Decent Literature, which drew up what it called "our black-list" for use in dioceses across the nation. Noll's organization issued the *Catechism Dealing with Lewd Literature*, which announced its purpose on the title page: "A Comprehensive Treatise for Use by Men and Women Engaged in the Drive against Indecent Literature and for Radio Broadcasts." The *Catechism* took pains to remind its readers that "there would be a danger if we designated 'indecent' the magazines on our black list. We have adopted a Code in keeping with that adopted by the Legion of Decency in relation to Motion Pictures, and we charge the magazines with violation of that Code." Bishop Noll urged readers to "Understand" that "we do not attach the 'immoral' charge to all these magazines. They are on our banned list because they offend against one or more of a five point Code adopted by the N. O. D. L." Among the magazines on the black list, in addition to *French Night Life, Illustrated Japanese Sex Relations, and Savage Arts of Love Illustrated* were *The Facts of Life* and *Your Body.*[41]

San Francisco neighborhood theaters were screening a short film called *The Birth of a Baby* in November 1938. First Lady Eleanor Roosevelt recommended the movie for its public-health value, but the Catholic Men of San Francisco "made a spirited protest" against this and other "indecent pictures" that violated their notions of decency, complaining directly to the nation's official movie censors in Hollywood. This was four years after the founding of the Catholic Legion of Decency and eight years after the adoption of a motion-picture production code by the film-industry trade association, a code that remained in effect for nearly forty years. The production code is often associated with Will H. Hays, the president of the Motion Picture Producers and Distributors of America, or with Joseph I. Breen, the head of the Production Code Administration, which did the actual work of vetting films. But the code was written by a Jesuit priest, Daniel A. Lord, S.J., with input from a Catholic Action advocate, Martin J. Quigley, and from George Cardinal Mundelein, the archbishop of Chicago. Joseph Breen was an active Catholic, and James Hagerty and Sylvester Andriano confided to him that they hoped for a sympathetic response from Breen's office to their complaint rather than, as in the clean-reading campaign, a situation where it was necessary to make "endless protest to parties who may be helpless to improve the situation or uninterested or irresponsible."[42]

The downbeat assessment of the clean-reading campaign by the San Francisco Catholic Men's organization matched that of Archbishop Mitty, who provided his own assessment of the campaign to the Vatican's apostolic delegate, Archbishop Cicognani.

Writing in March 1939, Mitty reported that he was happy to say that the results were quite satisfactory in the residential districts. A great deal of difficulty was encountered, however, in the business sections." Mitty's report was prompted by Cicognani's official notice that "the Supreme S[acred] Congregation of the Holy Office, in keeping with the competence conferred upon it by the Code of Canon Law (can. 247, #4), feels the need of reminding the Most Reverend Ordinaries of their obligation to censure pernicious writings (cf. can. 1395, #1) and to denounce them to the Holy See (cf. can. 1397)." The Vatican official's concern was prompted by "the continuous and constantly increasing diffusion of all kinds of publications which spread erroneous doctrines, deprave the mind and pervert morals, imposes an obligation upon the Shepherds of Souls to be ever more watchful and prompt in keeping the Faithful from such poisoned sources and so 'to defend sound and orthodox doctrine and to defend good morals' (can. 343, #1)."[43]

Mitty and his men's and women's Catholic Action organizations continued the decent-literature campaign "with greater zeal and thoroughness" by developing closer working relationships with the city's police department and by joining forces with their counterparts in Los Angeles. This strategy benefited from the fact that Sylvester Andriano was now a member of the police commission, having been appointed by Mayor Rossi in July 1937. Andriano's reputation for probity had been acknowledged by the president of the board of supervisors during the July strike crisis of 1934, and former Chamber of Commerce president J. Ward Maillard Jr. replaced two members of the commission who had been discredited in a grand-jury investigation into police corruption in the city. The report of the investigation by former FBI agent Edwin Atherton laid bare a variety of malfeasance (including abortion mills, gambling, and prostitution) that netted some sixty-seven crooked police officers and two dozen city officials an estimated million dollars per year. One hapless patrolman who was discovered on the take shot his wife and children and then took his own life rather than face up to his disgrace. The post-grand-jury police commission set out to demonstrate its trustworthiness, with two Catholic Action stalwarts on board: Sylvester Andriano and police chief William J. Quinn. Chief Quinn was not personally implicated in the Atherton report, and he had been a member of Andriano's organizing committee that worked with the archbishop to establish the new Catholic men's organization.[44]

The cooperative relationship between Catholic Action moral-apostolate activists and the city police department had been underway for several years when the archdiocesan chancellor Thomas A. Connolly received a tip from Joseph J. Truxaw, the chairman of the Los Angeles Campaign for Decent Literature. Truxaw's source, a Los Angeles municipal judge, passed on information about a printing firm in San Francisco that was allegedly "the 'HOME' on the Pacific Coast of pornographic cartoons and pictures. Distributions from that place are made by trucks to all parts of California, Nevada, Oregon and Washington." Connolly informed Chief Quinn that "it certainly would be an excellent move for public morals" to close down the firm, and replied to Truxaw that he could "rest assured that the police will not involve the Catholic Church in this matter in any way whatsoever." Three months later, Chief Charles W. Dullea (who succeeded Quinn when he retired after thirty-five years of service) informed the chancery office that the department's "surveillance and investigation" yielded arrests that he expected would close down "the source of the printing of indecent literatures, pictures and booklets, distributed throughout this city and the bay counties." Dullea assured the assistant chancellor, Father Edwin J. Kennedy, that the S.F.P.D. was "pledging to you our fullest support in the suppression of lascivious literature and other immoral booklets."[45]

The moral apostolate won another victory when the Catholic Men of San Francisco convinced the administration of the Golden Gate International Exposition to cancel an exhibit in the Hall of Science sponsored by the Birth Control Federation of America. Margaret Sanger happened to be speaking to the League of Women Voters of San Francisco the same week that the exposition announced the cancellation of the birth-control exhibit. Sanger expressed her disappointment to a reporter for the *People's World*, the local Communist Party newspaper: "Wherever I go I meet the same opposition—and I must say that it is most insidious and effective." Perhaps Anna E. McCaughey of Los Angeles, national chairman of the NCCW, had in mind that victory for the moral apostolate when she assured Archbishop Mitty that the members of her organization "look upon San Francisco as a focal point where East meets West in developing national service for God, Church, and Country."[46]

The San Francisco Catholic Action stalwarts practiced, in addition to the moral apostolate, a social apostolate, defined by Cardinal Pizzardo as "concerned with the spread of Catholic social teaching and the realization of Catholic principles in social institutions."[47] Archbishop Mitty used his office as a "bully pulpit" on behalf of Catholic social teaching, and he also delegated social-apostolate work both to laypersons and to clergy, appointing young Father Hugh A. Donohoe (1905–87) to be the unofficial and informal coordinator of this aspect of Catholic Action work. Donohoe began his work immediately after being ordained in June 1930; when the school year began that fall, the twenty-five-year-old Donohoe commenced teaching at St. Joseph's College, the archdiocesan preparatory seminary for aspiring priests. Two years later, he began doctoral studies at The Catholic University of America and received his Ph.D. in 1935, with a dissertation written under the direction of Monsignor John A. Ryan (1869–1945), the nationally eminent scholar of Catholic social-justice theory. Donohoe then began a seven-year tenure as a professor of social ethics at St. Patrick's, the archdiocesan seminary in Menlo Park, some thirty miles south of San Francisco. During that time, he helped organize the local branch of the Association of Catholic Trade Unionists, and he served as its chaplain from its founding in 1938 through the 1940s. Mitty appointed Donohoe rector of St. Mary's Cathedral, and in 1942 Mitty appointed him editor of the official weekly newspaper, the *Monitor*.[48]

When Donohoe moved from the *Monitor*'s editorial office to the chancery after being consecrated auxiliary bishop in October 1947, some seven hundred unionists attended a dinner in his honor at one of the city's premier hotel banquet rooms, the Gold Room of the St. Francis. The dinner was sponsored by the ACTU jointly with AFL, CIO, and independent union organizations in the Bay Area. John F. ("Jack") Shelley, president of both the California State Federation of Labor and of the AFL San Francisco Labor Council, and a former California state senator, praised Donohoe for having been "a champion who understands us perfectly; a man who has realized our rights; one who has fought for us." "He has made San Francisco realize," Shelley continued, "that we are not primarily interested in wages but rather we insist that our labor and the conditions of our labor be an expression of our human personalities . . . [He] has instilled in the minds of the public that we are not mere 'things' but human beings with personal interests clamoring to be recognized."[49]

Like Donohoe, Jack Shelley (1905–74) was a product of the city's Mission district, and they had known each other since boyhood, having been classmates at St. Paul's grammar school. Jack Shelley was one of nine children of Denis Shelley and Mary Casey. Denis was an immigrant from County Cork who worked on the docks as a longshoreman, and his mother was a native San Franciscan. Donohoe left St. Paul's for the preparatory seminary, but Shelley enrolled in Mission High School, where he was president of the debating club and the student body, captain of the rowing team, head yell leader, and ROTC commander. In 1922 Shelley shipped out as a merchant seaman, and by 1929, when he returned home because of a death in the family, he had worked his way up to first mate and was fluent in Spanish and Tagalog, a Philippine dialect.[50]

When the twenty-four-year-old Shelley started work that year, he immediately enrolled as a member of the International Brotherhood of Teamsters and drove bread trucks in the city. Restless and ambitious, he delivered bread during the day and studied law at night, and the University of San Francisco—a Jesuit institution—awarded him a law degree in 1932. He was elected vice president of his local union three years later, and then president the following year. In January 1937 he won election as president of the San Francisco County AFL Labor Council, the youngest man ever to hold that position, and in 1938 city voters sent him to Sacramento as their sole state senator, a position he held until 1946. Shelley also served as president of the Labor Council all through the 1940s, as well as president of the California State Federation of Labor. He would later serve eight terms in the U.S. Congress, from 1949 to 1964, and then one term as San Francisco mayor, from 1964 to 1968.

Shelley was one of the organizers, with Donohoe, of the local branch of the ACTU, and he drew explicitly on the principles of the Catholic encyclicals in his labor-union advocacy and as an elected official at the local, state, and federal levels.[51] Shelley's appeal to voters, from his run for the state senate in 1938 to his campaign for mayor in 1963, drew explicitly on Catholic labor teaching in several ways. He demanded justice for working people and at the same time advocated treating business as a partner, not an enemy of labor. Like Pope Leo XIII in *Rerum Novarum*, Shelley insisted that the community's well-being should take precedence over the interest of any specific interest group. A flyer from Shelley's first campaign for office included a quotation from his campaign manager, city supervisor James B. McSheehy, that illustrated his approach: "Speaking as a business man, Supervisor McSheehy said: 'Shelley's loyalty to the workers in the American Federation of Labor has never been open to question. At the same time, he has always been conscious of the general public welfare in labor–capital dispute. He knows San Francisco problems and is pledged to work for their solution.'"[52]

During his tenure as state senator, Shelley sponsored two pieces of legislation that put into practice the Ryan-Donohoe interpretation of the labor encyclicals, calling on state intervention for the furtherance of worker dignity: a labor-standards bill for apprentices in the building trades, and a disability insurance program. And in San Francisco shortly before being elected to the state senate, in his capacity as president of the county AFL labor council, Shelley helped put in place a business and labor cooperative arrangement that mimicked at a local level the industrial-council concept of Pius XI's *Quadragesimo Anno.* In 1937, faced with a labor victory in the 1934 waterfront strike and voter rejection of a twenty-year old anti-picketing ordinance, city chamber-of-commerce leaders met with Jack Shelley and together they negotiated an informal arrangement whereby employers would accept the legitimacy of picketing provided no violence took place. The chamber then disbanded its twenty-year-old antiunion Industrial Association, a subsidiary that had orchestrated the city's successful open-shop campaign. In its place was created a new cooperation-oriented subsidiary called first the Committee of Forty-Three and then, in 1939, the San Francisco Employers' Council.[53]

By 1940, the CIO unions had joined Shelley's AFL unions in this informal cooperative system for handling labor relations in the future. Disagreements persisted on the particulars, and numerous hard-fought strikes and negotiating sessions took place in the decade to come. Future conflicts would be settled, however, within an institutional framework informed by Catholic labor theory, the framework that Shelley (with Donohoe's advice and counsel) had spearheaded in 1937 and 1938.[54]

In the late 1930s, San Francisco lay activists built up Catholic Action's numbers and expanded the organization at the citywide and parish level. Andriano, William Lowery, and Harold McKinnon established a lawyers' guild, the St. Thomas More Society, with McKinnon serving as the first president. Parish councils, charged with organizing Catholic Action Circles in each of the city's sixty parishes, pursued a three-part agenda of devotional revitalization involving individual sanctification, sanctification of the home, and sanctification of society. The program included participation in parish holy-hour devotions, regular celebration of annual feast days, blessing of homes, grace before meals, family Communion, and renewal of marriage vows daily; parish Sunday Mass crusades aimed at increasing regular attendance and limiting latecomers and those leaving early; and the use of the missal and active participation in rosaries, benedictions, and Stations of the Cross.[55]

Catholic Action schools for parish priests and parochial-school teachers began operations in San Francisco, Alameda, San Mateo, and Santa Clara counties. And in 1939 the Catholic Men of San Francisco published *Catholic Action, The Church in Action: Official Handbook of the Catholic Men of the Archdiocese of San Francisco*, with forewords by Archbishop Mitty and Cardinal Pizzardo, as well as *Catholic Action and the Priest*, a booklet by Father John J. Hunt, the group's chaplain. The archdiocesan council published a monthly newsletter and operated a speaker's bureau that dispatched lecturers to meetings and radio programs in all the Bay area counties. St. Patrick's Seminary in Menlo Park added a required Catholic Action course to its curriculum. Even Catholic high schools in the Bay Area joined the campaign by establishing student Catholic Action Circles. By mid-1941, according to the official report, 160 of the 174 parishes in the archdiocese had established Catholic Action Circles involving 1,500 men and 300 women.[56]

Lay activism in San Francisco entered a new phase with the entry of the United States into the Second World War. As Archbishop Mitty devoted more of his attention to the pressing needs associated with the impact of wartime and postwar demands on the Church in the Bay Area, and to building the institutional infrastructure required by the rapid growth of the Catholic population during the postwar baby boom, he placed a lower priority on mobilizing the laity to accomplish the Catholic Action agenda of the previous pontiff, Pius XI. The work did continue, however, as the following vignettes indicate. In 1944 Sylvester Andriano directed Caritate Dei (For the Love of God), a program of Saints Peter and Paul church for war relief. Caritate Dei shipped packages of food and clothing to the residents of Italian cities.[57] And in 1947 attorney Maurice E. Harrison (1888–1951), another Catholic Action stalwart, who had organized the St. Thomas More Society with Andriano in 1939, formed an interfaith Bay Counties Committee for Displaced Persons. Archbishop Mitty endorsed the effort and in February 1947 cosponsored a public statement with Rabbi Morris Goldstein, president of the Northern California Council of Rabbis, and Abbott Book, secretary of the Northern California Council of Churches. They urged the public to lobby for "the liberalization of immigration laws" so "then this nation would be doing its bit to wipe out a bitterness in Europe that threatens to generate new conflicts."[58]

Mitty chose Father Bernard C. Cronin (1910–87), a protégé of Father Hugh Donohoe, to head the Catholic Resettlement Committee of the archdiocese. Cronin and Father James Murray, assistant director of the archdiocesan Little Children's Aid organization, recruited fifty laymen and laywomen to lay the groundwork. Soon each of the thirteen counties of the archdiocese had working resettlement committees, as did each of the parishes and all of the Catholic "nationality" organizations: French, Italian, Polish, Slovak, Croat, Slovene, and Lithuanian. In addition, each of the dozen or so Catholic religious organizations—such as the Knights of Columbus, the Guadalupe Society, and the Catholic Daughters—had established their own working groups, and so had Catholic members in the two major labor organizations, the AFL and the CIO.[59]

Father Cronin headed the Resettlement Committee for ten years, becoming known in the Bay Area as "the priest of displaced persons." He operated his agency on a cooperative basis with Jewish and Protestant counterparts; press photographs show him in numerous appearances, sometimes walking arm in arm, with local rabbis and Protestant ministers. They facilitated the settlement, and sometimes, as in the well-publicized case of the Shmerlins, a Jewish family who needed assistance in traveling from Shanghai to Israel, the transfer, of some 6,000 displaced persons from camps in Europe and Asia to new homes in the United States and beyond.[60]

By the time Archbishop Mitty appointed Father Cronin to oversee refugee resettlement work, Joseph L. Alioto was replacing his mentor Sylvester Andriano in the front ranks of San Francisco Catholic Action. Alioto's association with the program began with his 1936 "Catholic Internationale" speech at the Young Men's Institute. Four years later he wrote to his St. Mary's College philosophy professor James Hagerty about a *Moraga Quarterly* article "Catholic Action and the Lawyer." Alioto explained that, while he may have been living in Washington, D.C., while earning his law degree at Catholic University of America, he kept informed about San Francisco Catholic Action by reading the *Monitor*.[61] Later that year, Alioto became an associate in the San Francisco law offices of Brobeck, Phleger and Harrison. Partner Maurice Harrison, an activist in the California Democratic Party, had helped organize the St. Thomas More Society. Harrison believed that the exemplary public stand of the recently canonized St. Thomas More provided "to Catholics in general, and to Catholic laymen particularly, the true answer to the problems which confront the world today." After a brief association, Alioto left Brobeck, Phleger and Harrison for a position with the federal government's Board of Economic Warfare. In 1942, Archbishop Mitty invited the lawyer to address the First Regional Catholic Congress on the topic "The American Catholic Tradition." The event was organized by the archbishop in connection with the wartime Bishop's Committee to Unite the Catholic Youth of America.[62]

By the late 1940s, Alioto backed causes similar to those supported by centrist liberals elsewhere, such as school bonds, higher salaries for teachers, and removing a board-of-education ban against teachers participating in political campaigns after school. But Alioto also brought a distinctive Catholic Action emphasis to his post–Second World War urban liberalism. He critiqued the textbook-selection process, arguing that too much material sympathetic to communism was allowed to find its way to students in the city's public schools. Alioto's concerns about left-wing influence in San Francisco were realistic given the size and political activism of the city's Communist Party. Beginning in 1948 the local party launched an offensive to stem the tide of Catholic activism. At the party's county convention in 1948, CP delegates discussed strategies to combat Catholic power in local government, the press, and the labor movement and issued a single-spaced eight-page report on the subject. By the early 1950s, however, the city's CP was in decline, and nothing more than newspaper articles came of Joseph Alioto's charges, made at a meeting of the board of education, that several members of the faculty at San Francisco State College were sympathetic to Communism.[63]

Alioto also drew on principles of Catholic moral philosophy regarding organic communal solidarity when he served on the city's redevelopment agency, where he argued that land use policy necessitated careful balancing of the interests and needs of all residents.[64] By the time of his first inaugural address as mayor, in January 1968, the Vatican II–inspired calls for a revised concept of lay activism had attracted widespread attention, but Alioto's convictions represented more of an evolution of his pre–Vatican II views than a fundamental reorientation of his thinking. The new mayor urged San Franciscans to construct a just society and a moral economy, rejecting a standard derived from "the standard of Jeremy Bentham," which was "no longer acceptable as a criterion of government. Closer to the mark is the more ancient philosophy which views government as an ordinance of reason for the 'common good.'"[65]

During his two terms of office, from January 1968 through December 1975, Alioto continued to stress the common good and governed as a centrist, supporting both downtown commercial redevelopment and residential construction for moderate and low-income residents. He drew explicitly on the concept of subsidiarity when he argued—as he did in his second inaugural address—that "what our City needs, what every big city needs, is a 'Declaration of Independence' from unwieldy state control. What we need is more local autonomy, more local sovereignty, if you will, to meet our problems head on and seek our own unique answers to them." His call for charter reform, "expanding the City's grant of power" to insure that "the State Legislature be forbidden to mandate programs of any kind unless it provides the money to cover the cost of those programs," proved unsuccessful. He did manage, however, with support from the chamber of commerce and organized labor, to convince the state of California to transfer ownership of the port from the state of California to the city.[66]

The mayor also initiated more comprehensive urban-planning guidelines and endorsed strong measures to preserve the city's aesthetic beauty and environmental quality. He failed in his efforts to demolish the Embarcadero Freeway, but he convinced the federal and state governments to move a section of Interstate Highway 280 away from a proposed lakefront site along city-owned property in San Mateo County.[67]

Alioto supported the Catholic campaigns for racial equality in employment, campaigns endorsed by Auxiliary Bishop Donohoe in the late 1940s and expanded in the 1950s by Jack Henning in his capacity as head of the California State Labor Federation and by Father Andrew C. Boss of the Labor Management Program of the Jesuit University of San Francisco. Prior to his election, Alioto supported the calls for racial justice by the Catholic Interracial Council, which Archbishop Mitty established in 1960, and by the Catholic Social Justice Commission, which Mitty's successor, Archbishop Joseph McGucken, established in 1964. Once in office, Alioto appointed numerous African American, Mexican American, and Asian American officials to city government posts, and his administration worked with both city agencies and private employers to begin recruitment programs for minority workers.[68]

A supporter of organized labor since his days as Monsignor Haas's administrative assistant, Mayor Alioto defended the right of public employees to unionize and to strike, and he aggressively used his powers of persuasion to bring about several timely settlements between labor and management. His long-standing commitment to Catholic doctrines with respect to labor relations and his decades-long personal relationships with San Francisco's labor priests brought him the robust support of numerous AFL-CIO union leaders, many of whom had been active ACTU members.

Alioto's public commitment to a moral economy also led him to reach out to members of the independent, left-wing dockworkers and warehouse workers' union. He named Harry Bridges to a seat on the charter-revision committee and to the position of port commissioner of San Francisco. David Jenkins, a leader of the longshoremen's union and former Communist Party activist, was appointed to the city's Redevelopment Agency.[69] In 1989, Jenkins reported that diehard former comrades shunned him when, already having left the party, he compounded the perceived disgrace by becoming a collaborationist in Joseph Alioto's Catholic Action–inspired "grand urban coalition."

As Alioto's work indicates, the San Francisco Catholic Action lay and clerical activists promoted economic and social justice for labor and a democratic union movement, and they contributed an explicitly Catholic perspective to the resolution of a variety of prewar, wartime, and postwar public-policy debates. The reverberations from Archbishop Mitty's Catholic Action program persisted long past the thirties and the forties. After Monsignor Bernard Cronin stepped down as director of the archdiocesan resettlement program in 1958, he served twenty years as pastor of St. Matthew's Church in San Mateo, a suburb of San Francisco. He continued to preach after his 1979 retirement, and in a homily delivered the Sunday before Election Day in 1984, Cronin announced that "the separation of church and state is not absolute." "The Church," he argued, "has the right to express moral judgments about public policy, to add moral dimensions to public debate and form right conscience of its believers. In short, the government may encourage religion without establishing it."[70]

Three years after some 80,000 San Francisco Catholics had gathered to celebrate the anniversary of the Holy Name Society and to demonstrate against the Ku Klux Klan, the *Atlantic Monthly* published a controversial letter by an Episcopal attorney who criticized New York governor Alfred E. Smith. Smith, the attorney charged, should be rejected by the Democratic

Party as a nominee for the 1928 presidential campaign because he would undoubtedly put his fealty to the pope ahead of his loyalty to the Constitution. Smith replied that he was an American patriot as well as a Roman Catholic and that he had gone through parochial school as a boy without ever having even heard of the papal pronouncements that his critic claimed he would be duty-bound to obey.

The Al Smith anecdote may have been apocryphal, but his alleged ignorance of papal encyclicals would have troubled the men and women who rallied to Archbishop Hanna's and Archbishop Mitty's Catholic Action initiatives in San Francisco from the 1930s to the 1960s. In the second-largest city of the West, the laity active in Catholic Action paid close attention to Vatican teaching and to their archbishops' calls to action on numerous public matters, including the relations between labor and capital, socialism and communism, marriage and divorce, and the powers of the national state vis-à-vis the rights of individuals and families. Their lay activism was quintessentially a phenomenon of the preconciliar era; in building and deploying their Catholic Action movement, they expressed no discontent with, nor did they dissent against, the Church's structure of authority.

Lay Catholics in San Francisco subordinated themselves to their priests and archbishops even as they worked in what they considered a partnership relationship with the Church. Their social, moral, and educational apostolates emerged out of a genuine commitment to a distinctive Catholic Christian faith-based program for the reform of everyday life. They were fully cognizant of the nonestablishment clause of the First Amendment, and they had no wish to create a Catholic theocracy in California. At the same time, they were also fully aware of the freedom-of-conscience clause, so they did not hesitate to translate the principles of their Catholic moral convictions into the language of public policy. They realized that many of their fellow citizens did not share their convictions, and so they utilized politics to discuss, debate, lobby—and compromise when that proved necessary—in order to achieve as many of their policy goals as possible. The story of San Francisco Catholic Action was distinctive in many ways, but its residents were partaking in a venerable national tradition, a debate about the role that religious tradition and faith-based values should play in defining the public good and shaping the public policies of a major American city.

4 From Participation to Community

John Courtney Murray's American Justification for Catholic Action

CHRISTOPHER D. DENNY

> In no other way can one learn exactly what a layman is and what the
> Church today wants to make of him.
>
> *John Courtney Murray, referring to papal teachings about Catholic Action*[1]

Most of the essays in this current volume are written from the
perspective of the grassroots, detailing the contrasting strategies that lay
Catholics employed to sustain cultural identity, alleviate social problems,
and strengthen parochial life in the decades before and after the Second
Vatican Council. This chapter is different, for it is a theological portrait
of Catholic Action as seen through the writings of a priest who was a
member of the Catholic elite. John Courtney Murray (1904–67) was
a Jesuit priest who is the consensus choice for the most influential theologian in American Catholic history. Murray is best known today for his
contributions to Vatican II's *Dignitatis Humanae*, or *Declaration on Religious Freedom*. Indeed, his name has been recently invoked in theological
debates, by protagonists on both sides of the liberal–conservative divide
in contemporary American Catholic ecclesiology, as one who upholds
their respective views regarding the Second Vatican Council. While the
lion's share of attention to Murray's writings in recent decades centers on
his contribution to the Catholic Church's long-delayed embrace of religious liberty in the mid-1960s, his earlier writings on Catholic Action
developed a theology of history that understood Church history as a succession of communities in changing relationship to the world. While
other theologies of history often center on doctrinal developments or
changing power relationships, Murray's writings on Catholic Action place
this lay movement within a historical trajectory that demonstrates how
the Church moved from a predominantly institutional conception of itself
toward a self-definition of emancipated Catholic Christians acting for the

greater good within a properly differentiated society. Murray's vision of Catholic Action provided an example of what Robert Doran has called "a theological theory of history," albeit one in which history is not the movement of static principles or material forces but the organic development of the Catholic Christian community.[2]

This theological survey helps to explain to the readers of this volume the intellectual justifications that America's most influential theologian used to defend a more activist stance for the lay apostolate, providing support for religious developments that would eventually outgrow the original goals of the Catholic Action movement and spill over into what Vatican II's *Lumen Gentium* (*Dogmatic Constitution on the Church*) called the People of God. My chapter will examine contrasting European responses to the political changes of the 1920s and 1930s and their corresponding prescriptions for lay apostolates; Murray's early writings and lectures on Catholic Action's role in the historical relations between Church and state; and how Murray's distinctive American justification for Catholic Action was outpaced by social changes at midcentury that radically transformed the apostolate of the laity after the Second Vatican Council.

A United or a Diverse Lay Apostolate? Contrasting Solutions for European Crises

Murray's understanding of Catholic Action is best studied by comparisons to the European counterparts that were faced with social crises similar to and different from those lay American Catholics encountered in the 1930s. In 1929, Pius XI signed the Lateran Treaty with Mussolini's Partito Nazionale Fascista, bringing to an end nearly sixty years of Vatican isolation from Italian political life. Having conceded that direct ecclesiastical authority over Italians was no longer a possibility, Catholic clergy needed a new mechanism by which to effect change in society. Azione Cattolica had already been promoted by Pius X in the early years of the century as a restorationist project designed to reclaim the temporal power of the ecclesiastical hierarchy, but the price Pius XI paid to Mussolini for Vatican sovereignty in 1929 meant that Azione Cattolica's mission would have to be transformed to meet the exigencies of the new political order.[3] In November 1929, nine months after the signing of the Lateran Treaty, Pius wrote to the primate of Spain, Cardinal Pedro Segura y Sáenz of Toledo. Murray later referred to this letter as "one of the two most fundamental pontifical documents" on the subject of Catholic Action.[4] Building on themes that he had included in his first encyclical in 1922, *Ubi Arcano*, Pius's letter to Segura defined Catholic Action as "participation of the laity in the apostolate of the hierarchy of the Church."[5] The entire letter walks a fine line between political neutrality and promoting the social apostolate of lay Catholics:

> Catholic Action is not of a material but of a spiritual order, not of an earthly but of a divine one, not of a political but of a religious one. Nevertheless it must fully deserve the name of Social Action since its very object is to bring about the reign of Christ, thereby to provide society with the great benefits and advantages which flow from it. For the welfare of the nation, though called political, is the concern of the many rather than the few. This splendid object Catholic Action can and must achieve if the laws of God and His Church are obeyed— providing that party politics are carefully excluded.[6]

Segura failed to take the pope's words to heart. A stalwart supporter of Primo de Rivera's dictatorship in the 1920s, his agitation on behalf of the exiled Alfonso XIII and the monarchy's accompanying support of the Church led to his expulsion from Spain shortly after the Republicans came to power in early 1931. Pius asked for and received Segura's resignation in September of the same year.[7] By contrast, article 43 of the 1929 concordat between the Vatican and the Italian government excluded all opponents of Mussolini's regime from leadership positions in Azione Cattolica.[8]

Theological underpinnings for Pius XI's statements on Catholic Action were provided throughout the 1920s and 1930s by Luigi Cavardi, whose *Manuale di Azione Cattolica* went through several editions in those years. Cavardi served as a president of Azione Cattolica. His workmanlike presentation of Catholic Action proceeds in good neo-scholastic fashion, beginning with the definition of the movement and then moving to its goals, activities, and finally to its external relationships with the wider society. This last topic was one about which Cavardi's *Manuale* contained a great deal of ambivalence. On one hand Cavardi, taking a cue from *Ubi Arcano*, insisted that Catholic Action was consecrated to the Kingdom of

Christ and denounced the twentieth-century secularism "that had appropriated the cry of the Jews: 'We will not have this Man to reign over
us' (Luke xix.14)."[9] Military analogies abound in the opening chapters;
Catholic Action is a militia fighting on behalf of the Church Militant.
Tracing a line of social deterioration from the glorious days of the "Christian *civitas*" through "rationalist Protestantism" to the French Revolution
and its "child" Liberalism, Cavardi states that Catholic Action "represents, in short, in its origin, the Catholic reaction against the de-
Christianising work of the French Revolution."[10] On the other hand, this
army of laypersons is forbidden to fight as a collective unit. Cavardi's insistence that politics and religion are distinct but not separate had centuries of ecclesiastical theory behind it, but whereas in earlier generations
lay Catholics were called to coordinated political organization under
clerical auspices, Cavardi's instructions necessarily stop short of specific
tactical directives.[11] Members of Catholic Action are now left to their own
devices in joining political parties. Unlike Mussolini's Blackshirts, Azione
Cattolica's supporters had to enter the political realm with only indirect
support from their leader. Cavardi warned: "To drag the Church towards
one party, and to wish that she should lend a hand in defeating one's political adversaries—this would be a hideous abuse of religion."[12]

In France the Catholic political crisis of the late 1920s and 1930s revolved around Pius XI's 1926 condemnation of the integral nationalism of
Charles Maurras's L'Action Française. With no viable alternative to the
Third Republic emerging, writers such as Jacques Maritain, a former
member, took a course different from Cavardi's. Maritain's book *Human-
isme intégral* (1936) originated in a series of lectures given in Spain two
years earlier. The work confronts the sociopolitical ambivalence of Catholic Action as Maritain distinguishes his prescriptions for the apostolate
from Catholic Action, which he places on the side of "the religious and
apostolic order."[13] Maritain writes:

> If it has been said that Catholic action should lead to political action
> and prepare the solution of social problems, it is in the degree to which
> it belongs to it to shape, in the midst of their respective political com-
> munities, Catholics firmly and fully instructed in the common doc-
> trine of the Church, notably in social matters, and able to cause to pass
> into life an authentically Christian inspiration. But it would be to
> confuse the spiritual and the temporal to imagine that the common

doctrine of the Church success [sic] in itself to resolve the conflicts of temporal history and to provide the concretely determined solutions which men have need of *hic et nunc*.[14]

Following on this assertion, Maritain breaks with the Italian model of Azione Cattolica in making an additional distinction that transcends what he laid out in his book *Primauté de spirituel* (1927), written in the immediate aftermath of the papal condemnation and designed to refute Maurassian fusions of altar and throne.[15] Over and above the distinction between the neo-scholastic model of politics and religion, Maritain identifies a distinction between the Church and Christians and holds that it is only to the latter that "transformation and regeneration according to the Christian spirit" belong.[16] Rather than supposedly participating in a hierarchical apostolate, laypersons are called to take the initiative from below.[17] French Catholics seeking to justify their separation from the royalism of L'Action Française could appeal to Pius XI's decree, but laity who did not progress beyond a rationale of simple obedience to the papacy in doing so still acknowledged their subordinate position in society as they chose one hierarch over another, a situation little different from those faced by French laity in previous French–Vatican conflicts as far back in history as the struggle between Philip IV and Boniface VIII at the start of the fourteenth century.

Where Cavardi's model of Catholic Action envisaged two spheres of society, Maritain identified a third intermediary plane between the spiritual and temporal orders, between the earthly city and the Church. In this third zone, Christians are called to act as Christians but not in the name of the Church. The autonomy that Maritain grants to the temporal order is mirrored in earlier theological conceptions of relationships between Church and state, but in his further admonition that the temporal order imposes on those who live in it a necessary diversity, Maritain breaks with the Azione Cattolica ideal of a unified coordination of lay social apostolates. Maritain writes:

On the plane of the temporal, it is not union, it is *diversity* which is the rule. When the objective is the earthly life of men, when it concerns earthly interests, earthly goods, this or that ideal of the earthly common good and the ways and means of realizing it, it is normal that a unanimity whose center is of the supratemporal order should break up, and that Christians who receive Communion at the same table should find themselves divided in the body politic. It would be contrary to the nature of things, and therefore very perilous, to demand on this plane a union of Catholics which could be *there* only artificial, and obtained either by a political materialization of religious energies (as was the case too often with the 'Catholic parties' such as the German *Centrum*), or by a weakening of the social and political energies of the Christian, and a kind of escape into general principles.[18]

The following decade brought with it more diversity on the temporal plane than Maritain could have reasonably expected in the mid-1930s, and historians of French Catholicism can debate to what degree justifications like those offered by Maritain presage the post–World War II collapse of a unified French Catholic political front.[19]

Murray's Writings on Catholic Action and Historical Church–State Relations

While the Italian Catholic laity had to follow Pius XI's lead in the belated loss of the temporal authority of the Church, and while Maritain's followers struggled to reorient their social outlook in the wake of Maurras's demise, a different Catholic struggle was unfolding across the Atlantic in a society that had no Catholic confessionalist ancien régime to look back upon. In his book *Contending with Modernity*, Philip Gleason places the origin of the Catholic Action movement in the United States within the interpretative lens of Catholic attempts to recover from the landslide defeat of Al Smith's 1928 presidential campaign.[20] "Catholic Action as a proper noun," writes Gleason, "a technical term, was thus effectively introduced in the United States immediately after the defeat of Al Smith."[21] During the weeks immediately preceding and following the inauguration of Smith's opponent, Herbert Hoover, in March 1929, the bulletin of the National Catholic Welfare Conference, *America*, and *Commonweal* all ran stories attempting to explain Pius XI's plans for the Catholic Action movement.[22] In Gleason's retelling, from this point onward Catholic Action served as an umbrella under which to group a bewildering array of clerical and lay endeavors over the next decade: Virgil Michel, O.S.B., sponsored the first Liturgical Day at St. John's Abbey in Minnesota in 1929; the National Council of Catholic Men began a campaign of Catholic apologetics that give birth to Fulton Sheen's radio program *The Catholic Hour* in 1930; Sheed and Ward opened a new American branch in 1933; Dorothy Day and Peter Maurin founded the Catholic Worker movement in 1933; the Association of Catholic Trade Unionists was established in 1937; and the Catholic Art Association was formed in 1938 to promote traditional aesthetics in the visual arts. All of these activities provided a vehicle for Catholics to promote an alternative to the dominant Protestant culture that had rejected Smith and his Catholic supporters so resoundingly. For Gleason, the 1930s mark a formative period in American Catholic intellectual life, when the neo-scholastic movement was channeled into the quest to create a "Catholic culture." "The word *culture*," Gleason writes, "was more and more widely employed to designate the way of life of a people."[23]

Amid this American Catholic revival, John Courtney Murray returned to the United States from Rome in 1937 after completing his doctorate in sacred theology at the Gregorian University. Murray took up a teaching post in the small-town atmosphere at Woodstock College in Maryland, a Jesuit seminary physically separated from the urban milieu in which so many of the Catholic Action apostolates profiled in this current volume had their roots. By vocation and temperament, Murray was not an activist but an educator, and his contribution to the Catholic Action movement began by seeking intellectual grounding for the Catholic culture that the activist apostolates labored to create. In the late 1930s Murray provided spiritual direction to Edward Kirchner, who was the president of Pax Romana, an international Catholic student organization. Kirchner's work with American Catholic Action brought Murray into the circles of the movement.[24] Murray's first published remarks on Catholic Action are from a statement that he made at a symposium held by the National Catholic Alumni Federation in 1939. The title of the symposium revealed its oppositional stance: "Man and Modern Secularism—the Conflict of the Two Cultures Considered Especially in Relation to Education."[25]

In his contribution to the symposium, Murray took a minority point of view in responding to the remarks of two other priests who shared the podium with him: the Reverend Gerald B. Phelan of the Institute of Mediaeval Studies in Toronto (another new Catholic venture begun in 1929 by the philosopher Etienne Gilson), and the Redemptorist priest and Catholic University of America professor Francis J. Connell, who throughout the 1940s and early 1950s would clash with Murray over the issue of Church–state relations. While both Phelan and Connell advocated teaching theology to lay students in Catholic universities, reminding the audience of theology's preeminence as the queen of the sciences, Murray voiced doubts that the systematic theology of neo-scholastic seminary education was practical enough for the laity. "If you take Catholic theology as it is taught in our seminaries, and examine it," Murray said, "you cannot resist the impression (at least I cannot) that it does not adapt itself to becoming the basis of an effective program of Catholic action."[26] Murray's problem with neo-scholastic seminary theology was not doctrinal. Rather, Murray thought that neo-scholasticism lacked the necessary communitarian and social foundation that would make it relevant for lay students. Contrasting the "demonstrability of truth" with "the livability of the Word of God," Murray remarked:

> By Catholic action I think we agree in meaning, action that is coextensive with the spirit of Christ in this world, action, therefore, that is wholly positive, that has as its supreme purpose *aedifacatio Corporis Christi*, the building up of the Body of Christ; therefore in Catholic action that is what we are trying to inspire, vigorous social action, action that is characteristically social.
>
> If you look now at scientific theology as it is taught in our seminaries, you cannot deny the fact—and I say this not on my own authority but on the authority of many other theologians who are teachers, professors of scientific theology—that Catholic theology in its contemporary form is shot through with a very individualistic current of thought.[27]

Murray's next foray into the subject of Catholic Action took place before a very different audience. Early in 1942 at the Jewish Theological Seminary in New York City, he delivered four lectures under the heading "Religion and Society."[28] Given only weeks before the U.S. Postmaster General barred Charles Coughlin's anti-Semitic magazine *Social Justice* from the postal system, these lectures mark a further development in Murray's views on Catholic Action, offering a broader historical frame of reference, one extending back far earlier in time than the 1928 presidential campaign. Murray began his opening lecture by reiterating the social concern that he had emphasized at the 1939 symposium, stating that his goal was "to develop for you the fact that the Church does conceive herself to have a mission in the socio-temporal order, in the total field of human social life as it is lived here on earth." For the final lecture of the series, Murray placed Catholic Action within a sixth epoch of a historical periodization of Church history that he borrowed wholesale from an article by Henri Carpay in the *Nouvelle Revue Théologique* in 1935.[29] Sixfold divisions of Church history have been employed as far back as the fourth century A.D., but unlike patristic and medieval periodizations based on biblical exegesis, Carpay and Murray's novel delineation of historical epochs was governed by the relationship between the temporal and the spiritual orders of human societies.[30] According to Carpay, each of the epochs has been defined by a distinctive relationship of these two aspects of human social organization, and this relationship determined the Church's strategy for effecting religious change in the world. In epochs during which the temporal and the spiritual realms of society are in opposition, as in the pre-Constantinian age and in nineteenth-century Europe, the Church's apostolate necessarily relies on spiritual means rather than temporal power to spread the gospel message. In other eras, such as late antiquity and the Middle Ages, Carpay's two societies interpenetrate one another, leading to a different form of apostolate.

Carpay and Murray faced different political landscapes in appropriating such Catholic historiography. While Carpay wrote in the mid-1930s, in a political milieu in which the dying remnants of the Action Française sparred with left-wing secularists, the anti-Catholicism that Murray faced was not secularist but rooted in a rival version of confessionalism, an American Protestantism suspicious of the Catholic Church's commitment to religious disestablishment and democracy. Despite their different starting points, both Carpay and Murray interpreted their own age as part of the sixth era of the Church's history, inaugurated in the 1922 election of Achille Ratti as Pius XI and his advocacy of the Catholic Action movement. As a lay apostolate that respected the distinction between the temporal and spiritual orders while simultaneously working to reform temporal society, Catholic Action allowed the Catholic Church to transcend the sort of clericalist interference in political life that had already made Father Coughlin notorious, without turning its back on the secular realm altogether. Patristic and medieval periodizations of the sixth age of Church history were often laced with millenarian and apocalyptic expectations. While Carpay and Murray do not use such apocalyptic motifs to foretell the impending end of world history, each speaks of his present age with striking urgency. Carpay writes that "the question of an *accord between the church and the state* will decide the future of the world," while Murray told the audience at Jewish Theological Seminary that this is "the issue of human society on which all the future hangs."[31] For Carpay and Murray, Catholic Action, as promoted by Pius XI, was the distinctively modern apostolate that the Catholic Church required in the mid-twentieth century.

Murray's subsequent writings on Catholic Action, written for a primarily Catholic readership, return to the framework of educational reform. In an article in *Theological Studies* (1944), Murray wrote that religious training for Catholic laity "should start with intensive research in the papal theory of Catholic Action. . . . In no other way can one learn exactly what a layman is and what the Church today requires of him."[32] That same year, Murray taught a course at Woodstock entitled "Questions Regarding the Social Duty of the Church."[33] In both the *Theological Studies* article and his lecture notes for the course, Murray continued to draw on Carpay's 1935 article in claiming that Catholic Action served as a "bridge between Church and society," but he also expounded on Catholic Action's mediating function between the clergy and the laity.[34] In Murray's exposition, Catholic Action's ties to the Church hierarchy provided a new historical mechanism for ensuring that it would seek a goal "emanating, not from [an] individual will in pursuit of [its] particular good, but from a will of public character in view of [the] common good of the Church."[35] With its mediating function and its pursuit of the common good, Catholic Action assumed for Murray the role of social, political, and theological archetype, as he noted in his Woodstock course notes that it provided "in its generality [a] formula perfect per se, [that it] opens [the] way to [a] 'new era of Xtian civilization.'"[36] For Murray, Catholic Action also provided a meeting ground between theory and history. In his eyes "it solves [the] ancient problem of civilization, sc. [the] spiritual direction of [the] temporal order without violating [the] transcendence of [the] spiritual or [the] autonomy of [the] temporal."[37]

In explaining his views regarding the community of faith and the social responsibilities of the Church, Murray generally relied on time-honored juridical language in naming the temporal and spiritual as distinct "orders" or "powers" of society. Throughout the 1940s and the early 1950s, Murray's understanding of "order" was framed in terms of the neo-scholastic distinctions between the natural order of reason and the supernatural order of grace. In 1944, Murray relied on this distinction between nature and supernature in a pamphlet he wrote for the Catholic Association for International Peace, designed to secure support among Catholics for the Declaration on World Peace, which was signed by Catholic, Protestant, and Jewish leaders the previous year. Murray's address to Catholic lawyers during that same year relies on this same terminology in arguing for a juridical international organization. Throughout the Second World War, Murray's appeal for interreligious cooperation hinged on his claim that the basic moral truths recognizable by people from various religious traditions made social collaboration possible while at the same time leaving room for a supernatural order of grace that would guard against traditional Catholic concerns about religious indifferentism.[38]

While these time-worn theological distinctions may interest theologians and political theorists, it was Murray's interest in the lay apostolate that induced him to supplement this abstract terminology with a concrete focus on social organization. Murray's concern for lay organization served as a mediating topic in this area. He told his Woodstock students that social structure was the key contribution that Pius XI made in the area of the Church's apostolic endeavor. "Pius XI," Murray insisted, "saw that [the] key to [the] modern problem was *organization*."[39] J. Leon Hooper has commended the shift in Murray's thought "from the juridical and institutional to the realms of philosophical and theological meaning."[40] This shift, however, does not imply discontinuity between the institutional and theological foci of Murray's writings. In the early 1940s, his thinking on Catholic Action was in no way classicist, thanks to his borrowing from Carpay's exposition, and Murray's writings endowed Catholic Action with a historically conditioned yet privileged *theological* role in the Church.

The American melting pot also induced Murray to turn his attention to the ecumenical possibilities for the Catholic Action movement, moving well beyond the usual scope of Catholic Action concerns in Europe, where the long history of Catholic political establishment steered the hearts of many Catholic laity toward the different ideal of a parallel subculture. The Second World War brought with it exigencies that called for Americans to bridge their religious differences, and in 1943 Murray wrote an article on intercreedal cooperation, in which he claimed that the theological rationale for such cooperation was not in doubt.[41] Rather, it was the means of organizing such cooperative effort that required greater explanation. Engaging in a historical retrieval of Pius X's 1912 encyclical letter *Singulari Quadam,* which allowed German Catholics to join trade unions composed of both Catholics and Protestants, Murray used this German precedent to argue that Catholic Action was an ideal institutional vehicle to promote interreligious cooperation in a world scarred by war. Commenting on Pius XI's encyclical *Quadragesimo Anno,* Murray moves well beyond Pius's definition of Catholic Action as lay participation in the hierarchical apostolate and employs sacramental expressions to describe the community of faith:

> Behind [Catholic laity] is an organization, Catholic Action, that educates them to their responsibility, unites them in indispensable bonds of solidarity, and is the source of their spiritual inspiration, their integral Christian life, whose demands they are to realize concretely and in institutional form by the use of their professional abilities in the social field. And behind Catholic Action is the total sacramental reality of the Church, the Body of Christ, which powerfully deploys its sacerdotal action in prayer and sacrifice, to the end that the whole body may be filled to the fullness of God, and flow over in beneficent action for the common good of all men.[42]

Murray's description of Catholic Action bears resemblance to Pius XII's description of the Church as the "mystical body of Christ" in the encyclical *Mystici Corporis,* published the same month as this article of Murray's.[43]

Pleading for Community among Upwardly Mobile Catholic Laity

Henri Carpay taught Murray that undifferentiated societies, whether the religious society of medieval Christendom or the secularist societies of modern times, were threats to the human dignity that Murray would champion during Vatican II. Civil unity and a peaceful international social order were goals that Murray promoted in the 1940s and 1950s, but the ultimate human goals were not, according to Murray, to be achieved solely through the acquisition of more extensive civil rights. Murray's insistence on social differentiation is often overlooked, given his later theological contributions to Vatican II, but any adequate account of Murray's social thought must acknowledge that his would become a voice of protest within a postwar America that sought to enshrine what Murray's contemporary, sociologist Will Herberg, termed the "American Way of Life" as the common faith of the American body politic. In Herberg's characterization, the American Way of Life is an inner-directed, middle-class, secularized Puritanism that has dispensed with religious transcendence. In his 1955 book *Protestant, Catholic, Jew*, Herberg wrote: "Insofar as any reference is made to the God in whom all Americans 'believe' and of whom the 'official' religions speak, it is primarily as sanction and underpinning for the supreme values of the faith embodied in the American Way of Life."[44] David O'Brien has written of this same "Americanizing" impulse among mid-twentieth century American Catholics, in which aspiration for mobility and assimilation displaced the impetus to reorganize society.[45]

Murray sought to counter any such Americanizing tendencies among Catholic laity. For Murray, while civil society has its own proper degree of autonomy, humanity's final teleology is instead a matter for God's supernatural providence. Murray believed that Pius XI's central role in twentieth-century Church history was a consequence of his acceptance of the distinction between the civil and religious spheres of society. When Pius XI broke with over fifty years of papal precedent by going to the outside balcony of St. Peter's Basilica to give his first papal blessing to the city of Rome minutes after his election, the head of the Catholic Church recognized the positive value of a differentiated society. In Murray's account of history, Pius gave his blessing to Catholic Action as a new apostolate designed to achieve unity within this new historical epoch.

Though the prominence of Catholic Action in Murray's writings and in the Church's apostolate as a whole declined in the second half of the twentieth century, Murray's emphasis on organization and community as necessary underpinnings of the Church's apostolate within a differentiated secular society did not wane. After 1950, Murray took care to contextualize the idea of freedom by contrasting his understanding of the value of freedom with that of nineteenth-century continental liberalism as detailed in Carpay's fifth era of Church history, extending from the French Revolution to the papacy of Pius XI. In Murray's recounting, the bitter conflicts between Church and state in nineteenth-century Europe were conflicts in which each side fought for its own unitary conception of society. For its part, the papacy in the years of Gregory XVI and Pius IX longed for a return to the sacralized *ancien régime* of medieval Christendom, with its union of throne and altar. France's Third Republic, on the other hand, attempted to counter reactionary Catholic politics with a laicized state that subsumed all Church functions within a monistic body politic that Murray in 1952 had already labeled "totalitarian democracy."[46]

In Dwight Eisenhower's America, totalitarian democracy was not the problem that had confronted the Catholics in the Third Republic, but the problems of organizing Catholic laity remained, even in the absence of governmental suppression. In 1954, the same year in which the televised Army–McCarthy hearings brought the fiercely anticommunist Catholic senator into living rooms across the nation, Murray characterized the distinctive brand of American irreligiosity as follows: "It was not Continental laicism, superficially anticlerical, fundamentally antireligious, militant in its spirit, active in its purpose to destroy what it regarded as hateful. Unbelief in America has been rather easy-going, the product more of a naïve materialism than of any conscious conviction. . . . And this fact has been important in influencing the general climate in which our institutions work."[47]

When Murray returned to the theme of Church history in a 1957 symposium, "Christianity and Our Present Discontents," which was published in Russell Kirk's conservative journal *Modern Age,* he was emphatic that freedom per se is *not* the paramount problem of modern society as it had evolved since the European Enlightenment. The underlying trouble with the nineteenth-century stalemate between Catholic ultramontanists and continental liberals was not, according to Murray's essay "Freedom of Man in the Freedom of the Church," that this struggle frustrated the individual person's need to be free from constraint in religious matters. Rather, Murray interpreted the problem of modernity as one of organization, just as he had before his Woodstock seminarians some fifteen years earlier: "We confront again the dilemma which modernity resolved in its own sense. Is the life of man to be organized in one society or two?"[48] Just as the eighteenth-century beliefs in reason or inevitable progress were eclipsed by the hardships of experience, the modern doctrine of freedom had been found wanting because "it neglected the corporate dimension of freedom" and separated it from order.[49] What followed in the essay was another historical synopsis, not delineated in the manner of Carpay's outline, which treated the theme of freedom as a quality of the Church rather than of the individual. Unlike the earlier historical schematization that Murray borrowed from Carpay in the early 1940s, Murray's revised theological interpretation of historical Church–state differentiation defines the Church as both "the limiting principle of the power of government" and as "the ultimate directive principle of government."[50]

Over the span of three decades, the problems facing American Catholic laity had shifted markedly. Mary Brown's article in this volume reminds readers that the maintenance of Catholic immigrant subcultures was a concern in the United States well beyond the 1940s, but the Italian Catholic Action groups she profiles in Boston and Washington were throwbacks to the bygone era of Al Smith and accompanying Catholic concerns about religiously hostile surroundings. By contrast, the era of Christian Democratic parties in postwar Western Europe attracted Catholics who found them supportive yet autonomous allies in the political struggles against socialist and communist groups. In the United States, anti-Catholic sentiment continued, as seen by the success of Paul Blanshard's "Catholic Power" trilogy of 1949–54, but Catholics increased their proportion of the population throughout the 1940s and 1950s and saw one of their number finally elected president in 1960.[51] Affluence replaced exclusion as the prime threat to lay apostolates, and Murray's criticism of materialism blunts a Cavardi-like defensive stance toward the surrounding culture; totalitarian democracy was a threat from within the gates of American society that could not be blamed on "rationalist Protestantism" or liberalism. Like Cavardi, however, Murray lived to see his intellectual justifications for lay initiatives outpaced by unfolding events. Protestants and Catholics would cooperate on a greater scale as the Eisenhower era progressed, but the interwar cohesion of Catholic Action's prime never returned. The contributions from Mary Henold, Jeremy Bonner, Sam Thomas, and Andrew Moore in the second part of this volume demonstrate how the succeeding generation of American Catholics took their previous support for democratic structures outside the Church and carried it within the ecclesial precincts. In distinguishing among planes in his social model, Maritain did not anticipate the centrifugal force that a diverse lay apostolate could unleash. Murray's model of a differentiated society contained little material with which to construct a model for a more differentiated Catholic Church, which was not a priority for him during the years in which he spent ink fending off attacks on the Church's institutional independence.

Theological distinctions (such as that between nature and grace), ecclesiastical distinctions (such as that between laity and clergy), and social distinctions (such as that between a spiritual church and a temporal world) fell on hard times by the late 1960s, so it is not surprising that the Catholic Action movement vanished from lay consciousness after Vatican II, given the movement's initial formation as a way for laity to mediate the action of the hierarchy. By the late 1960s, the negative liberty to which Isaiah Berlin first referred in the late 1950s proved much more attractive to many American Catholics than Murray's theories about social organization, especially as the civil-rights movement, a new wave of feminism, and an emerging counterculture led many to equate social distinctions with segregation, and hierarchy with oppression.[52] Within the Church, many lay Catholics chafed under the enforced tutelage of the hierarchy, in a trend that came to a boil with the dissent from *Humanae Vitae* after that encyclical's promulgation in 1968.[53]

Murray died in 1967, before this tumult reached its apex, but his lectures and writings on behalf of Catholic Action made the movement more understandable to a theological elite that surely remembered the battles over lay trusteeship and ethnic rivalries in American Catholic history. In a country where lay Catholics could not appeal to a past ideal of a politically restored Catholic establishment, Murray was given an opportunity to explain Catholic Action in forward-looking terms in a religiously diverse milieu. Those liberals and conservatives who battle today to be certified as the rightful heirs of Murray's theological legacy can argue whether or not the internal transformations within the lay apostolate after Vatican II would have been welcomed by him. Regardless of the outcome of that debate, this chapter has tried to demonstrate that the bottom-up influence of the lay apostolates on the clerical and theological leaders of the American Church was already far advanced by the time that Vatican II was convened.

5 Azzione Cattolica in an American Setting

The Society of St. Charles–Scalabrinians and Catholic Action

MARY ELIZABETH BROWN

This chapter examines two postwar Catholic Action groups, which, though separated by distance, shared a common heritage. Established in parishes founded for Italian immigrants in the late nineteenth and early twentieth centuries, respectively, they drew a significant portion of their membership from those Italians who migrated to the United States during the 1940s and 1950s and brought with them a familiarity with Catholic Action as practiced in Italy. The form of Catholic Action that they developed, however, was less a mechanism of lay empowerment than a means of sustaining an ethnic culture that had largely vanished from the Catholic Church in the United States by the early 1940s. In this respect, it represents a significant departure from the model promoted by most of the proponents of American Catholic Action from the early 1930s onward.

The older of the two subject parishes, Sacred Heart of Boston, was part of the Archdiocese of Boston, itself founded in 1808 and raised to archdiocesan status in 1875, by which time Italian immigrants had begun to settle in the city, principally in the North End. Their first recorded worship site was St. Mary's Church on Thatcher Street, a parish that had been established in 1835 and entrusted to the Jesuits in 1847.[1] In 1873, Archbishop John Joseph Williams purchased the former Free Will Baptist Meeting House on North Bennett Street for the congregation. In 1875, the parish became the Portuguese parish of St. John the Baptist, prompting the Italian Franciscans and Italian laity to begin to worship at St. Leonard of Port Maurice on the corner of Hanover and Prince Street in 1876.

During the same period, however, the Italian community divided into northern and southern Italian factions. Until unification of the Italian peninsula in 1870, southern Italy had formed the Kingdom of the Two Sicilies, composed of the island of Sicily and the mainland of Italy to a point north of Naples. This region was linguistically and geographically divided, with the Straits of Messina and the Apennine Mountains forming natural barriers. Despite a shared Catholic faith, each community's religious life revolved around a particular patron saint. The principal unifying factor was poverty. Landowners claimed large tracts of the most fertile arable land and hired the local residents as their agribusinesses required. Most of the peasantry could neither find steady work nor go into business for themselves, nor, because they were obliged to pay a variety of high taxes in cash, could they rest content with subsistence farming.[2] By contrast, in northern Italy—despite pockets of poverty—a national government dedicated to promoting industrialization had produced a more robust proletariat. Northern and southern Italians regarded each other as distinct cultures, with the former adopting an attitude of cultural superiority. When sufficient numbers of people from the two regions migrated to the same location, they reassembled their regional communities, leading in Boston to the separation of the northern Italians—mostly from Genoa—from the southern Italians of St. Leonard of Port Maurice.

In 1884, a group of Genoese men resident in Boston organized the San Marco Society, with the object of establishing a new Italian parish. The name of the society reflected the group's effort to present themselves as *Italians* rather than as natives of a particular part of Italy, since St. Mark was and is patron saint of Venice, a northern Italian city across the peninsula from Genoa. The next year, the San Marco Society purchased a church, first erected on Boston's North Square in 1833 as "Father Taylor's Seamen's Bethel," the church of Edward Thompson Taylor, a sailor who became a Methodist minister serving his former colleagues in the maritime industry. The society's intention to use the building as a parish church nevertheless ran counter to the law of the Commonwealth of Massachusetts, which recognized Catholic ordinaries as the sole trustees of the parishes in their sees.[3]

In 1888, the San Marco Society departed from canon law by bypassing the local ordinary in its pursuit of priests for the planned parish. It resorted to an as yet unnamed order, founded the previous year by Bishop Giovanni Batista Scalabrini of the Diocese of Piacenza in the province of Emilia-Romagna in northwest Italy.[4] Born in 1839 in Fino Mornasco in the region of Lombardy, Scalabrini was appointed bishop of Piacenza in 1876. On his first pastoral visit to his new diocese, he noticed the high emigration rate and adopted migration as his cause. While Scalabrini's flock was migrating across Europe and into North Africa, he was most concerned with migration to the Americas; he envisioned South America as a jungle frontier and North America as dominated by either Protestants or secularists. To address this concern, he founded an order of priests to serve the migrants in transit and in their new homes. In 1893, he chose Charles Borromeo, sixteenth-century archbishop of Milan, as patron saint for his order, although the order has historically been known by the adjectival form of its founder's name.[5]

The first Scalabrinian priest to work with the San Marco Society, Father Francesco Zaboglio, advised society members to avoid antagonizing Archbishop Williams while they negotiated the archbishop's recognition of their parish. Zaboglio even suggested that the society find another building for worship during the negotiations, and space was rented on Beverly Street for a chapel named in honor of the Sacred Heart (of Jesus). In 1890, when the San Marco Society and Archbishop Williams reached an agreement, "Sacred Heart" became the name of the new North Square parish.

Thereafter, Sacred Heart developed in a fashion similar to that of most English-speaking parishes. Except for the San Marco Society, most of its parochial organizations could also be found in non-Italian parishes, the earliest being the married women's Confraternity of Christian Mothers, formed in 1889. In 1893 the League of the Sacred Heart of Jesus, a trans-parochial organization that cultivated its members' prayer lives, organized a chapter at Sacred Heart. In 1897, the men of the parish organized the St. Vincent de Paul Society to channel parish charity toward the parish poor. The Children of Mary, another trans-parochial organization, which promoted a deeper prayer life and more intense involvement with parish programs among girls and unmarried women, reached Sacred Heart in 1889, and a San Luigi Society for Sacred Heart's young men was organized in 1911. That same year, a parish mission resulted in the establishment of a society devoted to Our Lady of Mount Carmel, the patroness of Salerno.[6] The parish also maintained St. John's Parochial School.

Unlike Sacred Heart, Holy Rosary parish in Washington, D.C., was organized in the early twentieth century, and—since Washington was not a port city—the Italian immigrants who became parishioners tended to be manual laborers and skilled builders working on new construction projects, such as Union Station.[7] Their appearance at most parishes in the area around Capitol Hill prompted the apostolic delegate, the Vatican's representative in the area, to take an interest, and it was he who alerted the ordinary, at that time the archbishop of Baltimore, to the need for a new parish.[8] As a result, Father Nicholas De Carlo, a former Augustinian priest from southern Italy, who had just arrived at the Catholic University of America to take a course in preaching missions, found himself thrust into the role of pastor of Holy Rosary.[9]

There were no lay-led societies involved in Holy Rosary's founding, and the societies subsequently established at Holy Rosary were—like those at Sacred Heart—similar to those at non-Italian parishes, although Holy Rosary, which had Italian-speaking parishioners scattered across a wide geographical area, never established a parochial school. Teresa Poloni, a midwife active in Washington's Italian American community, organized the Society of Christian Mothers in 1914, but that organization did not long survive Poloni's death in 1920. The same year, the School Sisters of Notre Dame, who were conducting Holy Rosary's Sunday school, organized the young women into the Children of Mary, seeking to appeal to the English-speaking daughters of Italian immigrants. In 1915, Joseph Balducci, a local grocer instrumental in founding Holy Rosary, brought to the parish the Holy Name Society, a trans-parochial organization devoted to the prayer lives and parish participation of married men. Ten years later, the younger English-speaking men of the parish organized a Junior Holy Name Society, and as the older generation passed away, this organization became *the* Holy Name Society of the parish. Finally, in 1918, parishioner Maria Croccia founded the Union of Italian Catholic Women, for married Italian-speaking women. While a Catholic Action group did exist for a short period during the 1920s, it left no documentary evidence and only a single mention in a parish history prepared by the pastor and by a non-Italian friend of the pastor, who was also a professor at Catholic University of America.[10]

Although their parish organizations were not unique to Italian Catholics, both Sacred Heart and Holy Rosary were considered by priests, parishioners, and the local press to be distinctly Italian churches. Sacred Heart was housed in what was originally a Protestant building, but the parish mounted a statue of the Sacred Heart of Jesus in a niche above and between the two front doors, installed statues and images of saints around the interior, and hired an Italian-immigrant artist, Donato Buongiorno, to add additional frescos of the saints on the walls.[11] Holy Rosary's pastor approved the plans for the parish's building, which was designed in a style common to churches in town squares across southern Italy. On its facade was a mosaic of the Virgin and Child in a Byzantine style also common to southern Italy. Inside was a Carrera marble altar, pulpit, altar rail, and baptismal font, a terrazzo floor, Venetian-glass mosaic Stations of the Cross, and a giant painting of Our Lady of the Rosary stretched across the dome above the altar. Holy Rosary's elaborate Nativity scene stood out among the Christmas decorations displayed by Washington-area churches.

When Father De Carlo became concerned about who would replace him as pastor, it was to the provincial superior of the Society of St. Charles–Scalabrinians (courtesy of a mutual acquaintance) that he turned for an Italian replacement. In 1960, Archbishop (later Cardinal) Patrick O'Boyle of Washington invited the Scalabrinians to staff Holy Rosary. By this date, both parishes followed a model that historian James Hennessey summed up in the phrase "so certain and set apart," meaning that such American Catholics preferred to focus on what distinguished them from the rest of American society rather than engaging with it.[12] Also by this date, Sacred Heart already had a Catholic Action group, and Holy Rosary was soon to acquire one, raising the possibility of apostolates engaged in the political, economic, and social questions of the day, but these parishes' attempts at Catholic Action would prove very different from one another.

Beginnings of Catholic Action at Sacred Heart and Holy Rosary

The founding of Catholic Action groups at Sacred Heart and Holy Rosary was closely associated with post–Second World War Italian migration. Until 1952, U.S. immigration law had been governed by the Immigration Act of May 26, 1924. From 1952 to 1965 it was shaped by the Immigration and Nationality Act, also known as the McCarran-Walter Act. Both laws favored migration from northern and western Europe. While Italy was allotted roughly five thousand visas each year, Italian American migration was greater than these numbers would suggest, because McCarran-Walter permitted U.S. citizens to sponsor spouses and minor children without regard to the number of visas available, and additional visas were available for war brides and displaced persons.[13]

Although Catholic Action emphasized lay leadership, its local manifestations at Sacred Heart and at Holy Rosary also depended on the Scalabrinian clergy. The priest who brought Catholic Action to Sacred Heart was Pierantonio (Piero) Oddi, born on May 2, 1931, in Morfasso, a town in the province of Piacenza; his uncle was Silvio Angelo Pio Cardinal Oddi, a Vatican diplomat and future prefect of the Congregation of the Clergy. Entering the Scalabrinian order when he was twenty-two years old and had already completed much of his education for the priesthood, Oddi made his perpetual vows on May 19, 1956, was ordained three months later, and served at the Church of the Redemptor in Rome from October 1956 to February 1958. Arriving in the American mission field in March 1958, he was assigned as an assistant to Sacred Heart, where he soon earned the respect of the community. Indeed, when he was transferred to New York in 1967, Caesar Donnaruma, publisher of the *Post-Gazette*, New England's Italian American newspaper, wrote the Scalabrinians to see if Oddi might be allowed to remain in Boston. Oddi also found his new mission less than satisfying. In 1967, the Scalabrinians' general superior was dismayed to receive an unfavorable report from Oddi's local superior, blaming it on the freedom that Oddi had enjoyed in Boston, where his superior had not been particular about his activities. By January 1968, Oddi had announced his intention to leave the order and the priesthood. The Scalabrinians appealed to Oddi's cardinal-uncle for help in restoring his nephew's sense of vocation. A transfer of Oddi to a more satisfying mission back in Italy kept Oddi in the community for ten more years. He left the order in 1978.[14]

At Holy Rosary, Catholic Action was initiated by Joseph Spigolon, C.S., who was born in Baldaria di Cologna Veneta in the province of Verona on July 17, 1929. An early vocation to both the priesthood and the Scalabrinians, he left home at age eleven to begin his priestly education but did not make his first profession of vows until September 4, 1946. He made his perpetual profession on October 1, 1950, and was ordained to the priesthood in March 1954. Entering the mission field that year, he served at St. Anthony's parish in Everett, Massachusetts, until 1959, when he returned to Italy for a year as assistant master of novices. He was Holy Rosary's first assistant pastor, arriving with Father Giulivio Tessarolo in 1960. In 1963, Tessarolo was elected superior general of the Scalabrinian community, and Spigolon became pastor, remaining at Holy Rosary until 1970, when he was called to Rome to serve in the Scalabrinians' central administration. He remained in the Scalabrinian order all his life, and died on January 9, 2004.[15]

One other Scalabrinian must be mentioned. Father Dominic Rodighiero entered the U.S. mission field in 1961 and succeeded Father Spigolon as assistant at Holy Rosary in 1963. In Rome from 1966 to 1967, Father Dominic subsequently returned to the United States, this time as an assistant at Sacred Heart in Boston. He was transferred in 1972 but returned to serve as pastor of Sacred Heart from 1986 to 1990. He was the only Scalabrinian priest to appear in the records of the Catholic Action groups of both Sacred Heart and the Holy Rosary.

That neither parish's Catholic Action group persisted long after the departure of the clergy most interested in them suggests the importance of the clergy in such an organization. Both groups published newsletters early in their existence, and these carried regular columns from the priest-moderator of the Catholic Action group. Father Oddi's Scalabrinian personnel file contains correspondence, between the priest and his superiors, indicating that Father Oddi was indeed the engine of his Catholic Action group. Father Spigolon left no such correspondence, but there is evidence that he was seen as a kind of paterfamilias of community life. Parishioners interviewed for parish histories brought up his role unprompted and praised his work. When he celebrated the twenty-fifth anniversary of his ordination, a group of parishioners went all the way from Washington, D.C., to Canada, where he was stationed, to help celebrate.[16]

The first reported Catholic Action group was a single-women's group in Boston. Its earliest surviving meeting minutes are from Saturday, December 12, 1958, of a meeting of the four executive officers and the chaplain.[17] A men's meeting did not take place until October 12, 1959, and its first recorded activity was to ascertain the absence of a quorum and then to adjourn until October 26.[18] Women also led the way at Holy Rosary, when a group of about fifteen began meeting with Father Spigolon in the rectory basement in 1961. While they elected a president and began publishing a newsletter almost immediately, it was only in 1963 that Fathers Tessarolo and Spigolon had conducted enough outreach among the men to allow for the organization of a male Catholic Action group.[19] This sequence of events is consistent with the formation of many Catholic organizations but runs counter to the general history of the formation of Italian American Catholic organizations, since Italian migration before the First World War was predominantly male and men's organizations tended to precede those for women. Inasmuch as those men settled down and formed communities, they organized societies in honor of the patron saints of their hometowns, dedicated to reproducing hometown feast-day celebrations in the new setting, and also to providing insurance ("mutual aid") to their members.[20]

Meeting space was an enduring concern, although in the early days both groups met on parish property. Holy Rosary's Catholic Action groups continued to do so for most of their existence, sharing basement meeting space with other parochial organizations, but Sacred Heart's Catholic Action group acquired its own meeting room early in its existence. At a meeting in December 1960, it was announced that the facility would be open on December 23 and December 24 (Christmas Eve) for members to play bingo and dance to the "juk-box" (an English word for which there was no Italian equivalent).[21] By 1967, the first year for which a detailed balance sheet survives, Sacred Heart's Catholic Action group operated a bar that, for an outlay of $659.01, made them $1,790.99 in profit.[22] In April 1969, Catholic Action leaders announced major renovations to the club house: a ballroom (no record of size), meeting rooms, a room for watching television, and a new bar with a machine that dispensed cocoa, soup, and four kinds of coffee, all for a dime a cup.[23] The year that it opened, the club house grossed $19,921.25, with $11,316.00 of that derived from the bar. (The bar's profit margin rose, as it cost only $4,740.44 to run that year.)[24] The bar was the club house's main attraction and remained profitable through 1972, the last year on record.[25]

The Ethos of Italian American Catholic Action

The clearest articulation of a purpose for Catholic Action appeared in capital letters in the newsletter *Incontro* in 1965—namely, "to conserve human and Christian values in the Italian community."[26] The activities of the Boston and Washington Catholic Action groups serve to indicate how this was achieved. Holy Rosary's Catholic Action group left few records articulating a value system, although the group's activities suggest some consistent patterns of thought. Sacred Heart's Catholic Acton group published more, although not necessarily anything particularly definitive. Translated into English, the introduction to its bylaws read:

> Boston Catholic Action clearly has a different face than the organization with the same name that is prospering in Italy. However, it is inspired by the same ideal.
>
> Its juridical form is not definite and hasn't adapted itself to the existing scheme of parochial or religious organizations. It is born with a super-parochial spirit and with a marked tendency toward recreational social activities.
>
> Boston Catholic Action reflects the situation and the ambience from which it emerged: among the immigrants and for the immigrants who have rediscovered a certain social nucleus in the section of Boston known by the name of the North End, but is not limited to that neighborhood, it embraces the whole metropolitan region.
>
> Its religious activity is not unique; rather, it tends to the Christian ideal. Boston Catholic Action's style is a dynamic opening, fresh, not bound to plan, dynamism that implies constant research into the means and initiative adapted to diffusing the Christian message, and even before that to encourage and develop human values. Much of its work is simply social assistance that does not bear immediate spiritual fruits, but which is still the presence of the Church among the immigrants.
>
> In this sense every member is a committed Christian, that is to say an apostle, a testifier to Christ, who gives part of his time and his talents for the diffusion of the evangelical message.[27]

The same year that this statement appeared, Cardinal Richard Cushing died and Pope Paul VI named Umberto Medeiros to be the new archbishop of Boston. The first non-Irish archbishop since the first bishop of Boston, Medeiros was of Portuguese ancestry, and *Incontro* analyzed the transition accordingly:

> On October 7 Humberto S. Medeiros becomes the new Archbishop of Boston. After 26 years of untiring work, Cardinal Cushing retires.
>
> That's the chronicle of events in as few words as possible. However, this chronicle is a significant "changing of the guard." With Cardinal Cushing ends the era of the indisputable supremacy of the Irish. That's not a criticism, only a statement of fact.

Archbishop Medeiros represents another world. For the Catholics of
Boston, he's a bolt out of the blue, especially for those who represent
the "Establishment." He's a peaceful revolutionary, an embodiment of
the Gospel who espouses love and brotherhood, a nomination in tune
with the times. Humberto Medeiros is an immigrant, a man of the people, like us. A man who has known poverty and work. A man who, to
some degree, has known the same problems and the same humiliations
of others who are also strangers. A man who represents the face of the
church of today: without prejudice, without privilege, in evangelical
simplicity, with Christian courage. Courage that comes from his convictions, from the teaching, from the principles that Christ has carried into
the world and that have already operated to transform the world.

As Catholic Christians we should glory in the change to the new
Archbishop, and give him all our cooperation. He did not come in search
of honor, glory or riches. He came to work. A work few understand,
many criticize, always compensated by indifference or ingratitude, as
also happened to Christ.[28]

Although a recurring impression of ethnic Catholics is of a group focused
on maintaining their ethnic identity to the exclusion of all else, the peculiar
nature of postwar Italian immigration often made them sound as though
they were in the vanguard of both Catholic Action and Vatican II. Italian
American Catholic Action publications seldom took a prophetic stance, however, and even the political discussions in their publications tended to treat
issues as apolitical, assuming values to be commonly held rather than defined by a Democratic–Republican, liberal–conservative, or even Christian–
secular divide. In February 1970, Boston's *Incontro* commented on President
Richard M. Nixon's recent State of the Union address. The editorial translated into Italian a passage of the address that read: "But let us above all
recognize the fundamental truth: we can be the best clothed, best fed, best
housed people in the world, enjoying clean air, clean water, beautiful parks.
But we could still be the unhappiest people in the world without an indefin-
able spirit, the life of a living dream which has made America from its beginning the hope of the world." The article then summed up Nixon's speech
with the biblical passage: "Man does not live by bread alone."[29]

This editorial was closely followed by another, on Charles Manson's
murder of Sharon Tate, a story that was in the news because Manson
came to trial that February. The editorial hypothesized the Tate murder

as the logical consequence of a modern life, and especially modern media coverage, that liberated people from conventional morality. *Incontro's* concern for such morality was also revealed in editorials against "drugs," meaning recreational drug use, and abortion.[30] Its one political advertisement in 1972 endorsed Nixon—"Presidente Nixon: Ora Più che Mai!" (now more than ever!), a sentiment unlikely to be shared in progressive Catholic circles—but that was about the extent of its political coverage.[31] *Incontro* stuck to the issues that were closest to home and did not otherwise discuss party politics or national issues such as Vietnam. Holy Rosary's Catholic Action newsletter, *Voce Italiana,* was even more focused on encouraging individual commitment to the Church. Over time, it became a parish project rather than a Catholic Action project, reflecting the concerns of diverse groups of parishioners.

Catholic Action Activities

The earliest forms of Catholic Action sought to promote the spiritual life of Italian American women in Boston, but their methods departed from the stereotypical Italian-immigrant devotion to the Madonna or to a hometown patron saint. Instead, at its first meeting, the executive council called on members to receive Communion in a body on one Sunday a month, with a spiritual retreat on the preceding Saturday. Members met at 1:00 P.M. for meditation, broke up for individual confessions, and reconvened for benediction with the Blessed Sacrament at 4:00 P.M.[32] While the men's group also reported a monthly Communion, there seem to have been no accompanying activities.[33] Sacred Heart's priests frequently used the Catholic Action organization to encourage conformity with Church regulations. When the Archdiocese of Boston scheduled confirmations for adults who had not received the sacrament in their youth, Father Dominic Rodighiero publicized the event among the Catholic Action members and encouraged anyone interested to contact him to prepare for confirmation.[34] Although attendance at Mass was an obligation, Sacred Heart's Catholic Action group increased the likelihood of such attendance by scheduling the reception of new members as part of a Mass.[35]

Both the Boston and the Washington Catholic Action groups were active during the late 1960s and early 1970s, when the Vatican issued directives bringing the reception of the sacraments into conformity with the decrees of Vatican II. In Boston, the response to Vatican II was mixed. Catholic Action publications nominally accepted the call for greater participation in the Mass, and by June 1969, Sacred Heart had an Italian-language dialogue Mass at 11:00 A.M. on Sunday.[36] A group was organized to lead congregational singing, and by October 1970 the congregation had a repertoire of simple popular songs that members learned mostly by singing them repeatedly at Mass, but that was the extent of liturgical experimentation.[37] When Sacred Heart observed the Feast of Christ the King in November 1969, the Mass featured the Catholic Action choir singing a traditional *Te Deum*, but *Incontro* noted that the Mass lacked the liturgical oddities of recent Masses.[38] Although there is less information regarding the Catholic Action group at Holy Rosary, all indications are that its members also valued tradition in the reception of the sacraments. Holy Rosary was a small parish and did not schedule confirmations every year; when a bishop was scheduled to come in 1970, a member of Catholic Action petitioned the local ordinary to permit her son to be confirmed even though he had not reached the recommended age, because confirmation and the Mass at which it was celebrated were opportunities for the family to affirm its Italian culture.[39]

Catholic Action was intended to bring the *social teachings* of the Church to the world, but among the Italian immigrants at Sacred Heart and Holy Rosary it played a *social function*, allowing Italian immigrants to make friends and find partners. This was especially noticeable in Boston, where *Incontro* periodically announced marriages between members, and the babies resulting from such unions.[40] By 1969, Mothers Day was an occasion for partying.[41] In both Boston and Washington, married members continued to be active in Catholic Action in association with single members, rather than splitting off to form a unit of the Christian Family Movement. Both Sacred Heart and Holy Rosary Catholic Action did have other functions. Holy Rosary's Catholic Action group was much more interested in using the organization to perpetuate and promote Italian culture, raising money to stage Italian-language theater productions.[42] Most parish organizations organized dances, but Washington's Catholic Action group offered a masquerade ball at the traditional carnival time just before Lent.[43] The young men joined a soccer team that won a local championship, although the club disbanded when the parish assistant in charge of the team refused to emulate the other teams in the league and pay players.[44]

Sacred Heart's Catholic Action group has a more voluminous record of activities, only some of which focused on Italian culture. Like Holy Rosary, Sacred Heart had a soccer team, and soccer was a game more common among Italians than Americans, although there were enough soccer players in the area to organize a league. One year, Sacred Heart's Falcons played a Polish team called the Eagles, a Scandinavian team, and other teams identified by the names of the Massachusetts towns they represented.[45] There were also enough Italians familiar with skiing for the Catholic Action group to organize trips to nearby resorts.[46] The same sports report that listed the Falcons' schedule also described a bowling tournament, so apparently Italians did not confine their interest to bocce. Sacred Heart's Catholic Action group did not so much promote *Italian* sports as provide a way for would-be teammates and competitors to find one other. Under its auspices, one member organized a billiards tournament, and another organized two tennis teams that played against each other.[47]

The principal Italian cultural activity of the Catholic Action group at Sacred Heart was its Cine Forum, which involved screenings and discussions of Italian film, and in which it took some effort to keep participants interested.[48] However, its focus tended to be more on sponsoring activities that appealed to members, regardless of whether the activities had a particularly Italian flavor. Although it hosted dances, there is no mention of masquerade balls or of carnival time, and when it hosted a Christmas party, it was Santa Claus who showed up, not the Italian *Befana*.[49] While the group sponsored trips to Italy, the most common field trips took members to local landmarks and so provided opportunities to learn American history, as when the women's group visited Salem, scene of the 1692 witchcraft trials, to see the historic sites and to picnic.[50] Perhaps because Sacred Heart's church was located across from Paul Revere's house, Catholic Action also showed an interest in the *cavalcata di Paul Revere*. The women's group took a field trip along the route of the ride, and *Incontro* in 1973 published an article explaining how Paul Revere's compatriot climbed the *campanile* of the Old North Church to raise two lanterns to signal to Paul Revere that the *giubbe rosse* were crossing the Charles River to start their march to Lexington and Concord, whereupon Revere galloped out of Boston by road to alert the Minute Men (a phrase the author could not translate into Italian).[51]

Although members of Sacred Heart's Catholic Action group did not schedule many Italian cultural activities for themselves, when it came to events for other Bostonians, they were proud exponents of Italian customs. Sacred Heart's Catholic Action group sponsored an Italian-language radio program on Sunday afternoons on WNTN-AM 1550, and group members formed a choir that sang Italian folk songs at Summerthing 1969, a city-sponsored event in Paul Revere Park.[52] In May 1970, the group participated in the Festival Italiano, organizing a wine tasting that attracted six hundred tasters.[53] Representatives of Sacred Heart's Catholic Action group also joined with delegates from other organizations to welcome the president of the Italian council of ministers and the Italian foreign minister (Emilio Colombo and Aldo Moro) to Boston in February 1971.[54] Because Holy Rosary was located in Washington, D.C., it received visits from Vatican officials and Italian diplomats long before it established a Catholic Action group.

Both the Holy Rosary and the Sacred Heart Catholic Action groups performed longstanding service to the parishes that hosted them, not least in the newsletters they published. The earliest undertaking of Holy Rosary's women's Catholic Action group was a newsletter named, apparently without much discussion, Voce Italiana (or "Italian Voice"), whose first issue was described as a piece of paper folded in half to create four pages.[55] This paper grew to be one of Holy Rosary's most important services to the Washington-area Italian community, disseminating information about people and events and preserving it for the historical record. Its Sacred Heart counterpart, Incontro, first appeared in January 1968. The newsletter was intended to be a print meeting place, where Catholic Action members could exchange ideas and learn about community events.[56] In October 1971, Incontro adopted an eight-page tabloid format. The first issue in the new series lamented the lack of respect accorded Italian Americans, despite their contributions to American life, and then explained that united action was the way to gain respect and that it could best be secured through a newspaper.[57] Unlike Voce Italiana, however, Incontro was not meeting an unfulfilled need. There was already an Italian-language newspaper covering the Boston area, the Donnarumma family's Post-Gazette, originally the Gazetta del Massacusetts, and Incontro ceased publication in the 1970s.[58]

Although promotion of Catholic teaching on public issues was one of the purposes of Catholic Action groups in Europe, there is no record of the group at Holy Rosary taking a corporate stand on social issues. This is not surprising, however, as the migration to Washington after the Second World War included people from all kinds of occupations and social classes, but many immigrants had family in Washington to assist them when they needed help, and many were well-educated professionals who did not need much support. Sacred Heart's new parishioners, on the other hand, did include recent Italian immigrants who needed help securing services from the city, state, or federal government (or from Italy, as there were military veterans and retirees from the Italian workforce who were entitled to social-security benefits from Italy). As a result, the parish's Catholic Action group was more socially conscious. In the fall of 1971, Father Dominic Rodighiero presided over the opening of the Office of Information and Social Services at the Italian Catholic Action office, although the number of cases it subsequently handled is not clear.[59] By the 1970s, moreover, both Catholic Action groups were entering a new phase.

The End of Catholic Action in Boston and in Washington

Even as Sacred Heart's Catholic Action group marked its tenth anniversary with an anniversary booklet, a Mass, and a party, its members were moving on to a stage of life that left them little time for such activity. Father Peter Polo, C.S., who was Sacred Heart's Catholic Action moderator from 1978 to 1979, recalled attending meetings in the Boston suburbs because that was where most members had moved. The meetings were focused on spiritual activities, with a talk on a religious topic followed by a question-and-answer period.[60] In short, instead of being a force in the community, Sacred Heart's Catholic Action became an activity for a small group. As members moved out of the area or passed away, Catholic Action vanished from historical view.

Holy Rosary's Catholic Action group seems to have met one goal of Catholic Action, the creation of lay leadership. Holy Rosary's Catholic Action groups dissolved in the mid-1970s; however, members of the group took on responsibility for perpetuating and promoting Italian cultural activities through other Washington-area organizations.[61] Members of

Holy Rosary's Catholic Action group also remained active at Holy Rosary parish. In 1963, when the parish celebrated its fiftieth anniversary, the work of organizing the Mass and luncheon was done by "parish stalwarts and new parishioners recruited through *Azione Cattolica*."[62] Eventually individual members of Catholic Action emerged as parish leaders. Anna Neri became involved at Holy Rosary when the Scalabrinian fathers first came to the parish, and she moved from involvement in Catholic Action to the first parish council.[63] Joseph Lupo came to Washington in 1952, got involved in Catholic Action and then in regular parish activities, and finally became president of the parish council in 1997.[64]

By the 1980s, Holy Rosary was becoming more active in promoting Italian culture in the metropolitan area; it is not clear how influential the Catholic Action group was in this development. In 1963, Holy Rosary held its first Italian Fall Festival, a celebration of Italian food and folklore that served as a fundraiser for the parish and for Villa Rosa, a senior-citizens' home for Italian Americans.[65] In 1981, the parish opened its Casa Italiana, where it could hold Italian cultural events without waiting for the Fall Festival. The next year, Holy Rosary opened its Scuola Italia, where children and adults could learn to speak Italian or could keep up their language skills, a project funded not only by the payments of the students but also by an allocation from the Italian government. Over time, the Scuola Italia expanded to cover subjects such as Italian ceramics and opera, and it required more space, which led to the construction of an annex in 1992.

In Boston, the Italians who had arrived before the Second World War outnumbered those who arrived after, and it was their culture that prevailed. As Catholic Action grew more quiescent, there was a renaissance of interest in preserving the cults of the hometown saints, and area organizations united to create an August event that celebrated all of the patron saints and Madonnas whose traditions had been brought from Italy to the North End. In April 2004, the Scalabrinians withdrew from Sacred Heart, citing a shortage of priests to cover both the older, assimilated immigrant communities and the newer ones that were forming elsewhere.[66] The following month, Sean Cardinal O'Malley, who had become archbishop of Boston in the wake of a number of lawsuits seeking damages from the archdiocese for the sexual abuse of children going back a generation, announced that sixty-five parishes in the archdiocese would be closed, Sacred Heart among them.[67] The Franciscan clergy stationed at nearby Saint Leonard of Port Maurice took charge of the property, with permission to say Mass there as pastoral need (e.g., the funeral of a long-time parishioner) dictated.

Historiographical Considerations

The behavior of Italian American Catholic Action groups in Boston and in Washington, D.C., in the postwar era departs not only from descriptions of Catholic Action in Italy but also from accounts of Italian Americans involved in Catholic Action in other parts of the United States as well as from accounts of the work of non-Italian Catholic Action groups.[68] In the case of every Italian American Catholic Action group, the question arose as to what mattered most in its identity: being Italian, American, Catholic, or part of Catholic Action. The literature on Italian American history is voluminous but noteworthy for its omission of the post–Second World War migration. Most surveys of Italian American history get a running start, so to speak, by mentioning Italians in colonial or revolutionary America, but their story really commences with the mass migration between 1880 and 1920 before proceeding, depending on when the history was published, to discussion of the subsequent generations born in the United States.[69] There is little mention of additional Italian migration after 1920.[70]

Similarly, historiography on Italian American Catholicism also tends to omit the postwar migration. Instead, scholars have debated the "Italian problem" that historian and New York archdiocesan priest Henry Browne first described in 1946—namely, that Italian Americans did not attend Mass in high numbers, frequent the sacraments, contribute to parish support, join the priesthood or sisterhoods, enroll children in parochial school, or even seem to realize they should have been doing any of these things.[71] The late Rudolph Vecoli published the classic revision of Browne's interpretation, agreeing with Browne on every issue but pointing out that the real problem was not the Italians but rather that the Church in Italy joined with the landowners in oppressing the common laborer and that the Church in the United States—dominated by Irish Americans at the time of the Italian mass migration—disdained what devotion the Italians did show.[72] Robert A. Orsi followed Vecoli's lead in studying what the Italians did rather than what others thought they should do, and his *The*

Madonna of 115th Street uses the devotional culture of Our Lady of Mount Carmel in East Harlem to document the Italian Americans' understanding of their Catholic faith.[73] For the purposes of studying the *group* rather than the *individual* experience, Silvano M. Tomasi's *Power and Piety* is helpful, as it establishes a paradigm for the development of Italian American parishes in which Italian immigrants moved from perpetuating the cults of the patron saints of their hometowns in Italy to the establishment of parishes in which Italian Americans could control the pace of their assimilation to U.S. Catholicism.[74]

The pioneering immigration historian Oscar Handlin used the word "uprooted" to describe how immigration utterly transformed immigrants. It may be worth noting that an early example of research rebutting Handlin was Vecoli's aforementioned investigation, which was focused on the Italian community in Chicago. Italian American research is full of case studies showing that Italians were not "uprooted" and did not "melt"; after a lifetime of studying Italian Americans in Philadelphia, Richard Juliani questioned whether assimilation was even a useful concept, because even after generations in the city, Italian Philadelphians were still a distinct group.[75] Research into Italian American assimilation describes a two-way street. Italians adjusted to the United States, switching from Italian to English and choosing educational paths, careers, and even marriage partners without reference to their Italian backgrounds. Sufficient numbers of Italian Americans, however, remained attached to their culture so that they were able to organize and to preserve it, and so Italian Americans became one element of a larger multicultural society. Religion was one of the components of their culture that Italian Americans preserved, and the beginning of this chapter alluded to a few of the many studies documenting how Italian Americans began with their own religious organizations and then developed Italian parishes. The parishes were in place, however, when the postwar Italian immigrants at Sacred Heart and Holy Rosary organized Catholic Action groups. Why did these Italian immigrants feel the need for their own organizations when they already had Italian parishes?

There is not much literature on the function of immigration organizations in the process of assimilation of Italian Americans, but there is a clue in Lawrence K. Hong's study of post-1965 Chinese migration to San Francisco. The Chinese who settled in San Francisco after 1965 joined one of the United States' oldest and best-organized Chinatowns. New and old immigrants, however, came from different Chinas—nineteenth- and twentieth-century China, respectively—and so had different needs, and so the new immigrants formed different organizations.[76] Similarly, nineteenth- and twentieth-century Italians came from different Italys. The difference was clearest at Holy Rosary. The earliest arrivals came with few cultural resources: They could maintain their cuisine, and some had construction-work skills that allowed them to maintain their artistic heritage, but so few of them spoke or wrote standard Italian that English became the parish lingua franca early on. The immigrants who arrived after the Second World War benefited from a new educational system that increased literacy in standard Italian. They did not fit into Holy Rosary's existing parish organizations, and so they had to create their own, taking one they knew from Italy and adapting it to their new circumstances.

In his sociological analysis of Italian American parishes, Silvano M. Tomasi argued that the parishes allowed the Italian Americans to pace their own immigration, introducing English or dropping traditional devotions when they were ready to do so. Catholic Action groups may have fulfilled the same role for the more recently arrived Italian Americans at Sacred Heart and Holy Rosary. While neither Catholic Action group left a lasting organization, both assisted individuals in the transition from immigrant to Italian American Catholic.

A final reason for thinking of Italian American Catholic Action at Sacred Heart and at Holy Rosary as a function of immigrants' needs for community is that the Catholic Action groups were missing something— Catholic Action. Neither group followed a Catholic Action organizational model, prioritizing lay action over clerical leadership. Neither group practiced the observe-judge-act model, which led members of Catholic Action elsewhere to analyze society and then try to change it. While both groups published newsletters that decried aspects of modern society and encouraged traditional values, Catholic Action's interest in campaigning for decency in media is only one possible inspiration for that activity.

On the other hand, these Italian immigrants organized specifically Catholic Action groups. Why? First, they, and the priests serving them, were familiar with the name; the idea of Catholic Action first appeared in Italy in 1867.[77] By the 1950s and 1960s, however, they may have been more familiar with the name than with the thing. They were the generation after the events described in William Issel's chapter earlier in this book. They missed the confrontation between Pope Pius XI and Benito Mussolini that led to the "downsizing" of Catholic Action. While they came later in time, in terms of where they were on their path toward integration into U.S. society, these Italian immigrants can be seen as being at a stage before that of the descendants of those immigrants who created the Catholic Club of New York City, immigrants whom Patrick Hayes describes, also in an earlier chapter in this book. Like the CCCNY, members of Italian Catholic Action were distinct enough from other Americans that they felt the need to organize a group. Like the CCCNY, they used their organization to meet members' needs—in the CCCNY's case, the need for education; in Boston Catholic Action's case, the need for social services; and in both cases, by providing entertainment that brought group members together. Like CCCNY, Catholic Action had the ideology of helping to preserve Christian values in the larger society, but unlike the CCCNY it lacked the organizational structures to do so. The groups at Holy Rosary and at Sacred Heart thought of Catholic Action as a means to different ends, the ends being the preservation of their Italian and Catholic identities and their accommodation to American life rather than the transformation of it.

Part II: The People of God

6   Relevant Transformations

The Young Women of the Extension Lay Volunteers, 1961–1971

ELIZABETH DUCLOS-ORSELLO

In the oppressive heat of mid-August, 1968, in Chicago, just days before the opening of that year's infamous Democratic National Convention, nearly one hundred twenty young American women finalized preparations for what would be a life-changing experience. In days they would be putting their training, education, and convictions to the test as they set forth to face some of the most pressing social concerns of the day and to manifest deeply held beliefs about social justice, social change, and the need to be part of something larger than themselves. Among these recent college graduates were Ruth Poochigian, a sociology and economics major from Mooseheart, Illinois; Karen (Flottum) de Hartog, English major and new teacher from Glenwood City, Wisconsin; and Elaine (Olivier) Duclos, a sociology and philosophy major from Manchester, New Hampshire. They and dozens of others had come to Chicago—a city they found "alive with tension"—from small towns and cities throughout the country. Despite their individual hopes, dreams and motivations, each manifested a Catholic social activist identity and a vision of how to implement it. They shared, in the words of Mary Jones, another woman with them that summer, "the sincere desire to help," and like her they were willing to "put . . . life on hold for a purpose."[1]

Chicago 1968 has been a touchstone for much scholarship and many iconic images of both the 1960s and the youth-led social-change movements of that era. After all, that summer's convention was marked most notably by sometimes violent clashes between and among two apparently oppositional groups: the older status quo of Mayor Richard Daley's Catholic Chicago politics and the younger activists of the counterculture and such New Left groups as Students for a Democratic Society and the Yippies (among others), whose energetic actions bespoke their passion and have evoked ever since an almost singular representation of what it meant to be young and socially engaged in this era.[2] For women like

Ruth, Karen, and Elaine, however, Chicago 1968—and the 1960s in general—reflected a different and differently compelling story. They had left their university dorms, the city, and their training grounds at the University of Chicago on August 17, just days before the convention opened, to take up posts as teachers in some of the most racially tense schools in Detroit, as health-care and social workers serving Mexican migrant workers in Oklahoma, Kansas, and Texas, and as parish workers whose goal was to seek out need and meet it wherever they were in whatever way they could. They departed in twos, threes, and fours to share houses or apartments from which they assumed new and unexpected responsibilities, and in all this they were profoundly changed. They set forth as proud Catholics, not so much in the manner of earlier generations of Catholic women but as the inheritors of Vatican II's dramatic transformation of what it meant to be a lay Catholic. They were part of a little-noticed group called the Extension Lay Volunteers (ELV), and their six weeks in Chicago that summer had prepared them for their year of service in mission parishes and in both urban and rural communities throughout the United States, as part of a decade-long lay volunteer program of the Catholic Church Extension Society (CES).

At least 80 percent of the nearly two thousand ELVs who served from 1961 to 1971 were female, and so their story illuminates the role of young lay Catholic women in both the Vatican II Church and mid-century America—a Church and a nation in dynamic flux, to which these ELVs responded and whose character they helped reshape.[3] The women of the ELV program represent a population of American Catholics heretofore unacknowledged, existing as they do at the intersection of social groups and movements regularly discussed in isolation from one another in the historical scholarship: women, Catholics, young, socially active Americans. The motivations and experiences of the female ELVs of the class of 1968, and those of the more than fifteen hundred others like them who served during the ten years of the program, offer new insight into and understanding of the place of young Catholic women in the postwar era. Exploring their story enables scholars to answer important questions about the lay apostolate, female religious identity and faith, social change, communalism, intellectual history, and youth activism at a highly charged time in the United States, both within and outside of the Catholic Church. Thus, in large part, this project suggests that when either "the 1960s" or "the Vatican II Church" are explored from the vantage point of these young Catholic laywomen, both the storyline and our scholarly understanding of each is expanded and enriched.[4] This echoes the argument made elsewhere in this volume by Katharine Harmon vis-à vis the pre–Vatican II Catholic Action and Grail movements. Harmon draws attention first to the ways in which changes in the intellectual traditions of Catholic thought and the social world of the United States from the 1910s to the 1950s were played out and shaped by laywomen, and second to the ways in which, by midcentury, a growing tension between women's essentialism and their right to use that position to effect social change was leading the Grail away from its original identity as a Catholic-focused organization toward one that made social-justice concerns paramount. In this light it is possible to see the women of the ELV as seeking and creating something that was a mix of these models. They were unwittingly reenacting a tradition from the early twentieth century, even as they were pursuing a social-justice agenda linked to secular trends and seeking a Catholic framework for their labors.

While the ELV program was designed originally to serve the needs of mission parishes and, by association, serve the institutional needs of a diocese and the goals of the global Church, the experiences and memories of the female ELVs suggest that, in addition, the program ultimately served the volunteers' personal, spiritual, and professional needs and goals. ELVs generally entered their volunteer year focused on the service they wished to do, the social change they wished to effect, and a desire to integrate their faith with the wider world (as expressed in the Vatican II document *Apostolicam Actuositatem*, or the "Decree on the Apostolate of the Laity"). Frequently, they also wanted to gain work experience, put their university training to good use, and undergo a new and dynamic life experience. For many who served, all these goals—and more—were met. Both the Vatican II zeitgeist and the structure of the program, which gave them relative autonomy over their work and home lives, allowed ELVs to chart a new course wherever they went. From these experiences came careers, new conceptions of what was possible for women (personally, institutionally, and politically), and a transformative sense of community that emerged with and through those with whom they served.

The women of the ELV found themselves at the confluence of multiple and often oppositional historical transformations, social movements, and cultural discourses, a context that provoked responses and goals distinct from those of their non-Catholic socially active peers but also different from the women religious and married laywomen who had traditionally dominated Catholic parish life. A comprehensive study of the female ELVs remains to be written, but this chapter begins the conversation by offering a multifaceted look at the motivations and lived experiences of these women's volunteer years. At a historical moment notable for communal impulses, political activism, feminist awakening, and a revision of Catholic doctrine and practice, the women of the ELV program stand out.

Although often exhausting in nature (emotionally, spiritually, and even physically), the ELV program was transformative. The volunteers, the CES organization, and the Catholic Church were all recipients of something greater than anticipated, as the program created new spaces and opportunities for young American Catholic women. Through their commitment to living out both their faith and the social-justice ethos of the 1960s, the ELVs fully engaged—as women, as Catholics, and as young Americans—with each other and with the world at large. In so doing they transformed not only their own lives but also any conventional understanding of what it meant to be young, female, American, and Catholic in the 1960s and early 1970s.

What Was the Extension Lay Volunteer Program?

In its simplest terms, the ELV program was a domestic, full-time volunteer program serving some of the poorest Americans and run under the umbrella of the CES, an organization founded in 1905 and headquartered in Chicago. CES's mission was to support (with money and priests) the mission parishes of the United States that were located in parts of the country where Catholics were few in number or concentration and where the need for ministry was great.[5] For most of the organization's history this was primarily the rural Midwest, Southwest, and West, with some forays into the Deep South. From its earliest days, the modus operandi of CES was to preserve what was best in the Catholic tradition while moving in new directions, always seeking out needs in the real world and responding in ways befitting to the specific place and time.[6] Initially sparked by a call during the 1950s for more assistance with social services and education in Oklahoma parishes, the local initiative morphed into a national effort after a few years of recruiting small numbers of female graduates from East Coast colleges to minister to the social and educational needs of the poor, the lonely, and the underserved in the U.S. interior. Following a small-scale beginning in 1960, CES's *Extension* magazine (mailed monthly to a general Catholic readership and to CES supporters across the United States) ran its first call for volunteers to serve in its newly formed Extension Volunteer program in March 1961.[7] By the time the program ended in 1971, nearly two thousand volunteers had served.[8]

The ELV program fit perfectly with *both* the secular and the religious moods of the time. Young adults were not being asked to choose among key parts of who they were—Americans, Catholics, social activists, observant. Rather, the opening paragraph of the first formal call for volunteers published in *Extension* magazine called on lay Catholics to embrace the Extension Volunteer program as a variation of President Kennedy's campaign call (soon to be realized in the Peace Corps and VISTA programs) for "peace volunteers" at home and abroad. The article even pointed out that the ELV idea was finalized concurrently with Kennedy's appeal and, relying on their readers' presumed familiarity with the president's moving inaugural address, framed the ELV option as a viable way to participate in the "New Frontier for the '60s."[9] At the same time, readers were reminded of the long history of lay service within the Church (global and national) and of the recent papal encyclical, *Princeps Pastorum*, which called directly for more lay help in doing good works and serving the needs of the people in the Church's mission parishes—precisely where the CES had been laboring for more than half a century in the United States. CES was now appealing to the single or married Catholic between twenty-one and fifty-five who wished to give a year of his or her life to work in one of various challenging environments. Volunteers were promised a place to live, health insurance, and $50 a month.[10] Photographs of young men and women (current volunteers in smaller regional programs) in the settings in which new volunteers might serve completed the picture. They reveal young clean-cut Catholic Americans, dressed in perfectly appropriate Cold War-era attire, appearing healthy and happy. They were "eminently normal" American young adults who sought to make a difference in the world.[11]

Only a month later, *Extension* magazine printed what would become a nearly monthly report on the status of the program and its volunteers. Promoted by parishes and in the pages of a free booklet explaining the program, the call for volunteers proved more than successful, for both the program's pitch and scope resonated with younger Catholics eager for an opportunity to demonstrate their abilities. Over two hundred applications arrived in the first few weeks, interviews were soon in process, and training programs were being established.[12] By May, the number of volunteers had reached three hundred. The CES attracted inquiries from hundreds of mostly young college graduates wishing to voluntarily exchange their relatively middle-class lives for dramatically different and challenging work and who presumably pictured themselves as protagonists in the recruiting articles' accounts. Perhaps they also saw themselves reflected in the recurring visual symbol used to entice new volunteers (positioned at the top of each monthly column in the early years): a line drawing of a young man, sleeves rolled up, tie on, pants pressed, and ready to, as the

By the way, the young man in our *Extension Volunteer* "cut" at the head of this column is not "fixin'" to pick a fight" as one of our southern correspondents feared. He is a bit preoccupied, yes, and perhaps a little serious as he rolls up his sleeve to get into the layman's job in the American Catholicism of the '60s. He has his eyes wide open and his feet are on the ground as he faces the work to be done. He has signed up as an Extension Volunteer.

Early recruiting images and text published in *Extension* magazine. Note the central male figure. Over the life of the ELV program it would be women, pictured here half a step behind the male, who made up the vast majority of volunteers.

caption read, "get into the layman's job in the American Catholicism of the '60s." In the same drawing, a neatly coiffed young woman wearing a knee-length, A-line skirt and kitten heels strides along just behind this lay*man's* left elbow, apparently also ready to get to work but half a step behind.[13] As it would turn out, young women ultimately made up the vast majority of all volunteer "classes" and so the ELV experience is largely theirs to tell.

Women Seeking Relevance

How do we make sense of this level of interest for Catholic social activism among women? Was the ELV program tapping into a latent longing, or into the current moment? Was it just good public relations on behalf of the CES Chicago office? What emerges from the recollections of female ELVs is first and foremost a desire to do something important and meaningful with their lives in a way that felt authentic and allowed them to integrate their multiple identities as Catholics and young Americans at a particular moment in time. No matter when they graduated in the 1960s, but particularly so in the middle to later years of the decade, these young Catholic Americans faced graduation at a time of profound change in their society and their Church. The ELV program was well timed to offer something new and yet familiar at a critical moment. As Mary (Martin) Meyers, a volunteer from 1967 to 1969, recalls: "I perceived my choice as countercultural because my parents would have expected me to enter the convent if I wanted to work for the Church, but I really liked the idea of being a lay missioner and trying to integrate God's work with a 'normal' lifestyle."[14] The old and the new, counterculture and tradition, the balancing act between past and future generations—all are reflected here.

In many accounts (both contemporary and historical) of the 1960s, a quest for "the authentic" takes center stage. Scholars in many fields have remarked on the degree to which midcentury young adults in the New Left and the counterculture reacted to what they perceived as a "fake" or "inauthentic" modern American culture and of how quests for the "real" or the "authentic" could (and did) lead many young people into secular forms of protest, activism, self-actualization, and communalism of all sorts (activist groups, co-ops, communes, and collectives).[15] Recent scholarship has shown that for some of the leaders of the broadly defined youth movements, radical political activism had religious, philosophical and theological roots. In *The Politics of Authenticity*, his magnificent study of the existential Christianity of the mostly Protestant young founders of the New Left, Douglas Rossinow demonstrates that many of the "secular" leaders sought in the 1950s and 1960s to find a new way to feel connected to the world around them. Their philosophical and political reading, as well as their interaction with existential theologians of the day, led them to see that an engaged, active, communal and participatory stance in the world would bring this authenticity closer.[16]

For the Catholic women at the center of this study, the quest for relevance (if not "authenticity" narrowly defined) framed their decisions to become ELVs. Here was a way to effect a change as Americans generally and as Catholics and Catholic women specifically, perhaps not altogether unlike the motivations and worldview of the subjects of Rossinow's account, or those of the "new nuns" and even the early Catholic feminists. Yet theirs was a unique position. What was it like to be a young, lay, Catholic American woman during the 1960s? What did one do to live an "authentic" life with such a complex identity? While "religion" and "service" and "community" and "place in the Church" might all have meant the convent or a women's sodality for their mothers or grandmothers, and might have meant explicitly Catholic feminist ideology and gender-based unity for some slightly older women of the 1960s and 1970s, the call to live "authentically" led ELVs in a unique direction.[17] They were attracted to the program because it offered an experience that seems to have spoken to many parts of their lives simultaneously and was ultimately relevant because it served both American society at large, and the emerging social-justice mission of the Catholic Church.

Prospective ELVs were largely the products of Catholic colleges and universities and thus, while certainly aware of the social movements of the 1960s, were more likely than other young Americans to have been exposed to the theology and philosophy of such people as Merton, Bonhoeffer, Teilhard, and Tillich and to have come of age, literally, during the dramatic laicization of the Catholic Church as a result of the Vatican II reforms completed earlier in the decade.[18] By the time the changes of Vatican II had come into their full flowering in the mid-1960s it was becoming clear to many young Catholics facing college graduation that to be Catholic could mean, and in fact required—if one followed certain understandings of

Vatican II teaching and the theological currents of the day—that they be at the active center of social change and social-justice work that was a key part of "American" culture. As one 1965–67 volunteer recalled, "I wanted to 'do something for God and the Church' after graduation. I was inspired by the Kennedy years, Peace Corps, and the general enthusiasm for change during that period."[19]

The ELV program was attractive in part because the directors made sure to remind potential recruits time and again that it could help them engage with both their Catholicism and the secular social-justice efforts of the day, while doing something truly significant. From the Catholic side, ELV recruiting mantras from as early as 1961 anticipated Vatican II reforms by celebrating and proclaiming the unique and critical role of the laity in the universal mission of the Church.[20] More than once in the early life of the program did its advocates reproduce the adage of Pope Pius XII: "You do not belong to the Church, you are the Church."[21] After 1962, as Vatican II documents began to circulate, it became even easier to sell the ELV program as an embodiment of dictates from Rome.

At the same time, the consistent message of ELV directors was that the program was directly relevant to and comported with the social-reform moments that defined 1960s America. If the Peace Corps and (later) VISTA programs were the most popular ways for young college graduates to effect change in the world and their own lives in the 1960s, *Extension* articles repeatedly (and accurately) reminded readers that ELVs had been at work before their Peace Corps and VISTA counterparts, even calling the ELV program "the original home peace corps."[22] In similar fashion did ELV promoters link their program's work to the civil-rights movement, running a multi-page article in *Extension* magazine in 1964 framing the work of the ELVs in Chicago in terms of the 1963 March on Washington and Martin Luther King's *Letter from a Birmingham Jail*.[23] To serve their fellow Americans in the face of growing inequality in the United States *and* to engage what was most compelling and current in the Catholic Church in the post–Vatican II years were the twin trends that the ELV program reflected and capitalized on.

This message of relevance was central to the marketing of the ELV program; in both form and content it was everywhere in the monthly *Extension* magazine by mid-decade. In 1967, a free verse poem referencing pop culture and postmodernism was used to engage the emotions of readers. Its staccato phrases paint a fractured picture both of life in the urban heart of Detroit and of the complex and ever changing work of the volunteers who lived amid the fractures, *experiencing* life as much as *helping* anyone.[24] Even more compelling was an article published just months after the Chicago protests of 1968, in which program leaders drew on both the immediate sociopolitical context of that year and the immensely popular notion of *seeking* to highlight the impact of and need for ELVs. It began with an account of a world in crisis: "The face of 1968 is scarred. It looked good before its features were ripped by political and racial assassination, torn by international power politics, bloodied by the convention year demonstrating, stomped on by urban rioting, emaciated by widespread poverty and beaten raw by racism." Continuing, the author asserted that "as a year, 1968 is surviving [because] it has found a few who are willing to apply healing salve to its wounds."[25]

Those *few* included the women who had left Chicago for their posts in the heated days of mid-August. These women were solving social problems, to be sure, but, as the article made clear, they were *also* fulfilling their own personal search for meaning and relevance.

> Extension Volunteers are intelligent, sensitive young Christians who are usually persons in quest. They want to know who they are, why they are and where they're going. They're not satisfied with pat answers. They sense that life has great meaning for them and that they have importance in the world, but they are not always too sure what this meaning and importance are. They are usually deeply religious persons in the best and truest sense of the term, but they often feel that their religion lacks relevance to the lives they live and the world in which they live. It must be lived, not just studied and discussed.[26]

Above these words appeared an oversized, closely cropped photograph of a volunteer and a young child, with a caption promising that "Extension Volunteers experience so intense a human involvement in their work that the rest of their lives are profoundly affected."

The language of relevance and duality resonated with the volunteers. With significant frequency, the recollections shared with the CES in 1990 on the occasion of the thirtieth anniversary reunion reflect ELV interest in both social change and personal spiritual fulfillment. In response to the question "What inspired you to join the ELVs?" Elaine Knob DeAngelis (1965–67) wrote: "Maybe it was John Kennedy and the Peace Corps [but] I also wanted to see what it was like to really give up something for God."[27] This unique call to be American *and* Catholic and to be able to believe that they were bringing a new world into being (in both their Church and their country) is reflected in the recollections of women who joined the ELVs, especially in the second half of the program's ten year run.

"In the counter-culturalism of the times," recalls Elaine Duclos, who spent two years with the program, from 1968 to 1970, "my years as an Extension volunteer seemed to be one facet of that movement. People were expressing themselves in new and different ways. I deeply wanted to make a difference. I wanted to be active in civil rights, affirmative action, equal rights for women, equality in the Church and so much more. But I thought the best way I could accomplish these goals was to work from within the organization." To this end, she was "also greatly influenced by the major changes in the Church as a result of Vatican II. The new possibilities for the laity were exciting to me."[28] Karen de Hartog, also a two-year volunteer, concurs. "We shared that altruistic spirit that we could make a difference that was very prevalent at the time," she insists. "I think we saw ourselves as similar to VISTA and other volunteers at the time [but] with a Catholic component." The Extension experience allowed her and her fellow female volunteers in Price, Utah, to "[feel] like we were part of something larger than ourselves and if not mainstream American culture, it was a change to mainstream Catholic culture at the time."[29]

ELV recruiters also sold this message of relevance and substance to prospective volunteers, with program directors encouraging some dynamic ELVs to stay on for a second year as volunteer recruiters touring the East and Midwest, speaking to students and preaching at every Newman Center and campus ministry office to which their Extension-supplied cars could take them.[30] More than one ELV recalls meeting young recruiters like these and being drawn in by their compelling accounts.[31] While reports suggest that the recruiting priests were also effective, the power of the female ELV recruiters lay in the fact that they embodied the unique identity of an ELV: They were living, breathing, confident, young lay women in fashionable clothes speaking about their experiences, the real world, and their faith. Such women were walking billboards for the idea that ELV service allowed young Americans to weave together the many

Official photo of ELV volunteer recruiters Elaine (Olivier) Duclos
and Karen (Flottum) de Hartog. Extension management sent this
image to universities and Newman Centers in advance of the recruiters' arrival on campuses throughout the Midwest during their
1969–70 recruiting year. In 1968–69, Duclos and deHartog had
served as ELVs in Ulysses, Kansas, and Price, Utah, respectively."
Photo courtesy of Elaine (Olivier) Duclos.

threads of their lives in a meaningful way. That they helped shore up other
institutional messages is clear from a recruiting brochure entitled "An Intersection Called Relevance," which presented readers with a profound
question: "If there were a point where your talents, needs, Christian rights
and obligations . . . your search for a chance for genuine service to both
God and man . . . your need to be and do . . . if there were a point where
all these coincided . . . wouldn't this be a very important intersection?
Couldn't we call it an intersection of relevance?" Many young women answered "yes." This single brochure proved so powerful that one young
woman who reportedly read it "a million times" before joining the ELVs still
had it in her possession a quarter of a century later.[32]

Should any ELV have doubted the relevance of her work in 1960s
America, the required preservice training—in many ways the culmination
of the recruiting process—almost certainly disabused her of such thoughts
by providing the new recruit with a crash course in relevance. As the 1960s
moved on, what had been a week of training with lay and religious leaders as well as social workers and community members had blossomed
into a six-week "course" engaging with prominent ideas and leaders in
the Catholic, ecumenical, and secular worlds to help new volunteers

grasp the social and theological complexity of the place and people among whom they would be living and working.[33] During the Chicago '68 sessions, for example, ELVs recall being addressed by Saul Alinsky on issues of community organizing and hearing from a range of speakers on social justice, ethnic and racial diversity, and immigration/migration issues.[34] ELV Mary Jones's rich memories of those weeks are of a process in which pop culture, folk music, charismatic worship, dynamic young priests, and strong doses of contemporary political discourse (including the brewing discontent in advance of the Democratic National Convention) mingled in equal proportions.[35] What was not in equal proportion were the relative number of male and female volunteers present, for the overwhelming majority of the volunteers in Chicago and in all other summer training sites were women.[36]

Feminism, Catholic Women's Communities, and the ELVs

While no published *Extension* materials celebrate or emphasize the overwhelmingly female nature of the program, the ELV program can be understood as offering a way for female volunteers to craft lives that allowed them to be an "average" young American, an engaged Catholic, and part of a larger movement for change that included a readiness to contemplate expanded and alternative roles for women in both the secular and the religious realms.[37] "I wanted to serve," recalls Karen de Hartog. "I had no desire to be a nun, and I thought then, as I do now, that there should be greater opportunities for women in the Catholic Church."[38] While not all ELVs were motivated explicitly by a sense of gender equity, none could escape the fact that their volunteer years coincided with some of the most critical years for both the secular and the Catholic feminist movements.[39] These were years in which secular consciousness-raising groups were common and women's liberation discourse had begun to filter onto some Catholic college campuses. Female theologians were asking troubling questions about the Church's teachings and the place of women within the Church, many nuns and sisters modified their habits and stepped into social-justice work or left the convent altogether, and Sally Field performed pop music and coached baseball as part of her good works as Sister Bertrille in the hit TV show *The Flying Nun*, produced and supported by the Catholic Church.[40]

There is no body of evidence to suggest that ELVs were, on the whole, nascent feminists or even primarily interested in challenging the status quo in respect of gender roles, but they were carving out a new vocational path and they realized that, by their actions, they were creating something new in the Church. While aware of being Catholic women, they had the confidence to choose a way of life that might redefine what that meant, blending a shared experience of being female in an institution that limited female power with a youthful anticipation of how their individual and collective power as laywomen might effect change. All of this was combined with a hopefulness and confidence that they mattered dearly to the emergent Church of the 1960s and early 1970s.

In a 1964 *Extension* article one female volunteer summed up the complex dynamics of being a laywoman acting within and for the Church at that time. Commenting on her work (with a fellow female volunteer) to establish a program for teenagers in a poverty-stricken Chicago neighborhood, she noted: "We feel terribly inadequate in the face of all these problems, especially with the limitations of what a woman can do. But it is a start. We can do something, and if we reach just a few people it will be worthwhile. To live in this marvelous time of the emerging layman is just fantastic."[41]

This ELV identified herself first and foremost as a *lay* person working within the prevailing structure of the Church. Neither the female "sisterhood" rhetoric of secular feminism, nor the Catholic feminism of Mary Daly or Rosemary Ruether, nor the existing model of female religious communities captured her imagination or informed her understanding of her work. If one understanding of "community" in this era was tied to a belief in unmediated gender solidarity, female ELVs seem to have been latecomers to that conversation. Even in the final years of the program—coinciding as they did with a strong feminist commitment to a sense of universal sisterhood—the volunteers whose stories I have heard did not identify themselves as such.[42] In particular, female ELVs seem to have been wary of any clearly codified definition or manifestation of "feminism." Even Karen de Hartog, the ELV who felt a need for an expanded role for women in the Church, recalls that "I have never responded well to loud, brash advocates of any position and at the time I did not have a feeling of kinship with 'feminists.'"[43] Nor do the ELVs seem to have been shaped or influenced by specific Catholic feminist ideas or by other well-studied female lay communities and contemporary Catholic initiatives such as The Grail or women's work within Catholic Action.[44] This might ring strange but for the fact that there was both a precedent in the nature of midcentury women's lay apostolic activities detailed in Harmon's account in this volume and, perhaps more importantly, a contemporary resonance. As Mary Henold makes clear in her article in this volume, the distinction between "feminist" and "anti-feminist" among American Catholic women (as well as non-Catholic women) in the decade before 1970 was fuzzy at best. The terms had not been fully fixed. "Second wave" feminism was still emergent and many women, even those operating within women's organizations sanctioned by the church hierarchy, both employed "feminist" language, positions, and programs of action and denounced "feminism" per se. This is precisely what we find in accounts of former ELVs who at times adamantly denounce feminism while acting in ways that seem to connote "feminist" worldviews to outside observers.

And if "feminists" were one group the ELVs saw themselves as distinct from, so too were the religious communities of nuns or sisters many ELVs had known in parishes and in Catholic grammar schools, high schools and universities. When asked whether they considered their lives as ELVs similar to those of sisters or nuns, the majority of the former volunteers contacted to date have said "no" and although a number of them considered the convent at one time or another, extended responses describe the religious life as restricted, confined or limited, and thus undesirable. Confinement to strictly controlled communities with centralized decision-making and direction was neither what the ELVs wanted nor what they saw themselves as doing. Joining the ELV program was not the same as joining a convent or order, for ELVs did not take a vow of community living, intentional sharing, or poverty as part of this lay apostolate. Although working in or through parishes with priests and nuns as supervisors, they were not members of a religious community. And while recruiting materials and published accounts of ELV lives spoke of partnerships among volunteers in a city or region, ELVs were drawn to the program as individuals who understood that they would be part of a "Catholic" community in often largely non-Catholic places.

With the benefit of hindsight, it might be possible to identify commonalities between the motivations and experiences of ELVs and the "new nuns" of the 1950s and 60s, especially those in the "racial apostolate," who were directly engaged in addressing racism and promoting civil rights and racial justice while living together in small communities in apartments and neighborhoods physically distant from the convent and from their larger religious communities.[45] In practice though, this model, if known, did not seem to speak to ELVs as laywomen.[46] They knew and embraced the fact that they were defining a new and different way of being Catholic and female—if not "feminist." A sense of possibility, self-confidence, and desire to effect change emerges from their recollections. One volunteer linked her lack of interest in a traditional religious community directly with an emerging sense that her work in the ELV program might lead to something new:

> During my High School and early college years I sometimes thought of entering the convent. I had many relatives who were either nuns or priests. However, each time I considered the possibility, I find [sic] that the lifestyles were too confining, restricted, dominating and directed for my taste. I was also greatly influenced by the major changes in the Church as a result of Vatican II. The new possibilities for the laity were exciting to me. They also made me even more aware of the restrictions on women as compared to men who chose priesthood. . . . Extension offered me a chance to work as an equal with the men who volunteered.[47]

Female ELVs presented both the institutional Church and the non-Catholic world with a new example of lay female involvement. Their exact location in the structure of the Church and the community of women was complex enough that on at least one recorded occasion outsiders questioned whether they were religious Peace Corps volunteers or nuns. The ELVs knew that they were neither and both—and more—at the same time.[48] They were living with roommates and working full-time, but they did not have the freedom of other young professionals. They were working for social justice, but through a Catholic lens. They were women who believed that they were capable and had a key role to play in the world, but they weren't identifiably feminist. They worked in fairly traditional gendered roles and ultimately for priests and bishops, but they were not sisters. While the fact that the ELVs could have passed either as secular young people, lay Catholics, or women religious was perhaps a sign of the times, it also perhaps reflected a desire to rethink and problematize categories, affinities, and identities within and outside the Church during this era. If "Catholic Action" was past, what was next?

It is possible to view the women of the ELV as embodying and enacting a bridge between old and new, laity and clergy in the post–"Catholic Action" era. These women neither fully embraced the secular movements of the day nor unwittingly followed outmoded structures of the Catholic Church. Rather in their work and witness they found a new way to mediate and broker and assist—and in this way did change the Church, broadly defined. In a moment—just prior to and just following Vatican II—of much transition in personal, ecclesiastical, and social structures in the United States, perhaps the women of the ELV presented the world with a vision of how the various threads could combine and weave a new brand of American Catholic feminism, a new model for a lay apostolate, and a new example of female Catholic communities.

ELVs as Action Communities?

One way to understand the experiences of the ELVs as a new type of female Catholic community mediating and brokering among many different points on the Catholic and secular landscapes of the 1960s may be by way of some the most highly publicized Catholic activism of the era: the idea of the "action community," a term made popular by members of the Catholic Left who used it to define those individuals who had participated in or supported dramatic efforts to sabotage or publicly disrupt activities related to the execution of the Vietnam War, most notably the decision of the Berrigan brothers (as members of the Catonsville Nine) to burn draft documents in Maryland in 1968.[49] As is the case with many discussions of "community," the term also (and perhaps more importantly) defines the *relationship* among those individuals. According to scholars of the radical Catholic Left, being part of a group whose identity was tied to actions undertaken by its members created a frame of reference "that helped participants make sense of and respond to particular political situations."[50] When discussing women in Catholic Left groups, this latter fact appears to be even more critical.

In researching women within these original "action communities," one scholar has recently argued that even more than the actions themselves—which were ostensibly the "draw" for Catholic Left "action community" members—it was the sense of sharing the experiences, the danger and the struggles with others in the community—that most marked their participation. Knowing that there were other people taking the same risks as they were, as well as sharing with fellow-activists in reflecting upon and comprehending the process of civil disobedience, was key to an activist's self and communal-identity.[51]

Among female ELVs, too, this sense of an "action community" appears to have been present. Volunteers found themselves living in modest shared accommodations generally conforming to the social and economic status of their assigned parish, town or city. While these houses or apartments were adequate, the neighborhoods in which the vast majority of volunteers were placed and the work assigned to them brought them face to face with some of the most pressing and challenging social issues of the day and with human suffering that could be extreme. Time and again, over a decade, *Extension* accounts tell of the litter-strewn streets of urban America and rural poverty in the South and Midwest, especially among African Americans and Mexican migrant workers.[52]

Accounts of former volunteers are even more graphic. Mary Jones recalled that in her one year teaching in La Junta, Colorado, she witnessed discrimination toward the town's poorest residents by fellow Catholics, "saw a 10 month old Mexican American baby in a casket because of a botched tracheotomy performed at a substandard hospital," and recalls the disbelief when "[she and her fellow volunteer] went to give an eighth grader . . . some make-up homework only to discover that she lived in a brothel."[53] Using more general terms, Sarah Overmeyer Cody, a 1962–63 volunteer, summing up the feelings of many who have recorded their experiences, described her volunteer experience as "Delightful! Culturally shocking, spiritually awakening, emotionally stimulating, physically draining, yet rewarding."[54] These types of complex, intense, raw, emotionally charged experiences led volunteers to turn to each other for support and to see each other as partners on a rough journey into new and often unknown social-justice territory.

Descriptions of the relationships and sharing between and among volunteers in these intense environments echo those of other "action communities." "We were far from home for the first time," recalls one volunteer who worked with her partner doing a wide range of parish work, "away from family and friends, learning about a vastly different ethnic and cultural group, facing discrimination in the community for a wide variety of reasons; all this forced us to draw from within and find the way to build community [with each other]." She notes that she "gained courage from my partners and I learned over time that each of them would support me." In time, she writes, "we became friends, sharing our work, setbacks, and hopes."[55] Another volunteer, like many of her counterparts, mentions the close friendships that developed as a result of the shared experiences, making clear that relationships with fellow volunteers were a critical part of her ELV experience because "the work we did was frustrating, exciting, challenging—all of which needed to be shared and discussed. Our room-mates were the audience."[56]

Other volunteers recall ways in which shared entertainment and trips on meager budgets helped them make it through the personal and profes-sional challenges of the work. For Mary Jones, the experience of living with another volunteer was *the* most critical part of her ELV experience because "it was a recreation in some way of a family." This family feeling was tied at least in part to the fact that she and her roommates had "sen-sitivity about our students' lifestyles. The poverty and discrimination they faced. We all saw things that affected us and influenced the way we lived our lives afterwards. . . . We were living with the children and saw the effects of poverty every day."[57] For Sheila Vandercar Long, who served from 1963 to 1964, the year was "fun, frustrating, disillusionment, joy, conviction, and very much a discipline in personal relationships, espe-cially my partner who is still one of my closest friends despite the miles that now separate us!"[58]

Thus, partnerships that often began as or were considered instrumen-tal relationships (to accomplish tasks, make sure dinner was on the table or coordinate the car to get to work) in a number of cases morphed into important bonds that sustained these young, lay women in challenging and dynamic times.[59] "My housemate and I had extremely different per-sonalities," recalls an ELV, "but perhaps for this very reason, over the course of nearly a year we became very close. We shared our histories, confidences, hopes, joys, and stories about how we came to be the people we were."[60]

What is perhaps most fascinating is that while none of these women came to the ELV program with a plan or expressed desire to build com-munity or otherwise engage with the communitarian ethos of the era, the recollections of ELVs suggest that among the unintentional outcomes of the program was the emergence of communal experiences among lay Catholic women and, in numerous instances, with their male and female religious coworkers as well.

Unintentional Communities

Communalism was on the rise in the 1960s and early 1970s. Throughout the United States, the era was marked by hundreds of thousands of efforts (small and large, long-lasting and ephemeral) to build a sense of community and to institute social, political or economic change through collective efforts and lifestyles. While community-building among ELVs was never a goal of the program, its particular structure nevertheless allowed and even encouraged young Catholic women to create shared lives and form intense bonds that sustained them during their years of service and that have, in some cases, been sustained for decades.

Intentional community, then and now, involves an attempt at living in a group setting with goals that originate from a vision of shared outcomes and shared lives that extends beyond simply sharing space as roommates. Shared finances, shared belongings, and a shared political or philosophical worldview were often, although not always, key to such endeavors and the ELV era saw an unprecedented growth in attempts by diverse groups across the United States to create communities of their own design and live out their vision together in urban and rural settings. While it has proven impossible to confirm a precise number of communes, collectives, co-ops, and communal houses that sprang up across the United States at this time, scholars put the number somewhere between a few thousand and tens of thousands.[61]

The extent to which the ELVs understood their year(s) of service to be part of this larger trend is ambiguous. The language of community appears in certain recollections ("I liked the sense of community as we three teachers worked together with our pastor to run our little school") and in more general comments about making new friends or meeting good people.[62] At the same time, other volunteers are quick to identify what they did as unrelated to or different from other intentional communities (spiritual or secular) of the day and more like the activities of any ordinary set of roommates or VISTA volunteers, although the language of "community" can still appear even when such distancing is present.[63] For example, in response to a question about possible connections to intentional communities or communes of the era, Elaine Duclos linked her own experience of the ELV program to the larger communitarian trend but drew a clear distinction:

> I [knew] about the rise of secular communes and the interest in communal living [and] my lifestyle was similar in that we lived in community, shared what we had in common and worked for the greater good. But, as much as I knew, most communes at the time were based on removing oneself from society and creating a small community. My lifestyle was based on moving out and into the community every day, interacting with people in need and people in power, and trying to effect change for the better . . . Most communes that I was aware of were turned inward.[64]

What is intriguing here is that despite a perception that their lives were different from those of other communitarians, Duclos's account hints at some of what marked many communitarian efforts of the time, including a shared sense of being part of something larger than themselves and being critically engaged in the world at large. For the ELVs, what began as an individual quest for relevance for individual women seems to have helped forge the type of bonds among and between volunteers that might be called communal.

The way in which such communal bonds were forged is a testament to the will and creativity of the volunteers for there were no standard rules for communal living and there is no evidence that the topic was discussed at pre-service training. Furthermore, unlike traditional intentional communities of the era, ELVs did not seek out their living/working partners, nor did they select where they would live. As a result, the very things that seemed to mark so many intentional communities—the careful attention to and revisiting of "fit" between and among members—was not present in ELV houses, although volunteers still spoke with vigor and conviction about the bonds that formed and were sustained through and by their ELV experiences.[65] While their relationships were not always intense and fulfilling (there are accounts of personality clashes and some divisiveness in some groups), ELV recollections contain a consistent thread of stories of adjustment and of learning—over time—to get along both in close quarters and in joint work assignments with people who had been strangers mere weeks before.[66]

These bonds were fostered and even encouraged—unintentionally—by the nature and structure of the program. While ELVs did not share all of their belongings or household activities, and in published and unpublished accounts no one mentioned collective economics or any pooling of their meager incomes, they did live together, under often stressful circumstances far from family and former friends.[67] Volunteers in their recollections attest to a shared life that included working together to accomplish professional goals and fulfill mission assignments, eating meals together, taking turns cooking and cleaning, socializing together, and sharing clothes, personal items and time as needed and available.[68]

Perhaps the driving force behind this shared life was a compelling shared worldview—consistent with other intentional communities of the day. All of the volunteers were Catholic, to be sure, but the shared vision was more than this. Despite differences in temperament and degree of Catholic education, while Catholicism was the foundation, the rock of that foundation was something deeper, which helped link them to and with one another and mark them as alike. That something was an understanding of themselves as being part of a larger world and a larger mission. One former volunteer spoke of this as "wanting to be an apostle and the un-definable [sic] 'call' to do something." Another recalled her motivation as "wanting to serve the Church and those in need," while a third, in what might serve as a summary statement of many voices, articulated it as "mainly a desire to help make the world a little better in line with the volunteer spirit of the '60s."[69] What was repeatedly mentioned in close association with this call, was the fact that volunteers seem to have been generally motivated, and therefore connected to one another, by a desire to question and explore alternative forms of social justice and social and economic responsibility, and to reestablish connections in a splintering industrial and modernizing world that could be isolating and disillusioning.

Such understandings recall Elaine Duclos's articulation of the "community" of her ELV years, referenced above, and brings us to another interesting point: the way in which the ELVs created and experienced community as something that could and did include people outside of the ELV home itself. To move "out and into the community" meant defining "community" as including and relying on a range of individuals and groups for its existence. It is this understanding of "community" that marks many ELV accounts, where priests, nuns, other lay Catholics, and non-Catholics all shared space in the ELVs' lives. Mary Sue Maher-Orr recalled that her experience "provided rich opportunities to work with dedicated people—lay, religious and priests," while Mary Jones became connected, in ways she had not expected, to the other volunteers whom she met at her Chicago orientation in 1968. Karen de Hartog cites her students among those with whom she built a communal connection, and Lucille Di Domenico, who served for two years from 1967 to 1969, in and around Brownsville, Texas, echoes them all, recalling that she felt a sense of spiritual community with the dozens of volunteers each summer at orientations in Chicago, with other ELVs whom she and her roommates hosted in Texas on holiday weekends, and with the parish staff and members of the parish with whom she worked.[70]

Conclusion: Unintended Consequences and a New Chapter

The words and focus of the ELV program and volunteers suggest that these lay Catholics were able and willing to engage in a nuanced view of the relationship between hierarchy, freedom, laity, clergy, individualism, community, and gender that was uncommon for their time and place. As they worked to understand and make manifest their understanding of what it meant to be the people of God, the female ELVs demonstrated to themselves and others what a complex, challenging, and thrilling task that could be. While it is not possible to pigeonhole the ideological, theological, political, and social views of young lay Catholic women in the so-called "tumultuous" years surrounding Vatican II and the attendant social upheavals in the United States, perhaps the complexity is what these people of God brought to light. As evidenced by their unique (literal) position in Chicago during the 1968 DNC, ELVs were perhaps the very embodiment of the nuanced and complex place of lay Catholic women in the post-conciliar Church.

In the ELVs we see women whose desire to have adventures, live their faith, put their professional training to use, and move into and through the everyday American life led them into intimate and alternative living and working environments, where a sense of authenticity, shared vision, supportive living, and a desire to rectify and propose alternatives for a broken alienated world took root. As such, the ELV experience was life-giving and change-making for the women involved. At the same time, by finding a way to live both their faith and their individual social convictions at the same time, these ELVs also transformed the Church. As they lived their newfound lay apostolate *as* the Church, they left it different from what it was when they found it in Dubuque, Iowa or Provo, Utah or Brownsville, Texas or Ulysses, Kansas or Chicago, Illinois or Fresno, California or Violet, Louisiana. While more study certainly needs to be done, it seems plausible to present the ELV program as a lay version of the story of the "new nuns" within the Catholic Church, especially when the emphasis is on the long-term impact.

The ELVs bear comparison with the women of Amy Koehlinger's "racial apostolate," whose ministry in the organizations and issues of contemporary mainstream America "provided [them] with invaluable practice of the skills they would need in order to reconstruct religious life" and enabled them to face, without flinching, authority figures within the Church.[71] The ELV experience—emerging out of individual desires and growing in a uniquely intense, dynamic, and communal environment—also seems to have given the women of this lay apostolate the skills and confidence to make changes in themselves. Time and again, female ELVs speak emphatically of the long-term and wide-ranging impact of their service years, professionally, personally, and spiritually.[72] "It changed me for life," writes one volunteer. "I left teaching after a year and went into social services and have been there ever since [working] to bring diversity to our workplace for over 20 years."[73] Another volunteer notes: "My two years as an Extension volunteer changed me for life. . . . I wanted to find a faith/Church in action, not only one of word. That has continued to drive my spiritual search over the years. My desire to work for peace and social justice has never left me, but has forced me to continue to look for ways to implement these."[74] And, finally, a third speaks boldly of the work and experience catapulting her into a position of authority at the age of twenty. When a hurricane hit only days after arriving at her Texas placement, she found herself caring for over three hundred parishioners and residents alone because the diocesan priests and nuns were out of town at the time. "I believe that my experience . . . offered me a tremendous opportunity to exercise and hone my leadership skills," she observes of her year of service.[75]

None of the female ELVs quoted in this chapter or who appear in the published records identify as "radical" or even "feminist" in the sense in which those words were used in the era under investigation. I engage the terms here because, in ways both large and small, the work and experiences of these ELVs seem likely to have played a role in creating what other scholars have noted was an engaged body of laywomen in the U.S. that, by the 1970s, was reshaping the appearance, character, and hopes (often unfulfilled) of the post–Vatican II American Catholic Church.[76] In the words of one ELV, even one of the most traditional elements of the program—the fact that the volunteers were under the direction of diocesan priests and bishops—was felt to offer new possibilities for dynamic transformation. Recalling the often-close working relationships between volunteers and clergy, she declares that "our involvement with the clergy was . . . significant because it spoke to all the turmoil and religious and life style changes following Vatican II. It was a time that we all felt was full of possibilities, of positive change, and, dependent as we were on the clergy in both my locations for support, we were a part of that change. There was almost a feeling of celebration."[77]

That the leaders of the ELV program were aware of its transformative nature—for volunteers and for the Church—cannot be denied. In 1966, the executive secretary of the ELV program said as much in an article recounting the work and lives of the half-dozen female ELVs he met in Pueblo, Colorado. Speaking of them and the impact their service might have on their lives and in the Church he declared:

> [They] do exactly as Vatican II has taught. They live as Christians in the world, learning, living, sharing, discussing, worshipping, laughing, and loving with priests and religious, children and adults, young and old, rich and poor, Mexican and Anglo, Catholic and Protestant. When they go home after their Extension service they'll know things about being a Christian that you don't find in books."[78]

And they did. Thus, the "conclusion" to this chapter is still to be written. It is the story of how these young laywomen shaped the Church, *their* Church, following their Extension days, when, according to the available research to date, most returned to "mainstream" life and many married, had children, and in many cases continued to be active in their local parishes and in social justice work.[79] It would seem, then, that these ELV women—over fifteen hundred of them—presented the post-Vatican II Church with a new type of laywoman. By the mid-1970s, many former ELVs were lay women in their twenties and thirties who, because of their service, were experienced in the needs and challenges of contemporary America and American life, had professional work experience, and were skilled in lay ministry, social-service work, and parish and diocesan leadership. They were independent, self-confident and had already been, at a very young age, central players within the Catholic Church.

How did these laywomen affect the Church of the 1970s and 80s? How are they shaping it today? Are they among the women who emerged as Catholic feminists or the leaders of lay groups such as Voice of the Faithful? Were they among the ranks of parish workers and educators who taught and raised a new generation of Catholics who came of age in the 1980s and '90s? Are they the women everywhere still doing mission work and fighting for social justice? If they became women religious, how did their early lay mission work influence their vocation? And if they have since left the Church, like one of the ELVs in this study, how do their experiences as lay missioners in the United States half a century ago shape their work, their faith, and their visions of the world today? There is much more to ask and to understand. But what seems certain is that the ELV experience of these women transformed them as women, as Catholics, and as Americans, and in doing so also transformed America.

Reaching Out to the People of God

The Implications of Renewal for the Sisters of Mercy in Parish Schools

MARY BETH FRASER CONNOLLY

Introduction

In the spring of 1958, Father Thomas J. O'Brien, the pastor of St. Raymond Church in Mount Prospect, Illinois, wrote Mother Mary Regina Cunningham of the Sisters of Mercy, urging her to send him six additional sisters for the next school year, promising he would "never ask for more than twelve Nuns." He further grimly prophesied that if the Mother Provincial failed to fulfill his request immediately, the following year "will be too late":

> There is a time in the history of every parish and religious order, when if things are not done immediately, the parish and religious order would dry up and wither away. This is what I fear at the present time. These people [his parishioners] will not send their children to a school where the Sisters do not control the school. The school will deteriorate. The parish will dry up. And the vocations to your order will wither up and die.[1]

Despite the pastor's evident urgency, Mother Regina replied that she could provide only three additional sisters in September, adding that "this, in itself, is a most unusual commitment, since we are constantly finding it necessary to solicit the support of our Pastors in accepting more and more lay teachers."[2]

Father O'Brien's dire predictions notwithstanding, St. Raymond School did not close (at the time of this writing, it is still in operation), nor did the Sisters of Mercy have to withdraw completely from the parish until 1970. Rather, the pastor identified a serious concern regarding the consecrated religious life that was not wholly unfounded, for parish schools were historically a significant source of vocations. Many young women were inspired by their sister-teachers to seek out the religious life and, if taught by Sisters of Mercy, were naturally predisposed to join a Mercy community. Within a decade, this dynamic would be in tatters, as the female religious orders—particularly those devoted to teaching—responded to the winds of change emanating from the Second Vatican Council, which opened in October 1962. The very drama of the Council and the renewal process that derived from it have led many to view the mid-1960s as *the* critical turning point in the lives of Catholic women religious (or sisters) as well as those of clergy and the laity.

Up to this point, the restrictions governing a highly structuralized religious life had served to place inviolable barriers between laypeople and religious. The parishes in which many sister-teachers served were a point of intersection between them and laywomen and laymen at Mass, in parish-based devotional, social, and benevolent organizations, and in the education process. As lives crossed, clergy, sisters, and lay members of a parish held to their assigned role within the Catholic Church hierarchy, which located women religious in a separate and ill-defined "other" space, neither possessing the authority of clergy nor counted as members of the parish. Furthermore, it was the superior of the religious community who made assignments to teaching ministries, and little—if any—consideration was given to the discernment of individual sisters as to where God (or their natural talents) might intend them to serve.

For many sisters, their overriding desire was not to distance themselves from parish life but to become full members of their parish community and break down the artificial barriers that separated them from the People of God.[3] Vatican II was a turning point for all women religious, not only those ministering in parish schools. The changes of the mid-to-late 1960s seemed to derive not only from the decrees of the Vatican Council but also from the general radicalism of the times, in which feminism, student movements, civil-rights protests, and the growing call for the Church all played a part. Congregations of women religious, such as the Sisters of Mercy, embraced renewal by exchanging their traditional and "outdated" habits for modified ones or none at all. While many women simply left religious life, a significant proportion of those who remained moved away from traditional ministries in parochial education to take on new apostolates in the inner cities, frequently with secular organizations.

For over a century, the Chicago Sisters of Mercy filled the ranks of Catholic elementary and secondary teachers in Illinois, Iowa, and Wisconsin.

Clergy and laity often identified them by their ministry, not their founding charism or spirituality. Renewal of the Catholic Church during the 1960s threw that identity into crisis, particularly with respect to how their vocation tended to be viewed by lay Catholics. The reality of religious renewal, particularly as it relates to the education ministry of the Sisters of Mercy, is that while Vatican II authorized religious congregations to make distinct alterations in their constitutions, customs, norms, and apostolates, the process of change originated in the preceding decade. By the 1950s, the Sisters of Mercy (in common with many other female religious communities) had embraced the Sister Formation Movement, engaged in the dialogue of Catholic Action, and accepted the call of Catholic theologians to be "nuns in the world." By the time the first documents emerged from the Second Vatican Council, community leaders and many rank-and-file Sisters of Mercy already had a distinct understanding of what renewal entailed and embraced the process of renewal in all aspects of their vowed religious life. As a consequence, such women religious increasingly rejected the traditional form of their apostolate, particularly as educators.[4]

Origins of the Chicago Province

Catherine McAuley established the Sisters of Mercy in Ireland in 1831, to serve the poor, sick, and ignorant, especially women and children. Practically speaking, this involved the creation of schools, ministry to the sick in their homes, and the opening of a House of Mercy in Dublin to provide affordable shelter to poor working women of good character. This model of religious life was recreated in cities and towns throughout Ireland— where the Catholic Church desperately needed women religious to restore and expand the Catholic faith among the people—and had distinct application in other English-speaking nations, including England, Australia, Canada, and the United States.[5]

At the invitation of the bishop of Pittsburgh, the Sisters of Mercy first arrived in the United States in 1843 to minister to Irish immigrants. Under the leadership of Mother Frances Warde, who would go on to establish numerous other foundations in North America, the new Irish community soon established itself in Pittsburgh. Three years later, Mother Frances escorted a contingent of five sisters to Chicago to create a new congregation, or branch foundation. While the Mercys traditionally focused on free schools, visiting the sick, and shelter for needy women, they remained open to such ministries as select schools or female academies, care of orphans, and hospital work, all contingent on the needs of a particular location. Indeed, the Chicago congregation founded in 1846—the first religious congregation of women in this growing Midwestern city—soon established free schools for boys and girls, as well as the Saint Xavier Academy (a pay, or pension, school), which attracted girls from wealthier Catholic and Protestant homes.[6]

From this beginning, the expansion of the Mercys was rapid. To their growing network of Chicago schools was added a ministry to orphans and the acquisition of a Chicago hospital, which became Mercy Hospital in the early 1850s. Although their mission in Galena, in western Illinois, proved short-lived, they were more successful in Ottawa, Illinois, where they established a branch house in 1858. In succeeding decades, the Sisters of Mercy established branch houses in Davenport and Iowa City, Iowa, and Janesville and Milwaukee, Wisconsin. Such expansion was frequently the result of a request from a parish priest or local bishop to staff an emerging parish school, although health care was the predominant concern of the Iowa foundations.

Traditionally, branch houses of the Sister of Mercy became independent foundations once they were firmly rooted in new territories, particularly when the new houses fell within different dioceses. Independent motherhouses allowed local superiors to adapt to the needs and circumstances of their immediate environment while maintaining the initial intent of Catherine McAuley, who had never intended for her religious congregation to have a centralized generalate government. By the early twentieth century, pressure from within the Vatican to centralize authority and regulate religious congregations (including communities of male religious) pushed sisters like the Mercys towards amalgamation. Arguing that there was too much variation in religious rule and life, the Vatican instructed the Sisters of Mercy and other congregations to revise their constitutions and form new associations under the revised Code of Canon Law adopted in 1917, which also imposed new and stronger restrictions on women religious. Many of the loosely associated independent motherhouses scattered throughout the United States conformed to the wishes of the Vatican and came together to form the Sisters of Mercy of the

Union in 1929, becoming subject to a central authority located in Bethesda, Maryland, and adapting their Rule and Constitutions and Customs and Guide to conform to a more monastic and highly structured religious life.[7]

Each of the eight independent foundations that ultimately composed the Chicago Province derived from another motherhouse. The Chicago South Side gave birth to Ottawa and Davenport, while sisters from Davenport were the inspiration for the communities in Iowa City and in Janesville, Wisconsin. Sisters from Janesville established a short-lived convent in Fond du Lac and then later a permanent foundation in Milwaukee. The Chicago West motherhouse originated in Nashville but did not join with the already established South Side community. Ultimately, they all came together in 1929, when the Sisters of Mercy of the Union was formed and established a generalate system for the Sisters of Mercy, creating larger entities such as the Chicago Province. The Chicago Province was composed of Chicago South, Chicago West, Ottawa, Davenport (Iowa City had folded back into Davenport several years prior to the amalgamation in 1929), Janesville, and Milwaukee. Roughly a decade later, Aurora, Illinois, joined the Union.

The Burden of Vocation

In the face of an ever expanding number of parishes—particularly in the suburbs—during the 1940s and 1950s, religious congregations such as the Sisters of Mercy struggled to staff their assigned parochial schools and respond positively to the constant requests for more teachers while continuing to operate hospitals, homes for women, diocesan high schools, and other ministries. The number of vocations to the Mercys remained consistently high through the 1950s, when a little under two hundred women entered the community and made their profession into the community. (The number of entrants in the 1950s, however, was not as high as the 1930s, which were a little over two hundred.) Despite the high number of entrants, the pressure to place young sisters not yet fully formed in their religious life or educated in their professions continued unabated.[8] Requests for teachers came from all levels of clerical authority, from parish priests to cardinals, and while many asked only for one or two sisters, some requests threatened to make a substantial dent in the

Mercys' personnel resources. In 1946, for example, the Chicago Provincial Council received requests to place sisters in new parish schools in Madison, Wisconsin. A few months later, Cardinal Samuel Stritch asked the community to expand its presence in the Chicago parish of Holy Angels—which he had designated an African American parish—by thirty sisters and to take over the running of a new high school. In the latter case, the congregation balked, believing that they should expend their resources and personnel more wisely, and consequently a mutual decision was made by the provincial council and the cardinal for the Mercys to withdraw from Holy Angels entirely and to allow another congregation, the School Sisters of St. Francis from Milwaukee, to take over administration of the schools.[9]

Requests for teaching personnel persisted throughout the 1950s and 1960s, even as the number of sisters available continued to decline. Often these pleas for assistance were phrased in such a manner as to suggest that unless the Mercys complied with the request, not only the parish school in question but the fate of religious life—including that of the Sisters of Mercy—hung in the balance. The previously cited correspondence between Father O'Brien and Mother Regina illustrates the prevailing problem in two ways. First, it reflects the inability of religious congregations to keep up with the rapidly growing Catholic population. St. Raymond, established on the North Side of Chicago in 1949, was typical of the newer suburban parishes planted to serve white ethnic Catholics moving out of Chicago, who sought for their children schools that were adequately staffed, preferably by sisters. At this time, however, congregations such as the Mercys still had ties and obligations to traditional parishes in inner-city Chicago as well as to Davenport, Janesville, Milwaukee, and other communities throughout their province.

In the second place, Father O'Brien's characterization of the sisters' central role in the future of Catholic education placed an undue burden on the Mercys to save it. As O'Brien perceived the problem, the failure to do anything other than send him six more sisters would be irresponsible and would suggest that the Mercys were shirking their religious obligations. His tone, albeit dramatic, fitted with the larger perception of sisters during the first half of the twentieth century. Neither the pastor nor the lay Catholic, both of whom had defined roles in the parish dynamic, fully understood the position of the sisters who taught in their schools, catechized their children, and often performed such domestic tasks as cleaning the altar linens. Sisters of Mercy were an integral part of parish life, but, because of the nature of the religious life before Vatican II, they were far from equal members of the church community.

From the perspective of provincial leaders such as Mother Regina, the Mercys had to balance the demands of parish priests and bishops and the congregation's many other institutional commitments (hospitals and women's residences) against the the needs of individual sisters. As religious superiors sought to address this issue, many congregations looked to the Sister Formation Movement, which promoted the completion of degrees and full professional and theological development of sisters prior to their entering classrooms or hospital wards. Even as these developments percolated within the Chicago Province of the Sisters of Mercy of the Union, the larger Catholic Church was on the verge of a momentous change. Women religious who taught in parish schools were exposed to the currents of postwar Catholic Action that were transforming Catholic understanding of the role of laypeople in the life of the Church. Debates over the shape and meaning of the liturgy of the Mass, such as those examined by Katharine Harmon in "The Liturgical Movement and Catholic Action," a chapter in this volume, had meaning for sisters as well as laypeople and, as the structure of the religious life shifted from a more formalized uniformity to individualized ministry, many sisters sought ways to reach out to the People of God while still remaining servants of the Church.[10]

In the Parish, but Not *of* the Parish

By the mid-1960s, leaders of the Chicago Mercys (not to mention the larger Mercy Union) recognized the need to renew religious life and did not require direction from the Vatican to engage in reform, but coordination by the Roman authorities helped promote the revision of the Mercy constitution—with its adoption of new modes of living, government, spirituality, and opportunities for ministry—more than a decade later.[11] When provincial leaders asked Chicago sisters to imagine how their community should renew itself, they enabled the sisters to redefine their relationship with their parish communities, with an enduring impact on Mercy-staffed parochial schools.

At the opening of the Second Vatican Council, Mercy sisters staffed forty-seven parish schools in Illinois, four in Iowa, and seven in Wisconsin, many of which had been run by the community since their founding in the nineteenth century. By the end of the 1970s, however, the Sisters of Mercy had withdrawn from over half of these schools, and the number of teaching sisters in parish schools in the Chicago Province continued to decline in the 1980s and 1990s. Only a minority remained within the school system as the institutional Mercy presence was withdrawn and some sisters transitioned into religious education or found alternative educational settings, even if it meant working in another religious community's school or within a secular organization. While much of this transformation had to do with the aging population of the congregations and declining membership, many Mercys, when given the opportunity to decide their ministry for themselves, chose to abandon their traditional apostolate.

Before the 1960s, most women religious lived in a convent attached to their ministry, whether in a hospital or a school. Such convents were maintained by the host parish, in the case of parochial schools, or located "over the shop," in the case of high schools, academies, and hospitals, which were independent institutions. In such a context, the life of the religious community set it apart from the parish community. Rules governing the interaction of sisters with laypeople and clergy prohibited the opening of their convent home to parishioners except on such specific occasions as pantry showers thrown to raise funds and literally stock the sisters' pantries.[12]

Sisters were required to travel in pairs and could not ride alone in automobiles with men, even if the driver was a father or brother. Sisters could not "leave the convent grounds without permission of the Local Superior" even if they went out "on visitation, on business, [or] to the doctor." Provincials even chose a sister-companion when a Sister of Mercy was given permission to study at a college or university, finding someone whose own academic needs required further education. In 1936, for example, the provincial council permitted a sister to take a postgraduate course in pediatrics at Cook County Hospital in Chicago only if they could find her a companion. In this case, Sister Mary Magdalen Hartman was paired with "Sister Grace Marie Crahan who [took] advantage of the time to take a special course in laboratory work." Despite giving provisional approval, the rules of their religious life had to be followed, and the provincialate made arrangements for the pair of sisters to live either at a local convent in the Precious Blood parish in Chicago or to stay at the nurses' home of the Cook County Hospital, whichever allowed them to hear Mass early enough to fit their daily schedule. Despite the provincial council's authority in the local community, they still had to obtain permission from Mother General in Bethesda.[13]

The intricacies of this type of planning reflect the restrictions placed on the movements of women religious at this time. Permissions and religious rules cautioned Mercys to remember to guard themselves from too much social contact with the laity and clergy, even with respect to the celebration of Mass within the parish. While appearing at Sunday services and shepherding their pupils through Mass during school hours, sisters had their own daily Mass said either by the pastor or another priest, and sisters had to request special permission from their provincials to extend their involvement in Masses for the parish community. Even playing the organ at parish Masses required approval from the provincial council. In one exchange of letters between the sisters at St. Alphonsus Church in Mt. Pleasant, Iowa, and Mother Huberta McCarthy, the provincial assistant at the time, the sisters requested permission to play the organ at various Lenten services and forty-hour devotions. Mother Huberta granted permission but only on a case-by-case basis and only if no one else was available. She stated that the mother general did not approve of sisters' playing the organ for parish functions, which suggests that the matter may have been about more than simply what was acceptable behavior for Sisters of Mercy. It was possibly about abuse of the sisters' time and service (i.e., in cleaning the church). Despite an often harmonious relationship between the parish priest and Sisters of Mercy assigned to a particular parochial school, mother provincials and mother generals sought to institute a general policy whereby sisters were not drawn into performing extra duties beyond the school and the education of children. In the minds of community leaders, a clear definition of what sisters were permitted to do protected them from an abuse of their time and services. Consequently, when the sisters of St. Mary's School in Streater, Illinois, wrote for permission to help the parish priest count the weekly collection money, the Mother Provincial replied:

It would be better not to take over the counting of collections, church work, or extra affairs at school, as Mother General is not favorable toward taking on this work in New Parishes; in older Parishes, it is difficult to get away from what has been done in the past. The policy should be that the time is needed for the teacher to meet ever-increasing educational standards, class preparation, and intensification of her own spiritual life. My advice is that it is better to adhere to this policy.[14]

Such monastic-style rules of religious life inevitably, however, erected a barrier between sisters and the communities in which they worked and lived, reinforced only by the lay predisposition to view women religious as otherworldly. A decision by young Catholic women to enter a religious community involved a lifetime commitment, education, and professional development as well as a change in status within the Church. Young women were transformed from daughters, siblings, and friends to holy women and brides of Christ. While they may also have become teachers, principals, and administrators, when they professed their vows and clothed themselves in the religious habit, they occupied a different space and status within the Church.[15]

By the beginning of the 1960s, many Sisters of Mercy sought a different relationship with the rest of the Catholic Church and with the world—specifically, they sought the removal of barriers between themselves and the laity. Sisters at various stages of religious life, from novices to those with decades of service in the community, had been exposed to the new social and cultural ideas percolating through their classes in theology, religious readings, the mainstream news, and even their classroom environments. It was in the parish schools, moreover, that the Mercys for the first time experienced Catholic Action, the new lay apostolate of the 1940s and 1950s. Such lay-led groups as the Christian Family Movement and the Young Christian Students (YCS) had taken a particular hold in the Midwest, in places like Chicago, Davenport, and Mt. Pleasant, where lay Catholics had developed a unique understanding of communal responsibility, and Mercy-staffed schools both provided the space and helped facilitate the expansion of the YCS apostolate.[16]

Mercy involvement in parish-based YCS groups continued into the early 1960s, decades after the establishment of Catholic Action. According to the convent chronicle, the YCS chapter at St. Alphonsus School in Mt. Pleasant, Iowa, was particularly active, with sisters at this school and the neighboring St. Patrick School in Burlington, Iowa, participating in

Iowa-based YCS meetings, gathering information to assist the state chapters, and attending conferences in Chicago. St. Alphonsus's chronicler reported that sisters traveled to nearby Fairfield to attend a regional meeting of the YCS. The sisters who attended were moderators of chapters in their parishes in Mt. Pleasant and Burlington, Iowa. In October 1961, the *Catholic Messenger*, the diocesan newspaper in Davenport, reported on the "Fall Study Day" featuring the YCS chapter at St. Alphonsus. This student-led day of study included not only students from the parish schools but also young adults from the public high school. Throughout the 1960s, Sisters of Mercy in the Mt. Pleasant and Burlington parishes sought to engage their students in the changes of the Second Vatican Council. In one instance, sisters instructed their students to bring in newspaper clippings about the council and to study readings on Vatican II and the Liturgical Movement. Sisters at St. Alphonsus had encouraged the YCS members to read and discuss the conciliar documents, and the ensuing conversations about the impact of renewal impressed the Mercys with the level of understanding shown by many of the children.[17]

Sisters at St. Alphonsus and at other parish schools in Chicago served largely in an advisory capacity with the YCS, which was a student-directed movement that nevertheless benefitted from the assistance and cooperation of the parochial and high-school teachers. On at least one occasion, YCS members of St. Matthew School in Glendale Heights, a western suburb of Chicago, traveled in January 1966 to the South Side neighborhood of Chicago to visit children at St. Cecilia School. Through the YCS, middle-school and high-school students from suburban parishes visited and developed partnerships with inner-city parish schools such as St. Cecilia, providing tutoring and material aid through clothing drives.[18] The Mercys also fostered YCS chapters in such urban parishes as St. James Church, at 28th Street and Wabash, where a YCS group at Christmastime in 1964 visited and entertained elderly neighbors. In another parish, the YCS group delivered toys and Christmas baskets throughout the neighborhood.[19] Even as YCS flourished, the Sisters of Mercy were beginning to develop a new understanding of their role in these urban parishes, whose formerly white ethnic Catholic population had moved into the northern and western suburbs and given way to Hispanic and African American residents, many of whom were not Catholic. As the Mercys' students came to engage with the issues of urban poverty and racial injustice, so their teachers, in performing

what they perceived as relevant ministry, felt obliged to confront the traditional restrictions of the vowed religious life.

A New Vocation?

The conception of renewal disseminated slowly through the Mercy community, whether in the form of new theology courses offered to novices
and professed sisters at Saint Xavier College or through provincial correspondence (circulars) and lectures and conferences intended to keep sisters abreast of potential changes to the religious life. Individual Sisters of
Mercy also received a personal copy of community newsletters, but few
had access to the *National Catholic Reporter* or other outside newspapers.[20]
Until the implementation, in 1967, of changes in the restrictions on religious life, most sisters received their news through their community leaders, either from local superiors, who communicated letters from general
and provincial leaders, or through limited exposure to the radio.

Once information about religious renewal reached individual Mercys,
however, such new ideas—coupled with the preceding decade of exposure to Catholic Action experience and the persistent lack of choice and
agency in community life, apostolates, and spirituality—prompted, by
1968 and 1969, a wave of experimentation among the Chicago Sisters of
Mercy. The approved experimentation fell into two categories: local living
and self-government. The generalate allowed small groups of sisters to
create intentional communities to implement new thinking on religious
government. For the Chicago Mercys, this meant putting into practice the
idea of subsidiarity. Groups of sisters sought to keep authority at the local
level, and many wished to do away with the position of local superior altogether. Such experimentation also involved budgets, control of money,
negotiating household management, and determining prayer life and the
need for horariums of a local house.

Experimentation in ministries, however, did not occur until the 1970s.
Exposed to the poverty of their students or the violence in their neighborhoods, many sister-teachers felt prompted to articulate their doubts about
the value that traditional forms of education served. Some sisters understood the value of serving a Catholic population in more affluent suburban
parishes. At the same time, others pressed for a more authentic presence in
less privileged urban neighborhoods, regardless of the religious affiliation

of the students who attended the parish schools. Many sisters sought to live in local communities, in the manner of their neighbors, rather than in a separate convent. Furthermore, many sisters sought to break away from the traditional model of parish education altogether, by directly addressing the needs of inner-city children. When asked by the community's newsletter, *Agape*, what programs they would implement if they were superiors, one sister responded that she would "like to work in the capacity of a social worker for the Church," by creating, with three or four sisters, a community center in an impoverished neighborhood. Another sister spoke of her desire to become a community consultant in inner-city schools, implementing experimental plans in education formulated at the Mercys' Saint Xavier College.[21]

By 1966, many sisters were ready to make changes in how they conducted their ministry. Change, however, would happen only after the Sisters of Mercy reformed the structure of their religious life and government. This was done through a series of chapters held at the generalate level in the second half of the 1960s. In the early 1960s, however, the Chicago Mercys sought to answer basic questions about the motivations they had as religious and how they should live their "apostolate of mercy." Should they "hand themselves over in love to those they serve or to present a mere shadow of themselves by playing a role as teacher, nurse, or administrator?" Concerned with the question of how they as religious love others, one sister commented:

> If we are to affect those we serve, we must touch them as individual persons; and this happens only through an empathetic engagement, in which there is the warmth of mutual understanding and acceptance. . . . We must make this gift of ourselves to each person whom we serve, or else we fail to break down the authoritarian image that many have regarding religious. Our interest and concern for others does not compromise our total gift of self to Christ. This seems to be what we most fear in our relationship with those around us. We must constantly remind ourselves that it is the human love with which we serve our sisters and Christ's children which is the *very means* of expressing our love for Him.[22]

Subsequent issues of *Agape* addressed individual questions of the apostolate by focusing first on health care and issues of renewal. While not uniform in their understanding of the purpose and outcome of renewal, the Chicago Mercys fully engaged the process itself, debating in the pages of this newsletter the nature of the spirit of their foundress, Catherine McAuley, and the nature of how they as "Sisters of Mercy [were] an organism, living, sharing, growing tougher within the People of God—that every adaptation, every response to the needs of today find [them] not isolated individuals within high religious aspirations."[23]

In the Christmas 1965 issue, the Sisters of Mercy fully engaged in the question of the place of sisters in their contemporary world. Turning to its readers, *Agape* contributors asked in what way they acted as authentic witnesses and had true Christian encounters with the People of God. How did they understand the social apostolate? A deeper question was posed by Sister Mary Irenaeus Chekouras who asked sisters to consider their motivation in their ministry and to wonder what was truly needed by those they served. Did sisters presume to know what others needed? Or, put more plainly:

> Should we not rather be advanced enough in our thinking and in our respect for those we serve, to go to these prospective recipients of our generosity and ask them what we may do to serve them best? We cannot assume that they do not know their needs, that they cannot speak and speak well. We can only fear that we will not understand what they tell us, that we will not take time to listen.[24]

Through their understanding of their own education and professional development, their experiences as teachers, religious educators, and arguably peripheral members of parish communities, and their engagement with the theology of Vatican II, sisters began to embrace the idea of respect for the human person, whether within their own congregations or within the larger world as they lived their apostolate.[25]

The attitude toward change and the search for a more authentic religious experience fully engaged in their apostolate resonated with the larger trend among other women religious of this period. Like other congregations, Chicago Mercys embraced renewal to reform what they understood was an "outmoded style of life," and many desired a more mature adult relationship within the Church, with both clergy and the laity. Sister-teachers wanted a more authentic and genuine connection with the People of God in the classroom and in the parish communities in which they lived and worked. As Sister Mary Charles Borromeo Muckenhirn, C.S.C., articulated in *The Changing Sister* (1965): "It is obvious that the Christian apostolic endeavor simply must be person to person, in some sense. This does not mean necessarily one to one, for genuine group action can be intensely personal. But there must be genuine openness and sharing of one's own self, not a mask of formulae or actions which separate and confuse."[26]

The model of educator as social worker offered in *Agape* in 1966, mentioned above, represents one way a Sister of Mercy might have asked and answered the question "Why?" raised by Sister Mary Irenaeus. For Mercys to act as informal social workers was not entirely without foundation in the Chicago Province. Sisters had always found ways to provide material aid to students in need, by providing, for example, meals, clothes, or tuition breaks. Many sisters had provided support, but they did not break from the traditional model of parochial education. They maintained what was the traditional purpose of Catholic education through the 1960s: to form the "true Christian," who as a "product of Christian education, is the supernatural man, who thinks, judges, and acts constantly and consistently in accordance with the right reason illuminated by the supernatural light of the example and teaching of Christ." Sisters of Mercy within this tradition of Catholic education sought to form students, to contribute to their mental, social, and religious development, and thereby to help them search for intellectual Truth. According to the *Handbook of Educational Policies: The Elementary Schools*, the objectives of "Christian Education in American Democratic Society" are "moral and spiritual perfection in Christ, Intellectual and cultural development, social virtue, economic competency, and physical fitness." From this goal, teachers sought to build students' knowledge of God, the Catholic Church, their fellow man, nature, and self, to master skills, and to acquire desirable habits, attitudes, and appreciations. More than these aims, education was designed to "train the child" in many capacities, such as observation, thinking, self-expression, and acting "intelligently." All this would be accomplished through a system of education built, like the Catholic Church, on a hierarchical system.[27]

A closer examination of the *Handbook* used by Sisters of Mercy in the Chicago Province suggests that the education of children within Catholic parochial schools followed a specific plan or course of study, and the intention was that education would be transmitted uniformly, regardless of the parish. The *Handbook* assured its readers that

> the diocesan School Board, under the direction of the superintendent of schools, determines the course of study for the elementary schools. It is the responsibility of every teacher to acquaint herself with the requirements of the courses of study prescribed for the subjects she teaches and to familiarize herself with those of the entire curriculum, in order that she may view the total pictures of the subject matter areas.[28]

Through this uniformity, teachers would transmit Catholic culture and teachings to shape generations of young children and guide them into adulthood. Many Sisters of Mercy came to see the purpose and form of Catholic education in a new way as they engaged in renewal of their own congregation and considered the teachings and principals of Catholic Action, Sister Formation, and Vatican II as well as the changing society in which they lived.

Mercy parish schools, however, became filled increasingly by non-Catholics whose parents respected the Christian education and structure their children received at the hands of women religious, but the possibility of the students' conversion to Catholicism became less a concern with respect to their continued attendance. At the same time, sisters began verbalizing to one another their doubts about their purpose in the traditional classroom, particularly within the context of living an authentic apostolate, and by the end of the 1960s and early 1970s they sought new ways to conduct their education ministries or sought out new ministries. This change, owing in large part to religious renewal, resulted in the need for the sisters to reduce their involvement in parish schools. Community leaders had made difficult decisions to reduce the number of sisters assigned to various parish schools throughout their province, but by 1970 retrenchment had become a larger concern. The Chicago Mercys faced the heartache of leaving a ministry to which they as a community had been devoted for over a century. From the 1970s on, the Chicago Sisters of Mercy changed the manner in which they as a province conducted their education apostolate. Instead of sending out a large workforce of sister-teachers to staff and administer hundreds of parish schools, the Chicago Mercys, still committed to teaching, had sisters in fewer numbers— in some cases, one or two—in parish schools and reconceptualizing their role as teachers. Often this meant establishing religious-education programs, conducting adult-education centers, and cooperating with lay teachers and parents to create sustainable education for the needs of inner-city and urban parish schools. These new forms of connection within the parish, through the roles of women religious as religious-education teachers and later as pastoral assistants, began the process by which they altered their connection to the laity.[29]

Sister-teachers who remained in parochial schools needed the cooperation of lay teachers to continue their ministry. This was apparent as early as the 1940s, when they faced an ever expanding school population with a limited number of available teachers, but by the late 1960s and early 1970s the leadership of the Chicago Mercys no longer determined how many—or, indeed, which—sisters staffed a particular school. Gone were the days of a request for teachers such as that made by Father O'Brien in 1958. Parish priests continued to make appeals to provincial leaders for teachers to staff their schools, but by the 1970s sisters increasingly began to apply for positions in schools on their own initiative, whether as teachers, religious educators, principals, or administrators. This change occurred at the same time as the Chicago Sisters of Mercy were steadily reducing their involvement in the parish schools their community had long staffed.[30]

The decline in available sister-teachers by the mid to late 1960s had multiple causes. Yes, the need for fully educated and professional teachers had limited the number of new teachers for parish classrooms. The number of women leaving religious life had begun to rise dramatically. The Chicago Province lost thirty-one members in 1967, thirty-two in 1968, and thirty-eight in 1969. The year 1970 saw the departure of twenty-nine members. In the subsequent decade, the numbers leaving began to ebb, reduced to ten and under for each year of the 1970s. While no one left the community in 1979, no one entered either. Of the sisters who left the community in the 1960s, nearly all of them had entered religious life in that decade or the 1950s.[31]

The diminishing pool of readily available sister-teachers was further complicated by the loosening of the restrictions that had governed daily life after 1967. More specifically, the regulations that determined for sisters their ministry life had begun to be lifted, and by the early 1970s,

Sisters of Mercy could determine for themselves where and in what form they conducted their apostolic life. In the late 1960s the number of Chicago Mercys working in parish schools began a steady decline, and by the mid-1970s only 288 still worked as teachers, alongside 673 lay teachers. According to congregation statistics, a significant number of sisters worked in urban schools, where the ratio of teaching sisters to students was 1 to 54, while the ratio of lay teachers to students was 1 to 24. Conversely, only 38 sisters served in suburban parishes, where the ratio of religious to students was 1 to 120, as compared with one lay teacher for every 28 students. By the end of the 1970s, roughly half of those in active ministry (i.e., full-time ministry) were in education of some form. This declined to a little over 20 percent by the early 1990s.[32]

A 1974 study of the status of the Sisters of Mercy in education revealed that lay teachers were the dominant presence in parochial schools, whether inner-city, urban, suburban, or rural. It also revealed something that the community already knew—namely, that the number of sister-teachers was declining and few, if any, new entrants would replace those retiring or discerning alternative vocations. Yet these statistics also indicated that education remained a central identifying ministry for the Chicago Mercys, and many of those who left the classroom did not leave education; they simply found an alternative educational environment, such as religious education, in which to conduct their ministry.[33]

Those who continued as teachers faced a different landscape of students, particularly in the urban and inner-city neighborhoods. By the mid-1970s most Catholic schools, particularly in the Archdiocese of Chicago, understood that many of their students were not Catholic. The Mercys understood their continued support of parochial education and this population shift within the context of Vatican II and their revised religious constitution. As a community, they believed they were called by God "to serve mankind, especially the deprived and oppressed, in whatever ways their needs dictate and our capabilities allow." Vatican II had inspired them to listen to other "voices."

In an era when Christian values wane, educators help students to find a sense of values by which to judge and to use the gift of material civilization. Non-Catholics in our schools are not governed by constraints or smothered by indoctrination. They are asked to respect Catholic education and they are expected to be active participants in the study of Christian values. Knowledge without values is pagan; knowledge with relationship to morality seems the apostolic thrust for Catholic education in 1975.[34]

The goals of Catholic education articulated here are not that distant from those articulated in the 1953 *Handbook* mentioned above. The language used and the approach that Mercys took, however, reflected a changed attitude towards their education apostolate. The question that remained for much of the late 1960s and 1970s was how and in what role they would continue within parish schools.

Staying the Course

How did those sisters who chose to remain in education come to conceive of their role as women religious and as members of the parish communities? Informed by the teachings of Vatican II, including the new emphasis on social justice, Mercy educators attempted to envision a new framework for teaching. First, they endeavored to reconceptualize parish education by developing new curricula and instituting alternative models of education. Second, they found new ways to transform children and adults in parishes through religious-education programs. If the Mercys could no longer sustain a parish school, they might still evangelize the population by providing religious instruction, either in the school or in the church.[35]

By the early 1970s, the Mercys were engaged in an extensive study of their educational apostolate, seeking, among other things, to identify useful community resources and develop an "innovating curriculum according to the needs and interests of local areas and specific schools." In response to questions about their relevancy and effectiveness, Mercy educators developed targeted programs designed to preserve those Catholic schools that served a particular need. The decision to withdraw sisters from a particular school was based in part on the availability of other schools in the community and on whether the Mercys were the right people to operate the school.[36]

The congregation also developed plans to combine resources of surviving schools, as was the case with the Westside Network of Mercy Schools, which included Resurrection, St. Catherine of Siena, and Precious Blood

Schools on Chicago's West Side. The Sisters of Mercy had staffed all of the schools since the early 1910s. The needs and resources available for these schools had altered throughout much of the mid-twentieth century. In the case of Precious Blood, the once predominantly Irish American student body had shifted. In 1970 it was nearly 70 percent Mexican and Puerto Rican descent and 30 percent African American. Enrollment had declined since the late 1950s, when the Eisenhower Expressway was constructed through the middle of the parish neighborhood. By the mid-1970s, the African American student population increased and was now nearly 60 percent of the school's enrollment. Located in an inner-city neighborhood, the school faced continual financial shortages throughout the 1950s and 1960s, which reached a crisis point by the end of the 1960s. By 1969 there were rising costs, buildings in need of repair, insufficient support from the parish community, and a constant worry that if the Sisters of Mercy withdrew the school would fold. By 1970, demands for more sisters were not being answered in the affirmative, and school officials began to consider consolidation plans, such as the proposal to pool resources and merge Precious Blood with Holy Trinity, St. Callistus, St. Jarlath, and St. Malachy schools into one central school for the area.[37] While this plan did not materialize, combining financial and academic resources resulted in the new plan to create the Westside Network in 1974.[38]

Principals and teachers at Precious Blood had sought new alternatives for engaging their students and looked for new ways to cooperate within the school, seeking a "renewal of educational programs" and to develop dynamic a curriculum. Administrators applied and gained admission into the prchdiocesan pilot program Project START (Schools That Are Renewing Themselves). The purpose of START was to "train faculties and administrators to plan together to determine new directions for their schools and to find the means to implement them." The idea behind such programs was to find creative means of carrying on the mission of schools that served parishes facing economic and social challenges. At the heart of this discussion was the effort to determine what sort of education students need to develop into "responsible, thinking Christians who are able to cope with life" and to be "well prepared academically for the future." For Precious Blood, this meant continuation of programs that addressed the needs of the whole person, and the school provided English-language education for Spanish-speaking students, a tutoring program run by college students from the Illinois Circle Campus, counseling services for children and adults, and engaging parents in the school's continued existence.[39]

Resurrection School, engaged in similar efforts, instituted a Teacher In-Service Development program "designed to increase the number and stability of Black teachers on the staff." Attempting to determine who was most needed in their classrooms, Resurrection administrators believed that hiring black teachers would "overcome 'institutional racism' which [was] so rampant in school systems." According to a "Proposal for Teacher In-Service Development" of the Archdiocese of Chicago, hiring African American teachers from the local community, even if they did not have full teaching credentials, would combat this institutional racism. The program allowed for on-the-job training and time for teachers to obtain the necessary academic credits to become fully certified instructors.[40]

Resurrection School also faced reduced enrollment since the late 1960s. Like Precious Blood, it had a large Irish American population, but its Italian population was equally significant. According to reports, in 1967–68 the school's enrollment was about nine hundred, of whom about 12 percent were African American. Enrollment had dropped by three hundred in the 1969–1970 school year and was now 90 percent African American. Once a school with a significant number of sister-teachers, Resurrection now had fewer than a dozen sisters in the classrooms. Like Precious Blood, Resurrection at the beginning of the 1970s attempted to provide a dynamic education that stressed the cooperation of faculty and students "in creating and shaping new ideas," to develop "realistic means of forming wholesome attitudes and establishing rewarding patterns of interpersonal behavior." The Resurrection administrators sought "to humanize education and [they saw] the PERSON as the most valuable component of our 'system: or 'structure.'" Resurrection's philosophy included a stress on an evolutionary and liberalizing atmosphere in the school. The hope was to maximize diminishing resources. Administrators designed a curriculum that broke from the traditional education found in parochial and public-school classrooms before this period, stressing not what students learned but how.

> Process and classroom environment are as important as curriculum content. The characteristic of "process" is the availability of options which allow the pupil to make mistakes, to learn responsibility for his own

choices, and to experience freedom. These options allow great choice of the instruments of learning, such as teacher-presentation, texts and other printed matter, audio-visuals, manipulative devices, or a helping relationship. Option, as related to curriculum content, permits considerable selection, especially in the arts of language arts and sciences.[41]

Under this new philosophy and curriculum, choice was given to students, and education moved from being top-down and became conceptualized as a more democratic and "liberating" process. Along with these changes, the school offered the services of a social worker and stressed the importance of parental involvement in the school, including encouraging parent-volunteers acting as aides during social activities.

St. Catherine of Siena's School, first staffed by the Sisters of Mercy in 1917, continued to draw large numbers of students into the 1960s. The parish boasted that 2000 families were members of the parish and had an enrollment of 800 children in 1964. Nearly ten years later, parish membership had dropped to 800 families and only 247 students in 1973. St. Catherine of Siena's decline had in part to do with the changing demographics of the neighborhood. As more African American families moved into the area, white families left. St. Catherine's is located in Oak Park, roughly two miles from the rioting that occurred following the assassination of Martin Luther King, Jr. in 1968 and destroyed much of the property within the nearby St. Lucy parish boundaries in the Austin neighborhood. By 1974, as membership declined in both St. Catherine of Siena and St. Lucy, the Archdiocese moved to consolidate the two, forming a new territorial parish: St. Catherine of Siena-St. Lucy. The parish school, however, continued throughout this period and Sisters of Mercy attempted to maintain a presence in the parish school and community in keeping with the charge of their constitutions to serve those in need regardless of church affiliation. In one case, the established religious education program attempted to reach the African American members of the neighborhood. The religious education program attempted to acquaint parents of the school with the Catholic faith. By making them more aware of the teachings of Catholicism, they hoped that parents would "support the religious thrust in the school." No one was compelled to convert to Catholicism to enroll their children in the parish school, but the Mercys engaged in this ministry confessed within the pages of the community newsletter, *Exchange*, that some of the participants might "choose to continue into the program's second state, learning more about the Catholic faith and eventually entering the Church." Parents attended a four to five week seminar on Catholicism and how it was presented in the school. In the sessions, parents were asked to explore their own faith experience and participate in an examination of Catholic and Protestant traditions. Using Scripture the religious education teachers called attention to the distinctions between faiths, highlighting Catholic beliefs possibly to dispel any concerns parents might have or potentially persuade parents.[42]

Despite efforts to bolster schools facing economic and staffing needs, and mindful of recent withdrawals of religious personnel from parish schools, lay and religious staffing Precious Blood, Resurrection, and St. Catherine of Siena Schools sought a means of combining resources to guard against further school closings. Sisters of Mercy working in all three of these schools developed a plan with the support of lay personnel to cooperate across school lines in late 1973.[43] With the cooperation of all three school boards, parish councils, and teaching staffs (including lay and religious teachers), the three schools voted to unite their efforts along disciplinary lines. In the event of funding and classroom resource shortages, the network would create horizontal networks devoted to "discipline, activities, scheduling, [and] facilities." At the same time, vertical networks united the disciplines at all levels, by focusing on "curriculum matters." While preserving the autonomy of the individual schools, the pooling of resources would, ideally, help prevent future closures.[44]

The Westside Network worked for a time and did prevent the complete withdrawal of Sisters of Mercy from the three schools, but not forever. Mercys continued to staff Precious Blood School until 1979 and Resurrection school until 1981. A Sister of Mercy remained at St. Catherine-St. Lucy well into the twenty-first century. The Archdiocese of Chicago closed Resurrection Church in 1988, but Precious Blood and the combined St. Catherine-St. Lucy's remains. Did the presence of Sisters of Mercy have an impact on the type of education offered at these three schools, or for that matter their longevity? For the Sisters of Mercy who staffed these schools, the questions they wished to answer had more to do with how they could be most effective. In the case of this West Side neighborhood, as much as leaving a school to which they had dedicated much of their time and energy was heartbreaking, many saw new opportunities to serve a greater need in that area.

Sisters of Mercy discerned new avenues by creating a community education center in the West Side Austin neighborhood. The Austin Career Center established in 1977 grew out of a collaborative effort of sisters living and working on the west side of Chicago. Using the funds from the sale of the Mercys' then-closed Siena High School (a school which had developed from the St. Catherine of Siena Academy in the early twentieth century), they established a West Side Planning Network to support ministries in the area. In February of 1977, eleven sisters from Resurrection, St. Catherine of Siena, St. Thomas Aquinas, and other churches met to develop plans to work full-time to build a support system of people and services for the West Side, specifically the Austin and Oak Park neighborhoods. One out-growth of this planning was the development of the Austin Career Center in the former Siena High School. Established in 1977, the center was designed to reach older teens and adults looking to complete high school degrees and seeking assistance in employment opportunities for those who left school before graduation.[45]

A different approach was adopted by teachers at St. James School on the South Side of Chicago, where the Mercys had been dealing with "real problems" for a couple of decades. In the 1950s, the faculty of St. James School were focused on the "instruction and care of large Negro Population" and the successful baptism of the "neglected race" whom the Sisters of Mercy sought to serve. Throughout the 1950s, however, the sisters experienced declining enrollments and an increasing incidence of petty crimes and vandalism. In May 1957 the convent experienced the loss of their lawnmower, two typewriters, a phonograph, and four suitcases and "[t]wo sisters, a bell and a bat [kept] vigil" that night. Reports of shootings and other violence in the neighborhood also filter into the parish chronicles by the end of the decade. In the decade that followed, the sisters at St. James sought to address the problem by attending lectures and meetings regarding inner-city schools and new programs to help children. They also went to Catholic Interracial Council meetings and heard Martin Luther King speak, attended meetings of the Urban Apostolate, prayed for civil rights workers in Alabama in 1965, and set up a Head Start program.[46]

The Mercys at St. James, in conjunction with lay teachers, strove to "create the best possible environment for [their] students," recognizing that the classroom was not "the real world." They accepted that the school environment was "very different from the urban survival hassle of the streets, but [they] also believe[d] that [their] students should cope with the real problems in their world." As a part of the Student Affairs Committee, the Mercys helped promote a school-within-a-school in 1973, which provided a more concentrated, student-directed learning environment, and this "mini" school appears to have had many of the characteristics of the Montessori Method. The new religious education program also incorporated greater parental involvement and teachers reported increased reception of the sacraments.[47]

The initiatives pursued at St. James and at other schools represented a concerted effort to redefine the presence of women religious as educators. In the context of the immigrant Catholic population of the nineteenth and early twentieth centuries, the Sisters of Mercy had emphasized that education gave their children the opportunity for social betterment. In the second half of the twentieth century, the new emphasis on social justice led the Chicago Mercys to emphasize that this educational goal was not intended for Catholic children alone. Furthermore, the decline in their numbers obliged them to acknowledge the need for cooperation with lay faculty members and administrators as well as parents, a course that they were able to put into practice at St. Raymond School in Mt. Prospect in 1972, when the community letter of the Chicago Mercys reported that the Social Science Department and the school had reflected upon the need to "heighten [its] awareness of social justice issues among themselves and their students." During the school's Day of Renewal, the faculty discussed "social injustices" and planned to expose the students to "multi-ethnic experiences." Two years later, the Chicago Consortium of Colleges and Universities had selected St. Raymond to participate in a study funded by the National Institute of Education focusing on individualized educational program.[48]

During the early 1970s, a Sister of Mercy acted as the principal of St. Raymond School, while Sister Mary Loftus directed the efforts to provide religious education for children and adults and Sister Jean Shulte oversaw the pre-Cana program at St. Raymond parish. Both sisters occupied roles traditionally filled by priests, and, while not allowed to assume the title associate pastor, acted in a pastoral capacity. In a further demonstration of the changing times, a layman joined the religious education team as youth minister.[49] The efforts of Sisters Mary and Jean were not unusual for the Mercys serving in parishes after 1970. Emulating the growing number of laymen and laywomen inspired by Catholic Action to take an active role in parish life, the Chicago Mercys shifted from the rote catechizing of school children, to an entirely new form of religious education and assumed leadership positions within it.

The most visible and tangible change in the character of professed religious women, however, at least from the point of view of the laity, was the manner in which the two groups ceased to interact at the parish level. When sisters left the classrooms, many of them also seemed to abandon the religious life. Although the two were not directly connected, the media were quick to proclaim the existence of "New Nuns" and the crisis of the emptying of convents. One day school children saw their teacher in a full habit; the next she entered the classroom wearing a modified one; within a few years, she did not wear a habit at all, but instead dressed in secular clothing. By the 1970s, many sisters left schools, but were still present in their parishes, attending weekly Mass as if they were any other member of the parish.[50]

As the religious life changed and more and more sisters discerned their ministerial life to be somewhere other than in a classroom, lay teachers increasingly assumed control of Catholic parish schools. Between the early 1950s and the early 1980s, the Chicago Mercys (along with the entire Sisters of Mercy of the Union) worked through a process of renewal that involved re-conceptualizing many of their former motifs of ministry. In many ways this was a collaborative debate as to what religious life for the Mercys would ultimately become. The Second Vatican Council only confirmed the shift among the Mercys as to their understanding of their identity as religious women and how they related to and worked with the laity. In many ways this was a period of growth and maturity as well as a time of conflict and struggle for the congregation. The final result would be the departure of women religious from parish education and their replacement by laypeople who had previously treated their vocation with exaggerated reverence.

8 "This Is Our Challenge! We Will Pursue It"

The National Council of Catholic Women, the Feminist Movement, and the Second Vatican Council, 1960–1975

MARY J. HENOLD

In 2000 I began researching the history of the American Catholic feminist movement.[1] At the beginning of that project I knew very little about Catholic feminists or, indeed, Catholic women in the 1960s and 1970s. Quite early in my research I stumbled across a 1966 article about women and the Second Vatican Council. Its title, "The Buried Talents Symposium," suggested that I might find some Catholic feminists in its pages, and I was not disappointed. The article featured the perspectives of a number of prominent Catholic women, including Margaret Mealey, identified as the executive director of the National Council of Catholic Women (NCCW). Mealey's comments were striking:

> By the action and pronouncements of Vatican II, women have been given their wings. But too many pastors and bishops are reluctant to let them fly. If the church is to be relevant in the world, it must pay serious attention to the status of its women. Catholic women are growing tired of being ignored in this most important area of their lives, but they are still ready to step forward and assume an adult role in the Church with intelligence and grace when it is offered. It is not yet too late—but it is surely high time.[2]

Perhaps I can be forgiven for assuming that Mealey was a Catholic feminist; her support of Catholic women moving out of traditional roles is clear, as is her criticism of the hierarchy. As I moved forward with my research, however, I discovered that Margaret Mealey was not part of the Catholic feminist movement and that the NCCW was not considered a feminist organization. In fact, according to self-identified Catholic feminists, the NCCW was an antifeminist organization, dedicated to blocking the Equal Rights Amendment, curtailing abortion rights, and dominating any commission called by the bishops on the question of women's place in the church. Feminists' comments on the NCCW always seemed punctuated by a silent rolling of the eyes at best or, at worst, flashes of angry frustration at the organization's perceived backwardness. For example, the always outspoken feminist Sister Margaret Ellen Traxler once ripped into the leaders of NCCW, accusing them of being mired in the "parochial company of the Altar Society" and of possessing a "neanderthal self-image as women."[3] Taking them at their word, I classified the NCCW as a foe of the movement and turned my attention elsewhere.

More recently, I found my mind returning to the "buried talents," intrigued by the mystery surrounding Margaret Mealey's words. Why would an antifeminist write so eloquently not only of Catholic women's oppression at the hands of the Church but of her belief that Vatican II had given women "their wings"? That simple question led to some surprising conclusions, significant for both the history of American feminism and Catholic women's history in the twentieth century.

First, this story helps us better understand the complicated nature of feminism in the first years of its resurgence in the mid-1960s. The papers of the NCCW reveal that Margaret Mealey and many women in NCCW's leadership—its committee chairmen, conference speakers, editors, board of directors, and staff—did call for women's rights, leadership, and autonomy, not just in 1966 but well into the 1970s. While they did not self-identify as feminists, labeling them antifeminist is simply inaccurate and disguises the amorphous state of feminism in this period. Accepting the perspective of self-identified feminists on this issue helps conceal the willingness of moderate and even conservative women to espouse feminist ideas before the definition of "feminist" hardened into something they could no longer support. The NCCW's experience gives nuance to a historical narrative that regularly assumes that opponents of feminists' most cherished goals must have been opposed to feminism in its entirety.

The story of NCCW's feminism also helps us understand the experiences of Catholic laywomen in one of the American Church's most tumultuous periods. The National Council of Catholic Women was the official umbrella organization for local Catholic laywomen's groups at both the parish and the diocesan levels; it claimed to represent all laywomen in the United States. Therefore the NCCW provides an invaluable—and relatively rare—opportunity to investigate how rank-and-file laywomen of the American Church negotiated the simultaneous changes of Vatican II and the women's movement.

During the 1960s, the NCCW's leadership willingly, at times eagerly, transformed its organization to conform to conciliar principles. As it did so, it invited its members to evolve into a new breed of Catholic women. In support of this new ideal, NCCW leaders coaxed the rank and file to venture out of the parish hall, the altar society, and the Christmas bazaar and to seek the leadership and opportunities promised by the spirit of Vatican II. These changes were not drastic, but clearly NCCW was inclined to embrace change, not forestall it. They used the dual influences of the women's movement and Vatican II to fling open the doors to a larger world of adult responsibility, committed female leadership, and engaged spirituality. This call to empowerment, however, was not prompted by the desire to pursue a larger conservative political agenda, despite the group's official opposition to the ERA and abortion rights. Rather, it appears to have been an attempt to create a new, viable, responsive approach to Catholic womanhood, as the ground shifted beneath their feet.

Growing Up and Turning Outward

The National Council of Catholic Women was founded under the auspices of the U.S. bishops in 1920, its stated purpose being "to give Catholic women of the country a common voice and an instrument for united action."[4] At midcentury, NCCW functioned as an umbrella organization for thousands of parish-based women's groups across the country. In 1960, affiliates numbered 13,000.[5] Margaret Mealey (1912–2006) guided the organization through the transitional years at midcentury, serving as executive director of NCCW from 1949 to 1977. Due to her prominence in NCCW, Mealey was often asked to represent Catholic laywomen nationally and internationally. She served on Paul VI's Pontifical Commission on the Council of the Laity and observed at Vatican II. She also served on John F. Kennedy's Presidential Commission on the Status of Women and on the citizen advisory councils of three different presidents. Through Mealey's influential voice, NCCW women staked a claim for themselves in the broader world.

Through biennial conferences and numerous publications, the national organization provided a forum for laywomen to organize, discuss their priorities, highlight their service to the Church on the local and national levels, and foster laywomen's leadership. At midcentury, NCCW's loyalty to the nation's bishops and their policy positions was absolute, at least in its published and archived written materials. NCCW's leadership usually spoke in reverent tones when referring to the Catholic hierarchy.

As the Second Vatican Council neared, the NCCW looked much as it had in the 1950s. Publications were largely geared toward the promotion of parish-centered events and fundraising, and the NCCW continued to pursue a socially conservative agenda. For example, a Family and Parent Education Committee panel at the 1960 conference described its purpose as affirming that the "home was a worthy career for women" and instilling "respect for large families." The committee also set out "to fight the evils of artificial birth control, abortion, divorce and free love." The same conference passed a resolution supporting modesty: "The dignity of the individual woman demands that the Catholic women exert their influence in the fashion world to overcome styles which offend modesty and jeopardize virtue."[6]

The NCCW continued to view itself as an instrument of the nation's bishops. The organization's leadership spoke in very positive terms about the membership's willingness to serve in the bishops' larger program of Catholic Action. Bishops and clergymen were common keynote speakers at NCCW conferences and other programs, and they had an obvious relish for speaking to such dedicated Catholic laywomen, but their comments, meant no doubt to be supportive, could quickly veer into condescension. "My dear Catholic women," the Very Reverend Alexander Sigur told attendees of the 1960 conference, "you are really fortunate to be invited by Almighty God to join Him through the Popes and the Bishops, in the establishment of the Kingdom of Christ on earth. . . . I really congratulate you." Similarly, the Most Reverend John Spence gushed in 1964 that NCCW's president, a Council visitor, had been given "a place of honor close to [the pope's] throne."[7]

Such clerical speakers mixed their praise for the women's service with pronouncements on their essential nature. In the same address, Sigur insisted that "women must see to life, their essential domain. . . . Women must see to home and family, where they are the queens." In 1963, the Reverend Leo W. Duprey, O.P., told a group of NCCW leaders that "woman's nature represents those psychological endowments which are more or less static and without conscious motivation." The following year, the Most Reverend John Spence expounded on the theme "Woman's Particular Role" in the context of the Council. Outlining the new role of the laity, he nevertheless concluded that "perhaps what the Church needs today is more Indians. She may have enough chiefs." He encouraged the assembled women to be "privates, corporals or sergeants in the Army of Christ." Of course, the women themselves also spoke the language of essentialism. A 1963 NCCW fact sheet, "The Nature of Woman," warned that "struggles of woman for freedom have led her deeper and deeper into a state of conditions which continually frustrate her nature and her mission."[8] Such sentiments were not unusual in Catholic circles in the early 1960s, but what is so remarkable is how quickly they disappeared. NCCW's leadership was clearly ready to make a change. By 1964, such overblown essentialist rhetoric—that is, the assertion that men and women are fundamentally different and complementary—was largely absent from NCCW publications and conference proceedings.

What the membership heard instead was a new kind of talk about Catholic women, clearly inspired by Vatican II. NCCW's leadership approached the Council with great enthusiasm. Their positive response to Vatican II is all the more striking when you compare it to two other national Catholic laywomen's groups: the Catholic Daughters of the Americas and the Daughters of Isabella. These traditional fraternal organizations had a much more guarded, and at times oppositional, approach to the Council. For example, they were much less likely to promote Council reforms to their memberships.[9] The leadership of the NCCW, in contrast, displayed a committed enthusiasm, even zeal, when discussing Vatican II.

First, there was acknowledgment that Catholic women needed to get on board with the changes early or they would miss their chance. In a 1965 editorial, Margaret O'Connell urged women to "*make ourselves ready. We can so conduct our lives and prepare our minds that when the moment of change and opportunity reaches to the parish level—as it most certainly will—we shall be ready to act and to fulfill what is required of us. We must not be caught napping when the moment comes—lest we awaken to find that the moment has gone by.*"[10]

Others wrote not just of coming changes to parish or liturgy but of more profound implications. In a talk on the new liturgy at the 1964 convention, Mary Perkins Ryan spoke eloquently of the transformation Vatican II could make in the lives of women:

> No wonder the changes in the liturgy disturb many Catholics—for they constitute a call to conversion. . . . But once we realize that this is basically what the Church in our times is asking of us—to make Christ the real center of our interests; to make living His life the central drive of our lives; to meet Him and delight in Him as He reveals and gives Himself to us in the Church, in the Christian community, and then to meet Him and serve Him in 'the sacrament of the neighbor'—surely every serious Catholic will say 'Amen.'

Here we see enthusiasm mixed with a commitment to deepening women's spirituality through the Council.[11]

Those who might look to the NCCW for in-depth analysis of Council documents will come away empty-handed. For the most part, its leaders were not theologians and did not attempt close readings of the texts for the membership. They did, however, encourage members to read the documents on their own or in groups, and the 1966 conference "The New Pentecost" was dedicated to understanding the larger implications of the Council for laywomen. Overall, the NCCW's posture toward Vatican II was one of openness. In the NCCW, then, we find support for historian Mark Massa's argument that American Catholics stood ready to embrace the changes brought by the Council. In *The American Catholic Revolution: How the Sixties Changed the Church Forever,* Massa explains that American Catholics were particularly open to the central ideological shift of the Council, the acknowledgement of historical change: "Certainly Catholic Christians in the United States, where historical consciousness had won the day in so many parts of the culture . . . were ready when what Garry Wills termed the 'dirty little secret,' that the Church itself changes, was let out of the bag. . . . They had been waiting for precisely that little secret for some time."[12]

The rapidity with which the NCCW leadership embraced changes brought by the Council, and shortly thereafter began to question their own subservience to the hierarchy, suggests that these women rejected the fundamental immutability of the Church. "There is no doubt but that ten years ago, we were all oriented to the past," the chairman of the Church Communities Commission wrote in 1968. "The future, if it seemed to hold anything new and different, would just have to be re-formed and conformed to the sacred past, we thought, and our program-ming reflected that, too. . . . Today we know this is not sufficient."[13] Not until the mid-1970s do we find evidence that some members regretted the loss of the certainty that comes from unchanging tradition.

On the contrary, in the 1960s the NCCW saw itself as a key player in spreading its excitement about change by spearheading laywomen's edu-cation about the Council. In her 1966 report to the board, executive direc-tor Margaret Mealey wrote: "These are exciting times for the Church, for its members, and for its organizations. Careful thought must be given as to how we can best assist the membership in attuning itself to the Council Documents. . . . This is our challenge! We will pursue it."[14] Margaret Mary Kelly offered more practical suggestions to parish leaders in the or-ganization's primary publication *Word*. She urged local chapters to read the constitutions paragraph by paragraph and to create "a favorable climate—for understanding and acceptance of the Council's conclusions." She warned that the bishops' efforts would meet with failure "unless *we*, with sincerity and willingness, make the Council's reforms and renewals our own."[15]

If NCCW did nothing but champion the Council, one could argue that they were still operating in a preconciliar mode by simply rubber-stamping the bishops' agenda. We begin to see signs in the mid-1960s, however, that they were using Vatican II explicitly to question and chal-lenge both their traditional role in the Church and their relationship to the hierarchy. First, the documents show that NCCW's leadership believed the Council to be an invitation to reevaluate "woman's nature." For ex-ample, they interpreted the Council as a call to Catholic women to stop focusing exclusively on traditional forms of parish-level service. Discussing NCCW's revamped organizational structure in 1967, the editor of *Word* said bluntly that the new approach would have no "relation to such activi-ties as pot luck suppers, parish picnics, fashion shows, and the laundering of altar linens . . . and readers who look to *Word* for guidance and direction in these activities will continue to look in vain."[16] The older forms of ser-vice were referred to as the "little clique" and "the cozy sewing circle." As one commission chair insisted, "the new Catholic woman, God bless her, is a bridge between the Church and the World." It is worth comparing these statements to a 1962 address by John Tracy Ellis in which he called on the women of NCCW to "withstand the world's contagion."[17] In just five years, NCCW had largely abandoned the idea that Catholic women should flock to the parish to protect themselves from external threats.

Many reports and articles sought to provide an alternative to the old insular model of Catholic womanhood, one that called for openness and turning outward. At the 1964 conference, the chairman of the Spiritual Development Committee, Mary Perkins Ryan, declared:

> Catholic women need to see that the changes in the liturgy, the new shape and spirit in religious instruction, the new emphasis on our duties with regard to racial and social justice, the present developments of the Church's teaching about married love, the new emphasis on ecumenism, are all inter-related. They all open out to us and make available to us a more complete, more whole-hearted, more vital Christian life, the life to which we all are called.

Two years later, the national chairman of Organization and Development insisted that if members claimed their first duty was to their home and family, the job of the local Organization and Development chair was to "convince such women that they are placing too much emphasis on only one part of the truth." Such a statement is in striking contrast to the 1960 conference at which women were asked to protect home and family. She urged committee chairs to "raise the sights of the members, and to encourage them to reach out from their 'little world' into the 'big world.'" NCCW insisted that laywomen's call to service was larger than the home and parish hall.[18]

A second theme in the challenge to the traditional role of the Catholic woman was the exhortation that the membership grow up and assume adult responsibility in the Church. "In this day and age," Margaret Mealey asked the membership in 1970, "are we equipped to leap from our own dependency to realistic maturity?" Such a message was delivered frequently to both laymen and laywomen in the years surrounding the Council, but it held special meaning for laywomen who had traditionally been expected to surrender to the will not just of the Church but of their husbands as well. Margaret Mary Kelly neatly encapsulated the change in one long word: "The attitude of sit-with-hands-folded-until-someone-tells-me-(preferably in words of one syllable)-what-to-do-is-definitely-not-it."[19]

NCCW leaders tried to parlay this new sense of adulthood into concrete leadership opportunities. The membership was urged to get on the new parish councils and finance committees and to participate in the liturgy to the extent that they were allowed to do so, although there was certainly some naiveté about how successful women might be at this. "We can go home and get ready to get elected," one optimistic committee chair claimed at the 1966 national conference. "You know there will be a place for us," she went on. "The decrees have said so."[20]

This desire for responsibility also took the form of pointed comments about laywomen's fawning attitude toward their pastors, since challenging the ultimate authority of the clergy was a third theme in the attempt to redefine woman's role. In advising organizations on ecumenical programming, one leader commented on how she was tired of seeing "Father Smith will speak" in diocesan newspapers. "It doesn't seem to matter what Father Smith will speak on," she said. "If it comes from Father, it is bound to be religious." "Isn't it amazing," the editor of Word commented in 1968, "to realize that women, who . . . are teachers, lawyers, nurses, doctors, secretaries and manage the great institution called home . . . become simpering idiots in their communication and understanding with the parish priest?" Priests were not the only pillars of the Church under attack. At a panel on ecumenism at the 1964 conference, Rosemary Cass criticized laywomen for closed-mindedness. She claimed that the cause of this was "our own doctrinal heritage." Such public comments would have been unheard of in the mid-1950s and earlier.[21]

By the mid-1960s, then, NCCW women were becoming more attuned to the need to step outside their traditional roles, turn outward toward the world, and claim the right to leadership in the Church. They were also prepared to criticize clergy and to challenge Catholic *tradition* publicly. Since this looks, on the surface at least, like the stirrings of feminist consciousness, we must ask how much NCCW was influenced by second-wave feminism, then in its ascendency.[22]

NCCW and the Feminist Movement

Let's return, for a moment, to the original question driving this research: If Margaret Mealey and the other leaders of NCCW were antifeminist, as self-identified Catholic feminists claimed, why did they speak so eloquently about the power of the Council to liberate and empower women? This mystery proves how fruitless it is to employ such terms as "feminist" and "antifeminist," or even "moderate" or "conservative," when analyzing a time period in which such concepts were in flux.[23] It is not just that people are themselves complex and defy easy labeling. While this is true, we must also consider that the women in this story were living in a time before such ideas had hardened into labels. When Mealey made her comments about women and Vatican II in 1966, the feminist movement was just emerging in its newest incarnation and had not yet radicalized, the political right was regrouping and soon to surge, the political left was fracturing, and the Catholic Church, emerging from the close of the Council, was ripe for redefinition and experimentation.

Before exploring the limits of these labels and the exact nature of NCCW feminism, a little background is in order. Historians of second-wave feminism date the beginning of the movement to around 1963, the year Betty Friedan published her best-seller *The Feminine Mystique*. Friedan's book did not cause the movement single-handedly—second-wave feminism had its origins not only in the discontent of middle-class suburban women but also in the civil rights movement and the New Left—but it provides a handy starting point, since the book brought the movement its initial broad base of support. The Catholic feminist movement also began in 1963, but its origins were firmly rooted in the Second Vatican Council; the first Catholic feminist writers were equally inspired and infuriated by the clash between the Council's ideological promise of change for women and its actual treatment of women within the Council sessions. The Catholic feminist movement began its organizational phase in 1970, and by 1975 it included major organizations of women religious such as the Leadership Conference of Women Religious and the National Coalition of American Nuns. While many women religious flocked to the movement as their lives changed immeasurably in the wake of the Council, laywomen were less visible in Catholic feminism and were certainly underrepresented, given their numbers in the Catholic population.[24]

As we shall see, however, NCCW showed a remarkable openness to feminism in the latter half of the 1960s. This matches with the tone of Catholic feminism (and indeed the larger second wave) at that time, when the movement was in its ascendency and women across the country were hearing their first feminist ideas and finding themselves nodding in agreement. The radical wing of the larger feminist movement, and its counterpart in the Catholic movement, did not emerge until 1968. The national media seized on radicalism, highlighted its more outrageous manifestations, and painted all feminists with the same brush, causing many women who espoused more moderate ideas about equal rights to distance themselves from the term "feminist."

The media are not entirely to blame for this distancing. Radical feminists were quick to dismiss (and antagonize) women whose beliefs began and ended with straightforward liberal feminist goals such as equal pay for equal work or ending job discrimination. Around the turn of the 1970s, moreover, liberal feminists embraced two controversial goals as markers that defined a woman as a feminist: support for the Equal Rights Amendment and support for abortion rights. Regardless of what brought about the hardening of the definition of "feminist," it caused many early supporters of women's rights such as Margaret Mealey to opt out. By the early to mid-1970s, the brief window when "feminism" was fluid after a long dormancy was now closed.[25] In retrospect, we label Margaret Ellen Traxler "feminist," and Margaret Mealey "antifeminist," because the former self-identified and supported ideas that we now associate with second-wave Catholic feminists (such as the ERA, the ordination of women, and public protest), and the latter opposed the ERA, did not advocate women's entering the priesthood, and would never do anything so impolitic as to stage a rally in front of the National Conference of Catholic Bishops. But we can also see that in this time of extreme fluctuation, self-identified Catholic feminists on the political left and in the thick of the promise of renewal were actively trying to define and police the label "feminist." To Margaret Ellen Traxler, you were either on the side of the angels or you were on the side of Phyllis Schlafly; there was no in-between.

In reality, however, many women who served as the NCCW's leaders— that is, its executive director, its presidents, the chairs of its commissions, members of its board, and the editors of its publications—freely used the language of the women's movement to advocate for a change in women's status in the Catholic Church and in their roles at the national, diocesan, parish, and liturgical levels. Moreover, they used feminist rhetoric to argue for the survival of the NCCW as an autonomous women's organization. Mealey and the NCCW, however, clearly were not feminist *enough* to meet the emerging standard that would earn one the title of "feminist," not least because they still occasionally used the rhetoric of essentialism, arguing for women's essential difference. Their ideas lacked feminist theological underpinnings in any recognition of women's fundamental oppression. You would think that their call to preserve an autonomous national organization for laywomen would strike a chord, since women's autonomy and leadership was a goal these women shared, but the NCCW remained too backward on issues such as the ERA and abortion, in the eyes of self-identified feminists, to earn them a place in the sisterhood.

What is so intriguing is that Mealey did not choose to fight this battle. Despite a clear willingness to espouse feminist principles in the press in the mid-1960s, and with her own membership well into the 1970s, she ceded the label "feminist" to others. She agreed to stay on the other side of the fence, occasionally speaking of avoiding "militancy" and those "so-called 'Catholic' feminists," the mid-1970s equivalent of the now familiar "I'm not a feminist, but . . ." Eventually Mealey participated in the hardening of the labels by opting not to claim the title "feminist" for herself and her organization, despite her continued quiet—and ideologically complex—advocacy for women's rights in the Church and society.

The Nature of NCCW Feminism

What did feminism look like in the context of the NCCW? The first thing that strikes a researcher in the NCCW papers of this period is the sheer number of articles on feminist issues and the openly feminist articles in NCCW's primary magazine, *Word*. In 1967, the NCCW hired a young editor fresh from the recently launched, and quite liberal, *National Catholic Reporter*, hoping to use their own magazine as a more provocative platform to push their membership forward.[26] It featured many articles on social-justice issues, including women's rights. An NCCW member could read about the emerging female theologians, feminist biblical exegesis, or the first Catholic feminist monograph, *The Illusion of Eve*, all with a positive spin. Sarcastic comments on the editorial pages about blatant discrimination against women in the Church were not uncommon. In 1967, the magazine even featured a very evenhanded roundtable on Catholics and abortion rights, leaving readers with the surprising suggestion that intelligent Catholic women could differ on the subject.[27]

NCCW conferences and periodicals featured numerous self-identified feminist contributors from the 1960s through the mid-1970s. These included Sidney Callahan, author of *The Illusion of Eve*; Sally Cunneen, author of the sociological study *Sex: Female, Religion: Catholic*; and Frances McGillicuddy, founder of the American section of the Saint Joan's International Alliance, the first Catholic feminist organization in the United States. The most important of these contributors, though, was Arlene Swidler, editor of the *Journal of Ecumenical Studies*. Swidler was a woman who not only served the NCCW faithfully but also had her hand in nearly every Catholic feminist group in the 1960s and early 1970s— including the radical ones. She first appears in the proceedings of the 1968 conference as the only married woman listed under her own name (as opposed to "Mrs. Leonard Swidler," the style followed by all the other married women presenters), so presumably she made a special request to be identified by her given name.

Swidler wrote impassioned articles about embracing Vatican II as chairman of the Church Communities Commission, and in *Word* she encouraged members to "Make Theology Your Business." It was clear that she was an ardent feminist, and yet the NCCW still named her editor of *Word* in 1970. One of the first things she did as editor was to publish an article on the brand-new movement to ordain Catholic women as deacons. An inset on the side of the article gave directions to local leaders on how to plan a program on women and the Church, including extending an invitation to an ordained woman minister or deacon to speak to their affiliate. While she did not hold the post long, she clearly did not cut ties with the organization. When NCCW unveiled a new magazine, *Catholic Woman*, in 1975, its cover story featured Arlene Swidler on feminist liturgies, a subject that could not even have been fathomed just ten years earlier.[28]

Despite these prominent Catholic feminists who made occasional appearances, NCCW's publications rarely featured blazingly feminist rhetoric; even Arlene Swidler toned down her feminism for her audience. What we find, then, in NCCW publications and conferences as a whole during this period is a mild but still recognizable form of feminism, one of whose primary characteristics was a tendency to temper it in some way so as not to appear too radical. A prime example of this appears in "Children, Church,—and Lib" (1971), an article by Theodora Briggs Sweeney, who opened with this provocative sentence: "Traditional Marian piety has affected the Catholic woman's self-image badly." The author went on to claim that the male-dominated society was harmful to girls and boys, and to priests who were kept from "reaching their full human potential." She discussed the ideas of several prominent Catholic feminist writers, including the theologian Rosemary Ruether, and concluded that "after listening to these women, it seems as if we have reached a point from which there is no turning back." Yet she felt the need to add the caveat that "while there are, of course, the radical, bra-burning man-haters, none of the women quoted here would fall into this category." Her bona fides established, she felt free to end with a quotation from the favorite Bible verse of Catholic feminists: Galatians 3:28 ("In Christ . . . there are no distinctions between Jew and Greek, slave and free, male and female, but all of you are one in Christ Jesus").[29]

A second example of tempered feminist rhetoric comes from a conference talk in 1966 by Mrs. John Paddenburg. She related a disturbing story about a Mass, held as part of the meeting for a women's organization, at which she and another woman were asked to bring up the Offertory gifts. As they reached the foot of the sanctuary and prepared to hand the gifts to the bishop presider, the priest acting as the master of ceremonies stepped in behind them and hissed in a loud voice, "Don't you women dare put your feet in that sanctuary." Reflecting on this incident, she commented, "You think, 'when are we going to have our chance?'" But she went on to say, "I would request that you remember that time heals all wounds. This might be good to bear in mind in case our feminine feathers get ruffled. . . . So please don't be impatient."[30]

In addition to tempering their rhetoric so as not to ruffle feathers (those of others, and their own), NCCW feminists wrestled with the concepts of female essentialism and complementarity well beyond the time when self-identified Catholic feminists had rejected such concepts. While some might maintain that this made them less "feminist," I would instead argue that their persistent wrestling with the essentialism of their Catholic past made the nature of their feminism more complex.

When we discuss essentialism, it is vital to remember how much change these women were experiencing in so short a time. This change manifested itself in concrete ways (women experienced the Mass in a fundamentally different, more participatory way) and more amorphous ways (women were asked to question their identities, how they expressed their spirituality, and their vocations). In a world in which everything seemed to be in flux, these women were now being told, by their own leaders, that what they had been taught was their very essence was no longer true. No wonder Mrs. Louis Sweterlitsch went out of her way to assure the gathered members at the 1968 conference that "we are still the same women, the same persons, part of the same people of God. . . . We find the same women with the same loving hearts yearning to serve God with love and to reflect God's love to our fellowmen."[31]

It remained a tricky proposition, for those with an affinity for feminism but an unwillingness to make a complete break with the past, to determine what exactly of the old identity to discard and what to keep. Some tried to reject essentialism, others to downplay it. Still others tentatively embraced essentialism as proof of why women needed their own autonomous organizations; without them, women's special talents and leadership styles would be lost. A full range of these approaches can be seen in the papers of the NCCW between 1964 and 1975. What is clear, however, is that few leaders in NCCW after 1964 espoused or disseminated pure essentialist ideas as they so commonly did before then. Whatever their approach to the question of women's difference and complementarity, feminism had certainly left its mark.

Some writers had no trouble rejecting the notion of female difference outright, on the grounds that it was both untrue and harmful to women. One of the most eloquent denials of essentialism came from Lillian O'Connor in 1967. In a *Word* article, she described the old identity, focusing not on the trope that "woman's place is in the home" but on the persistent idea that women focus on the details to the detriment of larger ideas and, as a result, come to doubt their own abilities in the larger world: "Confused by the clamor of society . . . we generally have been content to let the world plunge on, steeling ourselves against every challenge, refusing to see the whole picture, busying ourselves with details until details themselves loom larger than ideas . . . Always the focus has been on the unimportant." She concluded that women were tired of being revered only if they limited themselves. The needs of the world were too great to perpetuate women's doubts about their own abilities. "As Catholic women no choice is given to us," Mrs. Louis H. Sweterlitsch wrote in 1968. "We must take up the leadership role." If leadership was not a choice for the new Catholic woman, everything else seemed to be for Joanne Moran, the editor of *Word*, in 1969: "Never before has the individual woman had more freedom to choose the manner in which she wishes to respond to change, and in so doing, to choose the type of person she wishes to become." She can be open and constructive, Moran argued, or she can follow "the more comfortable . . . course and passively drift along the surface of life."[32]

Moran is a great example of how NCCW leaders wrestled with essentialism. The following year, she wrote an editorial introduction to a special issue of *Word* focused on the role of women. She began with a clear feminist statement: "Remember that every individual, regardless of race, sex, or religion, has a right to equality of opportunity, a right to develop her potential to the fullest . . . This principle is at the core of the various women's liberation movements whether radical left or middle establishment." After criticizing "women's lib" for its style ("It is true that many of our brethren could approach the subject in a less distasteful and more sophisticated way"), she went on to state a very curious hybrid affirmation/denial of women's difference. "The intelligent woman seldom permits herself to be categorized," she wrote. "In fact, she has the 'knack' for performing all the roles traditionally and erroneously assigned to the list of 'masculine' traits while still retaining her femininity and charm." She added that "if women's liberation is to succeed, its members should note that the badly needed demasculinization of our institutions does not mean the masculinization of themselves." So a woman was the same in that she had the same traits as men, but she was different in that she had a unique feminine nature (and charm!) that she must retain. The membership might be forgiven if they emerged from this editorial more confused about feminism and women's identity than when they started.[33]

NCCW leaders, then, could reject essentialism in the name of feminism or affirm feminism and difference in the same breath. Some made a claim for women's difference outright, without the connotations of subservience and self-denial so common before Vatican II and the emergence of second-wave feminism. Their arguments reflected the idea that women had a unique way of doing business, which made the existence of women leaders and women's organizations essential in the modern world. Women tended to be "both synthetic and practical," one committee chair claimed. A report on the importance of women's organizations concluded that they preserve "those qualities of organizational life which are uniquely feminine," such as nurturing women leaders and paying attention to the people without power. While the author cautioned women against being "duped" into thinking they must give all to their families, he also warned NCCW against going to the other "extreme" advocated by feminists—namely, integrating with men.[34]

In 1968, the NCCW board of directors made an official statement on "the Identity of NCCW as a Woman's Organization," in which essentialist rhetoric freely flowed. The board argued that "the way women work" must be highlighted and preserved, including such traits as the tendency to nurture growing things, following projects through to completion, valuing committee work, and a commitment to climbing the organizational leadership ladder. Most important, women nurtured other women's potential and focused on community concerns. By the same token, the more unsavory side of "the way women work"—manipulation—emerged in "Cooperation with Vatican II," an article by Margaret Mary Kelly. "And remember," she wrote, "in this as in all things to use the 'feminine method;' not charging into the rectory with crusader banners flying, but the gentle (and persistent reminder)—'Father, do you think maybe if . . . ,' 'as you mentioned recently, Father (even if he didn't, he probably meant to!) . . ." Under patriarchy, manipulation had always been the resort of those, particularly women, who were without power, but even in a world where the NCCW had opened itself to feminist principles, old habits were hard to break.[35]

The key to understanding the NCCW's approach to feminism is a remarkable report written by Margaret Mealey for the organization's fiftieth anniversary in 1970. Published in *Word*, for the NCCW membership, the report defined a mild pragmatic form of feminism that reflected both the leadership's desire for justice and its aversion to self-identified feminist activity. What we learn from this document is that NCCW supported justice for women while rejecting organized feminism; that NCCW leaders considered Vatican II and women's rights to be strongly linked; and, perhaps most significant, that the NCCW viewed the confluence of Vatican II and women's rights as a means of securing women's leadership and autonomy at a time when the continued existence of separate women's organizations was under threat.[36]

First, the report makes a clear statement about the NCCW's relationship to feminism. "There can be no differentiation between male and female," Mealey wrote, "no unequal consideration and treatment, no relegation to demeaning roles." As we have seen with other leaders in the NCCW, however, she made an effort to distance herself from the people she thought of as feminists: "Certainly such drastic action as the revolution being staged by some secular and 'Catholic' organizations of women, the women's liberation front, and other militant groups, to draw attention to their treatment as second-class citizens is not the way chosen by all to highlight inequities." Note that she does not take issue with their beliefs, only their approach. She went on to say, "Because we acknowledge [that equal dignity has] long been denied, NCCW is deeply committed to the goal of helping women achieve their full stature, in justice and with an equal measure of dignity." As was true of much NCCW literature from the mid-1960s to the early 1970s, Mealey explicitly linked feminism and Vatican II reforms:

> Vatican II recognized women as persons possessing full dignity, and as having inherent rights to develop and perfect their natural and supernatural qualities. The documents state that no longer need woman's identity as a person be submerged because of her role as wife and mother. Her whole person must be developed to the fullest, so she may make the unique contribution she was meant to make, in the community and in the world, as well as in her family and in her parish.[37]

It could be argued that Mealey made such a connection to defend her position against those in the Church who might object to feminist beliefs, but I believe that the link served a larger purpose. Mealey tried to use both the language of Vatican II and of feminism to achieve her ultimate goal of autonomy for Catholic women's organizations at a moment when their continued viability was in doubt. By 1970, the NCCW was hemorrhaging members, losing 1,100 affiliated organizations in 1969 alone. In an unrelated development, NCCW was faced with the possibility of merging with the National Council of Catholic Men. Many in the leadership of the National Conference of Catholic Bishops and the United States Catholic Conference could not see the purpose of retaining separate organizations for men and women at a time when new possibilities for mixed lay organizations were emerging.[38] The bishops were also aware that support for traditional Catholic women's organizations was on the decline. Mealey had strong doubts about the merger, not only because she believed in women's autonomy but because the NCCM did not function on the same scale as did the NCCW. The former existed mainly as an advocacy group and did not have a large or active membership. She feared that NCCW's authority and purpose would be lost if it were forced to merge with NCCM.

Mealey's report must be read in the context of these two problems. It begins with a discussion of the upcoming national conference, the theme of which was "Celebrate Life! Choose Life!" This was a reference, not to abortion, but to the very existence of the organization. As Mealey noted quite frankly, "In this climate of change, and in this transitional period, NCCW's organizational strength has suffered." Listen, then, to how she interweaves feminism, the vital and continued importance of women's leadership, and the Council's mandate to open the Church to the world:

> Are we significantly equipped to bring the Church to the world? . . .
> Can women's organizations adjust to the new pattern? Is the NCCW
> leadership content to sit outside new structures, ignoring uneven or
> unequal representation of women in them, or sometimes no represen-
> tation at all? As women, are we secure enough to take our place, our
> rightful place, as an essential segment of the people of God?[39]

Was the leadership of NCCW, under Mealey's direction, moving forward as stealth feminists, flying under everyone's radar? Not exactly. Mealey wrote a second version of her report, this time for the board of directors, in which she tweaked her definition of NCCW feminism significantly: "Women must be encouraged, not to pursue equal rights, as such, but to take their place in society, as persons with dignity . . . with an opportunity to contribute what has been not only their experience but the particular temperament and complementary nature which women bring to the whole of society." It is unclear to me why Mealey spoke of complementarity in one document and seemed to reject it in the other. She may have been trying to appeal to a more conservative segment of the board with the second report, but it is more likely that this was the nature of Mealey's pragmatic feminism (or at least how she chose to interpret that feminism for the organization). The most important object for her was promoting and preserving women's leadership and autonomy. To gain it she would argue either position.[40]

We can view her approaches not as inconsistent but as logical responses to the situation with which she was faced. She strongly believed that separate women's organizations brought something unique to the table. Unfortunately, they had been stymied in the past by discrimination within the Church. The women's movement provided the impetus to challenge that discrimination. Mealey embraced that challenge, but the women's movement also insisted that all-female organizations such as the NCCW—with its parliamentary procedure, its white gloves, and bishops as keynote speakers—were out of date and on the way out. Despite the NCCW's efforts to reform itself for the new, postconciliar world, it could not make changes fast enough to attract the young women of the rising generation, for fear of alienating their core constituencies. By mixing moderate feminist statements, denials of "militant" activism, and comforting reassurance about women's nature, Mealey seemed to be trying to strike a balance that would allow the work of the NCCW to continue.

The Membership and Antifeminist Backlash

The term "leadership" has been used throughout this study when discussing the NCCW's response to Vatican II and women's liberation, but how did the rank-and-file membership respond? Such a response can be difficult to gauge, owing to a dearth of sources, as much more information flowed from the leadership to the membership than the reverse. Surely many ordinary members would have supported their leaders' interpretation of Vatican II (and feminism) as welcome catalysts for redefining Catholic women's roles and identities, but the vast majority did not respond to the national office in writing, and we can assume that many of them chose not to write because their leaders' efforts did not alarm them.

Some members did find their leaders' positions alarming, however, and manifested a definite strain of antifeminism. The first indication of a lack of enthusiasm about the new programming initiatives began in the mid to late 1960s. The NCCW leadership often noted that the membership needed prodding to embrace reform and that no one seemed to be responding to their efforts. *Word* editor Margaret O'Connell described "the uncomfortable feeling, probably akin to what an all-night radio announcer must occasionally feel, that . . . there is nobody 'out there' listening."[41] It did not help, of course, that the perception of NCCW leaders that their members were unsophisticated and difficult to prod forward undoubtedly filtered down to the membership.

For example, in 1970 the writer of a letter to the editor of *Word* complained about a change of format that emphasized substantive articles on justice and theological issues over "Program Pictures," which chronicled the doings of local affiliates. "Our Catholic women are hungry for growth at this time but let's keep the food *within their reach!*" the writer argued. The editor responded condescendingly. "Learning always involves a *reaching* or striving toward something before it is grasped," she explained. "WORD operates on the premise that our women *care enough* to exert the energy toward perpetual growth as persons. . . . A format filled with program pictures is not the answer." Perhaps more charitably, a local organizer observed that "our women are not terribly sophisticated, but they are truly the 'salt of the earth' and I sometimes think that perhaps part of our problem is that we have not challenged them enough."[42]

Responses from the rank and file in the form of letters to the editor indicate that many women had been challenged quite enough, thank you very much, and did not care for the results. The writer of a 1969 letter to the editor was frank: "About the nature of woman—our job is not out fighting poverty but rather in our homes preparing our husbands and our children with the means to reach heaven." Later that year, the writer of another letter simmered with anger. "Please send *Word* to Mrs. ——," she wrote. "It's too liberal for me to take. . . . Fr. Beckman's article on revision of Canon Law so women can work as priests, etc. should not be published by NCCW. *Word*, I hope, will someday have something to help us spread *God's* message, not someone's political ideas." "I'm ashamed to show it to any women," another member wrote.[43]

Conference evaluations also provide a rare window into the opinions of women in the pews. The 1968 national conference elicited some strong responses. "God help the poor affiliations who have to listen to these reports," one woman wrote, "provided their representatives can find something that won't shock. . . . Let the laity stick to their knitting and let the appointed clergymen run their end of the business." "Rather than clear the air for definite guidelines," another commented, "our women are more confused than when they left home." A third conference attendee tells us that the NCCW was trying to innovate in the area of liturgy as well, and this member was not pleased: "One such hand clapping Mass would have been more than enough." Such comments were balanced by positive responses, but in the few places where we see the membership allowed a significant voice, many do express opposition to the changes they were being asked to make, in the areas both of politics and of personal identity.[44]

The rank-and-file membership is not the only place where we find a strain of antifeminism within the organization. The opposition of the board of directors to the ERA in the 1970s was interpreted by many outside the organization as an antifeminist position. From 1956 onward, NCCW consistently opposed the ERA, on the grounds that it would eliminate special protections for women, although by the 1970s the leadership protested that its opposition was not indicative of hostility to women's rights. A report from the 1972 general assembly illuminates this issue. During a question-and-answer session with then-president Bernice Zilly, several members apparently questioned NCCW's official position on the ERA. Zilly replied that the women should just read the copy of "a superb article on the ERA" recommended by Bishop Harrison found in their conference packet. "It will be helpful for anyone who has to stand up and give the reasons why the NCCW has taken this stand and our position to this particular amendment," she added. She did not leave the subject, however, before insisting "we must keep stressing the fact that this is just an amendment, because we are not opposed to equal rights for women."[45]

In hindsight, one can see why NCCW members were uncertain about the ERA and what they should do about it. The NCCW's board of directors made strong position statements against the ERA, yet its president tempered this position with feminist rhetoric while speaking to its members. We also know that Margaret Mealey produced for the board one document that included a section espousing essentialism and yet omitted that section in her version of the document for the membership. It would appear, then, that the organization in the first half of the 1970s was divided on the issues of the ERA and feminism.

Further evidence for this division comes in 1974, when a tantalizing entry appears in the board minutes: "Motion made and seconded that a letter of commendation and encouragement be sent to Mrs. Phyllis Schlafly for the work she has done in her opposition to ERA." The motion was followed in the minutes by this note: "The committee felt that some of [Mrs. Schlafly's] statements were inaccurate and the motion failed."[46] That same year, the executive committee was also split over the matter of the International Woman's Year (IWY), to be celebrated in 1975. At the

1974 conference, the executive committee wrote a draft statement in support of IWY, and it contained clear essentialist language:

> The National Council of Catholic Women endorses in general the theme of International Women's Year, which is 'equality, development and peace,' and will cooperate in the program of activities proposed by the Economic and Social Council to implement the principles proclaimed in the United Nations General Assembly to evaluate the status of women throughout the world. . . . The NCCW believes that the greatest contribution most women can make to development is to fulfill their role as wives and mothers.

But when the resolution was brought to the general assembly for a vote, the language had been changed substantially: "While strongly supporting the need to elevate the status of women throughout the world, NCCW believes that equality, development and peace are best achieved when women pursue their individual roles in the home and society with honesty and integrity." The statement added that women should seek holiness in "whatever role they perceive as their particular call from God."[47]

The effect of these divisions, both among the leadership and the membership, was that NCCW did not emerge as a potent organizational force pursuing "conservative" women's goals in the 1970s or the 1980s. While NCCW opposed the ERA, the membership was not urged to fight the ERA in any organized way, and it was not a major part of the NCCW agenda. If the membership had been encouraged to take to the streets (or the halls of Congress) against the amendment, some evidence of it would appear in the publications or program initiatives, but it does not. This finding is significant because NCCW, if it was indeed as conservative as Catholic feminists believed, would have been in a prime position to take advantage of the growth of right-leaning women's organizations at this time, especially that of fellow Catholic Phyllis Schlafly, the Eagle Forum. NCCW leaders were in position to ride the wave of the growing "Moral Majority" coalition if they wanted to, but they did not, even as membership continued to fall.[48]

Instead, members were treated to a slate of mixed messages in 1975, reflecting the organization's ongoing confusion over women's role and its lack of a concrete agenda on women in the Church. There is some evidence that the organization's leadership, and membership, had swung more firmly to the right by 1975. For example, a resolution from the 1975 conference is a patchwork of feminist but ultimately essentialist ideas. The first line alone would have been incredibly confusing for anyone with even a cursory knowledge of feminist theology: "Whereas, men and women were created to complement each other, 'male and female He created them,' and firmly believing in Paul's statement that there is no distinction between 'Jew and Greek, male and female' . . . be it resolved that the NCCW fully respond to Christ's expectations of the ministries of women in the life of His Church, recognizing their special talents and abilities."[49]

The resolution's authors here mixed the notion of complementarity with the two Bible passages used most often by feminists to claim that it was not to complement each other that men and women were created. They then affirmed the limits on women's ministries (most likely a response to the first women's-ordination conference, to be held later that same month), yet they claimed that they would "continue to inaugurate programs that will strengthen women's positions in the Church." A member reading this resolution, and thinking back to the article on feminist liturgies in the first issue of the organization's new magazine that same year, might wonder what message she was supposed to take to heart. One can hear the desperate desire for direction in a resolution, to "reaffirm Mary," that was introduced at the 1974 general assembly: "Mrs. Rita Burke reminded the assembly that Mary never lost her way. Maybe some of us did in the last difficult years, but Mary never did."

Conclusion

Margaret Mealey's feminist statements in 1966 were not an anomaly. Her desire to promote justice, equality, leadership, and new roles for Catholic women was expressed consistently over time. The primary point of confusion is why someone who rejected the label "feminist" would continue to espouse feminist statements in public. The answer can be found at the intersection of the feminist movement and the Second Vatican Council at a time of extraordinary change for American Catholic laywomen.

Margaret Mealey and the leadership of the National Council of Catholic Women believed in the power of the Second Vatican Council to transform their church. They embraced what they considered to be the promise of renewal: an energizing force that would call Catholics to a world outside their comfortable parishes and their everyday experience. They craved a challenge that would move them beyond complacency to a new revitalized spirituality. Yet Mealey believed that promise would go unfulfilled without a change in the identity of Catholic women. For their own part, laywomen needed to turn outward to embrace the call of adult discipleship. They needed to reject their traditional subservience, but such openness would not be possible without the simultaneous demand for justice. Mealey therefore turned to a moderate form of feminism, one that self-identified feminists were reluctant to acknowledge, to liberate Catholic laywomen and promote their leadership so that they might respond to the call for renewal. In the end, NCCW demonstrates that if we as historians look only to self-identified feminists to understand the women's liberation movement, we will miss those who fell beyond "feminism's" parameters. In the heyday of second-wave feminism and the excitement following the Council, NCCW created a new vision for Catholic womanhood, using the language and ideology, if not the identity, of the feminist movement.

9   Who Will Guard the Guardians?

*Church Government and the Ecclesiology
of the People of God, 1965–1969*

JEREMY BONNER

For a brief interval between 1965 and 1969, a vocal body of Catholic laypeople n the United States sought to apply the new theology of the People of God, articulated at the Second Vatican Council, to the sphere of Church governance. Where earlier forms of lay activism had accepted the necessary subordination of ecclesiastical structures to clerical leadership, those of the late 1960s frequently embraced what might be termed a democratic ecclesiology, which had particular resonance both in the former center of Catholic devotional life, the parish, and in the organizational nexus of the wider life of the Church, the diocese. While it is doubtful that the priorities of most American Catholics included either the creation of parish councils answerable to the congregation or the obligation of their bishop to conduct diocesan referenda on the permissibility of birth control, the significance of this debate for the Catholic Church in the United States should not be underestimated. Even as the National Council of Catholic Women emphasized the limits of complementarity in wider American society and Catholic civil-rights activists challenged the presumptions of racial segregation, those who promoted the new vision of the People of God in parish and diocese posed a corresponding threat to the very essence of Church order.

It is a commonplace today for critics of the episcopal hierarchy to denounce the Church for preaching the virtues of lay responsibility while continuing to deny them a share in the *management* of power.[1] Such a critique first gained traction in the immediate aftermath of Vatican II, but while most Catholic laypeople understood democratic structures to be a central feature of American Protestant ecclesiology, few appreciated the degree of political conflict that such an approach invariably engendered. Majoritarian democracy, moreover, was no necessary assurance of support for other progressive causes. When the priest at St. Stephen's Church in McKeesport, Pennsylvania, sought to extend the hand of fellowship to the town's Negro community in 1968, he faced an angry reaction that left him unsure of the consequences of putting the matter to a vote. "If I were to present the question to our parish committee whether or not we should open our school to the poor, which in this case means a poor population predominantly Negro," he admitted, "I do not know whether I would receive support. So now in a democratic setup such as represented as the parish committee, what do you do?"[2] It was a poignant question.

Perhaps understandably, the practical implications of the theology of the People of God were contested from the moment *Apostolicam Actuositatem* (Decree on the Apostolate of the Laity) burst onto the world in November 1965. Even though most conciliar documents continued to emphasize the ultimate authority of the ecclesiastical hierarchy, laypeople already active in the Church laid increasing emphasis on references to consultation by priests of their congregations and by bishops of their dioceses.[3] Initially, however, even progressive priests struggled with the concept of consultation. "There are few fully developed intellectually grounded authentic profound Christians in the Church (including priests, I must add)," a priest in the Diocese of Oklahoma City and Tulsa sardonically informed Bishop Victor Reed in 1964. "You could not trust the care of the material Church to them, especially since it is so intricately connected with the spiritual mission of the Church."[4]

Becoming American: The Church, the People and the Bishops

Father Nerin's dismissive verdict of those consigned to his pastoral care must be understood in terms of the preceding 170 years of American Catholicism, which commenced dramatically enough with an unprecedented papal authorization for the election—by his clergy—of John Carroll, the first Catholic bishop in English-speaking North America, in 1789. "Carroll's vision," wrote historian James Hennesey in 1981, "was of a local church in communion with the bishop and see of Rome (a communion which he always emphasized as essential), but internally autonomous, self-perpetuating and free of the least taint of foreign jurisdiction."[5] Thirty years later, John England, the bishop of Charleston, South Carolina, took some tentative steps to foster lay consultation with the hierarchy, but the system lapsed at his death.[6]

Such innovations demonstrated the possibilities of enhanced lay participation, but they would not long endure. Bolstered by the growing numbers of European-born clergy who arrived in the United States after 1840 and alarmed by the inclination of certain Catholic congregations to assert their autonomy, the American bishops soon reasserted the principle that all church property inhered in the person of the diocesan bishop and that the incumbent pastor of a congregation—chosen by the bishop— was the supreme authority in matters parochial.[7] By 1870, the American Catholic Church, largely composed as it was of poorly educated immigrants from Eastern and Southern Europe, was considered more loyal to ecclesiastical authority at all levels than almost any other part of the Church Catholic.

Prior to the First World War, lay Catholics tended to find themselves shut out of the debates concerning the creation of a more democratic political order, and the wider Protestant culture offered little incentive to do otherwise. The general perception of Catholic voters (particularly the Irish) as creatures of the urban political machines (invariably viewed as corrupt) persuaded many American Protestants that Catholic voters could not be considered an informed voting bloc. From the outbreak of the Civil War to the election of Woodrow Wilson as president in 1912, American Catholics stood accused of susceptibility to authoritarianism not only in their politics but in the government of their church, owing allegiance to a pope (Pius IX) who was the byword for illiberalism in Europe, and subservient to the direct rule of bishops and priests.[8]

In the forty years that followed the signing of the Treaty of Versailles in 1918, however, Catholic America blossomed. Declining ties with Europe, greater access to higher education, the collapse during the 1930s of much of the mutual-aid system that had previously underpinned Catholic life, and the rise of a new alliance of Catholic-dominated industrial unions with the New Deal state all contributed to the decline of the Catholic ghetto.[9] From the Catholic elite who joined the Catholic Club of the City of New York, documented by Patrick Hayes, to the San Francisco labor activists so eloquently described by Bill Issel, American Catholics entered the political mainstream.[10] Such secular developments were accompanied by profound changes in the lay Catholic world. From the radical personalism of Dorothy Day's Catholic Worker movement to the exuberant activism of the Young Christian Students and the Christian Family Movement

(CFM), the flagship Catholic Action body of postwar suburbia, Catholic laypeople experimented with forms of religious life in which the clergy's leadership role was either muted or absent.[11] As Catholic parishes became increasingly less insulated from the Christian communities around them, the question arose as to whether the hallowed lay commitment merely to "pray, pay, and obey" was still valid. If not, what model of participation should replace it?

Historically, while American priests and bishops had from time to time sought the advice of prominent laymen, such consultations were generally on a one-to-one basis and carried with them no implication that laypeople were anything more than sources of practical information. The activities of Archbishops Hayes of New York and Mitty of San Francisco in the 1920s and 1930s, respectively, discussed earlier in this volume, demonstrate the point remarkably well. For Hayes and Mitty, Catholic Action was a well-ordered auxiliary that received its directions from the chancery and had little if any scope for independent action. The American Church, however, was already in a state of flux, as the Catholic middle class increasingly deserted the close-knit inner-city Catholic neighborhoods for more diverse suburban communities. While as late as 1968 the bishop of Pittsburgh might rail against class differentiation by and among Catholics,[12] the new middle class, composed largely of assimilated, native-born, and third-generation American Catholics, had ideas of its own. The Catholic intellectual revival that, as Katharine Harmon points out, made the move of the publishing house of Sheed and Ward from Britain to the United States a viable strategy carried with it the seeds of future dissent.[13]

For the Catholic Church in Europe—particularly conservative prelates in Italy and Spain—democratic politics in any form was anathema, not merely because it raised the specter of Communist triumph at the ballot box but because it threatened the Church's privileged status in majority-Catholic countries. While the Church tolerated Catholic deference to the principle of religious pluralism in countries where Catholics constituted a minority, such tolerance could not be permitted elsewhere. Even in the United States, as late as 1922, no less a figure than Monsignor John A. Ryan, later the symbol of Catholic intellectual commitment to the New Deal, argued that the "Catholic State" could logically "tolerate only such religious activities as were confined to the members of [non-Catholic sects]. It could not permit them to carry on general propaganda nor accord their organization certain privileges that had formerly been extended to all religious corporations, for example, exemption from taxation."[14]

By the early 1960s such views were no longer in vogue and Catholic conservatives watched with horror as the American hierarchy, to a man, pressed on the Second Vatican Council the principles of religious pluralism that came to be expressed in *Dignitatis Humanae* (Declaration on Religious Freedom). The former could not begin to appreciate what little appetite American Catholics, all too aware of how much more threatening the Protestant majority would have been if vested with state power, had for religious establishment. Indeed, when the phrase "regrettable separation" (referring to the separation of church and state) appeared in a document generated by the papal curia in 1963, the bishop of Oklahoma City and Tulsa, Victor Reed, commented that this "would not be an expression of the true feeling of the American hierarchy or American Catholics."[15] Nor could the charge plausibly be leveled that religious pluralism had sapped the vitality of the American Catholic masses. "It is not our people who miss Mass on Sunday, refuse the sacraments and vote the Communist ticket," thundered Bishop Steven Leven of San Angelo to his brother bishops. "We have not lost the working class. They are the foundation and support of the Church."[16]

It was scarcely surprising that endorsement by the American Church of religious pluralism would subsequently provoke a debate over self-government. Since the Revolution, American Protestants had fought not merely for the establishment of secular political democracy but for the development of ecclesiastical structures through which the laypeople might exert some influence over the day-to-day life of their respective denominations. By contrast, American Catholicism's early experiments with lay participation had proved less than happy, at least from the hierarchy's perspective, and few bishops prior to the 1940s showed much enthusiasm for devolving power, even at the parochial level. As early as 1963, however, Bishop John Wright of Pittsburgh derided the idea that the "Catholic Church is a 'clerical' church, as the expression goes, while the so-called Reformed Churches are churches somehow more suited to laymen."[17] With the emergence of an educated Catholic middle class, the American Church was obliged to confront the question of whether, and, if so, to what extent, to open up its counsels to the laity.

When the bishop of Pittsburgh addressed his newly formed diocesan Pastoral Council on June 17, 1967, it was evident that he was visibly struggling to control his emotions. "I need hardly say," he told the assembled delegates, "how deeply moved I am to open this first Pastoral Council in the Diocese of Pittsburgh and on this scale and with the magnitude of these objectives, the first, I think, in the United States and, therefore, in all probability, anywhere in the post-council church. I am aware, as are you, that in many Dioceses there have been appointed Pastoral Councils but the key word is *appointed*."[18] Wright's satisfaction was reflected by certain other members of the hierarchy, including his predecessor John Dearden, whose decade of service in Pittsburgh had earned him the sobriquet "Iron John" but who was, in the words of historian Leslie Tentler, "transformed by the Council—by exposure to a global church in all its variety, and new ideas too."[19] In 1966, Dearden announced plans for an archdiocesan planning board with lay and clergy representation, affirmed the right of laypeople to oversee the finances, the liturgy, and the education programs of their parishes through elected councils, and called for a synod to discuss reforms at the archdiocesan level.[20] Ten years later, Dearden would preside over the Call to Action conference in Detroit, considered by many progressive Catholics to mark the high point of lay interaction with the American hierarchy.[21]

Bishop Wright cannot have been unconscious of the irony of Dearden's epiphany. "Bishop Deaden," he explained, "left behind him a disciplined, united and justly proud Diocesan organization. Very early in my own term here it struck me as desirable that we lose no part of the blessings of discipline, unity and organization, but I did have the feeling that it was a trifle highly centralized and that it would be better gradually and quietly to deploy responsibility and especially with an increase of the lay voice and lay expertise."[22] Wright had also undergone something of a transformation in his attitude toward the laity, for while he had pioneered structural reform at the diocesan level during his years as bishop of Worcester, Massachusetts, his principal object had been the reduction of the power of the pastors of large parishes.[23]

Like Dearden, Wright had been greatly affected by the atmosphere of the Council (and possibly by the writings of Council peritus Father George Tavard), though he would not always prove as accommodating toward the laity as would the archbishop of Detroit.[24] Elected to serve on the Council's theological commission, which helped formulate *Lumen Gentium* (Dogmatic Constitution on the Church), Wright chaired the subcommittee drafting the fourth chapter on the laity. Of that chapter, he would declare publicly that it "will lay a solid foundation for authentic Catholic Action and will dissipate the prevailing erroneous impression that the Church is exclusively 'clerical.'" The bishop of Pittsburgh also understood it to be his duty to convey to European audiences the nature of Catholic American understanding of the Council and set a frenetic pace delivering addresses at seminaries and to national hierarchies as well conducting newspaper and radio interviews.[25]

In an environment very different from that of industrial Pittsburgh, the bishop of Oklahoma City and Tulsa reached much the same conclusions as did his Rust Belt brother in Christ. First exposed to the currents of Catholic Action while a student at the University of Louvain in the late 1930s, where he was a contemporary of Catholic Action pioneer and Oklahoma priest Don Kanaly (the founder of the first Young Christian Workers cell in the United States), Victor Reed emerged as one of the most permissive bishops in the American hierarchy during the early 1960s.[26] Although he underwent no violent epiphany on the subject of lay participation, Reed presided over one of the more dynamic Midwestern conciliar experiments and could boast his own "Little Council" as one of the fruits of the renewal era.

The experiences of bishops such as Wright and Reed contrast with traditional accounts of the manifestations of lay democracy between 1965 and 1975, during which many American bishops pushed back against what they viewed as an excessive focus on freedom of expression at the expense of authority, whether by clergy, religious, or laypeople. Notable confrontations included Patrick O'Boyle's sanctions against priests in the Diocese of Washington who opposed Paul VI's birth-control encyclical, *Humanae Vitae*; James McIntyre's struggles with women religious in Los Angeles; and the conflict-ridden episcopates of John Cody in Chicago and Robert Lucey in San Antonio.[27] With the possible exception of McIntyre, none of these prelates had been viewed as particularly conservative in the early 1960s—O'Boyle and Lucey had won liberal plaudits for their commitment to the civil-rights movement—but they demonstrated little interest in lay consultation when it came to the affairs of the Church. A bishop's responsibility for diocesan affairs remained absolute in their eyes, and he had no obligation to seek the advice, let alone the consent, of those whom he shepherded.

Such a perception, while unwelcome to lay activists, at least left little room for ambiguity. More complicated was the situation in which a bishop articulated the language of lay consultation but, inevitably, could do nothing to bind his successor (in many cases leading to the swift collapse of such consultation in the event of the promotion or death of the sympathetic bishop).[28] In the case of Pittsburgh, moreover, the development of structures for lay consultation remained very much under the oversight of chancery officials. Such caveats notwithstanding, Pittsburgh and Oklahoma City and Tulsa, though remarkably different in many ways, shared a common experience of developing a system of parish and diocesan government that, for a while at least, engaged the active interest of the laity.

Who Runs the Parish? Catholic Action and Parochial Government

While Catholic leaders generally agreed on the necessity of developing a Catholic commitment to civic participation, progressive Catholics took this point to extremes. Writing in 1963, journalist Daniel Callahan made the point starkly:

> The layman's obligation to adhere to the dogmatic and moral teachings of the Church is very different from his obligation to the Church as a sociological group with a particular set of temporal needs and problems. The obligation, for instance, that a Catholic accept the Church's teaching on divorce is clear; he cannot be a Catholic if he does not accept it. Yet he has no similar duty to support, say, a local chancery office's desire to have zoning laws changed in order that an extension may be built on a parochial school. In the first instance, should he dissent, he will be in direct conflict with the authority of the Church; in the second, he will not be disloyal to authority, but may, should he oppose the zoning change, be disloyal to the Catholics in that civil community. Put another way, the kind of personal conflict he may feel if he is tempted by the ease of civil divorce will be different from the one he will feel if, for the sake of civic principle, he opposes the chancery office's desire to change zoning laws. In the former case, the tension is between religion and secularization; in the latter, between institutional and civic loyalties.[29]

Callahan erred only in one particular. Within five years, many American Catholics would no longer be willing to embrace the proposition that they forfeited their Catholic identity even if they broke with the Church on *doctrinal* issues. His analysis nevertheless resonated with suburban Catholics, who constituted the core constituency of the Christian Family Movement and the majority of Catholic political activists. John F. Kennedy's victory in the presidential election of 1960, in the course of which the Catholic candidate would basically repudiate the authority of the Church to determine the moral tone of secular society, not only galvanized a younger generation of American Catholics but also served to accentuate lay Catholic commitment to personal autonomy. Well before Supreme Court justice William Douglas outlined the theory of a zone of privacy in family life in *Griswold v. Connecticut* (1965), a ruling with significant implications for Catholic moral teaching, many Catholic laymen had begun to articulate a belief in personal autonomy in their relationship with the episcopal hierarchy.[30]

Many CFM activists honed their leadership skills in suburban parishes and communities during the late 1950s and early 1960s. Where older urban parishes approached the spiritual life through the agency of devotional societies, the suburban congregations gloried in the outreach activities of their CFM chapters. In Tulsa, for example, the parish of St. Pius X was established in a barn on the outskirts of the city in 1955. While its first pastor made a nominal effort to help perpetuate the Catholic enclave (by hiring a builder to erect homes for Catholic families in the locality), it was soon clear that the center of parish life would be CFM. The parish boasted the largest chapter in the state, including several Protestant couples, and many of its lay programs, while still seeking to articulate a Catholic vision, were oriented outward.[31]

CFM activists were the advance guard of the Vatican II generation, deeply committed to the application of Catholic teaching to contemporary political and social problems.[32] "As sharers in the divine life of Christ," wrote a Pittsburgh reporter and active Catholic parishioner, "the laity must carry Christ into the world. . . . In the factory or the office, in the union or the management group, in the community group or the Little League, at the cocktail party or the picnic—only the layman can bring Christ into these spheres."[33] CFM enjoyed a strong following in Oklahoma, where in 1961 almost one-fifth of parishes maintained chapters that involved a total of 420 Catholic couples. Despite an obvious interest in marital counseling, CFM was also involved in the political debate over civil rights and helped school several rising politicians, including Dewey Bartlett, Oklahoma's first elected Catholic governor.[34] "Like the victory of John F. Kennedy," Bishop Reed wrote the governor-elect in 1966, "I believe yours in Oklahoma will accomplish much towards eliminating religious bias among our people. I was happy to see that religion did not become a public issue in the campaign."[35]

CFM activism was not limited to the sphere beyond the parish, however. Most members of CFM had been raised in parishes in which any consultation was at the behest of the priest and any "council" was an advisory body of parish notables constituted less to discuss the merits of a project than the best way to raise funds for it. Occasional exceptions did exist, including one unnamed "semi-suburban" parish in Wichita, Kansas, which in 1959 was reported to have six elected committees and a parish priest vested with "the power of veto, which he has never used," but many priests continued to harbor reservations about such experiments.[36] "In discussion with a priest whose work and conversation would mark him as a 'liberal,'" wrote one observer in 1967, "a layman was told, 'Don't worry about the Church—you take care of the temporal order.'"[37] In Lansdale, Pennsylvania, Monsignor Paul Cahill of St. Stanislaus Church also sounded a note of caution. "The priest is not free to preach the Gospel if he must concern himself with what his congregation's reactions would be," he insisted, "as is the case in many Protestant churches."[38] If Catholic clergy were to create consultative structures, how were they to resolve disagreements that pitted pastor against congregation? And what would the introduction of a lay voice imply if disagreements were to move beyond the parochial to challenge the authority of bishop and even pope?

For all such concerns, it was mostly clerical initiatives that produced the earliest elected parish councils in Oklahoma. In 1965, Monsignor Don Kanaly—who had built St. Patrick's Church in Oklahoma City from the ground up during the 1950s—organized no fewer than fifty-five voting districts for his parish, each of which sent one representative to the parish council.[39] Other urban and suburban parishes followed suit, although there was less enthusiasm in the smaller rural parishes of Oklahoma.[40] By the late 1960s, the diocesan pastoral board, responding to the facts on the ground, had established guidelines for the operation of parish councils, including quarterly meetings open to the whole parish, publication of the minutes, the right of council members to review all parish documents, and the restriction of parochial offices to laymen. All lay members of the council had to be "freely elected," the guidelines declared, while all clergy assistants enjoyed a vote, and the pastor was an ex-officio, nonvoting member with veto power.[41]

To these arrangements, Bishop Reed in December 1966 added procedures for the election of the eight deans who served as his administrative representatives. Each dean was elected from a slate of three nominees selected by a committee with representatives from across the diocese. Within each deanery, every priest cast one vote, and the laypeople of each parish enjoyed as many votes as there were clergy assigned to their parish. (A parish with three priests assigned, for example, cast six votes.) In one case, the "Fulton for Dean Club" even paid for an ad in the diocesan newspaper that praised Father Kenneth Fulton of Tulsa's St. Jude's Church as "Friendly, Uncompromising, Learned, True, On-The-Ball and Non-Committed."[42]

In Pittsburgh, by contrast, the revolution in parish government was implemented throughout the diocese by episcopal initiative in September 1965. Bishop Wright declared that the new requirements were "binding on all parishes without exception" and that the parish committees (in Pittsburgh, the elected body was referred to as a parish committee) should also expect to "represent the parish in the civil community."[43] Henceforth, nominations for parish committee seats would be made by congregational representatives rather than the pastor, women could both vote and run for office, and all parishioners over the age of eighteen (lower than the secular voting age) could exercise the franchise.[44] A diocesan secretariat printed no fewer than 533,000 ballots (including ballots in Hungarian for two ethnic parishes), and each pastor was required to display in his church vestibule a poster explaining voting procedures.

On February 6, 1966, Pittsburgh Catholics went to the polls, with 5,076 candidates vying for 2,500 seats. Given the snowy conditions and the lack of provision for mail-in ballots, the turnout of 42 percent (ranging from a high of 60 percent in some parishes to a low of 19 percent in others) was very respectable. Women candidates fared poorly, however, with only 160 women elected of the 492 nominated (9.7 percent of the candidates but only 6.4 percent of the winners).[45] Holy Rosary parish in Homewood witnessed particularly interesting electoral dynamics, including the defeat of two incumbents, the election of the first Negro to serve on the parish committee, and 71 of the 398 ballots cast for write-in votes for a total of 133 people, including 101 women. (Most of the write-ins failed to be elected.)[46]

The spread of elected parish councils in both Oklahoma and Pittsburgh compared favorably with the nation at large. A June 1967 survey in the *National Catholic Reporter* suggested that from 500 to 1,000 of the nation's 17,000 parishes had an elected council, while another 3,000 had appointed parish advisory boards. Other dioceses reported to be promoting lay participation included Buffalo, Cincinnati, Fall River, and Omaha. Individual priests such as Monsignor David Herlihy of Coronation of the Blessed Virgin Mary Church in Buffalo, New York, and Francis Eshweiler of Good Shepherd Church in Menominee Falls, Wisconsin, also promoted parish councils. Eshweiler maintained that he enjoyed a veto only because canon law required it and that he would much prefer his council to move beyond coordination of parish activities to formal planning, including the making of such fundamental decisions as whether to close the parochial school. Herlihy proved even more outspoken. "The Church takes the way of operating that the people are accustomed to," he explained, "and today is the democratic way. . . . Any pastor who dominates his parish is clearly not carrying out the spirit of the council."[47]

Creating a parish council was no guarantee of its ultimate effectiveness. Critics faulted the limited representation of young adults and women as well as the tendency of many councils to focus on brick-and-mortar issues.[48] Indeed, the rector of St. Margaret's Church in Pittsburgh's Greentree neighborhood argued in favor of being allowed to make committee appointments because only the popular people would be *elected*. "[We] speak so much of youth today," he explained. "Now a youth does not have a chance of being elected on a church committee, I don't think, and yet in this way it would give us an opportunity to appoint a few youths to the church committee and perhaps to take care of the younger element."[49]

One survey of Pittsburgh-area parishes reported that their committees varied in size, from four to ten members, with larger parishes tending to maintain larger committees. While 75 percent of parishes gave advance notice of the date and time of their committee meetings, a mere 38 percent published an advance agenda, and only 45 percent subsequently reported what actions had been taken. Decisions in most parishes were made either by consensus (46 percent) or by a combination of voting and consensus (36 percent), with only a minority (18 percent) reaching decisions mostly through majority vote.[50] In 1968, a random sampling of parish councils across the country (admittedly by the *National Catholic Reporter*, which made no secret of its critical view of the clerical establishment) suggested that around 40 percent of councils actually *made* decisions. The same report noted that while 96 percent of parishes reported education subcommittees and 80 percent had liturgy subcommittees, only 71 percent had finance subcommittees, and a mere 44 percent boasted subcommittees focused on community affairs.[51]

Where council decision-making involved management of financial assets, tensions between clergy and laypeople could swiftly escalate. Bishop Wright wryly described how he received a parochial finance report, which required cosigning by the lay members of the parish committee, that was submitted to the chancery with seven signatures, all of them in the handwriting of the pastor![52] Less blatant, but more disruptive, was an attempt by the pastor of St. Mary's Church in Tulsa to sideline his parish treasurer, who had been in office for five years, for protesting the omission of certain receipts from the financial report to the diocese and the priest's failure to report his discretionary-spending account. "It is my opinion," the incensed treasurer complained, "that if parishioners are to be expected to take more responsibility in church affairs and contribute to church support, the very least to be done is to send them an annual financial report that is adequate and complete."[53] Bishop Reed reluctantly agreed and transferred the priest to another parish; his successor wisely announced the formation of a parish council and pledged that it would make decisions on all matters not reserved to his office under canon law.[54] A few years later, however, Reed supported the appeal of the pastor of St. Barbara's Church in Lawton, Oklahoma, against a parish-council decision to require that all expenditures over $300 be cosigned by the treasurer, agreeing that this was not only contrary to diocesan practice but might make it difficult to issue checks in a timely fashion.[55]

"If someone were to ask me what should the parish committee mean to a priest," declared the pastor of St. Leo's Church on Pittsburgh's North Side, "my reaction would be: the parish committee is step number one toward permitting him to function as a Priest, to let him get away from administrative roles such as being the supervisor of janitors and an accountant keeping the parish books and all these other things."[56] Such a reaction was far from uniform, particularly when parishioners sought to shape the new ruling body in ways that ran counter to the vision of the priest in charge, such as occurred in Cushing, Oklahoma, in 1969. After Father Martin Reid attempted to ensure that equal numbers of men and women were elected to his parish council, he was denounced as an Irish-born cleric who knew nothing about the "democratic process." Under the chairmanship of a local lawyer, the newly elected council demanded absolute control of the parish's financial records and a check-voucher system with a lay co-signatory, refused to make payments into the pastor's petty-cash fund, and even declined an auto-repair bill on the grounds that Reid had used his car for personal reasons.[57]

Particularly demoralizing was the situation when a priest who had previously expressed a progressive view of parish democracy suddenly decided that it had begun to interfere with what he considered necessary projects. When Monsignor Don Kanaly, the grizzled dean of American Catholic Action, decided to close down the parochial school of Oklahoma City's St. Patrick's Church in 1969, the subsequent firestorm culminated in a dramatic four-and-a-half-hour council meeting. After the council rejected Kanaly's plans, the pastor exercised his veto and the council then attempted to appeal that decision to the diocesan Pastoral Board, falling short of the necessary two-thirds by just three votes (out of a total of fifty-four).[58] The real problem, though, was less Kanaly's veto than the way it had been exercised and on whom. "For eleven years," the former assistant at St. Patrick's at that time explains today, "these people had been told, it's our church, it's our parish, it's our grade school, and now you are telling us that even though we have established very clearly that the mind of the parish is to keep the school open . . . you're going to close it anyway. That tore the heart out of people."[59]

When a parish actually got to express its collective voice through the ballot, the results could be surprising. In April 1968 the adult members of four parishes in the Diocese of St. Cloud voted 835–100 to close the Catholic high school in Pierz, Minnesota. Only seventeen years earlier, after local clergy had successfully urged defeat of a public-high-school bond issue, the then-bishop of St. Cloud had been willing to excommunicate Catholic layman Henry Gau for the offense merely of taking a straw poll in his parish that revealed a high degree of lay Catholic support for the measure. (The excommunication was later lifted.) During the 1950s the public schools rented classroom space from the Catholic school system, but when the state instructed them to end that practice in 1962, lay Catholics took note of the spiraling costs of parochial education and new state laws on rural school consolidation and acted accordingly. Eighty years after Archbishop John Ireland of St. Paul had first explored Catholic cooperation with the public school system, his spiritual heirs had returned to their ecclesiastical roots.[60] Only a month earlier, in the Diocese of Rochester, New York, Bishop Fulton Sheen's proposal to turn over St. Bridget's Church to the federal government for the benefit of the poor provoked pickets at the chancery and a petition signed by 130 priests protesting the abandonment of the parish's two thousand Puerto Rican members, which ultimately led Sheen to reverse his decision.[61]

On occasion laypeople took a stand in defense of the clergy set in authority over them. Andrew Moore's discussion, in this volume, of the confrontation between Archbishop Hallinan and Atlanta's Community of Christ Our Brother reveals an extreme case of laypeople asserting authority over their congregation, but more moderate examples can also be documented.[62] When Monsignor Stanley Ormsby of Our Lady of the Rosary Church in Niagara Falls, New York, refused a directive from Bishop James McNulty to sign a note for $120,000 as his parish's share of the debt of the Diocese of Buffalo, the thirty-member parish council unanimously backed his decision.[63] The replacement of popular priests also provoked congregational protests in the dioceses of Saginaw, Michigan, and Dallas–Fort Worth, but while Bishop Stephen Woznicki responded positively to representations on behalf of the dismissed pastor, Bishop Thomas Gorman stood firm in his decision to terminate the contract of the Paulist Fathers at St. Paul the Apostle Church in Richardson, Texas.[64]

Catholic "Democracy" in Action: The Rise and Fall of Diocesan Councils

While changes in parish government had the potential to redefine the relationship between priest and congregation, liberal Catholics also looked to the higher levels of the Church for evidence that what they considered to be the rights of the laity would be fully realized. Noting the growing tendency of the bishops of national churches to act in a corporate fashion, they called for their bishops to embrace analogous forms of consultation with the laity at the diocesan level.[65] While such initiatives as Atlanta's lay congress convened by Archbishop Paul Hallinan in 1966 were welcomed, they did not constitute the sort of shared mode of governance that many progressives desired.[66] Far more appealing were the elected councils of religious and laity, which met in both Oklahoma City and Tulsa and Pittsburgh during the late 1960s. That these councils did not survive the death of Bishop Reed and the transfer of Bishop Wright does not deprive them of cultural significance, for they reveal a great deal about how some lay Catholics internalized their understanding of renewal and related it to the existing structures of the Church.

Even before the establishment of elected councils, American bishops had begun to experiment with lay representation on diocesan boards and commissions that had previously been solely the province of priests and religious. In 1960, the Diocese of Oklahoma City and Tulsa became the first Catholic diocese in the United States to appoint a "mixed" board of education—albeit one with only six laymen, compared with ten priests and four sisters—which Bishop Reed converted from an advisory to a regulatory body three years later.[67] In Pittsburgh, although a Catholic laymen's educational association had been organized as early as 1944 and was active in promoting parochial parent–teacher guilds, it was not until 1962 that a sixteen-person lay advisory council to the diocesan school board was created. Three years later, five laymen were appointed directly to the board, and by 1967 that figure had grown to eight, which, in contrast with the representation of laity on Oklahoma's board of education, constituted an absolute majority. That diocesan officials were sensitive to charges of a perceived lack of democracy is evident from the reminder by diocesan officials that the members of most *public* school districts were appointed and not elected.[68]

Other diocesan institutions also acquired a lay voice. In 1963, Bishop Wright installed two civil engineers on Pittsburgh's diocesan building commission, until then a clerical bastion, and three years later launched a program to provide Catholic attorneys with the necessary skills in canon law to serve as lay advocates before the diocesan marriage tribunals.[69] In

Wright's former diocese of Worcester, his successor Bernard Flanagan appointed a layman as diocesan controller, "in keeping with the mind of the Church to give lay people the responsibilities in which they have special competence," while Bishop Fulton Sheen announced the creation of a review board of the laity to assess the fitness of seminarians for the Diocese of Rochester.[70] "In the past," Sheen subsequently explained, "the parish accepted the priest who was sent to them by the bishop, now the laity will determine the type of priest who can be sent."[71] The most dramatic shift, however, came in 1968 in the Diocese of Oklahoma City and Tulsa, when Bishop Reed created a diocesan Pastoral Board to coordinate diocesan decision-making. The board, which included two members elected by the clergy and the laity, respectively, received the reports of all diocesan departments, held public consultations, and served as a final court of appeal against any decision to close a parochial school.[72]

By the late 1960s, however, such appointments struck certain activists as inadequate. At the inaugural meeting of the Chicago Conference of Laymen in April 1967, philosophy professor John Bannan suggested that conflict at the diocesan level was a systemic problem, not one revolving around the personalities of a few autocratic bishops. "Our legitimacy," he told the lay delegates, "lies in the right of a group of the members of the Church to organize freely to act in the interest of the Church as they see that interest. We shall not pretend to speak for the Church. We shall speak for ourselves. But we claim the right to speak to the Church on matters within our competence and to speak from within the Church."[73] In the Archdiocese of St. Paul and Minneapolis, the Association of Christians for Church Renewal produced for Archbishop Leo Binz in March 1967 an unsolicited report that recommended the convening of a lay congress and the division of parishes into "neighborhood church communities" with greater lay oversight.

A month later, the association issued a call for a meeting of the Vatican II "new breed" laity, attracting interest from Cleveland, St. Louis, Chicago, New York, Philadelphia, Milwaukee, and Iowa. While such activists were vocal, one should not assume that their opinions were any more representative of the "typical Catholic" than were those of conservative clergy. A conference in Minneapolis in July 1967 suggested that the new National Association of Laymen was composed mainly of married suburban professionals and managers in their thirties, with considerable experience in the work of parishes and dioceses, a group very much in the minority in rural and working-class parishes.[74]

The professional middle class was nevertheless likely to be heavily represented in the new diocesan councils, which posed the most tangible threat to the ecclesiastical status quo. Such councils had been on the agenda since October 1965, when the *National Catholic Reporter* interviewed ten bishops on the most important changes they planned for their dioceses in the aftermath of the Second Vatican Council. Four of those interviewed—Charles Buswell of Pueblo (an Oklahoma contemporary of Bishop Reed), Victor Reed of Oklahoma City and Tulsa, Archbishop Joseph Ritter of St. Louis, and John Wright of Pittsburgh—all insisted that a "little council" would be their most significant innovation.[75] Outside these dioceses most bishops complied with the Council requirement for bishops to establish a priests' senate but tended to favor more remote processes when it came to consulting the laity.[76] In the Diocese of Lansing, for example, Bishop Alexander Zaleski authorized a diocesan-wide questionnaire in December 1966. The 38,000 responses that it generated suggested that the laity favored state support for parochial schools, approved of priests who took stands on issues of social concern, and desired more lay-led parish councils.[77]

The first formal initiative in support of a diocesan council came in St. Louis in November 1964, when a group of laypeople, inspired by what they had read of Cardinal Ritter's contribution to the Second Vatican Council, discussed organizing a diocesan council, which would "give to our clergy, religious and laity a new sense of Christian dignity and responsibility . . . would foster free public opinion within the Church and would establish a dialogue of communication among our people bringing us all to a closer realization of the renewal of all things in Christ." An initial meeting with Ritter suggested that the cardinal was willing for them to proceed, but a written proposal submitted in January 1965 was rejected because it was said not to be centered in the parishes and failed to involve lay diocesan organizations. Requests for further meetings with the cardinal were declined, and a second proposal was rejected in August on the grounds that it might "promote petty criticism and uncharitableness." Then, in September, Ritter announced plans for parish groups to study the conciliar document *De Ecclesia* as a necessary preliminary to any council. "There it was," a laywoman involved in the preliminary discussions complained, "the usual pyramid chain of command, from the top to the trusted lieutenants and thus to the 'faithful' with tidy control all along the line. . . . We had suggested that each parish determine its own agenda in a democratic and open manner . . . in a way that was appropriate to the problems and needs which the people themselves had given top priority."[78]

Ritter's program, dubbed Operation Renewal, involved 32,000 Catholics in six weeks of study and discussion. Their recommendations were passed to parish-renewal committees that compiled them into a consensus report to be submitted to the archdiocese. The process of compilation was productive of further lay frustration, however, most notably over a form produced by the chancery that some laypeople charged with being shaped by a "Baltimore catechism approach" to Catholicism. Particularly resented was the inclusion of a question asking whether the group would express "obedience to the Church and your loyal acceptance of the liturgical changes." Critics focused on the unrepresentative character of the forthcoming 120-member assembly (with 72 appointed delegates against 48 elected, and 72 priests and religious against 48 laypeople) and that no priest study groups had been established. According to the *National Catholic Reporter*, not the most dispassionate of sources, frustration against the perceived "capture" of Ritter by the chancery old guard was widespread.[79]

While Ritter oversaw the initial concept of a diocesan council, it fell to Victor Reed in February 1965 to be the first American prelate formally to embrace the principle (before the Second Vatican Council had even concluded), though at the time he described it merely as "a particularly appropriate way of advising the people of the work of Vatican Council II and its results."[80] While Reed issued a number of pastoral letters on the subject, overall responsibility for the consultation process was assigned to the head of the diocesan Catholic Action committee, who supervised the publication and distribution of the discussion manuals used by as many as ten thousand Oklahoma Catholics who met that fall to discuss *Lumen Gentium* (Dogmatic Constitution on the Church). These discussions generated more than three thousand suggestions from the laity that were then submitted to the eight diocesan commissions that had been appointed to process them. The bishop's sole intervention was a warning that all topics raised for debate would be designated either as something on which he was willing to submit to the majority view without reservation or as a subject on which he was desirous of knowing the "consensus of the people" but on which he would make no formal commitment.[81]

Selection of delegates for the forthcoming "Little Council," with minimal coordination by diocesan authorities, ultimately yielded a grand total of 441 clergy and lay representatives who met in joint session but voted separately on issues brought before them. Executive responsibility was vested in a nine-member board of presidents, composed of one religious (appointed by the bishop), three clergy (two elected and one appointed by the bishop), and five laypeople (three elected and two appointed by the bishop), giving it an absolute lay majority. At a working session to approve a constitution, the sole proposed amendment (approved by a two-thirds majority) modified a clause stating that the Little Council functioned "at the pleasure of the bishop," adding the words "and the people of the diocese." After the establishment of a diocesan office for the Little Council during the summer of 1967, its various commissions began a review of diocesan policy in their areas of competence. Summaries of their reports were distributed to Little Council delegates, and responses from diocesan department heads were requested as the Little Council geared up for its first formal meeting in April 1968.[82]

An exuberant Confraternity of Christian Doctrine teacher from Oklahoma City running for a position on the board of presidents exemplified the public mood. "Oklahoma with its Little Council," she insisted with pardonable exaggeration, "is in a position to make great contributions to Christianity. The whole nation waits for its success or failure. It is at this level where the fate of the Vatican Council lies. . . . Since I'm originally from the East, I can fully appreciate the large responsibility Oklahoma laymen have in their church."[83]

On April 19, 1968, almost a year after Bishop Wright had opened the first session of *his* council, Oklahoma delegates assembled to discuss no fewer than 167 resolutions on topics ranging from the liturgy and mixed marriages to clerical celibacy and parish government. "At times," reported an Episcopalian observer of the proceedings, "the tedious and somewhat repressive rules of order seemed to defeat spontaneous expression, yet as the council session continued, it became apparent that the difficulties were being resolved and true democratic exchange of ideas was occurring."[84] Equally noteworthy was the sight of Bishop Reed "dressed like all his priests, unobtrusively sitting in the Little Council audience and attentively listening to the debates."[85] On paper, the Little Council enjoyed its own autonomous space, independent of the official diocesan machinery. Both conservatives and progressives soon learned something of parliamentary procedure, with the latter securing adoption of an open-housing covenant and the former resisting efforts to join the Council of Churches.[86]

For all its achievements, the Little Council enjoyed an uneasy standing in the life of the diocese. Complaints soon surfaced that it was an instrument of the larger urban parishes and that delegates were failing to articulate the concerns of those whom they were supposed to represent.[87] More fundamentally, it became increasingly obvious that while lay participants in the Little Council envisaged a long-term consultative body in which majority opinion would enjoy significant authority in diocesan affairs, the bishop conceived of it as a temporary forum that would allow lay input as to how the changes proposed in Rome for the renewal of the global Church could be refined to take account of diocesan peculiarities. "In the beginning," Bishop Reed confessed at one point, "I thought that the work of the Little Council would be perhaps a year or two. But it wasn't very long until I realized that the work of the Little Council is probably a work that is going to go on and on. I just don't know how long."[88]

In Pittsburgh, far from merely sitting among his clergy, Bishop Wright chose to preside over proceedings and made frequent interventions on issues of concern to him. In his opening address, moreover, he made very clear the constraints under which he expected his council to operate:

> We have said that the immediate purpose of the Pastoral Council for consultation and advice is, as the name indicates, consultation and advice with regard to the policies of the Diocese. There are certain points, therefore, on which many [are] very eager to be heard and to speak but which will not be in order. For example, we are not met to discuss the Reform of the Roman Curia. . . . There are other speculative points, some pertaining to the discipline of the church, some pertaining to morals, on which, I am certain, many would be passionately eager to be heard. It is not the business of this Council.[89]

Such explicit warnings did not sit well with many council participants, even many of those who acknowledged the essentially diocesan nature of the council. As in Oklahoma, critics questioned the council's representative quality, its freedom to deliberate, and its unstructured character.

Many members also resented the failure of diocesan bureaucrats to report on the extent to which resolutions adopted by the council had been implemented. Although the council secretariat did suggest that if the council moved from an advisory to a deliberative role, provision should be made for delegates to introduce action items, throughout its existence it was the bishop who assigned the subjects to be discussed. While it had never been proposed that council members were there primarily to represent the interests of a "constituency," the very fact of their election implied a need for them to at least convey the views of those who had selected them: "It is not necessary that elected representatives *solely* reflect the views of their constituents (whether in secular life or religious). Members were elected or appointed because of their backgrounds (parish committee membership, religious vows etc.) not because they would reflect the views of those electing them. But, it would be helpful that they should *know* these views."[90]

Responses to a questionnaire circulated by the diocese in the fall of 1968 provides fascinating insights into the mindset of participating delegates.[91] That the council was perceived to be a middle-class preserve was attested to by several participants. "A good cross -section of the professions," one delegate commented, while others complained of the dominance of "a small group of the elites" rather than the "silent middle," or noted the absence of those reflecting the "labor side" and the poor.[92] One Wright appointee specifically lamented the failure to elect young, female, and black delegates and urged that reforms adopted in the Archdiocese of Detroit be applied to Pittsburgh, including regional councils between the parish and diocesan level and a communications system that worked from the "bottom up." Parish nominating committees to choose council candidates, she added, should be elected rather than appointed, to avoid "inbreeding of the same personalities," and candidate biographies should be posted in advance.[93] One of her colleagues also criticized the fact that equal representation from each deanery led to underrepresentation for deaneries with a few large parishes.[94]

Nor was lack of representativeness the only complaint. "This Council in many ways reminds me of the United Nations," one exasperated delegate lamented. "We talk, we talk, but who knows, time may prove us valuable." For another, council deliberations seemed to be dominated by the same "few members (mostly by ones unhampered by knowledge on any particular subject)."[95] Some lay delegates complained that the lay perspective was frequently given short shrift and that the tendency of certain clergy to ignore lay initiatives at the parish level had perpetuated a "what's the use" fatalism among the laity.[96] Lay delegates were generally "anxious to approve whatever the establishment wants," argued one respondent,[97] while another charged that "too many seem afraid to take responsibility and are always looking over their shoulder and asking 'What do you think Bishop?'"[98]

Critiques of this nature illuminated the constitutional ambiguities inherent in the council structures. A body that met, debated, and passed resolutions implied something more than a council of advice. "It all probably comes down," wrote one lay observer, "to the degree to which extra-episcopal (and hence extra-deanery) voices shall be heard in the running of the Diocese. Unless they are heard—and all are aware thereof—then a sense of futility might set in."[99] One trade-union representative termed the council an effort "to recognize that the Church is by nature a democratic institution made up of human beings of equal dignity among whom the Holy Spirit breathes where He wills."[100] His insistence that Vatican II had called for "democratic" structures was echoed by another delegate who declared that a council without legislative power would be of little value. "If the Council from which all others are to take example, namely Vatican II, had no legislative power," he explained, "it would be, as all such important organizations and structures, *non productive*."[101] Given the much-publicized accounts of political maneuvering among the bishops in Rome and the resistance of the American contingent to attempts to dilute the Declaration on Religious Freedom, it is unsurprising that one anonymous commentator wrote of the need for a "loyal opposition, a kind of two-party system" within the diocesan council as a necessary prerequisite to the development of creative programs.[102]

Just as at the parochial level, the argument was made that the laity should be consulted on all financial decisions affecting the diocese and be allowed to vote the "go ahead decision" in all but exceptional cases.[103] It was generally agreed that a forum that allowed priests, religious, and laity to debate contentious issues together, in the presence of their bishop, did help to bring the differing perspectives to the attention of all, but even the superior of the Sisters of Mercy in Pittsburgh still voiced concern that diocesan officials were being less than frank in their dealings with the council and that delegates who challenged their evasiveness were being treated as disloyal.[104] Another delegate agreed. "I don't intend that the departments should be *put on the carpet* necessarily," he wrote, "but when they report they have had reason to study a whole area and presumably are in a position to explain the reasoning of this report (this, of course, depends on how much *full* knowledge the Council is intended to have)."[105]

The novelty of parliamentary procedure for some delegates was also clearly in evidence. One male religious complained that issues raised by council members rarely received the scrutiny they deserved: "One speaker brings up something and then the next speaker that comes up to the microphone brings up a totally different problem or idea and my first impression is that there are a lot of balls going out but we aren't really zeroing in on specific problems."[106] The most contentious debates inevitably involved discussion of measures intended to improve race relations. One measure requiring the diocesan school board to achieve integration by moving beyond open enrollment in parochial schools to embrace student exchange and busing was defeated on a show of hands by 45 to 25 in 1967.[107] The following year, a vote on establishing a one-year preparatory school for black children was declared adopted by a voice vote, but following a request for reconsideration, the chairman reported the motion lost on a show of hands by 24 to 17 and apologized for "improperly stating the result."[108] During the same debate, a vote on adding personnel to the Human Relations Commission was reported as evenly divided, requiring a recess and prompting Bishop Wright to urge delegates not to go home. "Tedious as this is," he told them, "it will teach you how complex this problem is and how complex the necessity of meeting it. Don't quit."[109]

By mid-1969, however, it was clear that many of those laypeople most committed to the democratic process had lost faith in the bishops' good intentions. Despite such initiatives as Archbishop Dearden's Synod/69, which, though nominally consultative, was marked by Dearden's pledge to allow the decisions of the majority to guide him, the gap between expectations and reality was now too wide.[110] "I personally doubt that the voice of the layman will be heard and acted upon to the extent I would desire if I were to act as chairman," observed Catholic layman Patrick McCarren in a letter declining an appointment to one of the commissions appointed by Bishop John Wright to prepare legislation for Pittsburgh's upcoming synod.[111] In the Diocese of Cleveland, a lukewarm response to the circulation of petitions in support of Pope Paul VI's encyclical *Humanae Vitae* also suggested that lay deference to papal authority had lessened considerably.[112]

Following his appointment as archbishop of St. Louis, Columbus bishop John Carberry announced that he planned to reschedule a vote by diocesan priests on a possible successor, to ensure that all votes would be signed and the result kept from the public, moves that hardly comported with the new democratic vision.[113] This perception was only reinforced by the lukewarm response of ten local bishops to the request of the Northwest Pennsylvania Conference of Laymen for a voice in the selection of their new bishop.[114] Perhaps in reaction, the calls of lay activists for greater diocesan accountability increased. In February 1969, lay groups in the Archdioceses of Washington and St. Paul–Minneapolis and the Diocese of Rockville Centre, New York, all called for full financial disclosure by their dioceses both to keep the laity informed and to meet criticism by outsiders of the Catholic Church's lack of accountability.[115] The following month, several lay groups in Minnesota opposed a proposed archdiocesan fund drive, on the grounds that only 9 percent of receipts had been allocated for social action (compared to a 60 percent allocation for parochial and diocesan schools) and that a diocesan audit had yet to be released.[116]

In Pittsburgh, Bishop Wright's appointment to head the Vatican's Congregation for the Clergy removed him from oversight of preparations for the diocesan synod that he had already set in motion. Much of what was initially produced by the diocesan commissions appointed to prepare synod legislation was so heavily rewritten by diocesan administrators as to be indistinguishable from what had been submitted.[117] "The concept of democracy in the Catholic Church," one Pittsburgh official explained in March 1971, "does not in any way reduce the singular and historically-conditioned authority of a bishop."[118] Authority had reasserted itself, and the expansive dreams of Catholic liberals were over.

Vice or Virtue? The Conundrum of Catholic Democracy

"I will bring to this appointment [to the Diocesan Pastoral Council]," one Pittsburgh laywoman wrote Bishop Wright in April 1967, "my knowledge that group deliberations and advice are based on dialogue, and that dialogue with members of one's own Church is sometimes the most difficult of all."[119] Roseanne Reiser was perhaps more realistic about the future than was John Wright only two months later. "I have occasionally heard," observed the bishop of Pittsburgh, "though not so much in recent years, the criticism that the present Bishop displays too great a tendency to rely on the opinions of laymen. An American Cardinal once told me in the middle of St. Peter's, and therefore, almost infallibly, that he had heard in connection with the parish committee elections, that I had turned the Diocese over to the laity. I told him I hadn't, that I had merely done in 1965 what his successor would do in 1968. He looked mortally wounded but we parted good friends."[120]

Wright's optimistic view of his relations with the laity failed to recognize that the laity's understanding (or, at any rate, the understanding of the middle-class professionals who dominated the elected councils) of the implications of the "People of God" theology could be very different from that of the bishops. At the very least, the former expected to have a dominant voice in financial matters, and many financial decisions had implications for the broader aspects of the Church's life, yet at the parish level, it was far from apparent how a priest who insisted on persistently exercising his veto could be constrained. Indeed, progressive clergy who frequently hymned the virtues of parish democracy showed little desire to accommodate the majority will when it sought to preserve traditional religious practices or resisted politicization of parish life. At the diocesan level, even the most liberal bishops were the first to acknowledge that no diocese was an island. A diocesan council might imitate a parliamentary system, but ultimately its decisions always required episcopal ratification.

In any case, few bishops were enamored of a purely democratic model. "I would be as resistant to a dictatorship of the left or of liberals," Bishop Wright declared in June 1967, "as I would be to a dictatorship of the right or fascists. I would resist, also, a dictatorship of democracy, unless I was positively certain of what the devil the term meant in a given case."[121] For progressive laity, such attitudes were understandably a continued source of frustration. Their vision of Vatican II–inspired empowerment demanded a seat at the table, and while most acknowledged a sphere reserved solely for clerical adjudication, it was far smaller than many bishops and priests appeared to think. The uncertain status of the new representative organs of the Church had clearly unsettled their earlier attachment to the ultimate authority of the Church in their daily lives. Catholic Democracy, it appeared, had been weighed in the balance and found wanting.

10 Empowering the People of God

John Cardinal Dearden's Church of Tomorrow

SAMUEL J. THOMAS

Hope and promise, agony and despair . . . controversy and confrontation.[1]

Historians and Hollywood draw on these descriptors of the American 1960s to express the ambivalence and confusion over what most believe was a watershed period in the nation's development. Historian William Chafe has cautioned only against using the term "'watershed' to describe a given moment" because it risks "oversimplifying the historical process." It applies primarily to signify "an end to domination by one constellation of forces and the beginning of domination by another."[2] In the scholarship of American Catholic history, "watershed" appropriately tags the 1960s as a period of unprecedented acculturation or, as some would argue, assimilation.[3]

A singularly important consequence of the Second Vatican Council (1962–65) was that many clergy, religious, and laity who still presumed the fundamentally transcendent and immutable character of their Church encountered extraordinary opposition. Coalitions of reform-minded faithful—clergy, religious, and a laity whose apostolate Council documents had greatly enhanced—voiced their preference for the Church's immanence, for its integral, sacramental link to human society and its profound responsibility to engage the modern world and the Church's ills. To buttress their positions, reformers internalized their new identity as the "People of God," the scriptural phrase chosen by Council fathers to express the inclusivity inherent in the meaning of "Church."[4] From the moment Vatican II commenced and throughout its deliberations during and between formal sessions, liberal reformers and their conservative counterparts contested the communitarian meaning of "People of God" as well as the meaning and spirit of the Council itself. So began the culture wars that have wracked the church ever since.[5]

One tactic of ecclesiological jousting after the Council was to heap praise or criticism on those whom each side identified as its respective leaders. By the late 1960s, liberal Catholic intellectuals and reform-minded activists hailed John Francis Dearden, archbishop of Detroit from 1959 to 1980 and, from 1966 to 1971, the first president of the newly constituted National Conference of Catholic Bishops (NCCB) and of its civic arm, the United States Catholic Conference (USCC). In both capacities and for most of his tenure as Detroit's ordinary, Dearden toiled to forge a Council-inspired ecclesiological consensus on restructuring the governance of the American Church. His written and spoken words and deeds point to an overriding concern with building a more inclusive ecclesiological community. More importantly, he envisioned one that joined Vatican II's emphasis on a Church that promoted its immanent nature and intimate connection to the world. In so doing, he continued to fully acknowledge but placed less emphasis on the Church's institutional dimensions and on the preconciliar concept of the Church as transcendent—expressed in the Pauline doctrine, "Mystical Body of Christ."[6]

Numerous sources document the strategy that Dearden followed to lay the foundation for his Church of the future, a Church built by leader-servants and the shared responsibility of laity, clergy, and religious. Among numerous addresses in which he promoted his ecclesiological convictions, three addresses, by virtue of their timing, clarity, scope, and content, stand out as particularly compelling examples of what he believed in and worked for: first, his "Celebration of Synod/69," the Detroit archdiocesan synod that he convened in late March of that year and that resulted in a decentralization of his authority; second, and two weeks later, his bold mid-April address to the NCCB, a plea in which he presented his prerequisites for a viable, vital, collaboratively fashioned Church; and third, his November 1971 presidential farewell address, again to the NCCB, in which he skillfully integrated the accomplishments of the bishops' conference with his unwavering faith in the necessity of a much less clericalized and more inclusively governed Church. Together, the addresses selected here encapsulate a concept of Church that he had begun internalizing at Vatican II and then refined during the next decade. They also offer a compact, accessible way to understand many, if not all,

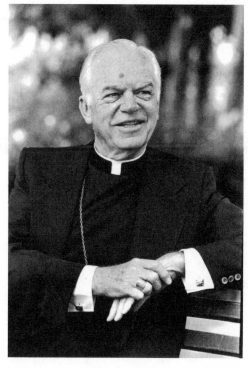

John Cardinal Dearden (1970s)
Courtesy of *The Michigan Catholic*, photo by Tony Spina

of the reasons for the kudos and criticisms that commentators have heaped on Dearden since his death in 1988.[7]

Before we begin an analysis each of them, the brief two and a half years—March 1969 to November 1971—that span the period in which Dearden delivered them require some background. More specifically, it is necessary to contextualize the circumstances that influenced the cardinal's evolving ecclesiology and in turn strengthened his determination to increase the collaborative role of the laity in an era that challenged conventional understandings of authority on all levels. How he articulated (and acted on) his stance toward collaboration will then follow by examining his three addresses and their logical culmination in the historic 1976 Call to Action conference. This essay will conclude with a reckoning of Dearden's legacy, the bequest of a man who, despite contrary forces that might have derailed other leaders, persisted and endured. By his own admission, he did so primarily because of an inborn—albeit cautious—optimism and unquenchable Spirit-sustained faith in the future of his Church.[8]

Episcopal Authority and Theological Dissent

Just as Vatican II formally ended the Church's largely self-imposed isolation from the modern world, so Archbishop Dearden acted on what he believed American Church leaders must do to engage the world in a critical-analytical manner. His answer, though not simplistic, was disarmingly simple: strengthen the essentially pastoral leadership necessary for success. "The whole world has been changing," he cautioned in 1969. "If we are to be a living church, a part and parcel of human lives, the church must be affected." A Rome-trained theologian, he was confident his Church could adopt a more independent, transparent, and participatory American identity, and he believed it could advance those goals without compromising the fundamentals of Catholic belief and practice.[9] His reform efforts were incomplete and only partially successful when a second heart attack forced him to resign as archbishop in 1980, but important earmarks of the Dearden era continued in Detroit and in the fabric of the American Church. Wherever "shared responsibility" continues to exist "in ways which support the mission of the church, strengthen, not weaken, the authority of pastors, and insure the integrity of the community of faith," there too the spirit of John Dearden continues to reside, inspiring his supporters and annoying his adversaries.[10] His promotion of a more collaborative and inclusive Church established the basis on which its transcendent and immanent charisms could meld into a unifying praxis. Such equilibrium was not just salutary; it was crucial to the stability and continuing vitality of Catholicism in the postconciliar United States. Though he excluded no one who was sincere of heart, Dearden's words and deeds suggest that he toiled hardest to rally the faithful—lay, religious, and clerical—who were moderately either left or right of center and who together constituted the vast majority of American Catholics. This goal proved harder than he may have anticipated, but he indisputably cultivated the ground and planted the seeds for future development.[11]

In the half-decade or so after the Second Vatican Council, ecclesiological differences sharply divided liberal and conservative bishops.

Among prominent conservatives were Bishop James A. McNulty of Buffalo, Los Angeles' James Cardinal McIntyre, San Antonio's Archbishop Robert E. Lucey, and Archbishop Patrick O'Boyle of Washington, D. C. Liberal-to-moderate episcopal leaders such as Dearden, Lansing bishop Alexander Zaleski, and USCC secretary Bishop Joseph Bernardin, along with a handful of theologians and canon lawyers, labored to mitigate the mistrust that after the Council had developed between their conservative peers and dissident or liberal parish priests, especially priest scholars. Quarrels between them were doctrinal and disciplinary in nature, and during the late 1960s and early 1970s there was no dearth of Cassandras.[12] Gloom occasionally snared even the normally sanguine Dearden. In January 1969, for example, he copied and filed in his personal papers this poignant assessment of the Church in the United States by a discerning American correspondent for *The Tablet*, the London-based progressive periodical:

> Priests and sisters are leaving their ministry at an increasing rate; the laity and many clergy, particularly the younger ones, have rejected *Humanae Vitae*, and are apparently unable to accept the leadership of the bishops in many matters. Liturgical experimentation far beyond the canon's present regulations is pervasive. So-called "underground" communities have sprung up in every diocese, some of them in opposition to the official leadership, and others simply not caring what the official leadership does and says. There is little apostasy in American Catholicism, but great dissatisfaction with the behaviour of the institutional leadership—a dissatisfaction which is increasingly making that leadership irrelevant to what is happening in American Catholicism.[13]

These observations were worrisome, yet neither they nor any other litany of woes undermined Dearden's consummate hopefulness or the fundamental loyalty of the bishops who stood by him. By some estimates, "Dearden bishops," those who shared at least his desire for greater concentricity and community in the Church's institutional structures, numbered about 70 out of 375 in the American episcopate. An estimated 125 were moderates or centrists. As many as 125 and probably more were theological and ecclesiological conservatives who privately and at times publicly conveyed a wary, even hostile attitude toward any changes that seemed to threaten clerical culture and authority.[14]

Dearden's Transformation and the NCCB

Scholarly and popular commentaries on Dearden concentrate on the years after his Vatican II transformation from a hidebound conservative to an "unobtrusive liberal." The nature and extent of his change produced interesting analyses, particularly among those who knew him personally. One plausible, arguably incisive, though adoring assessment came from Jane Wolford Hughes. She and her husband became close friends of the archbishop, particularly during her tenure as Dearden's director of the Institute for Continuing Education, "the first woman to be named to an executive diocesan position in the U.S.," an appointment she viewed as "significant testimony of his belief in the laity." In 1989 she recalled with both nuance and conviction the change from the old to the new Dearden:

> [Vatican II] irrevocably re-formed him. It was not so much that he was changed but that he was filled in to become more himself. His questions and his hopes were larger. His decisions and his actions displayed an unusual capacity for continued growth. He seemed comfortable with and unthreatened by ambiguity and diversity. Mentally, he had shed some of the traditional constraints walling in a bishop. The new life flowing from the Council was like his own breathing in and breathing out, yet he knew that if he did not give others the opportunity to embrace the new life, it would remain a grand but isolated experience. He did not pause long to begin.[15]

A year earlier, another close associate, Father Kenneth Untener—who with Dearden's support became bishop of Saginaw, Michigan, in 1980—provided other insights that nicely prefaced Wolford Hughes's assessment of the archbishop's transformative Council experiences. Writing for *America* magazine a few months after Dearden's death in 1988, Untener reflected on his mentor's evolution during and after the Council. To the cardinal's last breath, he reiterated his conviction that there were times, "dramatic moments," when the Holy Spirit moved the Council fathers in a particular direction. One such moment occurred during committee deliberations over *Lumen Gentium*—the *Dogmatic Constitution on the Church*. Before taking the document to the whole body of bishops, and after some debate, the committee inserted a chapter titled "The People of God" between a chapter titled "The Mystery of the Church" and a chapter on the hierarchy. That action, Untener mused, constituted a singularly important recognition "that the mystery of the church" lived foremost in the entire body of the faithful—laity, religious, clergy, and bishops—not only or even chiefly in the hierarchy. Here was Untener's explanation of the theological basis for Dearden's pastoral sensitivity and the opportunity for substantial participation that he would afford the laity during the reforms that marked his tenure in Detroit. Like Wolford Hughes, then, the future bishop contended that Dearden did not essentially change. Rather, just as the Church had evolved because of the Council, Dearden, "not without considerable effort," adjusted his outlook and leadership style and worked continually to engage the renewal embraced by Vatican II.[16]

His role as first president of a fractious national conference required him to cultivate the "unobtrusive" side of his liberalism. As numerous external or societal concerns demanded his attention, he labored tirelessly to transform a group of largely individualist bishops, each of whom was virtually (and canonically) sovereign in his own diocese, into an organization molded by consensus on a variety of important issues.[17] Among its central social concerns in the late 1960s were poverty, civil rights, collective bargaining (especially for migrant farm workers), and the war in Vietnam. Several months before his election as conference president in November 1966, Dearden anticipated what lay ahead for the American Church: "We, the People of God." he affirmed, "are intimately bound up with all the concerns [of those with] whom we live."[18] Three years later, that commitment reached a new plateau when the NCCB formed the Campaign for Human Development (CHD), a response to the "crisis of human needs and aspirations . . . in American society" and to the "impact" of Vatican II. In many ways, CHD simply institutionalized positions that Dearden and the bishops had taken on major social questions a year earlier, but it became the American conference's "most significant and longest-running experiment in U.S. social action." While not original in intent, CHD was unprecedented in the scope of Catholic activism for which it provided moral and financial assistance.[19]

Even though peace and social-justice concerns were significant and time-consuming, internal Church controversies and challenges absorbed most of Dearden's NCCB energies during the late 1960s. Key issues included liturgical reforms, confessional practices, divorce and remarriage, mandatory celibacy, inquisitorial directives from Rome, seminary curricula, Catholic education, hospital ethics, the suspect contents of a religious textbook, contraception, abortion, the establishment of due process in canon law, and the rise of Catholic Pentecostalism. Two dozen standing NCCB committees handled most problems and made recommendations to the conference or its executive committee. To Dearden's credit and that of his allies, whenever the bishops did issue a statement, whether from a committee or in a pastoral from the entire conference, they were able to muster the support of substantial majorities. Dearden also continually strove to build consensus—albeit less successfully—between bishops and clergy, including priest theologians, and by appealing to the nation's lay Catholics through key appointments on the archdiocesan staff and by broad consultations on questions of structural change and the exercise of authority.[20]

Dissent and Due Process

By early 1969, the year Dearden delivered two of the three addresses to be examined here, he had served as NCCB president for two and a half crisis-filled years. In spring 1967, he reassured archconservative Cardinal Alfredo Ottaviani, prefect of the Congregation for the Doctrine of the Faith (CDF), that there were no heresies in the American Church. Ironically, Dearden penned his response shortly before he and other trustees of the Catholic University of America initially refused to reappoint moral theologian Father Charles E. Curran because of the latter's allegedly suspect teachings on human sexuality.[21] That same year Pope Paul VI formally authorized a revision of the 1917 Code of Canon Law. Among the results were growing demands for due-process procedures that came to the bishops' attention. Early drafts of the new code, in which members of the Canon Law Society of America played an important role, actually included for the first time a bill of rights for Catholics, and American canonists and their episcopal supporters pressed for the establishment of due process and legal recourse not just for dissident or dissenting priests and religious but for laity too.[22]

A year later, at its fall 1968 meeting, the NCCB approved a formal set of guidelines for licit dissent as part of its conciliatory and compromise-generated pastoral response to *Humanae Vitae*'s prohibition of artificial contraception. Whereas the guidelines of an earlier draft of *Human Life in Our Day* had been addressed simply to "Catholics," the bishops could muster the required votes only by more narrowly stipulating that its criteria were for clergy and priest-theologians. For the reform-minded, of course, the effort was not adequate or broad enough. Respected canonist and Dearden admirer Father James Coriden argued the urgency of establishing procedures for due process throughout the Church: "Nearly every week, there is news of some conflict between a bishop and his priests, of some protest from the people, of some ruling from Rome. Often these items include a cry of rights denied, freedom restricted, lack of 'due process,' or adequate recourse. Not all of the outcries are justified, but the chorus cannot be denied."[23]

Indirect evidence strongly suggests that as archbishop of Detroit, where he wore the "liberal" part of his sobriquet more comfortably, Dearden agreed with Coriden. As a late-appointed member of the pope's birth-control commission in 1966, Dearden, along with most of his fellow bishops on the commission, had recommended a change in the Church's traditional teaching on contraception, partly on the conclusion that contraception was not intrinsically evil. After *Humanae Vitae's* release, he publicly acknowledged his acceptance, but privately was unhappy with the encyclical, and there is no evidence that he looked for archdiocesan priestly dissenters to discipline. Indeed, he allowed one conspicuous dissenter, Father Anthony Kosnik, to remain in his post at the regional seminary. Several years later, in 1974, he appointed to that seminary and made director of his Family Life Office a controversial Dutch theologian whose writing had run afoul of the Vatican because of allegedly heterodox views on divorced and remarried Catholics who had not received annulments but desired to receive the sacraments.[24]

First Address: A "Celebration of [Archdiocesan] Synod/69"

John Dearden was acutely aware of and pastorally sensitive to the problems cited by Coriden and others, even though effective solutions ultimately eluded him—perhaps for reasons more fully discoverable in his currently inaccessible archdiocesan papers. Whenever he wrote or spoke of his hopes for his beleaguered Church, he never distanced himself from the array of controversies that were fraying nerves and fracturing loyalties.[25] It was as archbishop of Detroit, not as conference president, that he took his first widely publicized action to resolve contentious issues and further the development of a Vatican II Church. Synod/69, held in late March in Detroit's Cobo Hall, was the tenth synod in the history of the archdiocese. It followed three years of planning, study, discussion, and dialogue among nearly 200,000 members of the archdiocese, including "80,000 adults [lay, religious, and clergy] and 100,000 students and young adults." In terms of preparation alone, the gathering was a unique experiment in shared responsibility.[26] Synod/69's express purpose was to "reflect the contemporary Church and implement the renewal of Vatican Council II." Its motto, "Seeking Progress Together," mirrored the "collective discernment" that brought it about. Dearden celebrated it as "a radical decentralization of authority" in the Detroit archdiocese and as a mark of greater involvement by the laity in the governing process, moves toward what then-Father Kenneth Untener described as "a process of participatory decision-making."[27] One respected news source commented that Dearden seemed to be "interpreting his office to mean presiding over the local church instead of dominating it."[28]

Canonically, the synod had only a consultative role, but Dearden turned it into something more by promising that the decisions of the majority would guide him. His pledge was the first concrete measure by which he conveyed his commitment to collaborative structural reform in the American Church. Synod statutes, recommendations, and related materials are available in an eighty-page booklet published by the archdiocese. Its provisions set a precedent for the kind of inclusiveness that Dearden repeated in later addresses to his episcopal confreres and to broader Catholic audiences. "The Church of the Archdiocese," he wrote, "will be stronger because we as a people were able to share responsibility for its growth in Christ." Symbolic of his message and of the synod's collaborative nature, Dearden's introductory address filled only the left half of each page. Adjacent columns contained brief, poignant quotes from various personages and other significant sources, a format followed throughout the booklet. Together, they impart an incarnational significance to the synod and denote respect for both the immanent and the transcendent qualities of the Church. Wisdom from Jesuit priest scientist Pierre Teilhard de Chardin—e.g., including the saying that "the world will belong to whoever offers it . . . the greatest hope"—appears four times on the pages of Dearden's address, more than any other source. Additional quotes are from Father Bernard Cooke, S.J.; scientist Robert

Oppenheimer; St. Paul's first and second epistles to the Corinthians; the Book of Revelation, and, predictably, Pope John XXIII.[29]

Dearden was confident that the synod would for a long time continue to inspire and motivate Catholics in his archdiocese. Reminding its participants of the rights and duties that flowed from their collaborative efforts to hold a "dialogue between God and Man," he began the conclusion of his remarks on a note that was upbeat and accommodating, as he almost always was when he wrote or spoke of the Church: "[For] all of us in this Archdiocese," he declared "[there must] continue . . . a state of Synodal co-responsibility, of constant searching . . . to identify and clarify what our Christian concerns should be and to find new and better ways to satisfy them."[30] Synod decisions, he reminded the participants, were not necessarily permanent. Opportunities would arise to modify them without compromising the synod's essential provisions: "We have dealt with people, and what people do, and the things of this world with which they do them. It is only the last of these that admits the government of laws or responds to sanctions. By our common effort we have found and named the ideals which command our acceptance. No further urging should be needed than the force of our love. The strictest law is finally the law of love of God and love of the Church."[31]

Waiting until the final paragraph to underscore his most important point, Dearden elaborated on the abiding "law of love," his greater understanding of which dated from the Council debates that produced *Gaudium et Spes, The Pastoral Constitution on the Church in the Modern World*. It was while he chaired the subcommission that drafted the sections on "Marriage and the Family" that he came to more fully appreciate the essential difference between a contract and a covenant. A contract, he noted, "may be modified by the people who have written [it]," but a covenant "is not something that can be changed once it is entered into . . . , because its nature is fixed by God, and the contracting parties . . . the covenantal parties, are . . . bound by its nature once they enter into it."[32] Thus sharing what he considered his central insight, he ended his address with the words of a leader servant at peace with the synod and with what it signified for the archdiocese: "While we have tried, insofar as it is possible, to specify this love, above all let this Synod stand as a covenant. It is a covenant of responsibilities to be fully what our Christian calling urges on us. It is a covenant whose force to command is what is in our hearts rather

Archbishop Dearden presiding at the celebration Mass at Synod/69.
Courtesy of *The Michigan Catholic*, photo by Tony Spina

than what can be imposed on us. It is a covenant of all of us entered into with God, and by it let all men know that we are Christians."[33]

A Synod/69 Afterword

Detroit's gathering was one of several important exceptions to the generally halting pace with which American bishops moved after Vatican II to implement pastoral changes in the exercise of episcopal authority and decision-making. Jeremy Bonner's chapter, "Who Will Guard the Guardians?" elaborates this point in considerable detail. He demonstrates the uniqueness and variable degrees of success with which other bishops provided opportunities for lay involvement, several of which began before and during Vatican II. Paths taken in such dioceses as Tulsa and Pittsburgh reveal both the strengths and weaknesses inherent in attempts to add democratic structures to large urban churches. In some cases the experiments, as Andrew Moore illustrates in "Christian Unity, Lay Authority and the People of God," his chapter on the archdiocese of Atlanta, were short-lived or turned contentious on many levels. Most dioceses, in fact, witnessed varying degrees of episcopal, clerical, and even lay reluctance to seriously begin the process, let alone implement it.[34]

Notwithstanding the mixed outcomes of diocesan attempts to broaden lay involvement, Detroit's Synod/69 gave the former "Iron John" an opportunity to develop and actually implement ecclesiological ideas that he had embraced at the Council. He reorganized the archdiocese to fortify a sense of pastoral community—to make it more *Gemeinschaftlich*, or communitarian, and less *Gesellschaftlich*, or bureaucratic. Eliminating the chancery, he divided his juridical territory into twenty-five vicariates, each composed of fifteen to twenty parishes. All vicariates were a mix of urban, suburban, and rural parishes designed to make each vicariate council think holistically about the needs of the Church. By launching a new organizational structure that initially included the popular election of twenty-five episcopal vicars, he deliberately moved in the direction of community renewal, solidarity, and subsidiarity. In doing so, Dearden reversed the chancery-centered organization nurtured by his two predecessors.[35]

Synod/69 drew national and international praise from progressive Catholics and influenced reorganizations in other dioceses. Dearden had accomplished his goal of incremental but not sweeping reform through compromise and shared decision-making, albeit not without criticism from some of the very Catholics whom he had hoped would embrace his actions. According to one sociological study, professionalizing the administration of the archdiocese provoked criticism by some laypeople who resented any new elite, whether lay or clerical, that seemed bent on imposing its will, particularly in liturgical matters. Specifically, the authors point to conflicts that arose "between the simple lay or ethnic Catholics and professional elites, especially liturgists" who felt entitled by their expertise to determine liturgical changes."[36]

Dearden offered a reasoned response to the uneven success of the archdiocesan reforms:

> To move to a period where you have to have endless consultations with great numbers of different people and organizations causes a major adjustment. . . . On the other hand, it isn't so much the end result anymore, as the fact that those who are affected by a decision have a voice in the shaping of it. And that's the reality of our time. I've had to learn to do those things, and it was no easier for me than for anyone else. I may have known the language, but that's all.

Problems aside, the organizational changes embodied in Synod/69 and the collaborative manner in which Dearden implemented them became among the most enduring parts of his legacy. Even after Dearden resigned in 1980 and his conservative successor recreated the chancery, reclaiming its pre-synod authority, the synod's spirit and some portions—e.g., the vicariate structure—of its concrete results have endured.[37]

Second Address: A Church for the Future (Spring 1969)

Shortly before Dearden celebrated Synod/69, news that Pope Paul VI had named him a cardinal lifted his spirits and must have seemed a blessing of his developing ecclesiology. Time magazine lost no time publicizing the ideological significance of the appointment, touting him as the "only outright progressive among the [thirty-five] new cardinals." Buoyed by his selection for the red hat and by the immediate post-synod glow in Detroit, Dearden opened the spring 1969 meeting of the NCCB with an address later published as "The Church of Tomorrow." Less than four standard pages, it was a bold, cogently argued case for a more collaboratively governed, less clericalized Church—that is, one in which the laity especially would play a significant role. At the same time, he chose his words carefully in order to "allay any concerns some bishops might have had about [the kind of Church] called for by Council teaching."[38] His opening assertion, for example, that the American Church was a microcosm of the universal Church was assuaging. So too was his admission that no one could predict the Church's future with certainty. Having created a conciliatory ambiance, Dearden affirmed the continued "vigor" of the postconciliar American Church, tactfully forecasting its continuing unity in all things essential and its "diversity" in all things that did not challenge the former. Some bishops may have thought he meant "diversity" in a way that did not compromise uniformity in belief and practice. Most likely, he used the word to express the strength of American Catholicism and to assure the conference that the reforms he supported did not constitute an impediment to ties with Rome.[39]

This does not mean that Dearden played down the ecclesial "tensions" in the American Church. Many of them, he readily acknowledged, would continue in the future. They did not, however, have to impede, and in fact could assist, the Church's continuing renewal. The juxtaposition of tension and renewal may have drawn inspiration from the model used by the Reverend Martin Luther King Jr. His 1963 manifesto, "Letter from a Birmingham Jail," attributed singular importance to the role played by "creative tension" as a means of promoting dialogue and achieving (in King's case, racial) reconciliation. Dearden seemed to agree that without such tension no authentic progress could occur. There is no thorough study of Dearden's theology of Church with which to substantiate this inference, but it is plausible that in King's paradigm he found consolation as well as sound advice for understanding and confronting the considerable turmoil in the American Church.[40]

For Dearden, confronting Church turmoil was chiefly the responsibility of the bishops, acting individually and as a conference. He added a point, however, that may have made some bishops balk: the assertion that a pastoral approach was vital to resolving conflicts. Ministry, he insisted, must be to persons— "priests, religious, or laymen"—not to institutions. Bishops must make others' "anguish and . . . concerns" their own, and "the bewildered, the uncertain and the frightened have a claim upon us side by side with the impatient, the impetuous and the demanding." Attending to the immanent and earthly was at the heart of Dearden's plan. As he put it, "apart from [institutions and structures] that are basic to the very nature of the Church,"—i.e., its transcendent elements—everything else was on the table. "There must be openness," he counseled, "to adapt those man-made structures that are less suited to the times. . . . Many things" need reexamination and reappraisal. "Some will undoubtedly survive with little or no change; others will call for radical change." In any case, he warned, not reexamining, not reappraising, not adapting where necessary would have dire consequences for the Church, possibly leading "to a rejection of the Church itself."[41]

Having proposed what he considered the only viable method of confronting Church crises, Dearden then addressed the boundaries of reform by implicitly juxtaposing the Church Transcendent and the Church Immanent. All "reappraisal" and change, he asserted, must derive from "the teachings of Christ and the good of his people." Notably, he did not include the word "magisterium," a loaded term that had become politically and theologically burdened with confusion and disagreement. *Humanae Vitae* in particular had dealt a devastating blow to that word's stature and credibility among activists as well as most "ordinary" Catholics. Keenly aware that established authority was under siege both in the Church and in the nation, Dearden prophetically cautioned that problems would only become worse if current practices of authority did not change: "[If] as is true in every order today, authority is challenged, we must recognize the challenge for what it is. Most often it is not authority that is questioned, but the way in which authority is exercised. And it is one of the basic realities of our time that in the Church, as in other institutions, if authority is to retain its credibility, it must function in a manner different from that of the past."[42]

During Vatican II, Dearden had come to understand authority as "a ministry of service" that required a more inclusive "decision-making process." Since he was now addressing a largely moderate to highly conservative episcopate, he wisely phrased his remarks in a way that conveyed both the Church's immanent and its transcendent qualities. A more inclusive approach to decision-making, he assured his confreres, would entail "no dilution of authority, no abandonment of authority. On the contrary, it means a more intelligent exercise of authority through the collaboration of those [laity, clergy, and religious] who with us are the Church." As if to then calm anxious listeners wondering what he might say next, he reminded the bishops that he did not support immediate change. What he wanted was "many intermediate steps," albeit without procrastination. The road to change, that is, must begin immediately with "concrete programs of action [established by the NCCB] that can help us to achieve at least some of our goals." Not doing so, he added, would be tantamount to treating only the symptoms of Church ills.[43]

Recognizing that the exercise of authority through collaboration required many steps, Dearden cited the central conciliar teaching about the meaning of Church among the People of God. Simply put, it was exercising authority in a way that conformed to "the mind of Christ." As he had done earlier in his address, he again referenced Christ, not the pope or the magisterium. As one who in June 1966 had voted with the vast majority of the pope's birth-control commission for a change in the Church's teaching on contraception, Dearden had private reservations regarding the exclusive identification of Christ's teachings with authoritative but noninfallible papal pronouncements. Still, he was confident that the Church was up to the task of genuine renewal and that, like the Council, the Church too, for all its troubles, remained under the guidance of the Holy Spirit.

With this assurance, he closed a "well received" address.[44] Measured and reassuring to the NCCB, Dearden nevertheless left no doubt about his commitment to what he believed was an authentic expression of Vatican II ecclesiology. Indeed, the fundamental message in his address meshed with another thoughtful, albeit less guarded, appraisal the same year by theologian Father Charles Meyer:

> Hopefully it [the Council, in Lumen Gentium, the Dogmatic Constitution on the Church] dealt a deathblow to the conception of the Church as an organization that is primarily and formally eschatological, transhistorical, immutable, omniscient, impeccable, invested with absolute and supreme authority, a surrogate for the divine, an idol in the fullest sense. Happily it excoriated an even more subtle and pernicious error, that the Church would be one frozen forever in the Tridentine paradigm. It is true enough: to refuse to respond to this teaching of Vatican II would not be heresy; but would it be ecclesiological suicide?[45]

Third Address: Presidential Farewell (Fall 1971)

Having circulated his Council-inspired message through the archdiocesan synod and the NCCB, Dearden spent much of his last two presidential years on new and continuing internal issues and controversies, most of which derived, directly or indirectly, from the crisis of faith and authority triggered by the dissent from Humanae Vitae.[46] All of the disagreements influenced his final annual report to the conference in the fall of 1971. It embodied his closing presidential recommendation for a more inclusive, less clericalized Church. With characteristic modesty—and an astute sense of realpolitik—Dearden stated at the outset that his comments were not going to be an exercise in narrow self-evaluation. Instead, his purpose was to "review and appraise" the accomplishments of the conference since its inception in 1966. Characterizing the previous five years as "extraordinary," Dearden clearly acknowledged the troubled condition of the American Church, a condition he linked to "our nation" and "our world," where there had been rapid, even "radical" changes. In connecting Church and society, he was likely doing more than simply drawing a parallel. He was prompting his fellow bishops, especially the most conservative among them, to recall that his own public preferences for the Church favored changes that would be incremental and gradual, not rapid or radical.[47]

While the Church, like much of the world, was in crisis, the former, he contended, was clearly experiencing a crisis "of transition, of adaption [and] of growth." All of the "many challenges . . . which unavoidably attend the Church" must be confronted head on. There was no time, therefore, for either "timidity or alarm." Indeed, Dearden entreated the bishops to see in the Church's crisis "great hope for the future."[48] One way to deal with the crisis, he implied throughout his address, was to continue incorporating into the Church appropriate facets of the nation's democratic institutions and ideals.In part, the bishops had already done this by reconstituting the National Catholic Welfare Conference into the NCCB/USCC. As a result, they had gained, if only for a time, not only greater autonomy on local matters through the conference's rejuvenation of "subsidiarity" but also an institutional base from which to address both societal and ecclesiastical problems. Notwithstanding its improved situation, the conference had to remember—and here there must have been a stir among the most conservative bishops—that it existed not primarily to be a governing body. First and foremost, the conference should act as the foundation for "the collaborative efforts [i.e., among all the People of God] that the future will demand of us."[49]

With pride, Dearden noted, without explicitly mentioning the influence of democratic ideals, accomplishments such as the conference's initial adoption of due-process procedures, its ecumenical outreach, the formation of an advisory council made up of "priests, religious, and laymen"; and the Campaign for Human Development. Not all was well, however. Friction and mistrust typified the relationship between many "bishops and priests" and between the latter two groups and "the laity." Ascribing blame to no one and mistakes to all, Dearden called for an end to the "breach" through greater efforts at collaboration, especially between bishops and priests. Perhaps most telling of all, he called for a deeper and stronger "theological" dimension to the conference's activities and decisions. "Religious conviction," not pragmatism, he stressed, must be the NCCB's motivating force. To that end, he welcomed the bishops' authorization of a full-time position for a theologian to advise the conference.[50]

Closing sections of his address pointed to the need for more "collaboration" throughout the Church. That word "collaboration" and its variations form a virtual litany throughout the eight double-spaced pages of his farewell. "Collaborate" and "collaboration" appear seven times in the address;

in between, the words "cooperation," "conciliation-arbitration," "due process," "participation," "shared responsibility," "sharing," "openness," and "communication" ring in harmony. Without abrogating his leadership responsibility or that of the conference, and while expressing respect for the Church's hierarchy, Dearden nonetheless opted for a much less clericalized approach, one that he believed synchronized with the spirit of Vatican II and with the world emerging in its wake. "[We] need to seek other ways of involving more fully other persons in the ongoing work of our Conference," he declared. "We cannot risk isolating ourselves or the Conference from other segments of the Church."[51]

Near the end of his remarks, he reaffirmed his strong faith in the Church's ability to navigate successfully through waves of crises, concluding on a note that was both heartfelt and faith-based. "I am confident of the future," he assured his brother bishops, "as I know you are, for our confidence is the confidence of those who follow Christ." With these sentiments, he completed his last presidential opportunity to promote what he had begun at Synod/69: an unceasing and essentially pastoral, personalist drive to restructure the Church in the United States.[52]

A Call to Action

Central as Dearden's three addresses are to the purpose of demonstrating his ecclesiological mission, nothing honors or disparages his legacy more vividly in both the popular and scholarly mind than one event, the Call to Action conference in the fall of 1976. It would be a serious oversight not to include it here, if only briefly, and in part because of the irony that the NCCB, not Dearden, commissioned it. Admirers and critics alike characterize the three-day gathering as the most concrete way to illustrate Dearden's approach to building an inclusive postconciliar Church. And although it took place under the auspices of the bishops' conference, Dearden chaired it and played a lead role organizing it. The late October assembly at Detroit's Cobo Hall—a result of nearly three years' planning and nationwide consultation—promoted "Liberty and Justice for All." Those who assembled were principally reform-minded Catholics—laity (both men and women, including religious), and clergy—including over one hundred bishops. As he was about to convene it, Dearden emphasized the meeting's historic nature, calling it part of a continuing exercise in

Cardinal Dearden speaking with Catholic laity (1970s)
Courtesy of *The Michigan Catholic*, photo by Tony Spina

"practical collegiality" that had begun in 1789 under Bishop John Carroll. Attendees with positive memories of CTA/76 recall it as *their* high point in hands-on, postconciliar praxis. For lay Catholics especially, it was the pinnacle of Dearden's effort to give them a voice.[53]

During its sessions, the voting delegates directed their attention and recommendations toward justice not simply in the world but also in the Church, an objective that stirred much of the resulting controversy. Two weeks after the event, Dearden assessed its effectiveness in a presentation to the bishops' conference and conceded its shortcomings. He admitted to an overly ambitious agenda and many impractical recommendations, but he also reminded the conference that many of the suggestions had come from individuals, especially laypeople, who in the past had rarely been given an opportunity to voice their convictions. Not one to spotlight the negative, he also praised the assembly's positive achievements in shared responsibility for both the internal and external life of the Church.[54]

The NCCB, led by his close friend and longtime disciple Cincinnati archbishop Joseph Bernardin, who did not attend the CTA, rejected a small percentage of its recommendations—one estimate is 14 of 182. Those they targeted as inappropriate or heterodox were not unexpected, particularly questions of mandatory celibacy, gender equality, and various teachings related to sexual morality. A year later Bernardin struck another dissonant note when he characterized the event as "polarizing." Nevertheless, in its 1978 report, the NCCB, while reaffirming the unique teaching authority of bishops, conceded that CTA had helped reinforce its commitment to continue listening and consulting—though not deliberating with—the whole People of God, as stipulated in *Lumen Gentium*. Perhaps the three most noteworthy later examples of the listening process were the consultations that preceded the pastorals on war (1983) and the economy (1986) and the first draft of an ultimately abortive effort to issue a pastoral on women in the Church (1992).[55] As for those recommendations that the NCCB rejected, they quickly resurfaced in Call to Action's second birth in Chicago in 1978 as a lay-run organization independent of the hierarchy—four years before Joseph Bernardin succeeded Cardinal John Cody as archbishop. CTA's continuing history cannot be told here except to note that its current stances strongly reflect those that failed to receive official support in 1976.[56]

Ironically, in 1996, Bernardin, as archbishop of Chicago, initiated his own effort to mitigate increasing polarization in the Church. But he did so in a more controlled fashion than marked the 1976 event in Detroit or the self-perceived successor organization that formed in his diocese two years later. His "Common Ground Initiative" in some ways echoed the spirit of CTA/76, but his goal of encouraging dialogue and co-responsibility within the Church met with stiff resistance from the outset, most adamantly from fellow bishops. And although Common Ground continues to receive plaudits, it has never experienced the kind of success or institutional support it aspired to in its original statement of purpose.[57]

A Measure of the Man

During the years since Dearden's presidency, CTA/76, and the founding of the Common Ground Initiative, the spirit and the substance of the cardinal's vision by those who learned from it have generated more debate than dialogue. Liberal Catholics, through their scholarship and organizations, have offered their own versions of a future Church. Much though not all of their discourse reaffirms Dearden's message. A steady stream of books, articles, and organizations have touted, pleaded for, extolled, and prognosticated the coming or emergence of a more democratic, collaboratively governed American Catholic Church.[58] Eugene Kennedy's *The Now and Future Church*, David O'Brien's *Public Catholicism*, David Gibson's *The Coming Catholic Church*, Peter Steinfels' *A People Adrift*, Robert McClory's *As It Was in the Beginning*, and John Allen's *The Future Church* contain a progressive schema.[59] In his monograph *What Happened at Vatican II?* and in a later essay, "Vatican II: Did Anything Happen?" Father John O'Malley, S.J., identifies an "epideictic genre" of "persuasion and reconciliation" in the documents of Vatican II, wherein words like "partnership," "collaboration," "dialogue," and "collegiality" played essential roles. Father Joseph Chinnici identified a similar spirit in the correspondence of mid-century reform-minded Catholics who pressed for greater "participation," "collegiality," and a recognition of the "priesthood of the laity." These and other studies, including many of those that have been flying off the presses in commemoration of Vatican II's fiftieth anniversary, may differ in focus, but all attribute importance to *the immanence of Christ's Church* and its continued assimilation of what is best in the American democratic experiment. Organizations such as Corpus, Future Church, Celibacy Is The Issue (CITI), and the Chicago lay-initiated Call to Action all endorse, to varying degrees, similarly grounded definitions of Church.[60]

Conservative or traditional Catholics have adopted more restrictive interpretations of the documents and "spirit" of Vatican II. Their understandings generally dispute the inevitability, desirability, and, at times, possibility of democratization or of a more thorough engagement with the modern world. Some conservatives do admit the necessity of reform and often sanction an agenda for change that endorses more substantive roles for laity, clergy, and religious, but their perspectives generally filter the process of change through a lens that accents *the transcendence of Christ's Church*—e.g., the divine nature of its hierarchical character and its canonically defined teaching magisterium. Many conservative organizations, some with fortress-like names—Catholics United for the Faith, the

Catholic League for Religious and Civil Rights—and others, such as the erudite Fellowship of Catholic Scholars, counter, dissipate, or try to discredit the positions of the liberals. As on the left, so also on the right, there has been no dearth of monographs. Beginning with James Hitchcock's *The Decline and Fall of Catholic Radicalism* and continuing with Msgr. George Kelly's *The Battle for the American Church*, Ralph McInerny's *What Went Wrong at Vatican II*, and George Weigel's *The Courage to Be Catholic*, all avow, more or less, the resolute *Roma locuta est, causa finita est*—Rome has spoken, the case is closed.[61] Similar publications, like those on the left, will likewise continue to promote this point of view in commemoration of Vatican II.[62]

Contending groups on both sides of the frequently fuzzy center have been at loggerheads over the pivotal theological question of Vatican II. Was the Council, as Fathers John O'Malley and Andrew Greeley have concluded, a major reform event, or was it, as scholars such as the late Ralph McInerny seem to suggest, the closing chapter in continuity with its unfinished predecessor, Vatican I (1869–70)?[63] Both interpretations derive much of their support from the same hermeneutic challenge: the compromised language that makes up the sixteen major Council documents. Compromises enabled the Council fathers to achieve consensus by an otherwise impossibly large margin of assent. Concessions helped them produce magisterially approved teachings whose language, notably in the four constitutions, is frequently elusive. Liberals and conservatives claim the validity of their respective understandings of those teachings, but the less ideologically bound on both sides concede that Council documents lend themselves to different yet arguably defensible perspectives. Much more than in the 1960s, however, today's liberal and conservative Catholic scholars and activists write, speak, and organize in an atmosphere of *Sturm und Drang* that Dearden would have deeply lamented. There is also today a stronger sense of urgency that occasionally resounds with the faint clatter of a death rattle as each side argues its respective ecclesiology. Massimo Faggioli in *Vatican II: The Battle for Meaning* (2012) provides an insightful perspective on the often intense scholarly debates over the meaning of Vatican II that have occurred in recent decades between liberals and conservatives. Similar studies will no doubt follow, but so undoubtedly will the battles, scholarly and otherwise.[64]

Conclusion

John Cardinal Dearden would have been very uneasy with the way liberals and conservatives have drawn their battle lines, but he would continue to agree with the liberals that "the death of ecclesiastical authoritarianism" is necessary. And he would support "a concept of authority that realizes itself" through "methodological collegiality" and consensus. Such goals, he granted in 1974, were well worth pursuing, though not easy to achieve:

> I know if I want to win the cooperation and the understanding of those with whom I am working, priests, religious and laymen, I must be prepared to participate with them in the process of moving toward the decisions that have to be made. It is a reality. And while I can grumble as loudly as any of you at unproductive meetings, I realize that this is the process that is important for the life of the Church. In our own

A Pensive Cardinal Dearden (1970s)
Courtesy of *The Michigan Catholic*, photo by Tony Spina

stumbling, bumbling way we are trying to reflect our understanding and faith of what it means to be a member of a Christian Community.[65]

Confident that his ecclesiology could reconcile *all except the most extreme* (my emphasis) positions in the Church, he saw it too as a via media that welcomed more than just liberals who believed that personal and societal salvation lay in greater and sustained acknowledgment of the Church's immanence. Dearden's ecclesiology also included genuine respect for conservatives who countered that Catholics must uphold and increase their recognition of the Church's transcendent qualities. He numbered both variegated groups among the "People of God" in the flexible divine and human entity that he advanced in response to Pope John XXIII's call for *aggiornamento*. John Dearden's response continues to resonate, if only through the fractious, obfuscating discourse of today's culture wars over the future of the Catholic Church in the United States.[66]

11 Christian Unity, Lay Authority, and the People of God

The Community of Christ Our Brother in the Archdiocese of Atlanta, 1967–1969

ANDREW S. MOORE

In 1967 the Archdiocese of Atlanta, under the leadership of Paul J. Hallinan, launched a bold experiment in parish organization. Rather than being defined by geographical boundaries, as Catholic parishes traditionally were, the new Community of Christ Our Brother would recruit its members from across the city, in the manner of the Protestant churches that dominated Atlanta's religious landscape. The Community would seek to address social-justice problems, experiment with liturgical changes, and eventually explore avenues for ecumenical dialogue and cooperation. The accounts, given in earlier chapters, of the experiences of Cardinal Dearden in Detroit, Bishop Wright in Pittsburgh, and Bishop Reed in Oklahoma all demonstrate the difficulty that bishops and activist laity faced in striking a balance between greater lay participation and ecclesiastical authority. Even ordinaries supportive of increased lay authority, as these men were, imposed limits on their openness, limits that in turn threatened to alienate some laity. Two ultimately insoluble problems confronted the Community of Christ our Brother. The first was the attempt to approximate Protestant organization and government while remaining identifiably Catholic. Like their counterparts elsewhere, the thirty to forty people who made up the Community were eager to exercise greater authority in Church leadership and social activism. Consequently, their second problem, familiar to observers of Catholic Action and lay activity in the Vatican II period, was to balance a spirit of experimentation and greater lay involvement with appropriate pastoral oversight and respect for Church authority. Their failure to resolve either of these problems satisfactorily would lead to the parish's demise in 1969.[1]

The Second Vatican Council generally affirmed the right of individual freedom and conscience and encouraged bishops, priests, and laity to interpret "the signs of the times . . . in light of the Gospel."[2] It also introduced liturgical innovations and deemphasized the notion of the Church as a hierarchical institution in favor of the image of the Church as the "People of God." As several essays in this volume illustrate, one unintentional result of the Council was that traditional lines of authority became blurred, and, in the mid-1960s, priests, nuns, and many laypeople looked for new ways with which to engage secular society. As bishops increasingly sought to backpedal and rein in overenthusiastic laity and religious, the latter, inspired by conciliar changes, increased their participation in civil rights demonstrations against racial segregation and criticized Church leaders for not reacting swiftly enough to social change. Such activists challenged their bishops openly, justifying their stand with appeals to the dictates of personal conscience and charges that the decrees of the Church sometimes ran counter to the needs of contemporary society.

Hallinan, the leader of the archdiocese from 1962 until his death in 1968, was a member of a relatively young, progressive-minded group of Americans who had become bishops after the Second World War. He participated in the Second Vatican Council as a specialist on the liturgy, and he was a prominent advocate of experimentation. He agreed that the spirit of Vatican II called for a greater lay role in archdiocesan affairs. To that end, he convened a lay congress to meet in 1966, "to provide a true channel for lay opinion, initiative and participation." That was important, he concluded, because the "consecration of the world—the prime responsibility of the layman can hardly take place unless priest and laymen really share in the prophetic, priestly and ruling tasks of the Church, each according to his calling."[3] Meeting after the lay congress, an archdiocesan synod created seven new councils and boards that would oversee archdiocesan affairs. Each parish selected a total of fifty-nine lay delegates to all seven boards, and laymen chaired each of the new groups.[4]

Encouraged by Vatican II, then, many American Catholics saw the importance of individual conscience increase as the Church's official authority diminished. The Community of Christ Our Brother embodied this emphasis on the importance of conscience and leadership by the Holy Spirit, both among the laity and in the person of its charismatic priest administrator the Reverend Conald Foust. Ordained to the priesthood in the early 1950s, Foust was eager to be on the leading edge of liturgical and social change in the archdiocese. He participated in civil rights demonstrations, and some original members of the Community first met him when he offered a "folk mass" at the Cathedral of Christ the King.[5] Over the course of the parish's brief existence, Father Foust and the Community's lay members substituted the authority of their own consciences and the democratic consensus of the Community for the authority of the archbishop and Church teaching. Indeed, the experimental parish empowered some Catholic laity, many of whom had grown disenchanted with traditional religious institutions and found in the Community of Christ Our Brother an intriguing alternative. They sought new understandings of Christian community and embraced the significance of the leadership of the Holy Spirit in individual lives. Although outside the mainstream of American Catholic thought and practice, the parish could be included in the "underground" movement that flourished in dioceses all over the country in the late 1960s. These unauthorized and experimental gatherings comprised laypeople, clergy, and women religious seeking a more authentic if informal liturgical experience. They met in homes, used for the Eucharist eccentric elements such as consecrated doughnuts or birthday cake, listened to secular music, and danced "folk dances." Unlike most of these underground movements, the Community of Christ our Brother at least began with archdiocesan support. This new parish can also be placed within larger movements in American religion. Many of its members were "seekers" exploring new avenues for spiritual expression.[6]

On the one hand, the Community of Christ Our Brother represented one way that the post–Vatican II Catholic Church flirted with more egalitarian lines of spiritual authority. Laypeople took seriously the Council's elevation of their role in the Church. On the other hand, the Community also embodied the convergence of the Vatican Council and the civil rights movement, which helped to reshape the American Catholic Church in the 1960s. In Atlanta, Archbishop Hallinan and prominent white laypeople embraced the goals of the mainstream civil rights movement. Their uncompromising arguments for racial justice and integration placed them in the company of civil rights activists who saw the movement as a religious event, a redemptive opportunity that would ultimately reconcile blacks and whites in what Martin Luther King Jr. called a "beloved community." Since the nineteenth century, the Catholic Church in the South had to balance its belief that salvation came only through the Church with the South's legal and social demands for racial segregation. As a result, dioceses in the South evangelized African Americans but built separate institutions for them. By the late 1950s, however, an increasing number of white Catholics were ready to challenge the Church's complicity in the sinfulness of Jim Crow. That stance put Hallinan and those like him among a minority of white Southerners, many of whom insisted that the black freedom struggle was simply a political movement.[7] Through his rhetoric and example, however, King made the movement a spiritual movement. Segregation, according to King, "is a blatant denial of the unity which we all have in Jesus Christ." From that perspective, the goal of the civil-rights movement was reconciliation, a reminder that all were one in Jesus Christ.[8]

The Second Vatican Council also encouraged Catholics to rethink the official relationship to ecumenism. In January 1966, for example, the archdiocese encouraged its churches to participate in a week of prayer for Christian unity. Archbishop Hallinan instructed priests to urge members of their congregations to attend a series of "unity services" at Presbyterian, Baptist, Lutheran, Orthodox, Episcopalian, and Methodist churches. "We go," Hallinan wrote, "not out of curiosity or even fellowship—we go to pray that, in God's good time, 'all may be one.' . . . We go as Catholics, in no way diminishing the certitude of our faith, but we pray as brothers."[9] Hallinan led by example on ecumenical issues. He befriended other racial moderates and liberals in the city, including Rabbi Jacob Rothschild and Ralph McGill, executive editor of the *Atlanta Constitution*. He represented the renewed, postconciliar Catholic Church, open to the outside world and to cooperation with non-Catholics on social-justice issues.[10]

Hallinan, the Ohio native and progressive archbishop, and Atlanta, the New South city, were a solid match. Hallinan was one of the South's most liberal archbishops, an avid supporter of both the civil rights movement and the Second Vatican Council. In the 1960s, Atlanta represented the progressive city of moderate race relations—the city too busy with economic development to be distracted by the Southern states' single-minded and reckless defense of segregation. No Atlantan in power (white or black, it seemed) wanted the city to appear divided—for civic leaders, appearances and the city's image were much more important than actually solving racial problems.[11] Despite its reputation for moderate race relations, white Atlanta originally refused to honor its native son Martin Luther King, Jr. after he won the 1964 Nobel Peace Prize. Only Archbishop

Hallinan and three other prominent Atlantans (two white, one black)—
Ralph McGill, Rabbi Rothschild, and Morehouse College president Ben-
jamin Mays—proved willing to sponsor a banquet in January 1965 in
honor of the civil rights leader. Racially liberal mayor Ivan Allen Jr. tried
but failed to rally the white business community, some of whom bought
tickets at the last minute only to avoid embarrassment.[12]

The archbishop left a hospital stay early in order to attend the banquet
at Atlanta's Dinkler Plaza Hotel ballroom. In his address, Hallinan praised
the civil rights leader as a "pioneer in a new dynamic of peace . . . a creative
leader in racial justice, as a man . . . who has raised justice through non-
violence from a tactic to a high form of authentic Christian love."[13] Two
decades later, Mayor Allen recalled that "Archbishop Hallinan was a
prime mover in seeing that the business community supported that dinner," and King himself wrote Hallinan "to express my deep gratitude for
your sponsorship of the dinner honoring me."[14] King described Hallinan's
brief remarks there as "both eloquent and moving and I shall treasure
them amongst the storehouse of memories as a light of encouragement for
the many dark and desolate days of struggle which are before us."[15]

Hallinan and the Archdiocese of Atlanta were leaders in liturgical development. Even during the Council, the archbishop encouraged experimentation in liturgical matters. As early as 1963, priests at St. Joseph's
parish in Athens, Georgia, removed the church's communion rail (where
parishioners had knelt to receive the Eucharist), implemented a "dialogue" Mass (where worshipers responded to priests in the service), and
celebrated Mass facing the congregation. All were innovations that would
become standard practice in the postconciliar Catholic Church, but in
1963 they were considered, in the words of one St. Joseph's priest, "way
out." These reforms signaled greater interaction between priest and laity
and marked the Church's recasting of its relationship to a new era.[16]

Prior to its formal establishment, planners of the Community of Christ
Our Brother sought permission for several liturgical changes that would
have more fully integrated their social activism with their weekly worship. They requested permission to replace scriptural readings with other
material more relevant to the activities in which the community was engaged, including "some selection from current literature." Father Foust
argued that this was important, "since one of the essential purposes in
forming this experimental community is to be directly relevant to the

city, and the community is focused on human needs." In addition, the homily would be followed by "breaking up into smaller groups to 'come to grips' with the word of God in relation to actual daily life." Congregants would then reassemble for the continuation of the Mass.[17] Foust and the Community of Christ Our Brother thus exemplified liturgical trends in Atlanta but pushed their innovations just a little too far, leading to the Community's ultimate demise and Foust's eventual dismissal from the priesthood.

The idea for the Community of Christ Our Brother came from Father Foust himself. In September 1966, Foust defended the necessity of experimentation, arguing that change was inevitable and that the archdiocese could lead or play catch-up later. He claimed that priests, seminarians, and the laity alike would move faster than the hierarchy and that experimentation would "go on 'underground'" if not formally sanctioned, while Catholics would ignore their bishop if he tried to legislate against experimentation. Indeed, any attempt to stifle creativity and exploration threatened to lead to "schism" and to separate otherwise well-meaning Catholics from "the Body of the Faithful." The archbishop, therefore, must demonstrate "courageous and creative vision [in] this rapidly growing city and diocese." Even if bishops feared the eventual outcome, they must trust priests and laypeople to do what was best for the Church.[18] Foust's idea of experimentation included the establishment of a nonterritorial parish, a congregation composed of Catholics from all over the city instead of just those living in a specific neighborhood. This experimental parish would be the locus for archdiocesan innovations in ecumenism and the liturgy.

Archbishop Hallinan agreed with Foust about the importance of experimentation, and he approved creation of a committee to explore the possibility of an "open" parish. His vision of what the parish should be clashed with Foust's, however, and the relationship between priest and prelate proved rocky until Foust agreed to Hallinan's guidelines for the parish. Father Foust's and the Community's uneasy relationship with the archbishop and the Church hierarchy mirrors the ordeal of the wider Catholic Church in the era of the Second Vatican Council. Initially, Foust demonstrated his and the Community's willingness (even eagerness) to submit to the archbishop's authority. At the first meeting of the planning committee of the would-be parish, the group agreed that they must not proceed without the support of priests and diocesan leaders. They decided that they must "submit our findings to the Senate of Priests and the Pastoral Council." "A kind of concensus [sic] is necessary," the group allowed, "working within these structures." Father Foust informally polled eight of his fellow priests, and, according to the minutes of the first meeting, "only one encouraged him" while "the other seven expressed fears and objections." The group found comfort, however, in the novelty of its challenge, since this sort of "discouragement is to be expected with something so new."[19]

That spirit of cooperation that initially characterized the Community would ebb as the new parish got off the ground. From the beginning, Father Foust was pressing against the boundaries of diocesan authority and challenging Archbishop Hallinan. In a letter written the week before the first organizational meeting of the experimental parish, Foust responded to his prelate's refusal to allow a Catholic wedding ceremony to take place in a Protestant church. Foust assumed that the archbishop's leadership style did not desire mere assent on the part of his subordinates. Instead, the independent-minded priest took for granted that Hallinan wanted his priests to challenge his decisions and share their differing opinions, as if sharing contrasting viewpoints would somehow make the archdiocese ideologically stronger if not more broadminded. Foust first charged Hallinan's decision with being "a step backward from what is already permitted in the Archdiocese." As a result of postconciliar decisions, Atlanta Catholics were already allowed to participate in Protestant worship, provided that they did not partake of Communion. Current Church regulations also permitted a Protestant minister to offer prayers—but not perform the ceremony itself—after a wedding between a Catholic and a non-Catholic. Foust claimed that his proposal would be less confusing to ordinary laypeople than would current regulations.[20]

Of course, Hallinan's refusal to allow the ceremony to take place remained final, but Father Foust's letter prefigured the opening of an ever widening rift between himself and the Church hierarchy. In his mind, the Church was in the midst of rapid change, and failing to react swiftly enough threatened its position in the modern world. He saw reaction rather than proper leadership in Hallinan's decision. Such reaction, Foust feared, "seems to me symptomatic of a fear which becomes concretized in many ways in the Church, so subtle at times that it is often disguised as an institutional operation for the common good, but is in reality for the good of the institution against the common good."[21] The apparent ambivalence that so bothered Foust, however, merely provided evidence of a Church in transition. Hallinan sensed a real problem of authority in the wake of Vatican II, and his challenge was to decide just how much to give in and just how much it was necessary to cling to. Foust obviously believed that Hallinan's concessions were inadequate.

For their part, the lay members of the Community argued that conventional parish structures hindered the development of true Christian community and relegated the laity to the status of observers rather than participants. They sought rather to live out the conviction that there was a direct connection between enhanced lay authority in the Church and ecumenism. In 1966, Foust explained his own understanding of what should be the relationship between the laity and official Church authority in the postconciliar world. He argued that a radical new understanding of authority lay at the heart of all Vatican II documents. The Council offered a "distinctly new emphasis" on the role of the laity. Laymen and laywomen should share in the "governing of the Church." "Christian love infused by the indwelling Spirit" should preclude an "authoritarian structure" that looked more to secular power than to the New Testament Church for its model. Foust believed that the spirit of Vatican II favored reorganization of archdiocesan structures as a series of concentric circles rather than vertical lines of authority. In his decentralized model, individual voices would be valued and "active, PERSONAL exchange of the WHOLE People of God" would be the outcome. Such a model would also include "open communication . . . between all members of the Church;" what was more, it "should turn OUTWARDS, promoting open communication with those who are not Catholic, and fostering a readiness to learn from them."[22]

The laypeople who started the Community shared Foust's view of their own place in the Church. This new parish belonged to them and those they would serve. They were not taking orders from Foust; he was simply their liaison with the archdiocesan leadership. Indeed, at their first organizational meeting, two laymen, Randy Rauton and Ray O'Neill, were named cochairmen of the exploratory group. Most of the group's members were critical of existing parish structures. O'Neill argued that "most of our parishes are so organized, classified and stratified" that it was not likely that they could provide "*direct* service to those in great need." Sheila

Tidwell identified "a need in each of us to bring a Christ-life into ourselves and our families. It follows that we will extend ourselves." The danger of traditional parish life was the "routine that we feel very secure and smug in." Elena De Give noted that "many organizations are really obstacles;" as a result, "we are lacking wholeness."[23]

At one early meeting, Mimi Fenlon warned against projecting a specifically Catholic image, for, as Lee Offen subsequently pointed out, many people, "reared in misunderstanding," believed "'Roman Catholic' is a frightening word."[24] Fenlon and Offen preferred to emphasize the broadly Christian rather than distinctly Catholic nature of their community. "Basically we are Christians," Offen argued. "This [ecumenism] brings the whole community of Christ's Church into one Church." Foust clarified the statement, adding that "regardless of our differences, in different denominations, we are united in Christ."[25] The group's ecumenical desires extended to their own practice at their organizational meetings. The first meeting began with Mass, celebrated by Father Foust. The second organizational meeting, a week later, opened with a scripture reading and brief homilies by Reverends Kim Dreisbach and Austin Ford, both Protestants. Discussion then continued about the extent of the new parish's ecumenism. Non-Catholics participated from the outset, and they and the Catholics alike downplayed their denominational differences and emphasized their shared Christian faith. Those participants who identified themselves as converts to Catholicism strongly supported Foust's ecumenical aims. Helen Keeling had been raised in the Baptist church, but "I am now a Catholic and feel very strongly that this [an ecumenical ministry] is the only approach." Similarly, Kay Blair argued: "From my own experience as a convert, I feel we must definitely be ecumenical, not only for those we serve but for us who are serving."[26]

At that second meeting, the group voted unanimously to make the new parish "ecumenical in ministry and total structure" from the outset. At least three non-Catholic religious leaders from the area expressed an interest in being part of the experiment if they were invited. The Episcopal bishop and the regional leaders of the Presbyterian Church (USA) and the United Church of Christ, the Episcopalian Dreisbach reported, would be willing to cooperate with the pilot project. Dreisbach's report to the group, however, suggests that Foust had misled them about Archbishop Hallinan's willingness to support an ecumenical parish. The Episcopal priest acknowledged that the non-Catholic regional leaders "would all have to go higher in six or seven weeks as you will to your Archbishop, but the readiness to explore is there."[27]

The experimental parish's ecumenical mission, as Foust and the Community members interpreted it, was contested from the outset. Archbishop Hallinan and Auxiliary Bishop (later Cardinal) Joseph Bernardin envisioned a Catholic parish not bound by geography, a parish that in time—but not right away—would explore ecumenical social projects. Evangelism would be one goal, but worship would remain exclusively Catholic. Foust and lay members of the exploratory group had other ideas. Foust's inclusion of Dreisbach in the group's first meeting suggests that he envisaged the Episcopal priest, and any other non-Catholic minister who joined the parish, sharing pastoral duties with Foust. One model for the group was a similar experimental parish in Kansas City. Four ministers— Roman Catholic, Episcopalian, Presbyterian, and United Church of Christ—staffed Kansas City's St. Mark's Ecumenical Church. Four different worship services served each constituency, and the four denominations cooperated in social-work projects. Even with an ecumenical team of co-pastors, Foust allowed, the new Atlanta parish would "operate in cooperative relationship with the Archdiocesan structure." The "Catholic aspects" of the parish "would be in totally open communication with the Pastoral Council of the Archdiocese."[28] In a letter to Bishop Bernardin, Foust baldly proclaimed his goal for the new parish. "I envision this," he wrote, "as an Ecumenical Church."[29]

Bishop Bernardin responded coolly to Father Foust. "Unless more has taken place than I am aware of," he declared, "I think it would be premature to extend the discussions formally beyond Catholic circles at this time."[30] Although he acknowledged that he was not directly responsible for the project, Bernardin fairly represented Hallinan's sentiments. A month later, Hallinan himself wrote Foust: "In all honesty, we could not subscribe to this, because our hope of Christian unity relies in part on our being honest about theological differences which exist." Hallinan allowed that cooperation was possible, but only as long as it followed the dictates of *Unitas Redintegratio*, Vatican II's Decree on Ecumenism.[31] For example, Hallinan could support an arrangement that provided for separate liturgical worship services and joint prayer or Bible-study services. "Perhaps at a later date," he wrote Foust, "it will be possible to enter into the higher levels of ecumenism." For now, however, the parish "should thoroughly absorb the Catholic corpus of faith and moral principles" and "seek its first strength within the Catholic format, not outside."[32]

Lay members of the exploratory group were impatient with the archbishop's plan that the parish be exclusively Catholic and only later open to ecumenical dialogue. Foust responded to Hallinan that "the group finds their thinking to be different from the thinking you have come to at this time."[33] Earlier, the priest had charged that "present ecumenical activities seem to me to be token efforts."[34] The rest of the group agreed. At their first organizational meeting, the new parish planners argued that other faiths would not feel that they were part of the community if they were not included in the planning stages and invited to join only later. Foust put himself in the position of non-Catholics: "If I were a Protestant or Jew I would object to coming in after the philosophy, goals, and means had already been established. Couldn't they help us to see our obligations, etc.?" Paul Dolan, one of the laymen involved, argued that defining something necessarily established needless boundaries. "If this is supposed to be an experiment," he asked, "why limit it at the start? Especially if you want to work ecumenically, you cannot begin with a definition and tell those of other faiths that this is our definition and we'd like them to fall into it."[35]

As a nonterritorial parish, the experimental group did not begin with a firm location and a church building. Instead, their primary concern was to spell out their purpose and specific design before proceeding. If ecumenism was the group's intended design, its purpose was just as broadly defined. Members of the group, Father Foust included, expressed dissatisfaction with current parish structures. One man identified in the group's minutes as Father Hein charged the prevailing parish structure with being "incapable" of "uniting . . . a community in the Word of God and the Eucharist." This experimental parish would be different because members would choose to join, and it "is the free choice of entering this community that is important in this matter."[36] Elsewhere, Foust expressed similar faith in parishioners' being allowed to choose where they served the Church. According to Foust's vision for this experimental parish, Catholics would join by choice rather than have their parish affiliation dictated by where they lived. Because members would choose to belong to the parish, they would assume more active roles in its ministries and not rely on the same few people to manage the church's affairs. Foust claimed this was the case with larger parishes, where "the routine of the same dozen or two leaders is the line of least resistance followed naturally by priest and laity alike."[37]

The emphasis on individual choice rather than geography as the criterion dictating church membership would contribute to a stronger sense of community, parish organizers believed. This Christian community would be ecumenical, and it would lead to heightened social concern and activism. Members would work more closely with the secular community to alleviate problems of poverty and to achieve racial integration. Such social activism was consistent with the unfolding effects that Vatican II had on priests, nuns, and many Catholic laymen and laywomen, who took the conciliar redefinition of the Church as the People of God to require a greater focus on civil rights and antipoverty activism. Such activism often occurred within ecumenical or secular contexts, since there were very few Catholic organizations dedicated exclusively to the black freedom struggle.[38]

The emphasis on freedom of choice at the expense of geographical parish boundaries in choosing church membership placed the whole Atlanta Catholic Church in a unique position. Although Foust did not seem to be aware of the irony, the model for church membership on which he relied was a Protestant one. Protestant churches are not typically organized along territorial lines, and it is common for their congregants to drive past churches of the same denomination before reaching the one they belong to. The congregational style of church government that characterized, for example, the Baptists more closely resembled the leadership style that the Community of Christ Our Brother would later assume. In addition, the stress on freedom of choice also demonstrated the shift from a "dwelling-oriented" spirituality to a "seeking" spirituality identified by sociologist Robert Wuthnow as characteristic of post-1950s American religion.[39]

The committee appointed to find a suitable location for the new church group reported at the fourth organizational meeting that "location" was not "vital" at that point. More important, the committee argued, was that the community promote "self-discovery and freedom to be oneself."[40] Representatives of the new parish investigated two other similar experiments, in Kansas City and Oklahoma City. Neither one offered the precise model the Atlanta group hoped to follow, but in each they found characteristics they hoped to emulate. Foust, Dreisbach, and Randy Rauton, a Catholic layman, reported that at the Community of John XXIII in Oklahoma City a "spirit of respect and freedom was evident to the three of us" during the Mass. Later, "the spirit of freedom, open discussion, and cooperation" character- ized an informal gathering at the apartment of the parish priest.[41] Such a model would naturally appeal to those future members of the Community of Christ Our Brother who might be dissatisfied with the traditional Church and attracted to the emphasis on "freedom" and "choice." Although Foust, Dreisbach, and Rauton neglected to explain why the Community of John XXIII did not correspond directly with what they were looking to accom- plish, one element of the Oklahoma City parish—as well as of another parish, in Tulsa, that was modeled on it—that probably did not appeal to the Atlantans was its exclusively Catholic leadership and worship. Non- Catholics were encouraged to attend, but as one Tulsa layman concluded, "we are not cutting ourselves off from the institutional church as such."[42]

The black freedom struggle also gave Atlanta's moderate and liberal Catholics the opportunity to put into practice the conciliar doctrine of the Church as the People of God. The relationship between liturgical practice and social ecumenism fostered by Vatican II served as the foundation for the Community of Christ Our Brother. From the start, the Community's participants wanted to locate in a poor (majority-Negro) neighborhood and make social work its primary goal. Several members had a history of outreach and activism across class, racial, and denominational lines. Some of the women had participated in the Volunteer Task Force, a city- wide ecumenical program that placed volunteers in a variety of situations, from day care-centers to cooking classes for poor women. According to the program director, Elinor Metzger, the only requirement was that vol- unteers "must have a deep interest in people and respect the dignity of those with whom they work."

"I had always lived in one section of town," explained Mary Rauton, a founding member of the Community of Christ Our Brother, "and knew little about other people in other environments," a fact that prompted her to help start a music program for preschool children. Mimi Fenlon, an- other member of the Community of Christ Our Brother, noted the oppor- tunities for ecumenism. For her the Volunteer Task Force was "a terrific way to work with people of other faiths." She helped in a day-care center at a Baptist church.[43] Rauton's husband, Randy, owned a construction company and in 1967 he helped his employees join a credit union. In that endeavor, the challenge for him "was convincing the president of the credit union that our company was a good risk, because of the high ratio of Negro to white employees." Rauton insisted that his African American employees "were men—and they should be treated like men. They have dignity and responsibilities."[44]

For such laypeople, the Community of Christ Our Brother gave them the opportunity to apply the Christian principles inspired by Vatican II and their own consciences. In addition to liturgical and ecumenical experimentation, then, was a third goal of the new parish, increased community service and social action. Indeed, the group defined ecumenism more broadly than just interdenominational cooperation; their ecumenism was to include rich and poor, white and black. They sought an integrated parish focused on smoothing the rough edges of poverty in a single community. Foust argued that, among his general objectives for the parish, there "will be an opportunity for more joint community focus of effort in poverty areas, Christian influence in the business world, etc., by democratic choice of direction of effort."[45] Later, he wrote Hallinan that the group intended "to study the areas of poverty with the goal of discovering the area of greatest need."[46]

During the planning stages, the archdiocese encouraged such goals. Bishop Bernardin proposed that the group consider using Our Lady of Lourdes parish as the basis for their experiment. This Negro parish was already nonterritorial (since it was devoted to African Americans, whose de facto exclusion from "white" parishes in the city created segregated worship patterns the Church was not proud of). Bishop Bernardin reasoned that Our Lady of Lourdes was "an inner-city parish situated in the kind of poverty and social need with which you are concerned." Joining the experimental group (whose members were white) with an existing black parish would automatically provide the integration that both the archdiocese and Foust's experimental group sought. Given that immediate integration, "OLL would offer an excellent opportunity for mutual exchange. Together, then, the Negro and white families could realistically and consistently work to improve the community." Bernardin worried that such a proposal might appear to the Our Lady of Lourdes parishioners as a "'white take-over,'" so the idea must be presented "very carefully and tactfully."[47]

The parish merger made sense for reasons beyond those spelled out by Bernardin. Since the late nineteenth century, in efforts to abide by the social customs of Jim Crow, bishops in Southern states had established separate parishes for African-American Catholics. They often invited into their dioceses religious orders such as the Society of African Missions and the Society of St. Joseph to staff those parishes. Coming out of the civil rights movement and Vatican II, Catholic leaders sought to correct that institutional segregation and reorganize parish boundaries to eliminate racial barriers to church membership, but such corrections proved diffi-cult to achieve in the face of persistent residential segregation. The merger of Our Lady of Lourdes and the experimental parish, therefore, would appear to solve two problems at once.

Members of the new parish's organizational group were not receptive to Bernardin's proposal. They expressed concern for the parishioners of Our Lady of Lourdes and how they would perceive the "take-over," insist-ing that the latter have first choice in this matter. The only way the merger would work, the group decided, would be if they changed the name of Our Lady of Lourdes and thereby developed a unique identity separate from the established parish.[48] There were other concerns as well, which stemmed from the ecumenical direction of the experimental parish. Herb Farnsworth, a Catholic layman active in the planning of the Community and former chairman of the ad hoc committee that prepared for the 1966 lay congress, wrote Hallinan that "this offer [of OLL] seems inconsistent with the direction our explorations have been taking."[49] In reality, the group no doubt feared that merging with Our Lady of Lourdes would too closely identify them with the Catholic Archdiocese of Atlanta and lessen their ecumenical thrust.[50] The parish merger never materialized. Al-though he did not say why, other than to note that it was "for reasons to-tally unrelated to the proposed parish itself," Bishop Bernardin later withdrew his earlier offer from consideration by the experimental community.[51]

The Community's ecumenical scheme was clearly not what Archbishop Hallinan intended for the Atlanta experiment. In April, Bishop Bernardin expressed the archbishop's concerns when he wrote the chairman of the Archdiocesan Pastoral Council that Hallinan was not "prepared at this time to undertake a project of this kind"; the archdiocese could "sponsor and support the new community only if it is organized according to the original plan which was authorized." Nor was Episcopal bishop Randolph R. Claiborne willing to cosponsor an ecumenical parish.[52] When the group requested parish status in late May 1967, however, Hallinan approved the request "despite obvious problems . . . and the unfortunate change of direction during February–April this year." Approval came, of course, with stipulations and a call for careful guidance. The nonterritorial parish would be recognized "*as a Catholic community* on an experimental basis of one year," with Foust as administrator. Catholics from throughout the archdiocese could apply for membership, but the total number of families would be limited to seventy-five.[53]

The new parish was expected to take part in all normal archdiocesan activities and to support financially the priest, parish, and archdiocese, as all territorial parishes did. Hallinan intended the parish—as did Foust and the group's original Catholic members—to be an occasion for exploring the implications of the various decrees of the Second Vatican Council. Hallinan instructed that "all efforts to explore a true ecumenism with those of other faiths should be used." These included periodic ecumenical worship services and shared social-action projects. The church also was expected to sponsor study courses covering conciliar documents on the liturgy, ecumenism, missions, and the Church's role in the modern world. "Thorough discussion shall be a vital part of the study-course, but the essential part is a full-grasp of the mind of the conciliar Church," Hallinan wrote one of the Community's members shortly after its establishment.[54]

In June 1967, the new parish took the name Community of Christ Our Brother, Hallinan celebrated Mass for them, and the experiment was launched. On Sunday nights, the Community met for eucharistic services in the Bethlehem Center of the Methodist Church's Gammon Theological Seminary in Atlanta. On Thursday nights, the group conducted "prayer, study, and work sessions" at the center.[55] Throughout the week, they celebrated the Eucharist in individual homes.[56] By July the Community of Christ Our Brother had approximately forty members, ten of whom were Protestant. Of that number, according to Foust, "a few of them are skeptical of all organized religion." The group was "attempting to be honest listeners to secular life—to the lives of especially those who cry out in human need and to those of other religious traditions and of no organized religious affiliation."[57]

The Community of Christ Our Brother expressed the post–Vatican II notion of the Church as the People of God and located worship in the liturgy of human experience. In August 1967, Foust wrote in *Commonweal*, a liberal, lay-directed Catholic magazine, that the Community wanted "to discover our Brother Christ in the midst of human life, to become His friends, to share life with Him and to serve Him there, in the people we meet, and with whom we live."[58] By December of that year Foust was praising members of the Community for demonstrating a "more mature integration of secular and religious life in the [their] attitudes." The Community operated the Pryor Street School Center on Saturdays, which was intended "to encourage Negro leadership." The parish sponsored programs in drama, arts, crafts, dancing, movies, and physical education. Foust himself lived in the black community that the Community of Christ Our Brother intended to serve, tutoring neighborhood children, playing truant officer during the week, and attending court in support of those residents who were in trouble with the law.[59] Sadly, available archival sources do not reveal whether the people the Community intended to serve actually attended the parish's worship services or sought active membership, nor have precise details of the Community's social-action projects survived in the archdiocesan archives.

The experiment continued through 1968, despite the increasingly erratic—and eventually heretical—behavior of Father Foust. Under normal circumstances Foust's behavior might have brought swift censure early in the Community's life, but Hallinan was slowed with hepatitis, cirrhosis, and diabetes throughout much of 1967 until his death in March 1968. This left much of the day-to-day administration to Bernardin, who became the archdiocesan administrator until the new archbishop could be appointed. This probably extended the life of the parish, since at times Hallinan was physically unable to keep close watch on Foust and the Community. In April 1968, Bishop Bernardin reported to the Apostolic Delegate in Washington, D.C., that the Community had "settled down somewhat and are trying to carry out their objectives." There were twenty-eight families who were active in the Community, with approximately forty adults and fifty to sixty children. Besides weekly Mass at the seminary's community center, there were Sunday adult-discussion periods and Confraternity of Christian Doctrine classes for children. Holy Day Masses were celebrated in individual homes. "In these somewhat troubled times," the auxiliary bishop conceded, "such a group—if properly controlled—can serve as a good safety-valve for those groups who have become disenchanted with our present structure." Since Bernardin had opposed the experiment from the outset, his acknowledgment that the community had stabilized into "some good work" no doubt was a grudging compliment.[60]

Foust's behavior, however, had become cause for concern. As early as July 1967, merely a month after the Community of Christ Our Brother's official inception, Archbishop Hallinan questioned Foust's commitment to the truly Catholic nature of the parish. Following an *Atlanta Constitution* article that, according to Foust, misrepresented the Community's liturgical ecumenism, Hallinan wrote the priest that the "impression is growing in me that you either cannot or do not want to move forward within the format of the Archdiocese."[61] Foust reaffirmed his fidelity to Church teachings and his willingness to submit to Hallinan's authority. "Let me again assure you," he assured his superior, "that I desire wholeheartedly to serve the Church in the Archdiocese of Atlanta with true obedience and honesty."[62]

By 1968 that spirit of submission had evaporated entirely. Indeed, Father Foust represented for the Archdiocese of Atlanta the wider struggles of the priesthood in the late 1960s. Men who had pledged their lives to God and the Church questioned the Church's teaching authority and its commitment to making itself relevant to the modern world. Foust proved no exception, insisting that he no longer wished to conform to archdiocesan regulations. Instead, he professed the need to be open to the leadership of the Holy Spirit and the democratic consensus of the Community of Christ Our Brother. His openness to the Holy Spirit led him to further liturgical innovations and open opposition to *Humanae Vitae*, Pope Paul VI's encyclical (1968) banning the use of artificial contraceptives by Roman Catholics.

In April 1968, Bishop Bernardin wrote the apostolic delegate that Foust "has revealed to me that he is having a great deal of difficulty with the structure of the Church for theological reasons." Foust felt "compelled to follow the inspiration of the Holy Spirit even though it may be at variance with the position of the recognized authorities of the Church." Bernardin worried that, pushed to its logical extreme, this line of reasoning "could well lead ultimately to a repudiation of the Church's visible structure and authority. I patiently tried to explain to him why his view of the Church is incorrect but I am not at all sure that I succeeded."[63] In response to Bernardin's warning that Foust's reliance on the independent leadership of the Holy Spirit would lead to a rejection of the visible Church, Foust responded, according to the bishop, "that I was living in a different world from him and that my world would have to be destroyed before the voice of Christ would really be heard by the contemporary world."[64]

Foust had become a church unto himself, answering only to the Holy Spirit and the members of the Community of Christ Our Brother. Instead of living in the apartment authorized by Archbishop Hallinan, he had taken up residence with a married couple from the Community of Christ Our Brother. When Bernardin asked why, Foust responded that he planned to live with different families within the Community "to get to know them better and to save on expenses." In Bernardin's mind, this could be dangerous, since the couple with whom Foust was currently living had a history of marital problems and the last thing they needed was "to have a priest around the house all day."[65] The renegade priest had also given up clerical garb in favor of sport shirts and casual clothes.

To Bernardin, Foust's refusal to follow the authority of the Church suggested a mentally unstable priest who needed to be watched closely by the new archbishop when he was appointed. Foust was to go a great deal further, however, especially after he pushed the Community's liturgical innovations too far and usurped the Church's proper authority in, among other things, legitimating marriages. In May 1968, Foust "blessed" an interfaith marriage that the canon law of the Catholic Church could not authorize. A Catholic woman had married a divorced non-Catholic, a union that the Catholic Church saw as illegitimate and refused to recognize. The Catholic woman would be viewed as adulterous and refused access to the Eucharist, effectively cutting her off from the sacramental ministry of the Church. Foust came to the couple's home, supposedly validated the marriage, and told the Catholic wife that she could once again receive the sacraments. The confused Catholic woman called the archdiocesan office to make sure that Foust's ceremony and authority were legitimate, but Chancellor Noel Burtenshaw confirmed her fears that Foust was out of line and that such a validation could occur only with special dispensation from proper Church authorities.[66]

Foust defended his action to Bishop Bernardin, using language and reasoning similar to what he used before. He was bound by his conscience to validate the marriage so as to allow the Catholic woman to return to the sacraments. According to Bernardin's summary of their conversation, despite the dictates of Church law, Foust "felt that Church law should be set aside in this case for the spiritual good of the persons involved." Bernardin conceded that Catholics were responsible for following their conscience, "but we also must have an obligation to form a correct conscience, and to do this we must look to the Church for guidance." Bernardin recognized the larger problem, however—namely, that Father Foust's "concept of the Church is different from ours." Archdiocesan leaders retained some authority over Foust and his Community. "We can permit you to function as a priest in the name of, and with the support of, the Archdiocese only if you are willing to go along with the Church as it is commonly understood by the magisterium, namely, as a visible structure with definite laws and lines of authority," Bernardin told him.[67] Foust's refusal to accept these lines of authority meant that he effectively separated himself from the Church. It would be only a few months before the new archbishop, Thomas A. Donnellan, would be forced to make that separation official.

Donnellan replaced the deceased Hallinan in July 1968 but did not act immediately to discipline his most prominent apostate priest. He consulted with Bishop Bernardin and several priests and, he later reported to the apostolic delegate, "decided to take no immediate action dissolving the Community." The consensus was that the parish was "not flourishing, that it showed no signs of growth, that repression at this time might attract support for it, and that for the present it simply be observed carefully."[68] In the meantime, in August, Foust became the first Atlanta priest to denounce the encyclical *Humanae Vitae*, and more evidence surfaced of his liturgical rebellion.

In July 1968, with the promulgation of *Humanae Vitae*, Pope Paul VI had reaffirmed the Church's traditional teaching against artificial birth control. While the encyclical did not carry the weight of infallibility, Catholics worldwide were expected to abide by the teaching. That the commission of priests and laity appointed by John XXIII to study the issue and make recommendations had voted to drop the ban meant little to Paul VI, but it did to many other Catholics, who charged that the pope had violated the spirit of Vatican II by, in effect, circumventing the role of

individual conscience in family planning.[69] In his own statement supporting the encyclical, Archbishop Donnellan seemed to acknowledge that
many laywomen and laymen would be upset with the papal decision. He
defended the statement by appealing to the pope's authority and noted
the wide range of experts consulted before the ruling (ignoring, however, that those same experts had reached a different conclusion from
that of Paul VI). The encyclical was "an exercise of his [the pope's] ordinary magisterium, of his office as chief teacher of the Catholic Church,
and therefore . . . it calls for a sincere adherence to his judgment."[70]

By August 1968, Foust had placed himself on the fringes of Atlanta
Catholic society, and his resistance to archdiocesan leadership and discipline hardened into outright defiance. His decision to support birth control "as a matter of conscience" came after working with Atlanta's poor.[71]
In a statement read to the Community of Christ Our Brother, Foust declared that there was disagreement among Catholic theologians about
contraception. He claimed objectivity in explaining the central issues to
his congregants: "In exposing both sides of the question, I wish to show
the divergence within the total Church, without overweighting the opinion which I myself hold." Foust explained that the main question surrounding contraception involved "the totality of marriage" instead of "the
biological act of intercourse as such." In this understanding artificial contraception "becomes good in the light of the total love relationship of wife
and husband, parents and children." *Humanae Vitae*'s outright condemnation fell "again into vacuum abstractions, which are superimposed upon
human experiences."[72]

Husbands and wives were expected, therefore, to form their own consciences about the matter. Foust advised them that they "are to look at all
the sources available to you, and then decide in the light of these." He assured those Catholics concerned about remaining loyal to the Church even
as they opposed papal authority that those positions were not mutually
exclusive. Instead, the "total Church has come to realize that the Spirit
reveals the truth to all, that the search for truth is a dialogue between all
the members of the church who are also open to the members of other
ecclesial bodies and indeed, to the whole world." Paul VI's encyclical con-
tradicted the spirit of the Second Vatican Council, Foust concluded. The
Council had redrawn the lines of ecclesiastical authority, and "the recent
papal document on birth control ignores the advance of the church." Foust

declared that it was "important that we do not regress, just as we are emerging from a long history of monarchical emphasis which was assumed in history by the church's too close identification with royal power."[73] The Community of Christ Our Brother issued its own statement supporting Foust and praising "the courage he has shown in addressing this issue."[74]

Foust was not alone in his opposition to what he perceived as an overextension of papal authority. Indeed, controversy over the laity's acceptance or rejection of Humanae Vitae beset the Church in the late 1960s. As much as support for or opposition to the civil rights movement a few years earlier had defined Catholic conservatism and liberalism, now Humanae Vitae assumed that pivotal role. By some measures, as much as 90 percent of American Catholic laity rejected the teaching in Paul VI's encyclical, and by 1970 an increasing number of Catholic women were using some means of artificial birth control.[75] Even so, Foust's instructions to his parishioners that they could in good conscience ignore the dictates of Humanae Vitae were not what ultimately brought the condemnation of the archbishop. Instead, in December 1968, Archbishop Donnellan suspended Foust from his duties as a priest of the archdiocese for serious liturgical violations surrounding the celebration of the Eucharist. Foust's ecumenical proclivities and renegade spirit forced the archbishop's hand. The priest was guilty of celebrating Mass without proper vestments or the proper prayers and of improper distribution of the Eucharist. Perhaps most seriously, he had included non-Catholics in the reception of Communion, thereby violating the exclusivity of the Church's most singular sacrament.[76]

Foust remained unrepentant and unaffected by his suspension. When Archbishop Donnellan called the priest to account for his actions, Foust informed him that he answered only to his individual conscience and to the will of the Community. In his own statement to the apostolic delegate, Foust invoked the Catholic principle of subsidiarity—that is, the notion that decisions were best made at the lowest level possible. He also recalled his reply to Donnellan. "I feel in conscience that I should consult with the Community of Christ Our Brother," he wrote. "After thorough discussion of the matter, the Community as a whole will decide whether or not to follow these orders exactly." Foust assured Donnellan and the apostolic delegate that his reply "is not made with any contempt for authority, but rather, with love for the Church and the true meaning of Liturgy as 'the work of the People' (of God)."[77]

That both Foust and Donnellan could support their respective decisions by appealing to the good of the Church was consistent with the
Church's struggles following the end of the Second Vatican Council. Disagreements over the nature of the Church led to disputes over the interpretations of Vatican II and the sources of proper authority. In January
1969, Hugh F. Fenlon, a Catholic layman and member of the Community
of Christ Our Brother, wrote Archbishop Donnellan to defend the parish
and its purpose. Fenlon made no apologies for Father Foust—indeed, he
failed even to mention the priest or his suspension. Instead, he noted that
he had been "drawn to the window" opened by Pope John XXIII through
Vatican II. The Community of Christ Our Brother allowed Fenlon "to find
a deeper meaning and more personal experience in my relation to God."
Freed from traditional parish structures to be allowed to "search for a
greater individual fulfillment in the love of Christ," the Community,
moreover, "found the reality of the living Christ in the sharing of the
Eucharist and each other." Fenlon placed the experimental parish firmly
within the spirit of Vatican II and accused the archdiocese of failing to
honor the community's expression of its faith "as Christ and Vatican II
have done."[78]

The parish struggled on, despite Foust's suspension. In late January
1969, Archbishop Donnellan met with lay representatives of the Community of Christ Our Brother to discuss the parish's future. Perhaps surprisingly, Donnellan expressed his willingness to allow the parish to
continue—and even appoint a new priest to assume leadership duties—
provided that the members agreed to abide by the original charter and
obey the laws of the Church. Parish representatives at the meeting expressed their inclination to follow those stipulations, but they acknowledged that there was division within the community and probably not
everyone would agree. Donnellan also revisited his struggles with Foust
and reiterated his expectations about his and the Church's authority. As
the archdiocesan chancellor, the Reverend Noel C. Burtenshaw, summarized Donnellan's statement: "Father Foust declared his unwillingness,
without the consensus of the Community, to obey the Laws of the Church.
The archbishop declared that the Laws of God and the Church are not
based on the consensus of any particular group." The meeting ended with
one of the laymen "suggesting that dialogue must take place now within
the Community itself and that another meeting would be requested with

the Archbishop soon."[79] There is no record in the archdiocesan archives of that meeting's ever having taken place.

Without formal leadership, the Community of Christ Our Brother eventually expired, and its members either returned to established congregations or ceased church attendance altogether. At the meeting of the archdiocesan board of consultors on March 26, 1969, Archbishop Donnellan, according to that meeting's minutes, "referred to the recent marriage of Father Foust." Evidently, he had become involved with a woman in the Community. A priest's marriage would not have been out of the question. Indeed, it would have been typical of the struggle of the priesthood in the late 1960s and 1970s, when men left the ordained ministry by the thousands.[80] Foust's marriage served as perhaps the most fitting denouement of a drama whose plot centered on the redrawing of authority's boundaries in the Archdiocese of Atlanta. Marriage would have underscored both his rejection of the influence that the hierarchy of the Catholic Church had over him and his embrace of the primacy of individual conscience and the leadership of the Holy Spirit.

In their liturgical and ecumenical interpretations of the spirit of Vatican II, Father Foust and the Community of Christ Our Brother moved out of the Catholic mainstream. But in other areas they operated closer to the conventional thought and action of contemporary Catholicism. Their struggle with the archbishop and papal teaching authority was more consistent with that of most American Catholics than Church leaders cared to admit. And the Community's concern for social-justice issues reflected the Church's overall position in the late 1960s. Indeed, by 1970 the Church in Georgia had survived its crisis of authority and institutionalized social concern, after officials of the Archdiocese of Atlanta acknowledged the economic component of segregation and combined social-justice activism with efforts to end racial discrimination.[81] That aspect of the mission of the Community of Christ Our Brother's was no longer such a bold experiment.

Notes

Introduction

JEREMY BONNER, JEFFREY M. BURNS, AND CHRISTOPHER D. DENNY

1. Quoted in Joseph Chinnici, *Living Stones: The History and Structure of Catholic Spiritual Life in the United States* (New York: Macmillan, 1989), 183.

2. See Philip Gleason, "Neoscholasticism as Preconciliar Ideology," *U.S. Catholic Historian* 7 (1988): 401–11.

3. See Michael J. Lacey and Francis Oakley, *The Crisis of Authority in Catholic Modernity* (New York: Oxford University Press, 2011).

1. Catholic Action in the Archdiocese of New York: The Case of the Catholic Club of New York City

PATRICK J. HAYES

1. Compare, e.g., Charles E. Curran, *The Social Mission of the U.S. Catholic Church: A Theological Perspective* (Washington, D.C.: Georgetown University Press, 2011), 1–13; Jay P. Dolan, *The Immigrant Church: New York's Irish and German Catholics, 1815–1865* (Baltimore: Johns Hopkins University Press, 1975), 121–40; and John McGreevy, *Catholicism and American Freedom: A History* (New York: Norton, 2003), 127–65. See also Patrick B. Lavey, "William J. Kerby, John A. Ryan, and the Awakening of the Twentieth Century American Catholic Social Conscience, 1899–1919" (Ph.D. diss., University of Illinois, 1986). A previous generation of historians also commented on the rise of Catholic involvement in urban social questions, including those in New York. See, for example, the large corpus of Aaron I. Abell, e.g., *American Catholicism and Social Action: A Search for Social Justice: 1865–1950* (Notre Dame, Ind.: University of Notre Dame Press, 1963); Abell, "The Catholic Factor in the Social Justice Movement," in *Roman Catholicism and the American Way of Life*, ed. Thomas A. McAvoy (Notre Dame, Ind.: University of Notre Dame Press, 1960), 70–98; Abell, "American Catholic Reaction to Industrial Conflict: The Arbitral Process, 1885–1900," *Catholic Historical Review* 41 (1956): 385–407; and Abell, "The Reception of Leo XIII's Labor Encyclical in America, 1893–1919," *Review of Politics* 7, no. 4 (1945): 464–95. For

a contrarian view, see Joan de Lourdes Leonard, *The Catholic Attitude toward American Labor, 1884–1919* (master's thesis, Columbia University, History Department, 1941).

2. See, e.g., James O'Connell, "Impressions of a Jocist Camp," *Irish Monthly* 78, no. 924 (June 1950): 257–61. Internationalism of the Jocist movement would begin before the Second World War, though it would not have significant influence until the mid-1950s as it spread through Europe. While in the United States 1938 is generally the date of its beginnings, Jocism hardly made a similar impact in North America and still less in the developing world. See further, Oscar Cole-Arnal, "Shaping Young Proletarians into Militant Christians: The Pioneer Phase of the JOC in France and Quebec," *Journal of Contemporary History* 32, no. 4 (July 1997): 509–26; Richard J. Crimens, "Jocist Diary," *Furrow* 6, no. 4 (April 1955): 215–27; Craig Prentiss, *Debating God's Economy: Social Justice on the Eve of Vatican II* (University Park: Pennsylvania State University Press, 2008), 125–42; and Mary Irene Zotti, *A Time of Awakening: The Young Christian Worker Story in the United States, 1938 to 1970* (Chicago: Loyola University Press, 1991).

3. See, e.g., Mary Elizabeth Brown, *Churches, Communities, and Children: Italian Immigrants in the Archdiocese of New York* (Staten Island, N.Y.: Center for Migration Studies, 1995); and Peter R. D'Agostino, *Rome in America: Transnational Catholic Ideology from the Risorgimento to Fascism* (Chapel Hill: University of North Carolina Press, 2004), esp. 132–57.

4. Pius X, encyclical letter *Il Fermo Proposito, Acta Sanctae Sedis* 37 (June 11, 1905): 741–767. An English translation is available on the Vatican website, http://www.vatican.va. *Il Fermo Proposito's* universal application is brought out in the commentary of Joseph V. Sommers, "Catholic Action—Lay Apostolate," in *A Symposium on the Life and Work of Pope Pius X Commemorating the Fortieth Anniversary of His Encyclical "Acerbo Nimis,"* under the direction of the Episcopal Committee of the Confraternity of Christian Doctrine (Washington, D.C.: Confraternity of Christian Doctrine, 1946), 119–36, here at 121.

5. See D. J. Geany, s.v., "Catholic Action," *New Catholic Encyclopedia*, 2nd ed. (Detroit: Gale, 2003), 3:275–78, here at 275. Geany further notes that Catholic Action's definitions often depend on the era during which they are constructed and the region to which reference is made. Cf. Francis Schüssler Fiorenza, s.v., "Church, Social Mission of," in *The New Dictionary of Catholic Social Thought*, ed. Judith A. Dwyer (Collegeville, Minn.: Liturgical Press, 1994), 151–71, here at 158.

6. Pius XI, *Ubi Arcano Dei Consilio, Acta Apostolica Sedis* (hereafter AAS) 14 (December 23, 1922): 673–700. An English translation is available at the Vatican website, http://www.vatican.va.

7. See John C. Joy, "The Schools and Catholic Action," *Irish Monthly* 58, no. 690 (December 1930): 615.

8. Pius XI, letter to Cardinal Bertram, November 13, 1928, in Odile M. Liebard, ed., *Clergy and Laity: Official Catholic Teachings* (Wilmington, N.C.: McGrath, 1978), 30–34, at 31; official text in *AAS* 20 (1928): 384–87. The pontiff reiterated the line again in 1931 with his encyclical letter on Catholic Action in Italy, *Non Abbiamo Bisogno, AAS* 23. An English text may be found at the Vatican website, http://www.vatican.va.

9. See Joseph F. Mooney, s.v., "New York, Archdiocese of," *Catholic Encyclopedia* (New York: Robert Appleton, 1911), 11:28, referring to a letter of Kohlmann now in the Georgetown University Special Collections. See Kohlmann to Anthony Grassi, March 21, 1809, Maryland Province Archives, box 57.5, folder 10: "Application [has been] made to all houses to rise [sic] a subscription for the relief of the poor by which neary [sic] 3000 doll. have been collected to be payed constantly every year."

10. For the Catholic Worker, see William D. Miller, *A Harsh and Dreadful Love: Dorothy Day and the Catholic Worker Movement*, 2nd ed. (Milwaukee: Marquette University Press, 2005); and Mel Piehl, *Breaking Bread: The Catholic Worker and the Origin of Catholic Radicalism in America* (Tuscaloosa: University of Alabama Press, 2006); for the Laymen's League, see Joseph M. McShane, "'To Form an Elite Body of Laymen . . .' Terence M. Shealy, S.J., and The Laymen's League, 1911–1922," *Catholic Historical Review* 78, no. 4 (October 1992): 557–80; for the Association of Catholic Trade Unionists, see Douglas P. Seaton, *Catholics and Radicals: The Association of Catholic Trade Unionists and the American Labor Movement, from Depression to Cold War* (Lewisburg, Pa.: Bucknell University Press, 1981); Kevin E. Schmiesing, "Association of Catholic Trade Unionists," in *Encyclopedia of U.S. Labor and Working-Class History*, ed. Eric Arnesen (New York: CRC Press, 2006); Philip Taft, "The Association of Catholic Trade Unionists," *Industrial and Labor Relations Reviews* 2, no. 2 (1949): 210–18.

11. For the early history, see John Jerome Rooney, "Catholic Club of the City of New York," *Catholic Encyclopedia* (New York: Appleton, 1913), 3:452–53. Rooney, incidentally, was the presiding judge for the court of claims in New York from 1913. Rooney was a member of the National Geographic Society, the New York Bar Association, American Bar Association, National Democratic Club, and the St. Vincent de Paul Society. He was also a poet of some renown. See also Michael J. Madigan, "The Catholic Club of New York," in *Catholic Builders of the Nation*, ed. Constantine E. McGuire (Boston: Continental Press, 1923), 3:412–27; n.a., "Catholic Young Men's Associations," *Catholic World* 18 (1874): 269–79; n.a., "Our Forty Years," *Catholic Club Monthly Bulletin* 5 (May 1911): n.p.; David E. Nolan, *History of the Catholic Club of the City of New York, 1888–1960* (master's thesis, St. Joseph's Seminary, 1995).

12. Catholic Club of New York, *Charter, Constitution and By-Laws of the Xavier Union of the City University of New York* (updated 1891), in New York Public

Library, Microfilm Division; a copy may be found in Nolan, *History of the Catholic Club of the City of New York, 1888–1960*, 74.

13. On the Club's interiors, see n.a., "The Decoration and Furnishing of the Catholic Club," *Decorator and Furnisher* 21, no. 1 (October 1892): 11–12; and n.a., "The Catholic Club House," *American Architect and Building News* 48, no. 1016 (June 15, 1895): 112 (with architect's renderings of both the interior and the exterior on subsequent pages). Photographs of the interiors may be found in the Granger Collection at the Museum of the City of New York. According to Madigan (419), the Club's library contained "fine specimens of Incunabula, Elzevirs and other celebrated publishers, also of sixteenth and seventeenth century editions of works profusely illustrated by the best Flemish and Dutch etchers and engravers."

14. See n.a., *Memorial of the Most Reverend Michael Augustine Corrigan, D.D.* (New York: Cathedral Library Association, 1902), 104–5. Fornes went on to vow that "to prove . . . our love and veneration for our late Archbishop, we must sacredly guard and foster the welfare of those institutions which his prayers blessed, and which exemplify his solicitude in any work for sweet charity's sake and for the benefit of mankind" (105). The effusive Fornes was perhaps playing to the crowd. Corrigan liked the fact that the Club was there in order to show visiting prelates the kind of thing that his laity were capable of doing, but he hardly invested in its success beyond meager contributions and an occasional blessing. This would change with the ascendency of Archbishop (and later Cardinal) John Farley.

15. See "Mr. John S. Sumner's Lecture," *Bulletin of the Catholic Club* 6 (September 1922).

16. The Brownson Monument by Samuel Kitson was at West 104th Street and Riverside Park, a stretch of the West Side then becoming exceedingly fashionable. It was dedicated November 24, 1910. See "Brownson Monument," *Bulletin of the Catholic Club* 9 (December 1910). From the CCCNY's opening at Central Park South, the bust was in the entrance foyer.

17. See Catholic Club Minute Book v. 20 (1926–1930), meeting of the Board of Management, February 24, 1926, in CCCNY Archives, American Irish Historical Society, New York.

18. Ibid., regular meeting of the members of the Club, April 15, 1926.

19. Ibid., meeting of the Board of Management, March 13, 1928.

20. See "Recent Discourses of Our Professors," *Catholic University Bulletin* (April 1926): 23.

21. See "April Events," *Bulletin of the Catholic Club* (May 1923).

22. See "January Chronicle," *Bulletin of the Catholic Club* (February 1924) and "March Chronicle," *Bulletin of the Catholic Club* (April 1924).

23. See "Other Events in December," *Bulletin of the Catholic Club* (January 1923).

24. See "November Chronicle," *Bulletin of the Catholic Club* (December 1923).

25. As on March 23, 1924, where "the attendance [of some four hundred members] at the Mass and breakfast was encouraging and inspiring. The virility of our Club manifested itself in this splendid demonstration of Catholic Faith." See "Annual Communion Mass and Breakfast," *Bulletin of the Catholic Club* (April 1924). Bishop John J. Dunne celebrated. Archbishop Hayes had gone to Rome to receive his red hat. The CCCNY was instrumental in a grand reception on his return.

26. See D'Agostino, *Rome in America*, 88.

27. Membership Book of the Xavier Union and Catholic Club of New York, in CCCNY Archives, American Irish Historical Society, New York.

28. See Hayes to Cardinal Farley, October 24, 1912, in Archives of the Archdiocese of New York (hereafter AANY), Farley papers, I–15. Hayes had been impressed with Mulqueen for over a year. On a previous occasion, Hayes had written to Farley, December 20, 1911: "Last evening the Catholic Club held its dinner, at the Club House. Msgr. Mooney and myself were at the guest's table. The affair was magnificent and brilliant in every way. Your Eminence would have been delighted with the dignified tone and high class that marked the occasion. Mr. Michael Mulqueen is the right man for the presidency. He has large ideas and cordially knows how to carry out what he conceives. Two hundred and fifty representative Catholic laymen were at the dinner. The speeches were excellent." See Hayes to Farley, December 20, 1911, in AANY, Cardinal Farley Papers, I–34, correspondence, folder 7.

29. See "Estelle Mulqueen Bride in Cathedral," *New York Times*, June 10, 1917; and "Miss M. Mulqueen Weds Paul G. Daly," *New York Times*, December 28, 1920. These ladies were granddaughters of Thomas F. Gilroy, a former mayor of New York (1893–94).

30. Addresses at the Friendship Dinner to Rt. Rev. Patrick J. Hayes, D.D., Bishop Auxiliary of New York, Tuesday Evening, December 15, 1914, Waldorf-Astoria, New York City, in New York Public Library, Microforms Division. The dinner was the idea of Congressman Herman A. Metz, who was forced to be absent, owing to duties that brought him to Europe. This was largely a CCCNY affair, merely in a venue near the Club's quarters.

31. Addresses at the Friendship Dinner to Rt. Rev. Patrick J. Hayes, D.D., Bishop Auxiliary of New York, Tuesday Evening, December 15, 1914, Waldorf-Astoria, New York City, in New York Public Library, Microforms Division, 34.

32. Ibid., 36.

33. Ibid., 37–38.

34. Ibid., 36. Hayes also gave to the representatives of the city's Jewish community a surprisingly eloquent compliment, which was a rarity at this time among not only the New York hierarchy but the national hierarchy as well: "I

also want to pay a tribute tonight; or rather, to make you realize that, while the Catholic Church, in her composite, knows that she is of God, she appreciates what she owes to the Synagogue that was before her in time and figure. I would go back and pay a tribute tonight to the patriarchs, the priests and prophets of the ancient people of Israel, whose books are on my table, whose leaves I kiss with great reverence and whose writings I have studied and are an inspiration to my life as a Catholic priest" (37).

35. On the contributions of the two hundred CCCNY members in the war, see "Dedicate Service Tablet: 200 Members of Catholic Club Enrolled for War Work," *New York Times*, June 18, 1918. The tablet is now lost.

36. See Nolan, *The Catholic Club of the City of New York*, 52, and Christopher Kauffman, *Faith and Fraternalism: The History of the Knights of Columbus, 1882–1982* (New York: Harper and Row, 1982), 217–18. Agar's son, John Jr., was killed in action during the war in France. See "Lieut. J. G. Agar Dead on St. Mihiel Front," *New York Times*, October 30, 1918.

37. On Hayes's involvement with the founding of the bishops' conference, see Douglas J. Slawson, *The Foundation and First Decade of the National Catholic Welfare Conference* (Washington, D.C.: The Catholic University of America Press, 1992).

38. See Parish Visitors of Mary Immaculate, *The Cardinal of Charities: An Appreciation* (New York: Parish Visitor of Mary Immaculate, 1927), 143. The program for the pallium ceremonies may be found in the archives of the University of Notre Dame, Philip Richard McDevitt Papers (CMCD), 1/30.

39. Parish Visitors of Mary Immaculate, *The Cardinal of Charities*, 159.

40. For the early development of the move toward scientific social work in the Catholic context, see Donald P. Gavin, *The National Conference of Catholic Charities, 1910–1960* (Milwaukee: Bruce, 1962); William J. Kerby, *The Social Mission of Charity: A Study of Points of View in Catholic Charities* (New York: Macmillan, 1921), John O'Grady, *Catholic Charities in the United States: History and Problems* (Washington, D.C.: National Conference of Catholic Charities, 1930); Dorothy M. Brown and Elizabeth McKeown, *The Poor Belong to Us: Catholic Charities and American Welfare* (Cambridge, Mass.: Harvard University Press, 1997); and Mary J. Oates, *The Catholic Philanthropic Tradition in America* (Bloomington: Indiana University Press, 1995). See also, with particular reference to the Archdiocese of New York, Robert F. Keegan, "Surveys of Catholic Charities," *Proceedings, Sixth National Conference of Catholic Charities* (1920): 30–36. While chancellor of the archdiocese during Cardinal Farley's tenure, Hayes became quite familiar with the Associated Catholic Charities, a kind of umbrella group that sought to avoid replication of services through coordination of the various offices connected with charitable work. This group never had the kind of overarching authority or oversight that would emerge through Hayes's efforts at organizing Catholic

Charities in the years following 1919. The Associated Catholic Charities would eventually be subsumed into the diocesan organization.

41. See Welfare Council of New York City et al., *Directory of Social and Health Agencies in New York City* (New York: Columbia University Press, 1921), 30:54–55.

42. See "Archbishop's Plan of Social Work," *Catholic News*, January 24, 1920, 3.

43. See Robert F. Keegan, "A Survey and Its Aftermath," *Catholic Charities Review* 5 (1921): 46–49, here at 47.

44. See "Details of the Charities Survey," *Catholic News*, March 13, 1920, p. 5; "Laymen to Aid Archbishop's Plan: During 'Enrolment Week,' April 18 to 24, a Great Committee Will Help Secure Supporting Membership for Catholic Charities," *Catholic News*, April 3, 1920, 1.

45. See Hayes, "Ready for the Charities Campaign," *Catholic News*, April 17, 1920, 1.

46. See Talley to Hayes, March 16, 1920, reprinted in *Bulletin of the Catholic Club of the City of New York* (April 1920): n.p. There is a microfilm of the original, with Hayes's reply of March 23, in AANY, Patrick Cardinal Hayes Papers, roll 2, 0–12.

47. See "Support Archbishop's Charity Plan," *Catholic News*, April 10, 1920, 3.

48. Hayes, "Unification of Catholic Charities," *Catholic World* 117, no. 968 (May 1923): 145–53, here at 150, where the archbishop exclaimed, "The experiment has succeeded beyond our most sanguine hopes and dreams."

49. Hayes, "Unification of Catholic Charities," 152. New York's special position in the reception of immigrants was typically coordinated through the various ethnic immigrant aid societies. The Catholic Immigrant Auxiliary grouped together the Catholic resettlement societies at the port, assisted in processing new arrivals, made sure their spiritual needs were met, worked toward family reunification, and later developed Americanization programs.

50. See the interesting claim made in the *Irish Catholic* (November 3, 1923): 4, where the unnamed author complained of a decline in reverence over the previous decade: "Many do not wait for the conclusion of Mass and the Benediction, a still larger number are well underway for the door while the Gloria is still being sung." Cited in Maurice Hartigan, "The Religious Life of the Catholic Laity of Dublin, 1920–1940," in James Kelly and Dáire Keogh, eds., *History of the Catholic Diocese of Dublin* (Dublin: Four Courts Press, 2000), 331–48, here at 347. Hartigan goes on to assert that while this lament was the exception, not the rule, it also suggests that laity were more interested in sacramental practice than in Catholic Action, which failed to emerge in Dublin as a powerful movement.

51. Madigan, "The Catholic Club of New York," 3:414–15.

52. Ibid., 3:427–28.

53. See Martin Conboy to Bishop Stephen Donahue, April 11, 1925, in Archives of the Archdiocese of New York, Patrick Cardinal Hayes Papers, roll 4, Q-10 (1925).

54. See, e.g., Edward Cuddy, "The Irish Question and the Revival of Anti-Catholicism in the 1920s," *Catholic Historical Review* 67, no. 2 (April 1981): 236–55; Lynn Dumenil, "The Tribal Twenties: 'Assimilated' Catholics' Response to Anti-Catholicism in the 1920s," *Journal of American Ethnic History* 11, no. 1 (Fall 1991): 21–49.

55. See, e.g., Martin Conboy, "Can a Catholic Be President?" for the *Bulletin of the Catholic Club* (July 1924): 4–6, cited in Nolan, *The Catholic Club of the City of New York*, 45. The *Bulletin* also condemned such groups as the Ku Klux Klan; see "Intolerance that is Un-American," *Bulletin of the Catholic Club* (June 1924): 5.

56. See National Catholic Welfare Conference, "Pastoral Letter on Mexico" (December 12, 1926), in Hugh J. Nolan, ed., *Pastoral Letters of the United States Catholic Bishops*, vol. 1, *1792–1940* (Washington, D.C.: United States Catholic Conference, 1984), 337–65. Hayes was one of five bishops charged with developing the document, though the coordination and final draft rested with Hayes. On Guthrie's extensive contributions, see Hayes to Archbishop Curley, November 23, 1926, in Associated Archives, St. Mary's Seminary, Baltimore, Cardinal Michael J. Curley Papers, H 565; and Hayes to "My dear Bishop," December 11, 1926, in AANY, Patrick Cardinal Hayes Papers, roll 10, Q-33 (Mexico), folder 1.

57. See *Pierce v. Society of Sisters*, 268 U.S. 510 (1925). For more on Guthrie's legacy in this landmark case, see further Paul Abrams, *Cross Purposes: Pierce v. Society of Sisters and the Struggle over Compulsory Education* (Ann Arbor: University of Michigan Press, 2009).

58. See "Oregon Public School Legislation," *Bulletin of the Catholic Club* (February 1923).

59. Periodically, as with protests against the Calles government in Mexico, the Catholic Club issued statements decrying attacks on religious freedom. See Martin Conboy and John E. Donnelly to the secretary of state, *Catholic News* (April 24, 1926): n.p.

60. See Nolan, *The Catholic Club of the City of New York*, 51.

61. The Archdiocese of New York made a loan of $69,000 to the Catholic Club of the City of New York, February 9, 1929, per letter of George Gillespie, February 23, 1929, in AANY, Patrick Cardinal Hayes Papers, roll 6, U-4 (1929). About $52,500 was paid off by February 23, but similar loans may have been made throughout that year.

62. See Bennett to Gillespie, February 15, 1933, in AANY, Patrick Cardinal Hayes Papers, roll X-2 (Cardinal Hayes, Institutions and Societies), folder 1.

63. Ibid.

64. Carroll Hayes to Dear Member March 11, 1933, in Board of Managers, Minute Book, minutes of March 15, 1933, in CCCNY Papers, American Irish Historical Society, New York.

65. Hayes had McIntyre write Thomas Reynolds at the National City Bank to have the note returned. See McIntyre to Reynolds, May 13, 1933, in AANY, Patrick Cardinal Hayes Papers, roll X-2 (Cardinal Hayes, Institutions and Societies), folder 1.

66. Guinan was a social-justice advocate in his own right. He pastored Blessed Sacrament Church, east of Broadway at 71st Street, a venerable neo-Gothic structure that continues up to the present Guinan's outreach to the homeless. See "Cardinal Presides at Guinan Funeral," *The New York Times*, May 24, 1933.

67. The Club held meetings and functions at the Waldorf-Astoria beginning June 30, 1933, when a lease of rooms was made. The Catholic Club vacated its Club house on that day per minutes of a special meeting of the board of managers, Minute Book, minutes of June 15, 1933, in CCCNY Papers, American Irish Historical Society, New York.

68. Leslie to Father John Casey, October 16, 1933, in AANY, Patrick Cardinal Hayes Papers, roll X-2 (Cardinal Hayes, Institutions and Societies), folder 1. Cashin, an old friend of his ordinary, later consented to be the new CCCNY chaplain, an office that he would take up in addition to the parochial duties he had as pastor of the Church of St. Andrew at City Hall Place, at what is today Cardinal Hayes Place. See Hayes to Carroll Hayes, October 25, 1933, in AANY, Patrick Cardinal Hayes Papers, roll X-2 (Cardinal Hayes, Institutions and Societies), folder 1. In that missive, the Cardinal stated: "I should regret exceedingly the discontinuance of the Catholic Club after its long and close association with the Archdiocese, not to speak of the valuable assistance it has rendered the Church in this City and State on occasions when the Archbishop of New York desired loyal Catholic Action."

69. See Gillespie, letter to Hayes, February 20, 1933, in AANY, Patrick Cardinal Hayes Papers, roll X-2 (Cardinal Hayes, Institutions and Societies), folder 1.

2. The Liturgical Movement and Catholic Action: Women Living the Liturgical Life in the Lay Apostolate

KATHARINE E. HARMON

1. Paul McGuire, "Discussion," *1940 National Liturgical Week Proceedings* (Newark, N.J.: Benedictine Liturgical Conference, 1941), 92. The National Liturgical Weeks, organized first by the Benedictine Liturgical Conference and later by the Liturgical Conference, met annually to bring presenters, writers, authors, religious, priests, and laymen and laywomen together to learn about, discuss, and experience the liturgy.

2. McGuire, "Discussion," 92. Here, and throughout excerpted material, the noninclusive language of the original text has been maintained.

3. Bernice Strasser, "Discussion," 93.

4. As Leo R. Ward, C.S.C. (1893–1984), commented in 1959, when reflecting on contemporary Catholic lay movements, the liturgical renewal in America was but "a drop in the bucket," but he thought that it was the most *universal* recent religious development within Catholic lay movements: "It is far from swallowing up other developments, but something of it is almost sure to be induced in others, such as the Legion of Mary or Grailville or any expression of Catholic Action." Leo R. Ward, "Living the Liturgy," in *Catholic Life, Catholic Life, U.S.A.: Contemporary Lay Movements* (St. Louis: B. Herder, 1959), 10.

5. See, for example, Mary Jo Weaver, "Who *Can* Find a Valiant Woman? American Catholic Women in Historical Perspective," in *New Catholic Women: A Contemporary Challenge to Traditional Religious Authority* (Bloomington: Indiana University Press, 1995), 1–36; and James J. Kenneally, *The History of American Catholic Women* (New York: Crossroad, 1990), 161–97.

6. Virgil Michel, "The Liturgy as the Basis for Social Transformation," *Orate Fratres* 9, no. 12 (1935): 545. This is a form of an address originally delivered at the Thirty-Seventh Annual Convention of the Minnesota Branch of the Central-Verein, held in Mankato, Minnesota, September 22–24, 1935.

7. William Busch, "The Liturgy, A School of Catholic Action," *Orate Fratres* 7, no. 1 (1932): 9.

8. For example, during the National Liturgical Week of 1940, Rev. William Boyd described the "cell-technique," in which the "technique" for a Catholic Action cell meeting among boys might effectively pair the trifold watchword "observe, judge, act" with a discussion of the liturgy and prayer. See William Boyd, "Catholic Action," in *The Sacramental Way*, ed. Mary Perkins (New York: Sheed and Ward, 1948), 323–36, especially 328–29.

9. A number of resources for liturgical study appeared that made explicit connections between the efforts of the liturgical movement and Catholic Action, some of which include John Fitzsimons and Paul McGuire, eds., *Restoring All Things: A Guide to Catholic Action* (New York: Sheed and Ward, 1938), and Gerald Ellard, *Men at Work at Worship* (New York: Longmans, Green, 1940). See also John J. Griffin, "Catholic Action and the Liturgical Life," *Orate Fratres* 9, no. 1 (1934): 360–71.

10. See, for example, James P. McCartin, *Prayers of the Faithful: The Shifting Spiritual Life of American Catholics* (Cambridge, Mass.: Harvard University Press, 2010), and Joseph P. Chinnici, "The Catholic Community at Prayer, 1926–1976," in *Habits of Devotion: Catholic Religious Practice in Twentieth Century America*, ed. James M. O'Toole (Ithaca, N.Y.: Cornell University Press, 2004), 9–87.

11. In the field of liturgical studies, historians and theologians alike have worked to resolve this "split" that followed between liturgy and justice. Among

the first significant studies was Don Salier's "Liturgy and Ethics: Some New Beginnings," *Journal of Religious Ethics* 7, no. 2 (1979): 173–89. That was followed by Mark Searle's edited volume, *Liturgy and Social Justice* (Collegeville, Minn.: Liturgical Press, 1980). Likewise, the Virgil Michel Symposia, held in 1988 and 1993 in Collegeville, produced volumes that addressed themes of liturgy and justice, in concert with Virgil Michel's vision for liturgy as the school of social reform. In the late 1990s, Margaret Mary Kelleher explicitly discussed this connection in "Liturgy and Social Transformation: Exploring the Relationship," *U.S. Catholic Historian* 16 (Fall 1998): 58–70. Finally, Bruce T. Morrill has contributed to the discussion of liturgy and ethics, most recently in "Holy Communion as a Public Act: Ethics and Liturgical Participation," *Studia Liturgica* 41, no. 1 (2011): 31–46.

12. While 1926 is often viewed as the beginning of the "organized" liturgical movement, activists with similar motives for liturgical participation had sought to find an invigorated spirit of the liturgy long before this time. For example, John Carroll, the first American bishop, promoted use of the vernacular at the close of the eighteenth century, and, in the twentieth century, Rev. William Busch, of St. Paul, Minnesota, had begun local initiatives that introduced laypersons to the liturgy as early as the 1910s. I am grateful to Thomas Fisch, of St. Paul Seminary, St. Paul, Minnesota, for this note regarding William Busch.

13. As Lambert Dunne, O.S.B., remarked at a National Liturgical Week meeting: "Membership in Christ's Mystical Body as in an organism permits man to retain his individual personality with all its dignity, and still operate as part of the whole. In fact, his personality is augmented by contact with the organism. . . . Like any organism, the Mystical Body has its proper sphere of activity. The natural activity of the Mystical Body is the sacred liturgy: Holy Mass, the Sacraments, the Divine Office, the sacramentals, whereby the life of grace is fostered and brought to maturity. See how beautifully the liturgy of the Mass exemplifies the idea of community of members living the same life." Lambert Dunne, "Toward Christian Order in Labor Relations," in *The Sacramental Way*, ed. Mary Perkins (New York: Sheed and Ward, 1948), 338–39.

14. Virgil Michel, "The Liturgy as the Basis of Social Regeneration," *Orate Fratres* 9, no. 12 (1935): 544–45. Here, Michel quotes an unnamed source attributed to social historian Christopher Dawson. The source is actually Antony Timmins, "Liturgy and Sociology—and Dawson," *New Blackfriars* 16, no. 181 (1935): 278–84. See also "The Apostolate," *Orate Fratres* 10, no. 3 (1936): 129, 136–37, which accounts for Michel's error. Some relevant essays that resonate with Michel's views include Dawson, "Prevision in Religion," *Sociological Review* 26, no. 1 (1934): 41–54; and Dawson, "Catholicism and the Bourgeois Mind," *Colosseum* 11, no. 8 (1935): 246–56. For more on Dawson and Roman Catholic liturgy, see Paul Marx, *Virgil Michel and the Liturgical Movement* (Collegeville, Minn.: Liturgical Press, 1954), 291n6.

15. Joseph Kreuter, "Catholic Action and the Liturgy," *Orate Fratres* 3, no. 6 (1929): 165–70.

16. The restoration of the physical reception of Communion far outstripped the taking of Communion during the appropriate "liturgical" location in the structure of the rite. Nonetheless, the encouragement for Catholics to receive the Eucharist physically, as opposed to relying on "spiritual communion," laid an important precedent for participation in the liturgy of the Eucharist. See Joseph Dougherty, *From Altar-Throne to Table: The Campaign for Frequent Communion in the Catholic Church* (Lanham, Md.: Scarecrow, 2010).

17. See, for example, William Busch, "The Liturgy, A School of Catholic Action," *Orate Fratres* 7, no. 1 (1932): 6–12, here at 9: "Personal piety is preliminary to personal action; and similarly the antecedent to social action is social piety, which, moreover, is something more than the mere sum total of the piety of individuals. . . . It should be plain, therefore, that the apostolate of Catholic social action must have as its antecedent the domestic work of Catholic social sanctification, which, in turn, is something more than the cultivation of private devotions."

18. L. Jaeger, "The Liturgical Movement in Relation to Catholic Action," *Catholic Mind* 33 (1935): 15. The article continued: "Catholic Action demands a true Christian spirit for its execution. Now the 'primary and indispensable source of the Christian spirit' is found in an active participation of the Liturgy of the Church." See Keith Pecklers, *The Unread Vision: The Liturgical Movement in the United States of America, 1926–1959* (Collegeville: Liturgical Press, 1998), 100n51.

19. William Boyd, "The Birth of the Catholic Action Cell," *Orate Fratres* 16, no. 3 (1941): 113.

20. See Pecklers, *The Unread Vision*, 283.

21. I am grateful to my student Joseph Smith, of Loyola University of Maryland, for his observation regarding the distinction between Irish and German immigrants with respect to the reception of reform initiatives. See also Jay P. Dolan, *The American Catholic Experience: A History from Colonial Times to the Present* (Garden City, N.Y.: Doubleday, 1985), 160–76, for a discussion of the backgrounds of Irish and German Roman Catholic immigrant populations.

22. Mary G. Hawks, *NCCW Monthly Message to Affiliated Organizations*, no. 97 (November 1929), National Catholic Welfare Conference/United States Catholic Conference, National Council of Catholic Women (hereafter NCWC/USCC, NCCW) 63, the American Catholic History Research Center and University Archives (hereafter ACUA), the Catholic University of America, Washington, D.C.

23. Ibid.

24. Mrs. Arthur F. Mullen, "Address to the 7th Annual Convention of the NCCW," 1927, p. 2, NCCW/USSC, NCWC 76/19, ACUA.

25. Topics include, for example, "Mexico," "Education," "Cooperation with Racial Groups," "Industrial Problems," "Literature," and "Field Work." See Mullen, "Address to the 7th Annual Convention of the NCCW," 1927, pp. 7–9, NCWC/USCC, NCCW 76/19, ACUA.

26. "A news item from Washington announced that the National Council of Catholic Women would make the liturgy of the Church the official program of study for its members during the coming year. Once our Catholic mothers are steeped in 'the true Christian spirit' as derived from the 'primary and indispensable source', we shall not have to wait for the grade school period, or even later, to have our Catholic children learn something of the high privilege and dignity to which every member of the Mystic Body is called through Christ." "The Apostolate," *Orate Fratres* 4, no. 2 (1929): 89.

27. *NCCW Monthly Message to Affiliated Organizations*, no. 98 (December 1929), NCWC/USCC, NCCW 63, ACUA.

28. Ibid.

29. *NCCW Monthly Message to Affiliated Organizations*, no. 107 (September 1930), NCWC/USCC, NCCW 63, ACUA.

30. Ibid.

31. Ibid.

32. Miriam Marks, quoted in "Catholic Women Are Studying the Liturgy," in "The Apostolate," *Orate Fratres* 7, no. 1 (1932): 30–31.

33. "Catholic Women are Studying the Liturgy," *Orate Fratres* 7, no. 1 (1932): 31. Liturgical subjects were also presented at state Councils of Catholic Women, such as that of Minnesota, held in St. Paul October 26–27, 1932, at which Rev. Joseph Lord spoke on a theme titled "German Young People and the Liturgical Movement" ("The Apostolate," *Orate Fratres* 7, no. 2 [1932]: 88).

34. Quoted in "The Apostolate," *Orate Fratres* 7, no. 3 (1933): 134.

35. Agnes M. Marceron of Washington, D.C., reported: "With a greater knowledge of the Mass, the members were instilled with a greater love and a deeper understanding of the beauty and value of the holy sacrifice. Realizing the beauty of the prayers and wishing to assist at Mass in the very best manner, many of the club members have ordered Missals." "Study Club on the Mass," *Orate Fratres* 7, no. 12 (1933): 570.

36. For a discussion of the rising use of missals among American Catholics, see Pecklers, *The Unread Vision*, 49–52.

37. See, for example, Therese Mueller, *The Family Life in Christ*, 3rd ed. (Collegeville, Minn.: Liturgical Press, 1946).

38. Mrs. John Bell Hood, "Shrines in the Home," *NCCW Monthly Message* 17, no. 12 (December 1937), NCWC/USCC, NCCW 64, ACUA.

39. Maisie Ward, "Maisie Ward," in *Born Catholic*, ed. Frank J. Sheed (New York: Sheed and Ward, 1954), 143.

40. Evidence of struggle also exists, of course, as witnessed in "A Study Club Demonstration," which reported on the recent Convention of the Minnesota Council of Catholic Women in Minneapolis. Demonstrations on effective methods for study groups prompted those who had "experienced difficulties in holding study club meetings" to leave the hall "feeling that many of their problems had finally been solved." The article further noted that study clubs were "among the most appealing means for fostering adult education, especially in matters of religion." "The Apostolate," *Orate Fratres* 9, no. 1 (1935): 35–36.

41. "Liturgical Briefs," in "The Apostolate," *Orate Fratres* 7, no. 8 (1933): 374.

42. Mrs. D. M. Walsh, "Study Club Activity," in "The Apostolate," *Orate Fratres* 7, no. 6 (1933): 275–76.

43. "Liturgical Briefs," in "The Apostolate," Orate Fratres 7, no. 8 (1933): 273.

44. "Activity" was taken to new heights by some of the resources created for members of the Daughters of Isabella in the 1930s. For example, *The Pocket Recreation Magazine* described itself as a go-to resource for planning Catholic recreation outdoors, be it hikes, treasure hunts, games, or catchy wholesome songs to sing around the campfire. "Kit 23, The Pocket Recreation Magazine," vol. 6, no. 3, ed. Katherine and Lynn Rohrbough (Delaware, Ohio: Church Recreation Service, 1930), Daughters of Isabella, box 11, folder "Kits and Recreation," ACUA.

45. For a discussion of the evolution in professional roles for women in the United States, see Nancy F. Cott, "Professionalism and Feminism," in *The Grounding of Modern Feminism* (New Haven, Conn.: Yale University Press, 1987), 215–39. For a discussion particularly of Roman Catholic women, education, and social roles in the United States, see Mary J. Oates, "Catholic Laywomen in the Labor Force, 1850–1950," in *American Catholic Women: A Historical Exploration*, ed. Karen Kennelly (New York: Macmillan, 1989), 81–124.

46. "Study Club Activity," in "The Apostolate," *Orate Fratres* 7, no. 6 (1933): 276–77.

47. For a consideration of the shift in social class for American Roman Catholics, see James M. O'Toole, "The Immigrant Church," in *The Faithful: A History of Catholics in America* (Cambridge, Mass.: Harvard University Press, 2008), 94–144.

48. Lisa Sowle Cahill, *Sex, Gender, and Christian Ethics* (Cambridge: Cambridge University Press, 1996), 67.

49. R. Scott Appleby, "Pioneers of Renewal, 1930–1954," in *Transforming Parish Ministry*, ed. Jay Dolan et al. (New York: Crossroad, 1989), 24–25.

50. See Margaret Mary Reher, "The Path to Pluralism, 1920–1985," in *Catholic Intellectual Life in America: A Historical Study of Persons and Movements* (New York: Macmillan, 1989), 114–41.

51. See Dana Greene, "Maisie Ward as 'Theologian,'" in *Women and Theology* (annual publication of the College Theology Society), 40, ed. Mary Ann Hinsdale

and Phyllis H. Kaminski (Maryknoll: Orbis, 1994), 51. Maisie Ward would later reflect that she could "hardly remember, from the time I could read, being unable to find my places in a missal." Maisie Ward, "Changes in the Liturgy: Cri de Coeur," *Life of the Spirit* 16, no. 183, (October 1961): 128.

52. A movement among "high Church" Anglicans, and often associated with the University of Oxford, the Oxford movement was interested in a retrieval of the liturgical and theological traditions of the early Church. To this end, it resonated with some elements of the liturgical movement. See "Romanticism: Orestes Brownson and the Young Isaac Hecker, 1830–1850," in *Catholic Intellectual Life in America*, 37–38.

53. For a history of the Catholic Evidence Guild, see Maisie Ward, *Unfinished Business* (New York: Sheed and Ward, 1964); Frank J. Sheed, *The Church and I* (Garden City, N.Y.: Doubleday, 1974); Henry J. Brown, *The Catholic Evidence Movement* (London: Burns, Oates, and Washbourne, 1921); and Debra Campbell, "'I Can't Imagine Our Lady on an Outdoor Platform': Women in the Catholic Street Propaganda Movement," *U.S. Catholic Historian* 26, no. 1 (2008): 103–14.

54. Debra Campbell, "Gleanings of a Laywoman's Ministry: Maisie Ward as Preacher, Publisher and Social Activist" (Colby College, 1985), Print General Collection (hereafter PGEN) 103/4549, University of Notre Dame Archives (hereafter UNDA).

55. She came to agree with her husband, Frank Sheed, who claimed to have met priests "who [were] more afraid of the laity than of the Communists." Frank Sheed, *The Church and I*, 283.

56. Maisie Ward, *Born Catholic*, 123. The Ward of Sheed and Ward was initially supposed to be Maisie's brother, Leo. However, owing to his poor health and lack of business acumen, it quickly became evident that he was not up to the work and that Maisie could competently take up the task. See Greene, *The Living of Maisie Ward*, 64–65.

57. Campbell, PGEN 103/4549, UNDA.

58. Frank Sheed, *The Church and I*, 87.

59. Ward, *Unfinished Business*, 142.

60. See Dana Greene, *The Living of Maisie Ward* (Notre Dame, Ind,: Notre Dame University Press, 1997), 86.

61. Bruce Publishing Company and Newman opened in the 1930s, along with Prentice Hall and McGraw-Hill, all of them adding Catholic lines during this time. See Greene, *The Living of Maisie Ward*, 85.

62. See Debra Campbell, "The Heyday of Catholic Action and the Lay Apostolate," in *Transforming Parish Ministry*, ed. Jay P. Dolan et al. (New York: Crossroad, 1989), 227.

63. Maisie Ward, "Problems of the Apostolate," *Orate Fratres* 24, no. 1 (1949): 28.

64. Ibid.

65. See Burton Confrey, "Reactions to Basing Catholic Action on the Liturgy," *Orate Fratres* 7, no. 1 (1932): 66–72, here at 68, who described a Catholic junior-college course on Catholic Action and based in the liturgy. As one student summarized: "I have learned something else during these three months. I have come to realize, at least in some small measure, the vital importance of holy Mass and the fundamental significance of the liturgy. How I managed to go through twelve years of Catholic school training, repeating yearly, 'The Mass is the unbloody sacrifice of the Body and Blood of Christ' and still be able to dream and be stupid in church, I do not know. . . . How the Mass joined Christians in Christ's Mystical Body was of about as much importance to me as the theory of relativity. I have just recently come to realize a little of the significance of the holy Sacrifice."

66. Maisie Ward, *Born Catholic*, 143.

67. Ward, "Cri de Coeur," 130 (emphasis in the original).

68. Ward, *Born Catholic*, 129. Ward continued: "Frequent communion did begin at once; but in Italy itself and most other European countries this meant, as I well remember, a priest rushing to the Blessed Sacrament chapel every half hour, in some churches even every time anyone chose to ring a bell, and distributing communion with no relation to the masses going on at perhaps half a dozen altars in the larger churches. In small churches communion was given out before and after—but seldom in its proper place in the mass." See also Dougherty, *From Altar-Throne to Table*, 197–204.

69. Ward, "Cri de Coeur," 130.

70. Maisie Ward, "Journal," 8–9, Sheed and Ward Collection 13/19, UNDA.

71. See Paul Bussard, "The Source of Christian Spirit," in "The Apostolate," *Orate Fratres* 10, no. 7 (1936): 325.

72. Greene, *The Living of Maisie Ward*, 144.

73. Michel, "The Liturgy as the Basis of Social Regeneration," 545. See also Virgil Michel, "Frequent Communion and Social Regeneration," *Orate Fratres* 10, no. 5 (1936): 198–202.

74. See Gary MacEoin, "Lay Movements in the United States Before Vatican II," in *America* 165 (3–10 August 1991): 61–65; and Mary Jo Weaver, "Still Feisty at Fifty: The Grailville Lay Apostolate for Women," *U.S. Catholic Historian* 2, no. 4 (Fall 1993): 3–12.

75. See Alden V. Brown, *The Grail Movement and American Catholicism, 1940–1975* (Notre Dame, Ind.: University of Notre Dame Press, 1989), 20.

76. William Busch, "Liturgy and Farm Relief," *Catholic Rural Life* 8 (April 1930): 2.

77. For a more complete history of the transition of the European Grail movement to the United States, see Brown, *The Grail Movement and American Catholi-*

cism, 1940–1975; and Janet Kalven, *Women Breaking Boundaries: A Grail Journey, 1940–1965* (Albany: State University of New York Press, 1999).

78. See Katharine E. Harmon, "The Need for a Liturgical Movement, Beginnings in Europe, Preparations for America (c. 1870–1926)," in *There Were Also Many Women There: Lay Women in the Liturgical Movement in the United States* (Collegeville, Minn.: Liturgical Press, 2013), 22–72. See also Herbert Antcliffe, "A Dutch Catholic Pageant," *The Ave Maria* 36, no. 1 (1932): 49–52.

79. A brief review of the discussion of women as liturgical subjects and advocates can be found in Teresa Berger, "The Classical Liturgical Movement in Germany and Austria: Moved by Women?" *Worship* 66, no. 3 (1992): 231–50. For a more sustained discussion, see Teresa Berger, *Liturgie und Frauenseele: Die Liturgische Bewegung aus der Sicht der Frauenforschung,* Praktische Theologie heute, Band 10 (Stuttgart: W. Kohlhammer, 1993); and Katharine E. Harmon, "The Need for a Liturgical Movement: Beginnings in Europe, Preparations for America (c. 1870–1926)," 4–27.

80. Virgil Michel, "The Liturgy and Catholic Women," *Orate Fratres* 3, no. 9 (1929): 274. Another venue for discussion of women's role can be found in *Altar and Home,* a short bulletin produced by the monks of Conception Abbey, Conception, Missouri, and begun in the 1930s. Women's role in Catholic life long had been the subject of novels, newspapers, and instruction books, promoting a domestic ideology and touting the important role women played in sustaining a family's spiritual life. See Colleen McDannell, "Catholic Domesticity, 1860–1960," in *American Catholic Women: A Historical Exploration,* ed. Karen Kennelly, (New York: Macmillan, 1989), 48–80.

81. For a more sustained discussion of this shift in practice and attention of the liturgical movement, see Katharine E. Harmon, "Cooking for Christ in the Liturgical Kitchen: Liturgy, the Home, and the Liturgical Apostolate (c. 1945–1959)," in *There Were Also Many Women There: Lay Women in the Liturgical Movement in the United States* (Collegeville, Minn.: Liturgical Press, 2013), 264–347.

82. In concert with national efforts of Catholic Action, devotional structures at large, including novenas, eucharistic adoration, or praying the Divine Office, became increasingly connected to nationally organized efforts to promote and express Catholic identity and, often, to denounce unacceptable social institutions, especially communism. See Chinnici, "The Catholic Community at Prayer, 1926–1976," 62.

83. In fact, the National Liturgical Week meeting of 1946 chose "The Family in Christ" as the title of its organizing theme. See *1946 National Liturgical Week Proceedings* (Elsberry, Mo.: Liturgical Conference, 1947).

84. See Chinnici, "The Catholic Community at Prayer, 1926–1976," 53. Resources produced by and for members of the liturgical movement equally expressed

these sentiments. For example, in Florence S. Berger's *Cooking for Christ: The Liturgical Year in the Kitchen* (Des Moines, Iowa: National Catholic Rural Life Conference, 1949), she described a variety of "ethnic" (mostly Western European) recipes for Catholics to use throughout the liturgical year. With regard to recipes for Christmas, Berger (who was of German ancestry) advised her readers: "To my mind, the ultimate Christmas bread is the famous German *stolen*. If you were French, you would choose *brioche* or *galette*. If you were Scotch, you might long for a Yuletide *bannock*. If you were a Bohemian, you would want *vanocka*. But, since you are American, you may have all five. I advise that you use one sweet bread one year and another the next." Berger, *Cooking for Christ*, 20. Regarding views of the cold war, see, for example, Peter A. Nearing, "Making All Things New," in *1948 National Liturgical Week Proceedings* (Newark, N.J.: Liturgical Conference, 1949), 110–18.

85. "Grail Offers Courses in 'Lived' Christianity," in "The Apostolate," *Orate Fratres* 19, no. 7 (1945): 325 (emphasis in the original).

86. Grail leaders Janet Kalven and Lydwine van Kersbergen each wrote a book describing the subject of women: Janet Kalven, *The Task of Woman in the Modern World* (Des Moines, Iowa: NCRLC, 1946), and Lydwine van Kersbergen, *Woman: Some Aspects of Her Role in the Modern World* (Loveland, Ohio: Grailville, 1956).

87. Janet Kalven, "The Grail Spirit in Action," in "The Apostolate," *Orate Fratres* 15, no. 8 (1941): 383.

88. Ibid.

89. Robert B. Heywood, "The Spirit of the Grail," *Orate Fratres* 15, no. 8 (1941): 360.

90. Theodore Wesseling, *Liturgy and Life* (New York: Longmans, Green, 1938), 119.

91. Heywood, "The Spirit of the Grail," 361.

92. A news note in *Orate Fratres* praised the work of the Grail women: "Although only one of the courses is explicitly devoted to the liturgy, every day spent at the Grail brings a new awareness of the richness and practicality of the liturgical life. Two weeks will mean an unforgettable, formative experience in full Christian living, in learning initiative and in welcoming the responsibility of the lay apostolate. We recommend the courses enthusiastically and without reserve." "Liturgical Briefs," *Orate Fratres* 17, no. 7 (1943): 328.

93. Virginia Bogdan, "The Grail Training Course," *Orate Fratres* 17, no. 10 (1943): 464–66.

94. Janet Kalven and Grail Members, "Living the Liturgy: Keystone of the Grail Vision," *U.S. Catholic Historian* 11, no. 4 (1993): 29–38.

95. Kalven, "Living the Liturgy," 32. Others include: *Epiphany* (Loveland, Ohio: Grailville, 1946); *The Twelve Days of Christmas*, book and kit (Loveland, Ohio: Grailville, 1955); *Are You Ready? A Four-Week Advent Program in Preparation*

for Christmas (Loveland, Ohio: Grailville, 1956); and *The Paschal Meal* (Loveland, Ohio: Grailville, 1956).

96. Some of the pamphlets included are *This Is Marriage: A Simplified Version of the Encyclical 'Casti Connubii' (On Christian Marriage) by Pope Pius XI*, introduction by Emerson Hynes (Loveland, Ohio: Grailville, 1946); *This is Social Justice: A Simplified Version of the Encyclical 'Quadragesimo Anno' (On the Reconstruction of the Social Order) by Pope Pius XI*, introduction by Carl F. Bauer (Loveland, Ohio: Grailville, 1946); and *Families for Christ* (Loveland, Ohio: Grailville, 1949).

97. See also Brown, *The American Grail Movement*, 60–61; *Restore the Sunday*, ed. Janet Kalven, Mariette Wickes, and Barbara Ellen Ward, with James M. Shea (Loveland, Ohio: Grailville, 1949); *Toward a Christian Sunday, an Apostolic Program Based on the Volume, Restore the Sunday* (Loveland, Ohio: Grailville, 1949).

98. Kalven, "Living the Liturgy," 32–33.

99. Lydwine van Kersbergen, "The Restoration of Sunday: Goal of the Modern Lay Apostolate," *1949 National Liturgical Week Proceedings* (Conception, Mo.: Liturgical Conference, 1950), 35.

100. Ibid.

101. Campbell, "Reformers and Activists," in *American Catholic Women: A Historical Exploration*, ed. Karen Kennelly, (New York: Macmillan, 1989), 177. The Grail opened "city centers" in Brooklyn (1947), Cincinnati (1951), New York (1952), Philadelphia (1954), Lafayette, Louisiana (1957), Queens, New York (1958), and San Jose (1961). See Debra Campbell, "Both Sides Now: Another Look at the Grail in the Postwar Era," *U.S. Catholic Historian* 11, no. 4 (1993): 13.

102. Janet Kalven, et al., "The Grail in America, 1940–82," (unpublished manuscript), p. 4, quoted in Dolan, *The American Catholic Experience*, 414.

103. Dolan, *The American Catholic Experience*, 415.

104. Campbell, "Reformers and Activists," 178. Later, the Grail would prove to be a precursor of the linking of Catholicism and feminist movements of the last quarter of the twentieth century. See James O'Toole, *The Faithful: A History of Catholics in America*, 165. See also Mary Henold, *Catholic and Feminist: The Surprising History of American Catholic Women* (Charlotte: University of North Carolina Press, 2008), 66–67, 142–43. Henold notes that both so-called "new nuns" and communities such as Grailville were places where women were "committed to prayer and liturgy as instruments for communal worship and personal development. These women provided some of the first forces for feminist liturgical exploration."

105. As James O'Toole notes, by the 1930s there were about seventy Catholic colleges and universities in the United States, providing training for careers—in fields including accounting, engineering, medicine, and management—that would not have been possible for earlier generations of marginalized Catholic

immigrants. See James M. O'Toole, *The Faithful: A History of Catholics in America* (Cambridge, Mass.: Harvard University Press, 2008), 160.

106. Here, "mainstream" refers to "normative"—that is, to the most common attitude among liturgical movement advocates.

107. Beginning in mid-nineteenth-century England, the Oxford movement sought to intellectually and ritually support the "re-Christianization" of society and culture. See Geoffrey Wainwright and Karen Westerfield Tucker, eds., "The Liturgical Movement and Catholic Ritual Revision," in *The Oxford History of Christian Worship* (New York: Oxford University Press, 2005), 697.

108. See Godfrey Diekmann, "Is There a Distinct American Contribution to the Liturgical Renewal?" *Worship* 45, no. 10 (1971): 578–87; Gerald Ellard, "The Liturgical Movement: In and for America," *The Catholic Mind* 31 (1933): 61–76; and Ellard, "The American Scene, 1926–51," *Orate Fratres* 25, no. 11, no. 12 (1951): 500–8.

3. "The Priesthood of the Layman": Catholic Action in the Archdiocese of San Francisco

WILLIAM ISSEL

1. Sylvester Andriano, "The Program of Catholic Action in the Archdiocese of San Francisco," a paper read at the Diocesan Theological Conference, September 13, 1938, *Moraga Quarterly*, 9, no. 1 (Autumn 1938): 3–6.

2. San Francisco increased in size from 634,394 to 775,357 from 1930 to 1950. Only Los Angeles among Western U.S. cities ranked higher in population than San Francisco; ranking eleventh in the nation in 1930 and 1950, it had twice the population of Seattle in 1930 and was 25 percent larger than Houston (ranking fourteenth) in 1950. For demographic and social history, see William Issel and Robert W. Cherny, *San Francisco, 1865–1932: Politics, Power, and Urban Development* (Berkeley: University of California Press, 1986), and *San Francisco: Presidio, Port, and Pacific Metropolis* (San Francisco: Boyd and Fraser, 1981). Jeffrey M. Burns has written a three-volume history of San Francisco Catholic life: *San Francisco: A History of the Archdiocese of San Francisco*: vol. 1, *1776–1884, From Mission to Golden Frontier*; vol. 2, *1885–1945, Glory, Ruin, and Resurrection*; vol. 3, *A Journey of Hope, 1945–2000* (Strasbourg: Editions du Signe, 1999–2001). The term "lay apostolate" is from "Catholic Action Aims Are Defined in Letter of Cardinal Pizzardo" (hereafter Catholic Action Aims), National Catholic Welfare Conference News Service, July 4, 1938, copy in Catholic Action, folder 1936–1940, Chancery Archives of the Archdiocese of San Francisco, St. Patrick's Seminary, Menlo Park, Calif. (hereafter Chancery Archives).

3. Generalizations about attendance at Mass and similar indicators of participation in parish and archdiocesan life are based on data available in census and

financial files of the Chancery Archives. For an account of the status, prestige, and political influence of Catholics in San Francisco public life, see William Issel, "Business Power and Political Culture in San Francisco, 1900–1940," *Journal of Urban History* 16 (November 1989): 52–77.

4. The official archdiocesan newspaper, the *Monitor*, printed *Rerum Novarum* verbatim, June 17, 1891, pp. 1, 4. The paper ran an editorial, "The Grand Encyclical," along with the Laborers' Union letter to Pope Leo XIII, July 29, 1891, p. 4. On Hanna, see Richard Gribble, C.S.C., *An Archbishop for the People: The Life of Edward J. Hanna* (Mahwah, N.J.: Paulist Press, 2006).

5. The English text of *Il Fermo Proposito* is at the Vatican website, http://www .vatican.va. For all subsequent references to papal documents in this chapter, see this website.

6. When not otherwise indicated, biographical information about Sylvester Andriano is derived from his fifteen-page single-spaced typewritten autobiography contained in a letter to James L. Hagerty (hereafter Andriano autobiography), dated March 10, 1943, and from biographical data in other letters from Andriano to James Hagerty, all in box 237, James L. Hagerty Papers, Archives of the College of St. Mary's of California, Moraga (hereafter Hagerty Papers).

7. *San Francisco Examiner*, February 2, 1928; *San Francisco Chronicle*, October 17, 1929; Andriano to Hanna, December 7, 1928, *Monitor* file, Chancery Archives.

8. Andriano autobiography.

9. Andriano autobiography.

10. See Tracy H. Koon, *Believe, Obey, Fight: Political Socialization of Youth in Fascist Italy, 1922–1943* (Chapel Hill: University of North Carolina Press, 1985), 116–42.

11. The role of the National Catholic Welfare Conference (NCWC) in encouraging and monitoring diocesan implementation of papal Catholic Action theory is described in a personal handwritten letter from Rev. John J. Burke: the General Secretary of the NCWC to Archbishop Mitty, June 1, 1932, in NCWC 1932–1935 Correspondence file, 1 of 2 folders, Chancery Archives; see also excerpt from the minutes of the NCCW, Nov. 16, 1933, quoted in "Department of Catholic Action Study, National Catholic Welfare Conference," file NCWC Catholic Action Study, folder 3 of 3, Chancery Archives.

12. Jeffrey M. Burns, "Mitty, John Joseph," in *The Encyclopedia of American Catholic History*, ed. Michael Glazier and Thomas J. Shelley (Collegeville, MN: The Liturgical Press, 1997), 967–68; "Life Summary of Archbishop Mitty," *Monitor*, August 31, 1935, 2.

13. Sermon by Coadjutor Archbishop John J. Mitty to the Council of Catholic Women, May 7, 1932, Mitty Sermon Collection, Chancery Archives.

14. "Catholic League for Social Justice in the Archdiocese of San Francisco," pamphlet in Chancery Archives; "Report of Progress in the Crusade for Social

Justice, Bulletin 6, June 16, 1933," mimeographed newsletter, file Crusade for Social Justice file, folder PR118, Chancery Archives.

15. Amleto Giovanni Cicognani to Edward J. Hanna, date illegible, file NCWC Correspondence, 1933, folder 1 of 2, Chancery Archives.

16. "Program for the Year," August 11, 1933, file Catholic League for Social Justice, folder A46.9, Chancery Archives; Roy A. Bronson to John J. Mitty, September 28, 1933, file Catholic League for Social Justice, folder A46.9, Chancery Archives.

17. "A Revolution by Professors," the *Monitor*, January 27, 1934.

18. Andriano autobiography; memorandum (July 19, 1934) of a telephone conversation of July 15, 1934, between Roger Lapham and Frances Perkins, Papers of Secretary of Labor Frances Perkins, National Archives, Record Group 174, box 42, file Conciliation—Strikes—Longshoremen—1934; *Leader*, July 28, 1934.

19. *Leader*, July 21, 1934.

20. *Monitor*, May 11, 1935; Sylvester Andriano to Archbishop John J. Mitty, March 2, 1936, Italy/Italian folder, Correspondence files, Chancery Archives.

21. *Monitor*, April 6, 1935; Monsignor Luigi Civardi, *A Manual of Catholic Action* (1935; reprint, New York: Sheed and Ward, 1943).

22. Andriano to Mitty, March 2, 1936, Correspondence files, folder Italy/Italian, Chancery Archives.

23. *Monitor*, April 6, 1935; Mitty to Andriano, March 4, 1936, Correspondence files, folder 1936–1937 "A," Chancery Archives; "Plan for Catholic Action," Correspondence Files, folder Catholic Action 1936–1940, Chancery Archives.

24. Archbishop Mitty to Rev. Thomas N. O'Kane, letter marked "Confidential," Correspondence files, folder Catholic Action 1936–1940, Chancery Archives.

25. Biography file, Hagerty Papers, St. Mary's College Archives.

26. Joseph L. Alioto, "The Catholic Internationale," *Moraga Quarterly* 7, no. 2 (Winter 1936): 68–72.

27. Alioto, "Catholic Internationale," 72.

28. Andriano to Mitty, December 22, 1936, folder Catholic Action 1936–1940, Chancery Archives; "Catholic Action Group," January 6, 1938, uncorrected draft marked "News item: *The Monitor*," Chancery Archives.

29. Mitty to various addressees, December 22, 1937, Correspondence files, folder Catholic Action, 1936–1940, Chancery Archives; "Catholic Action Group," January 6, 1938, uncorrected draft marked "News item: *The Monitor*," and attached typewritten notes of meeting of January 6, 1938, folder Catholic Action, 1936–1940, Chancery Archives.

30. Archbishop John J. Mitty, "Address on Catholic Action," October 29, 1938, Mitty Sermons and Addresses, Chancery Archives; Andriano to Mitty, May 19, 1938, Correspondence files, folder Catholic Action 1936–1940, Chancery

Archives; *San Francisco Call Bulletin*, October 27, 1938, *San Francisco News*, October 28, 1938.

31. Pizzardo, "Catholic Action Aims"; Sylvester Andriano to Brother S. Edward, December 30, 1938; *Student Catholic Action* 1, no. 5 (November 1941): 2; *Catholic Action for You*, box 170; *Student's Handbook of Catholic Action*, 27; box 346.02—all in History of Catholic Action Collection, Christian Brothers Archives, Mont La Salle, Napa, California (hereafter Christian Brothers Archives).

32. Josephine J. Molloy to Archbishop Mitty, July 10, 1936; Genevieve E. Manning to Archbishop Mitty, July 2, 1937—both in Correspondence files, folder YMI/YLI 1936–1937, Chancery Archives; "Y.L.I. Grand Institute," July 18, 1937, Mitty Sermons, Chancery Archives.

33. For more about Agnes G. Regan, see Dorothy A. Mohler, "Agnes Regan as Organizer of the National Council of Catholic Women and the National Catholic School of Social Service," in E. Catherine Dunn and Dorothy A. Mohler, eds., *Pioneering Women at the Catholic University of America* (Washington, D.C.: Catholic University of America Press, 1988), 21–35.

34. Eugene J. Shea to Archbishop Mitty, August 9, 1939; Margaret McGuire to Reverend and Dear Father, March 3, 1937—both in Correspondence files, Youth Programs, 1937–1941, Chancery Archives; Agnes G. Regan to Archbishop Mitty, January 6, 1937, Correspondence Files, NCCW/M, 1938–1939, folder 2 of 2, Chancery Archives.

35. Margaret McGuire to Rt. Rev. Thomas A. Connolly, October 4, 1936; Memorandum, "Catholic Action"—both in Correspondence files, NCCW/NCCM, 1938–1939, folder 2 of 2, Chancery Archives; "NCCW Archdiocesan Council Hold Annual Meet in San Francisco," May 29, 1937, Mitty Sermons.

36. Memorandum from Monsignor Connolly to Archbishop Mitty, March 9, 1938; Maude Fay Symington to Archbishop Mitty, January 14, 1939—both in Correspondence files, NCCW/NCCM 1938–1939, folder 2 of 2, Chancery Archives; "N.C.C.W. Fifteenth Conference Ends With Luncheon at City Club—Archbishop Mitty," *Monitor*, May 27, 1939.

37. Pizzardo, "Catholic Action Aims"; "Address of His Holiness, Pope Pius XII, to the Congress of the International Union of Catholic Women's Leagues, Rome, April, 1939"; Agnes Regan to Most Rev. Thomas A Connolly, D.D., November 4, 1939; "Memorandum from Representatives of N.C.W.C. to Congress, I.U.C.W.L. Rome—1939"—all in Correspondence files, NCCW/NCCM 1938–1939, folder 1 of 2, Chancery Archives.

38. Pizzardo, "Catholic Action Aims"; "Proposed Project for San Francisco Archdiocesan Council: Clean Reading Campaign;" "Motions Relative to Magazine Rack Clean-Up Campaign" [February 1938]—both in Correspondence files, NCCW/NCCM 1938–1939, folder 2 of 2, Chancery Archives.

39. "Report of the Committee on Indecent Literature," May 5, 1938, Correspondence files, Catholic Men of San Francisco 1938–1941, folder 1 of 2; James Hagerty to Archbishop Mitty, May 18, 1938, Correspondence files, Catholic Men of San Francisco 1938–1941, folder 1 of 2; Margaret McGuire to Archbishop Mitty, June 11, 1938, Correspondence files, NCCW/NCCM 1938–1939, folder 1 of 2—all in Chancery Archives.

40. Archbishop Mitty to Reverend and Dear Father, June 10, 1938, letter marked "Official," in Mitty Sermons, Chancery Archives.

41. Florentine Schage to Rev. Harold E. Collins, February 28, 1939, Correspondence files, NCCW/NCCM 1938–1939, folder 2 of 2; Rev. John Francis Noll, *Catechism Dealing with Lewd Literature* (Huntington, Ind.: Our Sunday Visitor Press, 1939), 8; "Magazines Banned by the National Organization for Decent Literature," October 12, 1939, Correspondence files, folder National Catholic Welfare Conference Catholic Action Study, 1939—all in Chancery Archives.

42. James L. Hagerty to Joseph Breen, Esq., November 18, 1938; James L. Hagerty to Archbishop Mitty, November 18, 1938; Rt. Rev. Thomas A. Connolly to James L. Hagerty, November 19, 1938—all in Correspondence files, Catholic Men of San Francisco 1938–1941, folder 1 of 2, Chancery Archives; for more on the production code and Breen's role, see Thomas Doherty, *Hollywood's Censor: Joseph I. Breen and the Production Code Administration* (New York: Columbia University Press, 2007), and Gregory D. Black, *Hollywood Censored: Morality Codes, Catholics, and the Movies* (New York: Cambridge University Press, 1994).

43. Archbishop Mitty to Most Reverend Amleto G. Cicognani, D.D., March 30, 1939; A. G. Cicognani to Your Excellency, March 19, 1939—both in National Catholic Welfare Conference, folder Catholic Action Study, 1939, Chancery Archives.

44. The text of the Atherton Report was reprinted in the *San Francisco News*, March 16, 1937; for more on the investigation and its outcome, see Robert W. Cherny and William Issel, *San Francisco: Presidio, Port, and Pacific Metropolis* (San Francisco: Boyd and Fraser, 1981), 61–62.

45. Joseph J. Truxaw to Most Rev. Thomas A. Connolly, January 13, 1940; Rev. Edwin J. Kennedy to Honorable William J. Quinn, January 26, 1940; Rev. Edwin J. Kennedy to Rev. Joseph J. Truxaw, January 31, 1940; Charles W. Dullea to Rev. Edwin J. Kennedy, April 2, 1940—all in National Catholic Welfare Conference, folder Catholic Action Study, 1940, Chancery Archives; Anna E. McCaughey to Archbishop Mitty, June 5, 1941, folder National Council of Catholic Women / National Council of Catholic Men, 1940–1941, Chancery Archives.

46. Margaret Sanger, quoted in Sue Barry, "News and Views," *People's World*, May 22, 1939; Anthony B. Diepenbrock to Board of Directors, Golden Gate International Exposition, March 4, 1939, Golden Gate Exposition, folder 1 of 2, 1939–1940, Correspondence files, Chancery Archives.

47. Pizzardo, "Catholic Action Aims."

48. Donohoe Personal Record, Chancery Archives; *San Francisco Chronicle*, February 7, 1948, 9; August 12, 1958, 12; August 18, 1987, 22; Sister Patrice Donohoe, interview with Michael Kelly, April 28, 1999, Belmont, California, quoted in Michael Kelly, "Reverend Hugh A. Donohoe" (seminar paper, San Francisco State University, 1999), copy in author's possession.

49. "S.F. Labor Honors Bishop Donohoe," *Monitor*, October 24, 1947: 1–2.

50. *Who's Who in Labor* (New York: Dryden, 1946), 323–24; *San Francisco Chronicle*, October 2, 1974; *California Living* (supplement to *San Francisco Examiner*), April 30, 1967; *San Francisco Examiner*, September 23, 1963.

51. See William Issel, "A Stern Struggle: Catholic Activism and San Francisco Labor," in *American Labor and the Cold War: Grassroots Politics and Postwar Political Culture*, ed. Robert Cherny, William Issel, and Kieran Taylor (New Brunswick, N.J.: Rutgers University Press, 2004), 154–76.

52. A copy of the election flyer with the quotation is at The Virtual Museum of the City of San Francisco, http://www.sfmuseum.org/hist1/shelley.html. For the official congressional biography, see *Biographical Directory of the United States Congress, 1774–Present*, http://bioguide.congress.gov/scripts/biodisplay.pl?index=S000327.

53. Issel, "Business Power and Political Culture," 72–73; see also William Issel, "New Deal and World War II Origins of San Francisco's Postwar Political Culture," in *The Way We Really Were: The Golden State in the Second Great War*, ed. Roger W. Lotchin (Urbana: University of Illinois Press, 2000), 68–69.

54. William Issel, "Liberalism and Urban Policy in San Francisco from the 1930s to the 1960s," *Western Historical Quarterly* 22 (November 1991): 431–50.

55. Various reports and correspondence in Correspondence files, Catholic Men, folders 1–2 of 2, 1938–1941, Chancery Archives.

56. Andriano to Mitty, August 18, 1941, Correspondence files, Catholic Action 1938–1941, folder 2 of 2; "Summary of State of Organization Following Spring Series of District Meetings, 1941," Correspondence files, Catholic Action 1938–1941, folder 1 of 2—all in Chancery Archives; John J. O'Connor, "Emphasis on Action," *St. Anthony Messenger* (February 1942): 3–5, 55–56.

57. Sylvester Andriano to Dear Jim [Hagerty], November 12, 1943, box 327, Hagerty Papers; Sylvester Andriano to Dear Jim, August 1, 1945; John J. Mitty to Sylvester Andriano, March 2, 1946, Catholic Action File, 1945–1946, Chancery Archives.

58. (Monsignor) Howard J. Carroll to Mitty, January 24, 1947; Father James M. Murray to Mitty, January 10, 1947; Mitty to Caroline MacChesney, February 6, 1947; Mitty to Eric Cullenward, February 12, 1947; "Proposed News Release," February 12, 1947—all in Displaced Persons folder 2 of 2, Correspondence files, Chancery Archives.

59. Details of Cronin's biography in this paragraph and the next are from the Cronin Personal Record, Chancery Archives.

60. "Jewish Refugees: 488 Leave for N.Y. by Chartered Train—Thence to Europe, Israel," *San Francisco Chronicle*, February 23, 1949; "DP Twins Baptized," *Monitor*, October 28, 1949.

61. Joe Alioto to My dear Mr. Hagerty, [1940], Hagerty Collection, St. Mary's College Archives.

62. Alioto's position as an associate with Brobeck, Phleger, and Harrison is listed in *Brobeck, Phleger, and Harrison—The Earlier Years*, a booklet dated November 1973, in carton 2, Herman Phleger Papers, Bancroft Library, University of California, Berkeley; Maurice Harrison, "St. Thomas More," *Moraga Quarterly* 12 (Autumn 1941): 26; "'Youth and America's Crisis' Subject of Forum," *Monitor*, March 21, 1942.

63. "Catholicism in San Francisco," subject file, Communist Party, 1948, Southern California Library for Social Studies and Research, Los Angeles.

64. Unidentified newspaper clippings, September 17, 1948; February 28, 1949; June 22, 1949, April 5, 1950; *San Francisco Chronicle*, February 4, 5, 7, 8, 1953, "Joseph L. Alioto" news clippings envelopes, San Francisco History Center (SFHC), Main Public Library, Civic Center of San Francisco; *San Francisco Call Bulletin*, August 14, 1956; *San Francisco News*, [1957].

65. "Inaugural Address by the Honorable Joseph L. Alioto, Mayor of San Francisco," January 8, 1968, Joseph L. Alioto Papers, box 17, folder 35, SFHC (emphasis in the original).

66. Inaugural address by the Honorable Joseph L. Alioto, "For American Cities—A Declaration of Independence," January 8, 1972, Alioto Papers, box 17, folder 36, SFHC; Frederick M. Wirt, *Power in the City: Decision Making in San Francisco* (Berkeley: University of California Press, 1974), 198–99.

67. See William Issel, "'Land Values, Human Values, and the Preservation of the City's Treasured Appearance': Environmentalism, Politics, and the San Francisco Freeway Revolt," in *Pacific Historical Review* 68 (1999): 630, 644–45.

68. The Catholic racial-justice movement prior to the 1960s is described in William Issel, "Jews and Catholics against Discrimination," in *California Jews*, eds. Ava F. Kahn and Marc Dollinger (Waltham, Mass.: Brandeis University Press; and Hanover, N.H.: University Press of New England, 2003), 123–34, and in William Issel and Mary Anne Wold, "Catholics and the Campaign for Racial Justice in San Francisco from Pearl Harbor to Proposition 14," *American Catholic Studies* 119 (2008): 21–43. See also "Black Church–Labor Endorsements, Ingleside for Mayor Committee," [1971], box 18, folder 2, Alioto Papers; Rev. G. L. Bedford, "The November Election and the Blacks of San Francisco," October 13, 1971, box 18, folder 5, Alioto Papers; Joseph L. Alioto, "State of the City Message," October 5, 1970, box 17, folder 54, Alioto Papers.

69. Wirt, *Power in the City*, 175–76. David Jenkins at the conference "Labor and Politics: Who Pressures Whom?" San Francisco, February 7, 1989. Audio TS, side two, in Northern California Labor Archives and Research Center Collection, San Francisco State University.

70. Separation of Church and State," October 28, 1984, Cronin Papers, homilies, papers folder, Chancery Archives.

4. From Participation to Community: John Courtney Murray's American Justification for Catholic Action

CHRISTOPHER D. DENNY

1. John Courtney Murray, "Towards a Theology for the Layman: The Pedagogical Problem," *Theological Studies* 5 (September 1944): 347.

2. See Robert M. Doran, "System and History: The Challenge to Roman Catholic Systematic Theology," *Theological Studies* 60 (1999): 652–78.

3. See J. Carroll-Abbing, "Catholic Action in Italy: The Beginnings of Italian Catholic Action," in *Restoring All Things: A Guide to Catholic Action*, ed. John Fitzsimons and Paul McGuire (New York: Sheed and Ward, 1938), 98–106; Gianfranco Poggi, *Catholic Action in Italy: The Sociology of a Sponsored Organization* (Stanford: Stanford University Press, 1967), 14–18.

4. Murray, "Towards a Theology for the Layman: The Problem of Its Finality," *Theological Studies* 5 (March 1944): 43–75, at 67.

5. "Laetus Sane Nuntius," in AAS 21: 664–68. For an English translation of the letter, see Luigi Civardi, *A Manual of Catholic Action*, trans. Luigi Civardi (New York: Sheed and Ward, 1943), 254–58.

6. "Laetus Sane Nuntius," in *Manual of Catholic Action*, 256.

7. For more on Segura and the background of the Catholic Church's struggle with the new Republican government in the early 1930s, see Hilari Raguer, *Gunpowder and Incense: The Catholic Church and the Spanish Civil War*, trans. Gerald Howson (Routledge: New York, 2007), 15–35.

8. See Carroll-Abbing, "Catholic Action in Italy," 119–20.

9. Cavardi, *A Manual of Catholic Action*, 17.

10. Cavardi, *A Manual of Catholic Action*, 107–8.

11. See John Witte Jr., "Facts and Fictions about the History of Separation of Church and State," *Journal of Church and State* 48, no. 1 (Winter 2006): 15–45; Cavardi, *A Manual of Catholic Action*, 183–98.

12. Cavardi, *A Manual of Catholic Action*, 191; see also 202–6.

13. Jacques Maritain, "Integral Humanism," trans. Joseph W. Evans, in Jacques Maritain, *Integral Humanism, Freedom in the Modern World, and A Letter on Independence*, ed. Otto Bird, trans. Otto Bird, Joseph Evans, and Richard O'Sullivan, vol. 11 of *The Collected Works of Jacques Maritain*, ed. Ralph McInerny,

Frederick Crosson, and Bernard Doering (Notre Dame, Ind.: University of Notre Dame Press), 322.

14. Ibid.

15. See Maritain, *The Things That Are Not Caesar's*, trans. J. F. Scanlan (London: Sheed and Ward, 1930).

16. Maritain, *Integral Humanism*, 322.

17. See Maritain, *Integral Humanism*, 322–23.

18. Maritain, *Integral Humanism*, 342 (emphasis in the original).

19. See John Hellman, "The Opening to the Left in French Catholicism: The Role of the Personalists," *Journal of the History of Ideas* 34, no. 3 (July–September 1973): 381–90.

20. See Philip Gleason, *Contending with Modernity: Catholic Higher Education in the Twentieth Century* (New York: Oxford University Press, 1995), 146–66.

21. Gleason, *Contending with Modernity*, 154.

22. See "'Catholic Action' Defined by Pope Pius XI," *NCWC Bulletin* 10 (March 1929): 9–10; Wilfrid Parsons, "A Papal Slogan: Catholic Action," *America* 40 (February 2, 1929): 400–1; John J. Harbrecht, "What Is Catholic Action?" *Commonweal* 9 (April 24, 1929): 708–10.

23. Gleason, *Contending with Modernity*, 148 (emphasis in the original).

24. See Patrick J. Hayes, *A Catholic Brain Trust: The History of the Catholic Commission on Intellectual and Cultural Affairs, 1945–1965* (Notre Dame, Ind.: University of Notre Dame, 2011), 44–45, 309n44.

25. See National Catholic Alumni Federation, ed., *Man and Modern Secularism: Essays on the Conflict of the Two Cultures* (New York: National Catholic Alumni Federation, 1940).

26. John Courtney Murray, "Necessary Adjustments to Overcome Practical Difficulties," in *Man and Modern Secularism*, 152. See Gerald B. Phelan, "Theology in the Curriculum of Catholic Colleges and Universities," in *Man and Modern Secularism*, 128–42; Francis J. Connell, "Theology in Catholic Colleges as an Aid to the Lay Apostolate," in *Man and Modern Secularism*, 143–51. Gleason summarizes the manner in which John Montgomery Cooper and others sought to transform the catechetical instruction prevalent in nineteenth-century Catholic colleges into a course of study in "religion," designed to supplement the existing devotional and apologetic foci. See Gleason, *Contending with Modernity*, 142–44. Murray's response in 1939 represents a further development of Cooper's position.

27. Murray, "Necessary Adjustments," 152–54.

28. Transcriptions of these unpublished lectures can be found in the archives of the Jewish Theological Seminary in New York City (record group 16, box 2 of the Institute for Religious and Social Studies, folder 16–2–1). Murray's own notes for the lectures are located in the Woodstock College Archives (box 6, file 419) at Lauinger Library, Georgetown University, Washington D.C. For more on these

lectures, see my essay "The Laity and Catholic Action in John Courtney Murray's Vision of the Church," in *Vatican II: Forty Years Later*, ed. William Madges, vol. 51 of The Annual Publication of the College Theology Society (Maryknoll, N.Y.: Orbis, 2005), 55–77, which I have drawn on for this section of the present essay. For Coughlin, see Alan Brinkley, *Voices of Protest: Huey Long, Father Coughlin, and the Great Depression* (New York: Random House, 1982).

29. See Henri Carpay, "La Nouveauté de L'Action Catholique," *Nouvelle Revue Théologique* 52 (1935): 477–95. Carpay later expanded on this article in a book. See *L'Action Catholique: Essai de justification historique et de précision doctrinal* (Tournai: Casterman, 1948). For Murray's praise of the book, see John Courtney Murray, "Contemporary Orientations of Catholic Thought on Church and State in the Light of History," *Theological Studies* 10 (June 1949): 224. Their historically informed exposition of Catholic Action stands in contrast with other works from the mid-1940s that approach Catholic Action from a dogmatic angle. See James Voss, *De Fundamentis Actionis Catholicae ad Mentem Sancti Gregorii Magni* (Mundelein, Ill.: Our Lady of the Lake Seminary Press, 1943); Theodore M. Hesburgh, *The Theology of Catholic Action* (Notre Dame, Ind.: Ave Maria, 1946).

30. See Auguste Luneau, *L'histoire du salut chez les pères de l'Eglise: La doctrine des ages du monde*, vol. 2 of *Théologie Historique* (Paris: Beauchesne, 1964), 283–383; E. Randolph Daniel, "Joachim of Fiore: Patterns of History in the Apocalypse," in *The Apocalypse in the Middle Ages*, ed. Richard K. Emmerson and Bernard McGinn (Ithaca, N.Y.: Cornell University Press, 1992), 72–88.

31. Carpay, "Nouveauté de L'Action Catholique," 488 (emphasis in the original).

32. Murray, "Towards a Theology for the Layman: The Pedagogical Problem," 346–47.

33. Source materials for this course, consisting of handwritten lecture notes, are located in the Woodstock College Archives (Murray Papers, box 5, file 381), Lauinger Library, Georgetown University. From dates written in the lecture notes and from the publication dates of other materials present in this file, Murray appears to have given this course at Woodstock on more than one occasion during the mid and late 1940s. A typed course outline is dated "Sept./Oct. 1944."

34. Woodstock College Archives, Murray Papers, box 5, file 381, in the packet "Epochs in the Church's apostolate," 6.

35. Ibid.

36. Ibid., 7.

37. Woodstock College Archives, Murray Papers, box 5, file 381.

38. See Murray, "The Pattern for Peace and the Papal Peace Program," in J. Leon Hooper, ed. *Bridging the Sacred and the Secular: Selected Writings of John Courtney Murray* (Washington, D.C.: Georgetown University Press, 1994), 6–27; "The Juridical Organization of the International Community," in *Bridging the*

Sacred and the Secular, 28–41. For Murray's continuing use of the language of "two powers," see Murray, "The Problem of 'The Religion of the State,'" *American Ecclesiastical Review* 124 (May 1951): 330–31.

39. Woodstock College Archives, Murray Papers, box 5, file 381, lecture 2 (emphasis in the original).

40. J. Leon Hooper, ed., in *Bridging the Sacred and the Secular,* 5.

41. See Murray, "Intercredal Co-Operation: Its Theory and Its Organization," *Theological Studies* 4 (June 1943): 257–86. In the following year Paul Hanley Furfey, a sociologist at the Catholic University of America who had met with Dorothy Day in the mid-1930s, challenged Murray's appropriation of *Singulari Quadam* for the purposes of interreligious cooperation. See Furfey, "Intercredal Cooperation: Its Limitations," *American Ecclesiastical Review* 111 (September 1944): 161–75. Furfey in his book *Fire on the Earth* (1936) promoted what he termed "supernatural sociology," and began with his contention that "a solution for all the problems of modern life" could be found in the Catholic Church. See Furfey, *Fire on the Earth* (New York: Macmillan, 1936), 1.

42. Murray, "Intercredal Co-Operation," 278.

43. See Pius XII, *Mystici Corporis* (June 29, 1943), AAS 35 (1943): 193–248.

44. Will Herberg, *Protestant–Catholic–Jew: An Essay in American Religious Sociology* (Chicago: University of Chicago Press, 1983), 82–83.

45. See David J. O'Brien, "What Happened to the Catholic Left?" in *What's Left? Liberal American Catholics,* ed. Mary Jo Weaver (Bloomington: Indiana University Press, 1999), 259–62. O'Brien characterizes Murray's social thought as a "republican" position concerned for the public welfare of the nation, in contrast to "immigrant" and "evangelical" positions that are less interested in patterns of social organization beyond the boundaries of ethnicity and church. See 265–69.

46. See Murray, "The Church and Totalitarian Democracy," *Theological Studies* 13 (December 1952): 525–63. Murray would return to the same characterization of this historical era in 1964. See Murray, *The Problem of Religious Freedom* (Westminster, Md.: Newman, 1965), 58–59.

47. Murray, "Civil Unity and Religious Integrity: The Articles of Peace," in *We Hold These Truths: Catholic Reflections on the American Proposition* (Kansas City, Mo.: Sheed and Ward, 1988), 58. Republished a few times throughout the 1950s in different periodicals, this essay previously appeared as "The Problem of Pluralism in America," *Thought* 24 (Summer 1954): 165–208.

48. The essay was later republished as Murray, "Are There Two or One? The Question of the Future of Freedom," in *We Hold These Truths,* 197–217 at 212. This essay originally appeared as "The Freedom of Man in the Freedom of the Church," *Modern Age: A Conservative Review* 1 (Fall 1957): 134–45. Kirk characterized the ideological balancing act of the symposium's contributors as follows: "It also is of some interest that though all three of these contributors [David McCord

Wright, Wilhelm Röpke, and Murray] have some reservations about describing themselves as 'conservatives,' they all part company decisively with the liberalism of the Enlightenment and the Utilitarians. A century ago, Walter Bagehot wrote that liberal conservatives and conservative liberals must soon join forces for the protection of their common principles. That fusion of thought now seems far advanced." See Russell Kirk, "Religion and Society: Christianity and Our Present Discontents," *Modern Age: A Conservative Review* 1 (Fall 1957): 120.

49. Murray, "Are There Two or One?" 200; see 198–201.

50. Murray, "Are There Two or One?" 204–5. For a similar historical summary, see Murray, "On the Structure of the Church–State Problem," in *The Catholic Church in World Affairs*, ed. Waldemar Gurian and M. A. Fitzsimons (Notre Dame, Ind.: University of Notre Dame Press, 1954), 11–32.

51. See Paul Blanshard, *American Freedom and Catholic Power* (Boston: Beacon, 1949); *Communism, Democracy, and Catholic Power* (Boston: Beacon, 1951); *The Irish and Catholic Power* (Boston: Beacon, 1954); Roger Finke and Rodney Stark, *The Churching of America, 1776–2005: Winners and Losers in Our Religious Economy*, rev. ed. (Piscataway, N.J.: Rutgers University Press, 2005), 253; Murray, "Separation of Church and State: True and False Concepts," *America* 76 (February 15, 1947): 541–45; "Paul Blanshard and the New Nativism," *Month* 5 (April 1951): 214–25.

52. See Isaiah Berlin, "Two Concepts of Liberty," in *Liberty* (New York: Oxford University Press, 2002), 166–217.

53. The decline of the Catholic Family Movement during this period provides a specific example of how clerical direction of the lay apostolate broke down in one particular movement within the Catholic Action family. See Jeffrey M. Burns, *Disturbing the Peace: A History of the Christian Family Movement, 1949–1974* (Notre Dame, Ind.: University of Notre Dame Press, 1999); Kathryn A. Johnson, "A Question of Authority: Friction in the Catholic Family Life Movement, 1948–1962," *Catholic Historical Review* 86, no. 2 (2000): 217–41.

5. Azzione Cattolica in an American Setting: The Society of Saint Charles–Scalabrinians and Catholic Action

MARY ELIZABETH BROWN

1. See William M. DeMarco, *Ethnics and Enclaves: Boston's Italian North End*, (Ann Arbor, Mich.: UMI, 1981), 92–96.

2. The standard work on the Italian economy that led to the great migration is Robert F. Foerster, *The Italian Emigration of Our Times*, (Cambridge, Mass.: Harvard University Press, 1924).

3. Ibid., 98.

4. The most extensive biography of Scalabrini is Mario Francesconi, C.S., *Giovanni Batista Scalabrini: Vescovo di Piacenza e degli Emigranti* (Rome: Città

Nuova Editrice, 1985). For an English-language biography, see Marco Caliaro, C.S., and Francesconi, *John Baptist Scalabrini: Apostle to Emigrants*, trans. Alba I. Zizzamia (New York: Center for Migration Studies, 1977).

5. Since 1978, the English name of the order has been the Society of St. Charles–Scalabrinians, and its members will be referred to as Scalabrinians here.

6. See [Vittorio Gregori] *Venticinque Anni di Missione fra gli Italiani Immigranti di Boston, Mass.* (Milan: Tipografia Santa Lega Eucaristica, 1913), 179–98.

7. See Howard Gillette Jr. and Alan M. Kraut, "The Evolution of Washington's Italian-American Community, 1890–World War II," *Journal of American Ethnic History* 6, no. 1 (Fall 1986): 7–27; and Gillette and Kraut, "The Evolution of Washington's Italian-American Community," *A Multicultural History of Washington, D.C.*, ed. Francine Cuo Cary (Washington, D.C.; and London: Smithsonian Institution Press, 1996).

8. For the first appearance of Italian immigrants in Washington, see Mary Elizabeth Brown, *An Italian-American Community of Faith: Holy Rosary in Washington, D.C., 1913–2003* (New York: Center for Migration Studies, 2005), 272. For Vatican diplomats' involvement in Italian immigrant pastoral care and Father De Carlo's early years, see [C. E. McGuire], *The Parish of the Holy Rosary in Washington, D.C.: Twenty-Five Years of Mission Work, 1913–1938* (n.p., 1938).

9. See Gino J. Simi, *Golden Jubilee, 1913–1963: Holy Rosary Parish, Third and F Streets, N.W., Washington, D.C.* (n.p., 1963).

10. For the Holy Name Society, see The Sixteen[th] Annual Communion Breakfast of the Holy Name Society of Catholic Men, program dated March 8, 1987, Holy Rosary parish, Donanzan Papers, Holy Name Society, folder 1987. For other parish societies, see *Holy Rosary Parish*. The mention of the Catholic Action society is on page 9.

11. For the exterior, see *Venticinque Anni*, 101. For the interior contrast, see 97 and 99.

12. James Hennessey, S.J., *American Catholics: A History of the Roman Catholic Community in the United States* (New York: Oxford, 1981), 221.

13. See Immigration and Naturalization Service *1998 Statistical Yearbook of the Immigration and Naturalization Service* (Washington, D.C.: Government Printing Office, 2000), A.1–6, available http://www.dhs.gov/xlibrary/assets/statistics/yearbook/1998/1998yb.pdf.

14. See Center for Migration Studies, New York, New York, Collection 078, box 88, folder G-GV 50. (Hereafter all references to this collection are noted as CMS Coll.) For the letter expressing satisfaction with Oddi's work in Boston, see Caesar Donnaruma to Caesar Donanzan, C.S., Boston, August 11, 1967. For the letter claiming Oddi enjoyed too much freedom in Boston, see Giulivio Tessarolo, C.S., to Donanzan, Rome, January 26, 1968. For the letter regarding Oddi's

plan to leave the Scalabrinians and recruiting Silvio Cardinal Oddi's assistance, see Tessarolo to Silvio Oddi, Rome, October 28, 1968. The last communication with Oddi was Silvano M. Tomasi to Oddi, New York, March 10, 1978.

15. See Isaia Birollo, C.S., circular announced Father Spigolon's death, Rome, February 13, 2004, CMS Coll. 078C, box 92, folder G–GZ 58.

16. See *Voce Italiana* 18, nos. 7–8 (August–September 1979): 3.

17. See CMS Coll. 062, box 3, Azione Cattolica Italiana minutes, 1958–1963, December 12, 1958. The women's minutes were kept in a spiral notebook.

18. See CMS Coll. 062, box 3, Azione Cattolica Italiana minutes, 1958–1963, October 12, 1959. The men's minutes were typed and filed in a red folder, which is preserved in the archival box.

19. For the history of Catholic Action, see *Decimo Anniversario, Azione Cattolica Italiana* (n.p., 1972). For the inauguration of *Voce Italiana*, see *Voce Italiana* 11, no. 1 (January 1971).

20. See John W. Briggs, *Italian Passage: Immigrants to Three American Cities* (New Haven, Conn.: Yale University Press, 1978), who discusses the transplantation of mutual-aid societies from Italian villages to the American setting.

21. See CMS Coll. 062, box 3, Azione Cattolica Italiana minutes, 1958–1963, December 21, 1960, women's meeting.

22. See Congregazione dei Missionari di San Carlo–Scalabriniani, S. Carlos B. (New York), Azione Cattolica Italiana–Boston, CMS Coll. 078C, folder Q–QF14.

23. See *Incontro* 2, nos. 1–4 (April 1969).

24. *Azione Cattolica Italiana*—Boston—12 North Square, *Resoconto ecnomico* [*sic*] 1 Settembre 1968–31 agosto 1969, CMS Coll. 078C, folder Q–QF14.

25. Azione Cattolica Italiana—Boston, Resoconto economico 1 Sett. 1971–31 agosto 1972, Coll. 078C, folder Q–QF14.

26. "PER LA CONSERVAZIONE DEI VALORI UMANI E CRISTIANI NELLA COMUNITÀ ITALIANA," in "Perché?" *Incontro* 1, no. 1 (Gennaio 1968), 1.

27. "Azione Cattolica Italiana, Boston, Mass., Statuto, Regolamente," [1970], typescript in CMS Coll. 062, box 3, folder Azione Cattolica Italiana, Statues and Regulations.

28. *Incontro* 3, no. 10 (Ottobre 1970). My translation.

29. *Incontro* 3, no. 2 (February 1970). See also "Transcript of President's State of the Union Message to Joint Session of Congress," *New York Times*, January 23, 1970.

30. See *Incontro* 3, no. 4 (April 1970).

31. *Incontro* 2, no. 11 (November 1972).

32. See CMS Coll. 062, box 3, Azione Cattolica Italiana minutes, 1958–1963, December 12, 1958, women's meeting.

33. See CMS Coll. 062, box 3, Azione Cattolica Italiana minutes, 1958–1963, November 23, 1959, men's meeting.

34. See *Incontro* 2, nos. 8–9 (Agosto–Settembre 1969).

35. See CMS Coll. 062, box 3, Azione Cattolica Italiana minutes, 1958–1963, November 23, 1959 men's meeting.

36. See *Incontro* 2, nos. 6–7 (June–July 1969).

37. See *Incontro* 3, no. 10 (October 1970).

38. See *Incontro* 2, no. 11 (November 1969).

39. See Anna Neri to Patrick Cardinal O'Boyle, Washington, D.C., April 1, 1970, Archives of the Archdiocese of Washington, Holy Rosary, Washington, D.C., 117, Administrative correspondence, 1916–1997.

40. For wedding announcements, see *Incontro* 2, nos. 6–7 (June–July 1969). For both wedding and birth announcements, see *Incontro* 3, nos. 6–7 (Giugno–Luglio 1970).

41. *Incontro* 2, no. 5 (Maggio 1969).

42. See "Risate All'Italiana," n.d. Clipping found in Gino J. Simi, Holy Rosary Newsletter file, September 1968–June 1976, folder at Holy Rosary parish, Washington, D.C.

43. See *Decimo Anniversario, Azione Cattolica Italiana* (Washington, D.C.: Privately published, 1970), unpaginated.

44. See Mary G. Catucci, Parish Council minutes, October 20, 1970. Copy in Gino J. Simi, Holy Rosary Parish Council folder, at Holy Rosary parish, Washington, D.C.

45. See *Incontro* 2, no. 5 (May 1969).

46. See *Incontro* 4, no. 2 (February 1971).

47. See *Incontro* 2, no. 11 (November 1969).

48. See *Incontro* 3, no. 4 (April 1970); 3, nos. 8–9 (Agosto–Settembre 1970).

49. See *Incontro* 2, no. 12 (December 1969).

50. For trips to Italy, see CMS Coll. 062, box 3, Azione Cattolica Italiana minutes, November 17, 1961, men's group; *Incontro* 2, no. 5 (Maggio 1969); and *Incontro* 2, no. 5 (May 1969).

51. For the women's-group's trip along the route of the midnight ride of Paul Revere, see ibid. For the essay, reminiscent of Art Buchwald's effort to explain Thanksgiving to the French, see *Incontro*, n.s. 3, no. 4 (April 1973).

52. See *Incontro* 2, no. 10 (October 1969).

53. See *Incontro* 3, nos. 6–7 (Giugno–Luglio 1970).

54. See *Incontro* 4, no. 3 (March 1971).

55. See *Voce Italiana* 11, no. 1 (January 1971).

56. *Incontro* is the Italian word for "a meeting."

57. See *Incontro* n.s. 1, no. 1 (January 1971).

58. For more on the *Post-Gazette*, see Stephen Puleo, *The Boston Italians: A Story of Pride, Perseverance and Paesani from the Years of the Great Immigration to the Present Day* (Boston: Beacon Press, 2007), which is based largely on the business

archives of the Donnaruma family. The archives are now housed at the Immigration History and Research Center of the University of Minnesota, Minneapolis.

59. See *Incontro* n.s. 1, no. 2 (November 1971).

60. See Peter Polo, e-mail message to author, January 11, 2010.

61. See *Voce Italiana* (November 1980 and May 1981). The Associazione Comunità Italiana had the same initials as the name the members of the Holy Rosary Catholic Action group used for the organization, Associazione Cattolica Italiana.

62. Gino J. Simi, *Golden Jubilee, 1913–1963: Holy Rosary Parish, Third and F Streets, N.W., Washington, D.C.* (privately published, 1963), unpaginated.

63. For the parish council, see Leo L. Balducci to Gino J. Simi, Washington, D.C., July 5, 1968, Holy Rosary Parish, Gino J. Simi Papers, folder Parish Council. For Scuola Italiana, see Patricia Brizzi, interview, Washington, D.C., June 14, 2002.

64. See *Voce Italiana* (April 1997): 3–4.

65. See "Holy Rosary Church to Hold Italian Festival," *Evening Star* (September 16, 1963).

66. See Christine MacDonald, "North End: Full Family Press to Save a Church," *Boston Globe*, April 18, 2004.

67. See Michael Paulson, "65 Parishes to Be Closed," *Boston Globe*, May 26, 2004.

68. See William Issel, "'Still Potentially Dangerous in Some Quarters': Sylvester Andriano, Catholic Action, and Un-American Activities in California," *Pacific Historical Review* 75, no. 2 (2006): 231–70; and "Faith-Based Activism in American Cities: The Case of the San Francisco Catholic Action Cadre," *Journal of Church and State* 50, no. 3 (Summer 2008): 519–40.

69. Examples include Erik Amfitheatrof, *Children of Columbus: An Informal History of Italians in the New World* (Boston: Little, Brown, 1973); Alexander DeConde, *Half Bitter, Half Sweet: An Excursion into Italian American History* (New York: Scribner's, 1971); Patrick J. Gallo, *Old Bread, New Wine: A Portrait of the Italian Americans* (Chicago: Nelson-Hall, 1983); Luciano J. Iorizzo and Salvatore Mondello, *The Italian Americans*, 3rd ed. (Youngstown, N.Y.: Cambria, 2006); Jerre Mangione and Ben Morreale, *Storia: Five Centuries of the Italian-American Experience* (New York: HarperCollins, 1992); Humberto Nelli, *From Immigrants to Ethnics: The Italian Americans* (New York: Oxford, 1983); Andrew F. Rolle, *Italian Americans: Troubled Roots* (Norman: University of Oklahoma Press, 1984); Giovanni Ermenigildo Schiavo, *Italian American History*, 2 vols. (New York: Vigo, 1947–49); and Allon Schoener, *The Italian Americans*, commentary by A. Bartlett Giamatti (New York: Macmillan, 1987).

70. For an older exception to the rule, see Thomas Kessner and Betty Boyd Caroli, eds., *Today's Immigrants Tell Their Stories* (New York: Oxford 1982), 205–32.

71. See Henry J. Browne, "The 'Italian Problem' in the Catholic Church of the United States, 1880–1900," *U.S. Catholic Historical Society Records and Studies* 35 (1946): 46–72.

72. See Rudolph J. Vecoli, "Prelates and Peasants: Italian Immigrants and the Catholic Church," *Journal of Social History* 2 (1969): 217–67.

73. See Robert A. Orsi, *The Madonna of 115th Street: Faith and Community in Italian Harlem, 1880–1930* (New Haven, Conn.: Yale University Press, 1982).

74. See Silvano M. Tomasi, C.S., *Power and Piety: The Role of Italian Parishes in the New York Metropolitan Area, 1880–1930* (New York: Center for Migration Studies, 1975). Mention should also be made of Stephen J. Shaw, *The Catholic Parish as a Way-Station of Ethnicity and Americanization: Chicago's Germans and Italians, 1903–1939* (Brooklyn: Carlson, 1991), who has a similar thesis.

75. Rudolph J. Vecoli, "*Contadini* in Chicago: A Critique of *The Uprooted*," *Journal of American History* 51, no. 3 (December 1964): 404–17; Richard N. Juliani, "A Usable Past: Analysis and Application," *Italian Americana* 26, no. 1 (March 2008): 5–20.

76. See Lawrence K. Hong, "Recent Immigrants in the Chinese-American Community: Issues of Adaptations and Impacts," *International Migration Review* 10, no. 4 (Winter 1976): 509–14.

77. See Roberto Italo Zanini, *By God's Own Power: Scalabrini, a Bishop in the Difficult Years of the Nineteenth Century*, trans. Saint Charles Province of the Society of Saint Charles–Scalabrinians (forthcoming), chapter 25.

6. Relevant Transformations: The Young Women of the Extension Lay Volunteers, 1961–1971

ELIZABETH DUCLOS-ORSELLO

1. Information on Karen, Ruth, and Elaine comes from the following: Karen de Hartog, response to "Female Extension Volunteer Community Project Questionnaire" (hereafter FEVCPQ), April 29, 2010, in author's possession; Ruth Poochigian, response to FEVCPQ, May 2, 2010, in author's possession; Elaine Duclos, response to FEVCPQ, April 19, 2010, in author's possession. Quotations are from Mary Jones, response to FEVCPQ, October 24, 2010, in the author's possession. "Mary Jones" is a pseudonym. This questionnaire was completed in confidentiality, and the name of the respondent is withheld by mutual consent. Please note that all references to FEVCPQs in this chapter refer to documents that are in the author's possession, and so too with references to "Female Extension Volunteer Community Project Follow Up Questionnaire" (hereafter FEVCPQ-FU). I wish to thank Karen Kocich, formerly of the Catholic Extension Society Chicago, (CES), for her willingness to locate and make available to me scanned copies of all *Extension* magazines cited in this essay as well as other

archival materials held in an informal archive at the CES headquarters (hereafter referred to as the CESA). Without her support this research would have been impossible. Thank you, too, to my colleagues at Salem State University who read and commented on this project as part of a 2011 RWI workshop, and particularly to Patricia Johnston of Salem State University, whose editorial eye has made this much better than it might have been. Most notably, I wish to thank the six former ELVs (including my mother) who graciously and generously reached back into their memories and their pasts and shared their journeys with me. Their words and stories were the inspiration for this essay and serve to make it come to life. This is for them; I hope that they find that I have told their story well.

2. For an entry point into this vast scholarship, see first David Faber, *Chicago '68* (Chicago: University of Chicago Press, 1994), and Tom Hayden, *The Whole World Was Watching: The Streets of Chicago: 1968* (Davis, Calif.: Panorama West, 1996). Faber's multivocal exploration of the Democratic National Convention (DNC) and its lead-up showcases the various ideological positions and also points out Mayor Daley's Irish Catholic roots. See also James Miller, *Democracy Is in the Streets* (New York: Simon and Schuster, 1987), and for a popular account see Charles Kaiser, *1968 In America: Music, Politics, Class, Counterculture, and the Shaping of a Generation* (New York: Grove, 1988).

3. In the absence of an official accounting of the ratio of female to male volunteers—not currently available from the CES—the claim about percentages comes from the following data: (1) a 1990 directory of former ELVs produced for the thirtieth anniversary (although representing only about half of the total numbers who served) indicates that no more than 10 percent of the ELVs were men; 2) the lists in *Extension* magazine (the monthly magazine of the CES) for the years 1967 and 1968 (the height of the program) reflect slightly higher percentages but never more than 20 percent.

4. This project builds upon and adds to the excellent work emerging of late to try and place lay Catholics and female Catholics into a broader context of both the institutional Church and the cultural milieu and social-cultural politics and history of the postwar era. Among the most crucial to this effort are Mary Henold's groundbreaking *Catholic and Feminist: The Surprising History of the American Catholic Feminist Movement* (Chapel Hill: University of North Carolina Press, 2008); Amy Koehlinger, *The New Nuns: Racial Justice and Religious Reform in the 1960s* (Cambridge, Mass: Harvard University Press, 2007); and James O'Toole's survey of the lay Catholic experience in the United States, *The Faithful: A History of Catholics in America* (Cambridge: Belknap Press of Harvard University Press, 2008). See also Patrick W. Carey, *Catholics in America* (Westport, Conn.: Praeger, 2004); Jeremy Bonner, *The Road to Renewal: Victor Joseph Reed and Oklahoma Catholicism, 1905–1971* (Washington, D.C.: The Catholic University of America Press, 2008), especially chapter 12, "Out of the Ghetto: The Conscience of the

Catholic Layman"; and John Beiter, "'Lay People Can Teach': Rural Life, Edwin O'Hara, and the Confraternity of Christian Doctrine, 1920–1960," *American Catholic Studies* 120, no. 2 (2009): 53–69. For a slightly older but important look at the many links between Catholicism and American culture, see Mark Massa, *Catholics and American Culture: Fulton Sheen, Dorothy Day, and the Notre Dame Football Team* (New York: Crossroad, 1999). My study adds to this emergent conversation about women, laypeople, and the twentieth-century Church by telling part of the story of young single laywomen whose voices and histories are largely absent from the organizations, movements, and ideological discourses covered by this new wave of scholarship.

5. The Extension Society often used the term "Peace Corps" (sometimes with lowercase *p* and *c*) in the printed materials during the early years of the ELV program. For example, see *Extension* 55, no. 12 (May 1961): 40; *Extension* 56, no. 3 (August 1961): 40.

6. Bishop John May, "Something Old and Something New," *Extension*, 63, no. 2 (July–August 1968). For more on the early institutional and founding history of Extension and the lay volunteer program in its pre-1961 days, see the following: David Bovee, "Extension Society, Catholic Church," 493–94; James P. Gaffey, *Francis Clement Kelley and the American Dream* (Bensenville, Ill.: Heritage Foundation, 1980), and a more recent account in Bonner, *Road to Renewal*, 171–72, which also offers an excellent overview of the rural and mission churches, Catholics of the Midwest, and the progressive nature of Catholicism in this region during the period leading up to and following the Vatican II changes.

7. The dates 1960 and 1961 appear in different places as the "start date" of the program. It appears that 1960–61 was a small pilot year. For internal and contemporary published accounts of the early years, see "History," n.d., typewritten document in files of CESA (appears to be ca. 1965–66); script of slide presentation presented at ELV reunion, 1990, typewritten document in files of CESA; John L. May, "Extension Volunteers," *Extension* 55, no. 10 (March 1961): 13–14; May, "Extension Volunteers," *Extension* 55, no. 11 (May 1961): 46; May, "Extension Volunteers," *Extension* 55, no. 12 (June 1961): 30; May, "Extension Volunteers," *Extension* 56, no. 2 (July 1961): 33; and May, "Father John J. Sullivan Appointed to Organize Extension Volunteers from Coast to Coast," *Extension* 56, no. 3 (August 1961): 40. To date, there is no academic history of the Catholic Church Extension Society. There is also no formal archive of Catholic Church Extension Society records for the decade 1961–71. Materials from those years are held in storage at the offices of the Catholic Church Extension Society in Chicago. The formal Catholic Church Extension Society records, covering the period 1920–61, are at Loyola University, Chicago.

8. According to CES documents, the program ended in 1971 when the Society began supporting new programs across the nation. See *Welcome Home, 30 Year*

Anniversary Reunion (booklet), 1990, 3, CESA. It is worth noting, however, that in 1969 the *Extension* magazine published reports noting the dramatic (50 percent) decrease in applications that year over the previous one. *Extension*, 64, no. 11 (June 1969): 7. The ELV program began to dissolve about the same time that the New Left did. See Douglas Rossinow, *The Politics of Authenticity: Liberalism, Christianity, and the New Left in America* (New York: Columbia University Press, 1998), on the New Left's dissolution.

9. *Extension* 55, no. 10 (March 1961): 13.

10. The upper age limit seemed pretty flexible, yet available records indicate that nearly all ELVs were in their twenties. *Extension* articles and publicity documents consistently refer to volunteers in their twenties and suggest that while a college degree was not required most were college-educated. Note too that one of the most popular recruiting pamphlets of the Extension program made explicit the central role of the laity in the wake of Vatican II. On this point and age range and benefits see the brochure "An Intersection Called Relevance: Fast Facts on the Extension Volunteer Program" n.d., CESA. Finally, note that in 1966 the Vatican II focus on ecumenical efforts resulted in the first Protestant ELV to be accepted into the program. Mary Jane Kern served as a teacher at a Catholic school in Leesville, Louisiana. William Jacobs, "Can A Protestant Extend the Catholic Church?" *Extension* 61, no. 11 (November 1966).

11. See *Extension* 55, no. 10 (March 1961): 13–14. The claim about ELVs being "eminently normal men and women" appears in a recruiting brochure available by the second half of the decade and referenced by former ELVs as powerful. See "An Intersection Called Relevance."

12. See *Extension* 55, no. 11 (April 1961): 46.

13. See *Extension* 55, no. 12 (May 1961): 46.

14. Mary Meyers, response to FEVCPQ, April 28, 2011.

15. On the ideological and even spiritual similarities between these disparate elements, see Rossinow, *The Politics of Authenticity*. He refers to the New Left and the counterculture as "two parts of a larger white youth existential movement of the cold war era—two parts of a larger historical formation with common roots, even if they were not close tactical allies" (249). On the white youth counterculture see Theodore Roszak, *The Making of a Counter-Culture: Reflections on the Technocratic Society and Its Youthful Opposition* (New York: Doubleday, 1969); Rosabeth Moss Kanter, *Commitment and Community: Communes and Utopias in Sociological Perspective* (Cambridge, Mass.: Harvard University Press, 1972); John Case and Rosemary C. R. Taylor, eds. *Co-ops, Communes and Collectives: Experiments in Social Change in the 1960s and 1970s* (New York: Pantheon, 1979); and Timothy Miller, *The Hippies and American Values* (Knoxville: University of Tennessee Press, 1991).

16. See Rossinow, *The Politics of Authenticity*. See in particular part 1 for the ways in which the Christian Faith and Life Community, the YMCA, and the works of Reinhold Niebuhr, Paul Tillich, Dietrich Bonhoeffer and Albert Camus combined in a way that led to a search for justice and faith through action and influenced such key "movement" texts as the Port Huron Statement. See also Sydney E. Ahlstrom, "The Radical Turn in Theology and Ethics: Why It Occurred in the 1960's," *Annals of the American Academy of Political and Social Sciences* 387 (January 1970): 1–13. Note as well that David Faber, in his important close look at the events surrounding the DNC in Chicago in 1968, makes the case that during that week there was another thread/undercurrent running through the actions of the National Mobilization Committee to End the War in Vietnam and even Students for a Democratic Society: a moral quest that linked back to a liberal Protestant tradition of bearing moral witness in the world. See *Chicago '68*, 232–34.

17. While there are some links to be made between ELVs and the Christian Family movement, new nuns, and Catholic feminists when the era is painted with broad strokes, recent scholarship by O'Toole, Henold, and Koehlinger leaves open the specific question of where and how young laywomen fit into the new Catholic energy and activities of the postwar era. For the activities and roles of Catholic lay women in the twentieth century see O'Toole, *The Faithful*. Among women religious, the 1960s were a decade of dramatic decrease in numbers. In 1965, there were 181,421 U.S. Catholic nuns; in 1970, there were only 153,645 nuns, with over 4,000 nuns leaving the convent in that year alone, a rate six times higher than had been seen just ten years befor. See Rodney Stark and Roger Finke, *Review of Religious Research*, 42, no. 2 (December 2000): 125.

18. Accounts from *Extension* magazine and ELV recollections about recruiting practices indicate that the majority of ELVs were from Catholic colleges and universities from the Midwest and East Coast. This was confirmed by the recollections of two ELV recruiters, Elaine Duclos and Karen de Hartog, in responses to the FEVCPQ and FEVCPQ-FU in April and May 2011. Those volunteers not from Catholic institutions seem overwhelmingly to have been involved in Newman Centers at their secular institutions. The reading habits and theological/philosophical influences or training of Catholics graduating from colleges and universities in the 1960s has not been systematically examined to date. The recollections of some female ELVs in this study, however, and responses (both on- and offline) to a May 2011 discussion on H-Catholic about the topic suggest that each of these scholars/writers appeared (some more than others) in college theology and philosophy courses, in Newman Centers, and in the personal reading of some significant proportion of Catholic young adults. Elizabeth Duclos-Orsello to H-Catholic, May 9, 2011, http://h-net.msu.edu. See also chapter 6, "Secular

Sanctity," in Donald J. Thorman, *American Catholics Face the Future* (Wilkes-Barre, Pa.: Dimension, 1968). Thorman, then publisher of the *National Catholic Reporter*, claimed that Bonhoeffer and Teilhard de Chardin were "immensely popular in both religious and secular educational circles" (145). The influence of these Christian theologians (as well as thinkers ranging from Freud and Jung to Harvey Cox), changes in policy and theology, and the larger principles of Vatican II's call for Catholics to engage with the world were all present in ever increasing intensity on college campuses throughout the decade of the ELV program. On the transformations in Catholic higher education in these years, see Sandra Yocum Mize, *Joining the Revolution in Theology: The College Theology Society, 1954–2004* (Lanham, Md.: Rowman and Littlefield, 2007), especially chapters 4 and 6, and Alice Gallin, O.S.U., *Negotiating Identity: Catholic Higher Education since 1960* (Notre Dame: Ind.: University of Notre Dame Press, 2000).

19. From Sister Mary Lynne Wrocklage in *Welcome Home*, 5.

20. The second paragraph of the important *Decree on the Apostolate of the Laity* (1965) pronounced specifically that, in addition to a generally expanded role for and recognition of the apostolate of the laity, "in . . . places where priests are . . . few or . . . deprived of due freedom for priestly work, the Church could scarcely exist and function without the activity of the laity." *Apostolicam Actuositatem* (Decree on the Apostolate of the Laity), http://www.vatican.va.

21. See *Extension* 55, no. 10 (March 10, 1961): 14; and *Extension* 56, no. 11 (April 1962): 34.

22. In March 1961, *Extension* magazine ran an article identifying January 1, 1961 as the first day of the program's formal existence. See *Extension* 55, no. 10 (March 1961). For one of many additional examples of articles that point out the chronology of the ELV as compared with the Peace Corps and VISTA, see *Extension* 63, no. 2 (July–August, 1968). The quotation is from *Extension* 55, no. 1 (May 1961): 46. According to the Peace Corps' website the executive order establishing the Peace Corps program was issued on March 1, 1961. See "1960s" at http://www.peacecorps.gov/about/history/decades/1960. The VISTA program was funded in 1964 with the first volunteers beginning in 1965. See "The History of the Americorps VISTA" at http://www.americorps.gov/about/programs/vista_legacy.asp.

23. See Jerome Earnst, "In Remembrance of The March on Washington," *Extension* 59, no. 3 (August 1964): 36–38. The bold sidebar to this article read: "On August 28, 1963, 200,000 people marched for justice. One year later, on the same date, Extension Lay Volunteers will be traveling to 'missions' to help bring about that justice."

24. See *Extension* 62, no. 5 (October 1967): 34–35.

25. *Extension* 63, no. 4 (October 1968): 5.

26. Ibid.

27. *Welcome Home*, 5.

28. Elaine Duclos, response to FEVCPQ, April 19, 2010.

29. Karen de Hartog, response to FEVCPQ, April 29, 2010.

30. Descriptions of recruiting practices generally appeared repeatedly in *Extension* over the life of the program. The recollections of ELVs corroborate these accounts, as do the accounts of two ELVs who were recruiters in their second year of volunteering. Karen de Hartog, response to FEVCPQ-FU, May 11, 2011; Elaine Duclos, response to FEVCPQ-FU, May 5, 2011.

31. Mary Jones, response to FEVCPQ-FU, May 10, 2011; Elaine Duclos, response to FEVCPQ-FU, May 5, 2011.

32. "An Intersection Called Relevance." This brochure and another, "Try Extending Yourself," were immensely influential for Anne Mahunder, who served in 1966–67 and is quoted in *Welcome Home*, 5.

33. For detailed discussions of training in published materials see Jerome Ernst, "Extension is A Comin,'" *Extension* 59, no. 5 (October, 1964): 22–24, and "52 Weeks," *Extension*, 62, no. 4 (September 1967): 30–33.

34. The Catholic Extension Society does not have formal records of these training sessions but three 1968 volunteers independently recalled and commented on Alinsky's presence and his powerful admonishment to the ELVs to let go of any sense of superiority or knowledge of those they would serve as they began their mission work. Mary Jones, response to FEVCPQ, October, 24, 2011; Elaine Duclos, response to FEVCPQ-FU, May 5, 2011; Karen de Hartog, response to FEVCPQ-FU, May 11, 2011.

35. Mary Jones, response to FEVCPQ, October 24, 2010.

36. The overwhelmingly female makeup of the volunteer corps seems, in fact, to have been of some concern to the leadership who appear to have wanted to increase the number of men in the program, as suggested by recruiting tactics such as the placement of an article titled "LayMEN in the Home Missions," by Peter Gallagher, *Extension* 57, no. 6 (November 1962): 8.

37. For examples of profiles of women and discussions of teamwork and partnership, see for example Sharlene Shoemaker, "School's In," *Extension* 57, no. 1 (June, 1962): 20–21; James L. Everett, "In Betsy's Wake . . . A New Community is Born," *Extension* 61, no. 12 (May 1967): 28–33; George Lundy, "Extension Volunteers Help Put the Wheels in Motion in Bayou Country," *Extension* 63, no. 9 (April 1969): 5–11. In "Face to Face with 1968," *Extension* 63, no. 4 (October 1968): 6, the organization made clear that potential volunteers "must have a strong sense of teamwork."

38. Karen de Hartog, response to FEVCPQ, April 29, 2010.

39. See particularly Henold, *Catholic and Feminist*, chapters 2 and 3.

40. On these topics generally, see Henold, *Catholic and Feminist*; O'Toole, *The Faithful*; and Koelinger, *The New Nuns*. For details on the changes among women

religious and the loss of women religious, see Massa, *Catholics and American Culture*, chapter 8; Bonner, *The Road to Renewal*, chapter 11; and Carey, *Catholics in America*, 119–120. On *The Flying Nun* see Rebecca Sullivan, "Gidget Goes to the Convent: Taking the Veil as Girl's Adventure in *The Flying Nun*," *Canadian Review of American Studies* 31 (2001): 15–30. The claim here about gender equality or women's-liberation ideas on Catholic college campuses emerges from the very specific recollections of Elaine Duclos, response to FEVCPQ, April 19, 2010. Other former ELVs recall becoming interested in women's rights or feminist issues but do not tie them to particular events or moments.

41. Lucy McMahon, "Chicago Mission," *Extension* 58, no. 11 (April 1964): 28–30.

42. The idea of "sisterhood" was prevalent throughout the late 1960s. For a brief history of the ideology and the ultimate cracks that emerged, see Wini Brienes, "What's Love Got to Do With It? White Women, Black Women, and Feminism in the Movement Years," *Signs* 27, no. 4 (2002): 1095–1133.

43. Karen de Hartog, response to FEVCPQ, April 29, 2010.

44. This statement reflects the sum of the responses to such questions among the six ELVs who responded to questionnaires in 2010 and 2011 for this study. It seems certain that among the volunteers there was a range of knowledge and involvement in Catholic activities prior to joining the ELVs, but these "older" types of connections do not emerge as the predominant message.

45. See Koehlinger, *The New Nuns*, especially 235–36.

46. There was one exception among those who responded to questionnaires in 2010 and 2011 for this project. Elaine Duclos referred broadly to the new movement of nuns and sisters out of convents in the 1960s and 1970s. Interestingly, her account suggests that women religious were beginning to act more like the laity of the era rather than vice versa.

47. Elaine Duclos, response to FEVCPQ, April 19, 2010.

48. *Extension* 61, no. 12 (May 1967): 30.

49. The term "Catholic Left" (coined by the media) generally refers to Roman Catholic religious and laypeople involved in the antiwar movement in the 1960s and early 1970s. On this and the general activities of this group, see Charles A. Meconis, *With Clumsy Grace: The American Catholic Left, 1961–1975* (New York: Seabury, 1979). For specifics on the notion of an "action community" see Meconis, 43, and Marion Mollin, "Communities of Resistance: Women and the Catholic Left of the Late 1960s," *Oral History Review*, 31, no. 2 (2004): 29–51, 37–38.

50. Mollin, 38.

51. See Mollin, 39.

52. On Detroit, see *Extension* 61, no. 8 (January 1967); on the Louisiana bayou, see *Extension* 63, no. 10 (April 1969); on the boot heel of Missouri, see *Extension*

64, no. 5 (November 1969); on public health nursing in Oklahoma, see *Extension* 58, no. 8 (January 1964); on migrant worker camps in the cotton fields of Texas, see *Extension* 59, no. 7 (December 1964).

53. Mary Jones, response to FEVCPQ, October 24, 2010.

54. Sarah Overmeyer Cody, *Welcome Home*, 7.

55. Elaine Duclos, response to FEVCPQ, April 19, 2010. Other female volunteers who responded to a 1990 survey mention the intensity of the work/experience and how that related to a sense of connection to others. Said Judy Humowieki (63–64) of her volunteer year: "Wonderful and difficult. . . . Made life-long friends with similar values." And from Mary Sue Maher-Orr (65–66): "It was a growing time. I experienced poverty first-hand. It was disturbing to see the human cost of poverty. My experience also provided rich opportunities to work with dedicated people—lay, religious, and priests." For these 1990 responses, see *Welcome Home*, 6–7.

56. Karen de Hartog, response to FEVCPQ, April 29, 2010. This sentiment was echoed also in the recollections of Mary Meyers, response to FEVCPQ, April 28, 2011. For Meyers, who spent a year as a teacher in Fresno, California, the living together was critical and going it alone would have been difficult.

57. Mary Jones, response to FEVCPQ, October 24, 2010.

58. Sheila Vandercar Long (1963–64), in *Welcome Home*, 7.

59. Mary Jones, response to FEVCPQ, October 24, 2010.

60. Mary Meyers, response to FEVCPQ, April 18, 2011. In the case of some of the women who responded to questionnaires for this essay, it was the relationships that came to define the year(s) for them more than Catholicism or the nature of the service.

61. For an overview of this movement and its growth, see some of the following: Marguerite Bouvard, *The Intentional Community Movement: Building a New Moral World*, National University Publications (Port Washington, N.Y.: Kennikat, 1975); Terry Anderson, *The Sixties* (New York: Longman, 1999); John Case and Rosemary C. R. Taylor, eds., *Co-ops, Communes, and Collectives: Experiments in Social Change in the 1960s and 1970s* (New York: Pantheon, 1979); Keith Melville, *Communes in the Counterculture* (New York: Morrow, 1972); Timothy Miller, *The 60s Communes: Hippies and Beyond* (Syracuse: Syracuse University Press, 1999); Timothy Miller, *The Hippies and American Values* (Knoxville: University of Tennessee Press, 1991); Roszac, *The Making of a Counter-Culture*. For these numbers, see the excellent overview and debate in Miller, *The Hippies and American Values*, xviii–xx.

62. Avis Cotter Mannino (1963–64) in *Welcome Home*, 7; see Mary Heezen Smith; (no year listed) and Ann Moore Crowly (1965–67), in *Welcome Home*, 7.

63. Of the six ELVs who completed questionnaires for this project none linked their experience to other contemporary forms of community in an unqualified way. Four simply indicated no connection.

64. Elaine Duclos, response to FEVCPQ, April 19, 2010.

65. The import given to "fit" in other intentional communities of the era is suggested in an article devoted to the issue in *Communities* 1 (December 1972): 12–15.

66. All former volunteers who responded to questionnaires for this project speak about the need to develop and negotiate relationships with their assigned partners/housemates/coworkers. Karen de Hartog recalled that she and her three housemates "all learned tolerance and patience living with three other women in a one bathroom house. We shared household activities and had the common bond of being four well-educated Catholic females in a western, primarily Mormon town." Karen de Hartog, response to FEVCPQ, April 29, 2010.

67. This may be seen as not unlike accounts of "urban communes" or collective houses attractive to young singles and increasing in number by the late 1960s. These collective houses offered young people an opportunity to maintain family connections while enjoying the freedom to pursue independent work or a career outside of either a parent's home or a marital relationship. See Rosabeth Moss Kanter, "Communes in Cities," in Case and Taylor, *Co-ops, Communes and Collectives*, 112–35. Urban collective homes were attractive also to families in this era, according to an article in *Communities*, a magazine for describing communal and collective efforts and offering advice for those trying to live in such a way. "Middle Class Commune," *Communities* 1 (December 1972): 8–11.

68. The stories of sharing as well as living and working together can be found in articles in *Extension* magazine year after year, as well as in the accounts of former volunteers. Among the women contacted for this project, Ruth Poochigian recalls sharing meals; Mary Jones, Mary Meyers, and Elaine Duclos describe taking turns cooking and cleaning; others discuss sharing bedrooms or indicated that they worshipped or prayed together on occasion. See also the range of responses in *Welcome Home*, 6–9.

69. The three quotations here are from (in order) Nan Nader Koob (1966–67) in *Welcome Home*, 5; Mary Meyers, response to FEVCPQ, April 28, 2011, in author's possession; Mary Ann Voss (1965–66), in *Welcome Home*, 6–7.

70. Mary Sue Maher-Orr in *Welcome Home*, 7; Mary Jones, response to FEVCPQ, October 24, 2010; Karen de Hartog, response to FEVCPQ, April 29, 2010; Lucille DiDomenico, response to FEVCPQ, March 23, 2011.

71. See Koehlinger, *The New Nuns*, 237–38.

72. This is the summary sentiment of the dozens of former ELVs who responded to a 1990 questionnaire. Responses were published in *Welcome Home*.

73. Mary Jones, response to FEVCPQ, October 24, 2010.

74. Elaine Duclos, response to FEVCPQ, April 19, 2010.

75. Lucille DiDomenico, response to FEVCPQ, March 23, 2011.

76. See O'Toole, *The Faithful*, and Henold, *Catholic and Feminist*.

77. Karen de Hartog, response to FEVCPQ, April 29, 2010.

78. William J. Jacobs, "The People of God in Pueblo," *Extension* 60, no. 12 (May 1966): 30–31.

79. Both the results of the 1990 survey for the thirtieth-anniversary celebration (published in *Welcome Home*) as well as my recent intensive questioning of six female ELVs support this assessment.

7. Reaching Out to the People of God: The Implications of Renewal for the Sisters of Mercy in Parish Schools

MARY BETH FRASER CONNOLLY

1. Rev. Thomas J. O'Brien to Mother Mary Regina Cunningham, February 1, 1958, St. Raymond School, Archives of the Sisters of Mercy Chicago (hereafter ASMC).

2. Mother Mary Regina Cunningham to Rev. Thomas J. O'Brien, February 27, 1958, St. Raymond School, ASMC.

3. See Amy L. Koehlinger, *The New Nuns: Racial Justice and Religious Reform in the 1960s* (Cambridge, Mass.: Harvard University Press, 2007), 1–20; and Debra Campbell, "The Heyday of Catholic Action and the Lay Apostolate," in *Transforming Parish Ministry: The Changing Roles of Catholic Clergy, Laity, and Women Religious*, ed. Jay P. Dolan, R. Scott Appleby, Patricia Byrne, and Debra Campbell (New York: Crossroad, 1990), 222–52.

4. "Nuns in the World" refers to Leon Joseph Suenens, *The Nun in the World*, trans. Geoffrey Stevens, (Westminster, Md.: Newman, 1963). Cardinal Suenens's book instructed sisters and nuns to leave their convents and engage in the world. Suenens's top-down call for women religious to be "in the world" built on Pope Pius XII's urging for sisters and nuns to become better prepared educationally for their apostolic ministries. Communities of women religious, such as the Mercys, who engaged in active ministries were not "cloistered" behind convent walls and did conduct ministries in the world in classrooms and on hospital wards. They were restricted by religious rules and monastic-style customs. Mercys appreciated and were inspired by Suenens's work, as is reflected in various discussions in the minutes of the provincial council of the Chicago Mercys in the early 1950s. June 10, 1952, and March 15, 1953, Minutes of the Provincial Council Meetings, 1951–1954, 88 and 157, Provincial Council Minutes, section 2, Governance I, Chapters, ASMC; Regina Siegfried, ASC, "Religious Formation Conference: 'Educating for Deepening Relationships: Theological/Communal/Societal/ Cultural/Ecological,'" *American Catholic Studies*, 120, no. 1 (2009): 55; and Amy Koehlinger, *The New Nuns: Racial Justice and Religious Reform in the 1960s* (Cambridge, Mass.: Harvard University Press, 2007), 8–9.

5. For more on the founding of the Sisters of Mercy in Ireland and Catherine McAuley's intent for her religious community, see Mary Sullivan, R.S.M., *The Path of Mercy: The Life of Catherine McAuley* (Washington, D.C.: Catholic University Press, 2012), as well as her *Catherine McAuley and the Tradition of Mercy* (Notre Dame, Ind.: University of Notre Dame Press, 1995), and "Catherine McAuley in the Nineteenth and Twenty-First Centuries," in Elizabeth Davis et al., *"Fire Cast on the Earth-Kindling": Being Mercy in the Twenty-First Century* (International Mercy Research Conference, November 9–12, 2007). See also Kathleen A. Brosnan, "Public Presence, Public Silence: Nuns, Bishops, and the Gendered Space of Early Chicago," *Catholic Historical Review* 90, no. 3 (July 2004), 474–78. For a discussion of the emergence of active congregations of women religious in Ireland during this period of the founding of the Sisters of Mercy, see Mary Peckham Magray, *The Transforming Power of the Nuns: Women, Religion, and Cultural Change in Ireland, 1750–1900* (New York: Oxford University Press, 1998).

6. Pension or select schools were academies that had tuition fees. Most active religious congregations like the Mercys intended to open free schools for the children of immigrants in the nineteenth century, but found the need of a pension or select school for elite girls of the community or surrounding area. More cloistered communities like the Ursulines, Sisters of St. Joseph of Carondelet, and the Religious Sisters of the Sacred Heart had a more established reputation of providing academy education with paying students. See Brosnan, 473–85; and Suellen Hoy, *Good Hearts: Catholic Sisters in Chicago's Past*, (Urbana: University of Illinois Press, 2006), 35–40.

7. Not all of the Mercy communities voted to become a part of the Union in 1929. While they revised their constitutions to conform to the directives of the revision of the Code of Canon Law, they were not obligated to amalgamate into the generalate system of government created by the Union. In some cases, local bishops expressed concern about a new centralized authority that underscored that the Mercys, instead of being diocesan congregations as it was presumed, were in reality under papal approbation. Cardinal George Mundelein in Chicago initially forbade the Mercys within his archdiocese from discussing amalgamation. Despite Mundelein's objections, both Chicago congregations voted in favor of amalgamation. The Pittsburgh Mercys, the first community of Sisters of Mercy in the United States, however, did not elect to enter in 1929. For a complete and detailed discussion of the amalgamation, see Justine Sabourin, R.S.M., *The Amalgamation: A History of the Union of the Religious Sisters of Mercy of the United States of America*, (Saint Meinrad, Ind.: Abbey Press, 1976). For a complete history of the Sisters of Mercy of the Union see Mary Regina Werntz, R.S.M., *Our Beloved Union: A History of the Sisters of Mercy of the Union*, (Westminster, Md.: Christian Classics, 1989).

8. Throughout the 1940s and 1950s, nearly 400 women entered the Chicago Province in these two decades. In 1952 alone, nearly thirty women entered the congregation and went through formation, making their first profession. While the number of women to enter and reach profession fluctuated throughout this period, in general the entrants remained high. These numbers are based upon the Sisters of Mercy of Chicago Registry Database, which recorded entrance date, reception date (about six months later), and first profession (or temporary vows taken about two years after reception). See Registry Database, ASMC. The average ratio of sister-teachers to students in the 1950s was anywhere from 1:39 to 1:42. At times, it could be as high as one teacher for sixty students. Darra Mulderry, "'What Human Goodness Entails': An Intellectual History of U.S. Catholic Sisters, 1930–1980," (PhD diss.: Brandeis University, 2006), 36.

9. The creation of a high school department at that parish school was intended to address the educational needs of African American children in that area of the city, as opposed to incorporating them into territorial parish schools. While Stritch made some efforts to integrate schools in Chicago, he largely upheld the practice of segregating white and black parishes. See *Minutes of the Provincial Council of the Chicago Province*, (1939–1951), 105, 107–8, ASMC; Hoy, *Good Hearts*, 98; and Patrick W. Carey, *Catholics in America: A History* (Westport, Conn.: Praeger, 2004), 106.

10. See chapter 2 in this volume, Katharine Harmon, "The Liturgical Movement and Catholic Action: Women Living the Liturgical Life in the Lay Apostolate"; Karen Kennelly, C.S.J., *Religious Formation Conference 1954–2004* (Silver Spring, Md.: Religious Formation Conference, 2009), 14–16; George C. Stewart, Jr., *Marvels of Charity: History of American Sisters and Nuns*, (Huntington, Ind: Our Sunday Visitor, 1994), 444–45; and Amy L. Koehlinger, *The New Nuns: Racial Justice and Religious Reform in the 1960s* (Cambridge, Mass.: Harvard University Press, 2007), 30–1

11. The renewal process begun with Vatican II did not conclude for the Sisters of Mercy of the Union until the early 1980s, when the Vatican approved their revised Constitution. By the end of the 1970s, various groups within the Chicago Province had conducted experiments in religious government, local community living, and the exploration of new ministries that provided individual sisters with a choice in their apostolates.

12. Each local house (i.e., parish convent) submitted a percentage of its earnings to the provincial to help support the larger community, but teaching sisters throughout the first half of the twentieth century did not receive large monthly salaries and mother provincials often wrote parish priests requesting an increase to enable them to support themselves. In 1943, the mother provincial of the Mer-

cys sought an increase from a parish priest for sisters teaching in his Iowa parish. At the time, the Chicago Archdiocese paid sisters $35 a month, which was in itself insufficient, but the letter suggests that this parish priest may have been paying even less. Pantry showers hosted by the laywomen in a parish helped bridge gaps in their budgets. Mother Provincial to Reverend James J. Welsh, July 29, 1943, St. Alphonsus School; *St. James Chronicles,* 1959–1964, 40, and November 9, 1960; *Chronicles of St. Gabriel Convent,* September 1960 to June 1968, ASMC.

13. According to the Constitutions of the Sisters of Mercy of the Union, sisters were required to go out in pairs and they could not travel alone. While this restriction applied primarily to ministerial works, like visiting the sick and imprisoned, it also applied to all travel beyond the convent. Sisters were not permitted to participate in evening events, except when they occurred in their institutions connected to their convents, as in the case of a high school or hospital where sisters' living quarters were within the building. Sisters could accompany their students to a celebration such as confirmation, but whenever their travels encountered "seculars," sisters needed to guard their interactions carefully to avoid too much familiarity. Sisters of Mercy of the Union, *Customs and Guide of the Institute of the Religious Sisters of Mercy of the Union in the United States of America* (Bethesda, Md.: Sisters of Mercy General Motherhouse, 1957), 24, 29–30, quote 83, and 84–89. The records of the Provincial Council do not indicate whether this permission was granted or denied. See September 30, 1936, *Book of Minutes Provincial Council, Chicago, Sisters of Mercy of the Union in the United States of America,* (1929–1939), 57, ASMC.

14. For a discussion of permissions to play the organ, see correspondence between Sister Mary Loyola and Mother Provincial, Feast of Christ the King (November 18), c. 1951. Feast of St. Valentine, 1952, with response, September 5, 1952; Feast of St. Lawrence, with response, September 10, 1952; Feast of St. Nicholas Tolentino, February 22, 1954, with response from Mother Huberta, Mother Provincial Assistant, March 15, 1954. In her final response, Mother Huberta states that permission is given this one year only and that "Mother General does not approve, and too, we may not always be in a position to supply Sisters who can take over this work." Saint Alphonsus, Mt. Pleasant, Iowa, 1914–1968, ASMC. Sister Mary Hiltrudis Klug, RSM to Mother Domitilla Griffin, RSM January 19, 1954, St. Mary's School, ASMC.

15. See Patricia Byrne, "Saving Souls and Educating Americans, 1930–1945," *Transforming Parish Ministry: The Changing Roles of Catholic Clergy, Laity, and Women Religious,* edited by Jay P. Dolan, R. Scott Appleby, Patricia Byrne, and Debra Campbell, (New York: Crossroad, 1989), 115–16.

16. See Jay P. Dolan, *The American Catholic Experience: A History from the Colonial Times to the Present,* (New York: Doubleday, 1985), 389, 395, and 407.

17. Chronicles of St. Alphonsus, 1959–1965; and "All Studies Can Aid Apostolate, YCS Told," (Davenport) *Catholic Messenger*, October 12, 1961.

18. The Sisters of Mercy staffed St. Cecilia School from 1901 to 1971, which was located at 45th and Wells Streets on the Southside of Chicago. In 1971, it merged with St. Anne's, another neighborhood parish, and became St. Charles Lwanga, by which time it had long been an African American parish. A Sister of Mercy remained in some capacity at St. Charles Lwanga until 1984. *St. Cecilia Chronicles*, August 1964–September 1968, 28–29.

19. The Sisters of Mercy staffed St. James School from 1866 to 2003. In a manner somewhat similar to the St. Matthew-St. Cecilia relationship, YCS members from St. James School traveled to a Lake Forest suburban school to visit with a YCS chapter in that location. See *St. James Chronicles*, 1964–1971, 6–7 and 38–39.

20. One sister reported to me that her family in the 1960s gave her a subscription to Catholic news magazines, which she shared with members of her community at a time when sisters were not allowed to have personal subscriptions to magazines.

21. "Into One Bread," *Agape* 2 no. 2 (Easter 1966). *Agape* was the first community newsletter sent to each member of the Chicago Province. Prior to this, provincial and generalate leaders communicated with the rank-and-file of the congregation through letters and circulars, one sent to each house, to be read aloud by the local superior and posted in a common area of the convent. First sent in Advent 1964, it ran for three years, issuing three volumes a year: Advent or Christmas, Easter, and Pentecost. *Agape* was visually rich, full of discussion of the developments of renewal, the potential impact of Vatican II on ministries, religious government, and spiritual life, it provided a space for the provincial leaders to convey news and information, and allow for community-wide debate. It also featured sisters' poetry and artwork. It was replaced by *Exchange*, which sisters received more frequently, but it was also much more straightforward in its presentation, consisting of simple typewritten columns with few illustrations. Later it would incorporate more community photographs. *Exchange* ran from the late 1960s to the 1980s. It was replaced by a more journal or magazine styled communication, *Dimensions*, which lasted through much of the 1980s. Pagination was not always present in the issues of *Agape* and was not consistently done in *Exchange*.

22. Underline in text. "Into One Bread," *Agape* 1, no. 1 (Advent 1964). The discussion in this article answered the question: "In order to be most effective in our apostolate, why is it necessary that we be genuinely interested in others, that we overcome the fear of permitting ourselves truly to love others?" The various answers from members of the community were interspersed with quotes

from philosophers and theologians, such as Gabriel Marcel, Barry McLaughlin, S.J., and Adrian van Kaam, as well as Pope John XXIII and excerpts from Scripture.

23. "Currents of Thought: Toward the Coming Chapter," *Agape* 1, no. 2 (Easter 1965).

24. Sister Mary Irenaeus Chekouras, "Let's Ask Them Why," *Agape* 2, no. 1 (Christmas 1965).

25. Much of the ongoing discussion in the pages of *Agape* dealt with their own community renewal process, seeking to answer basic questions of how religious superiors should treat the members of their congregation, how sisters should interact with one another, and what form Mercy ministries should take. Respect for the individual was a dominant theme at this time and it permeated many sisters' understanding of how they should approach ministries like parochial education, especially as the chapters' decisions on how to revise their constitutions in 1967 and 1968 loomed on the horizon. See *Agape*, 1966–67.

26. Mary Charles Borromeo Muckenhirn, CSC, "Aposotlic Holiness: The Christian Dynamics," in *The Changing Sister*, M. Charles Borromeo Muckenhirn, C.S.C., ed., (Notre Dame, Ind.: Fides, 1965), 69.

27. Pius XI, *The Christian Education of Youth*, quoted in Committee of Elementary School Principals, *A Handbook of Educational Policies: The Elementary School*, (Chicago: Sisters of Mercy, Province of Chicago, 1953), 2, 4–11 passim, and 12.

28. *Handbook*, 51.

29. When the Mercys withdrew from parish schools, not all of them were in urban and inner-city neighborhoods. When the first wave of withdrawals hit the Chicago Province in the early 1970s, they left in equal numbers suburban and urban schools. "Teacher Shortage: Nuns to Leave 10 Schools," *Chicago Daily News*, Tuesday July 14, 1970. The prevailing wisdom among women religious of the mid to late 1960s was that as members of the laity and as life-long members of parishes, they could benefit from a more authentic connection to all the People of God. Mercys sought to interact with lay men and women and their families, whether as outgrowths of their classroom and YCS experiences, as directors of religious education programs, or as neighbors in the pews on Sunday. See M. Angela Seng, O.S.F., "The Sister in the New City," *The Changing Sister*, 254–56.

30. By the mid-1970s, within the Archdiocese of Chicago, for schools staffed by Sisters of Mercy the majority of financial support came from parental contributions. Roughly a third came from the larger parish community. Sisters contributed roughly 14.5 percent of the whole and the Archdiocese funded only 3 percent. Sisters' contribution often meant donated services or reduced salaries

and contributions from the province itself. Lay teachers also received lower salaries than they would have earned in public schools, and many parents acted as volunteers and conducted fundraisers. Other sources of financial support came from government funds, such as the Elementary and Secondary Education Act, Title II, and free lunch programs. See "Show Special Concern for the Needs of Those Who Are Poor in Goods of This World . . ." *Exchange* 61 (October 1975): 13.

31. See Registry Database.

32. Registry Database. Part of this decline, of course, had to do with the aging of the population of the Sisters of Mercy. Those engaged in full-time ministry decreased in numbers because sisters either retired or passed away. Of the sisters who retired, they did not truly retire, but found part-time or volunteer work and continued in apostolates of a different form.

33. "Statistics Provide Insights About Education Ministry," *Exchange* 53 (February 1974): 4–5. In the 1970s alone, the Mercys withdrew from over twenty schools. This trend continued into the 1980s and 1990s, and by the early 2000s individual Mercys continued to work at only three elementary schools.

34. Mercy Covenant, quoted in "Show Special Concern for the Needs of Those Who Are Poor in Goods of This World . . . ," 12.

35. See "Apostolate Education Commission," and Sister Mary Honora, "Ministry," *Exchange* 32 (May 1971).

36. "Apostolate Education Commission," Exchange 32 (May 1971), quote. When the Mercys withdrew from St. Thomas Aquinas School in the 1970s, they were accused of prejudice for abandoning a largely African American school while keeping white suburban schools open. At the time of this closing, however, the Mercys closed nine other schools, an equal number in suburban areas and urban neighborhoods. In this case, the Mercys concluded that if St. Thomas Aquinas was forced to close because of their withdrawal, African American children could find a Catholic education at the larger and better equipped nearby Resurrection School. St. Thomas Aquinas Survey, n.d., ASMC.

37. St. Callistus Church closed in 1994 and St. Jarlath Church closed in 1969.

38. Untitled Proposal at Meeting, February 6, 1969, Report: Precious Blood School, January 1979; Report: Precious Blood School, 1972; and Happenings, 1972–1973, Precious Blood School, in Precious Blood School, ASMC.

39. "Happenings—1972—1973," and "Principal's Report, March 1974," Precious Blood School.

40. Mary Sullivan, RSM, "Social Justice Activities: Resurrection," *Exchange* 38 (March 1972). This In-Service Development program models an earlier mode of operation in many Catholic parochial schools. In preceding decades, young sisters, often with temporary vows, entered classrooms prior to completing a

bachelor's degree. As young as nineteen or twenty years of age, these junior sisters received on-the-job training and supervision from older more experienced sisters in their schools. The Sisters of Mercy, like many other religious congregations, moved away from this practice by the 1950s with the Sister Formation Movement, stressing that sisters needed full professional development before entering classrooms. This decision impacted Catholic education systems like the Archdiocese of Chicago, making fewer teachers available and compelling many parochial schools to hire lay teachers. This required larger annual salaries paid to lay teachers than to women religious.

41. "Resurrection School," January 27, 1970, Resurrection School, ASMC.

42. The Mercys had conducted a girls' high school in this parish, known as Siena High School, until 1973. At the time of this publication, a Sister of Mercy, Marion Cysper, RSM was the principal of St. Catherine-St. Lucy School. Rev. Msgr. Harry C. Koenig, STD, ed., *A History of the Parishes of the Archdiocese of Chicago*, vol 2 (Chicago: Archdiocese of Chicago, 1980), 1432–33; and "On Four Parish Programs: Mercys Involved: St. Catherine of Siena–St. Lucy, Oak Park," *Exchange* 66 (October 1976).

43. Sisters of Mercy, Chicago, Executive Department Minutes, 1973–1976 (July 6, 1973–June 8, 1976), 31, ASMC.

44. "Westside Network Links Resurrection, Precious Blood, and St. Catherine of Siena," *Exchange* 54 (March 1974): 2–5.

45. Sister Colette Jolie, who had worked at Siena High School, helped develop this center and continued to direct its efforts through 2008. Sisters of Mercy, Chicago, *Province Team Minutes* (June 1976–June 1979), 96–97, 106, and 283, ASMC; Mary Catherine Daly, RSM, "Moving Along—Together," *Dimensions* 2, no. 3 (Summer 1980): 3; Mark Zambrano, "School a Beacon of Hope in Austin," *Chicago Tribune*, May 27, 1985, http://articles.chicagotribune .com/1985-05-27/news/8502020711_1_dropouts-job-training-center-students (accessed December 1, 2012); "Thank You for Your Service," *Catholic New World*, July 17, 2011.

46. "Saint James Catholic School," October 1950; *St. James Chronicles*, 1954–1957, 192; August 3 and 6, 1958, *St. James Chronicles*, 1957–1959; *St. James Chronicles*, 1959–1964, 175, 179; and *St. James Chronicles*, 1964–1971, 13, 35, 42, and 44, ASMC.

47. Margaret Lyons, RSM, "Saint James School!" *Exchange* 48 (April 1973).

48. Social Justice Activities," *Exchange* 38, (March 1972); and "Str. Raymond Wins Recognition," *Exchange* 56 (October 1974).

49. "On Four Parish Programs: Mercys Involved," *Exchange* 66 (October 1976).

50. Michael Novak, "The New Nuns," *Saturday Evening Post*, July 30, 1966, 22.

8. "This Is Our Challenge! We Will Pursue It": The National Council of Catholic Women, the Feminist Movement, and the Second Vatican Council, 1960–1975

MARY J. HENOLD

1. This research resulted in the book *Catholic and Feminist: The Surprising History of the American Catholic Feminist Movement, 1965–1980* (Chapel Hill: University of North Carolina Press, 2008).

2. "The Buried Talents Symposium," *Sign*, 15–19 October 1966, 17.

3. Margaret Ellen Traxler, statement before the Illinois House, 22 March 1973, National Coalition of American Nuns Records, 2/2, Marquette University Archives, Milwaukee.

4. The National Council of Catholic Women, The National Council of Catholic Women, http://home.catholicweb.com/NCCW/index.cfm.

5. Margaret Mealey, report to the board of directors, December 1959, National Council of Catholic Women Collection (hereafter NCCW), American Catholic History Research Center, Catholic University of America (hereafter CUA), 1; Margaret Mealey, report to the board of Directors, January 1964, 10/NCCW/CUA, 5.

6. "Family and Parent Education," 1960 Conference Proceedings, 23/NCCW/ CUA, 52–53; Margaret Mealey, letter to Catherine Schaefer, 2 August 1967, NCCW–Mealey, exec dir Corr/161/NCWC/USCC OGS/CUA.

7. Alexander Sigur, "Women in the Apostolate of the Church," 1960 Conference Proceedings, 23/NCCW/CUA, 73; John S. Spence, "Woman's Particular Role," 1964 Conference Proceedings, 23/NCCW/CUA, 50.

8. Sigur, 73; Leo W. Duprey, "Challenge to the Nature of Woman," May 1963, 34/NCCW/CUA, 1; John S. Spence, "Woman's Particular Role," NCCW National Conference Proceedings, 1964, 23/NCCW/CUA, 53; "Nature of Woman" fact sheet, 1963 NCCW Institute, 34/NCCW/CUA, 3.

9. The Catholic Daughters of the Americas and the Daughters of Isabella were originally one organization, the women's auxiliary to the Knights of Columbus. The collections of both organizations are housed at the American Catholic History Research Center at CUA. I am currently researching the response of these two organizations to the transitional period of the 1960s and 1970s.

10. Margaret O'Connell, editorial, "Women at Vatican II," *Word* 2, no. 12 (November 1965): 3.

11. Mary Perkins Ryan, "The Liturgy," 1964 Conference Proceedings, 23/ NCCW/CUA, 86.

12. Mark Massa, *The American Catholic Revolution: How the Sixties Changed the Church Forever* (New York: Oxford University Press, 2010), 158.

13. Arlene Swidler, "Church Communities Commission: Overview," 1968 Conference Proceedings, 1968/24/NCCW/CUA, 88.

14. Margaret Mealey, Report to the Board of Directors, January 1966, 10/NCCW/CUA.

15. Margaret Mary Kelly, "Cooperation with Vatican II," *Word* 2, no. 1 (October 1964), 11 (emphasis in the original), 1964/66/NCCW.

16. Margaret O'Connell, editorial, *Word* 4, no. 8 (May 1967): 3, 1967(1)/66/NCCW.

17. Mrs. Louis H. Sweterlitsch, "NCCW: People and Structures," 1968 Conference Proceedings, 1968/24/NCCW, 77; John Tracy Ellis, "The Catholic Laywoman and the Apostolate of our Time," NCCW National Conference, November 6, 1962, 34/NCCW/CUA, 3.

18. Mary Perkins Ryan, Report of the Spiritual Development Committee, 1964 Conference Proceedings, 23/NCCW/CUA, 190; "Organization and Development," *Word* 3, no. 5 (February 1966):7, 1966(1)/66/NCCW/CUA.

19. Margaret Mealey, "50th Executive Director's Report," *Word*, ca. 1970; Kelly, 11.

20. Workshop Session Notes, NCCW National Conference Proceedings, 1966, 24/NCCW/CUA, 82; Mrs. John A. Paddenburg, "Opportunities in the Church Communities, Myth or Reality?" NCCW National Conference Proceedings, 1966, 24/NCCW/CUA, 56.

21. Arlene Swidler, "Church Communities Commission: Overview," National Conference Proceedings, 1968, 24/NCCW/CUA, 88–89; "Signs and Wonders," *Word* 5, no. 4 (January 1968): 3, 1968/66/NCCW/CUA; Rosemary Cass, "A Catholic Point of View," 1964 Conference Proceedings, 23/NCCW/CUA, 146.

22. The only scholarly work on NCCW in this period can be found in Ruth O'Halloran's dissertation on NCCW's history. In it O'Halloran argues that NCCW was not antifeminist in the 1960s and 1970s and did express feminist ideas. Her dissertation does not pursue the nature of that feminism or its relationship to Vatican II, however. See Ruth O'Halloran, "Organized Catholic Laywomen: The National Council of Catholic Women, 1920–1995" (PhD diss., Catholic University of America, 1995), 221.

23. Mark Massa makes a similar argument about the difficulties in employing political labels in the postconciliar period. See *The American Catholic Revolution*, 160–62.

24. See Henold, *Catholic and Feminist*.

25. I refer here to the period of feminist dormancy in the United States between the ratification of the Nineteenth Amendment in 1920 and the beginning of the second wave in the early 1960s.

26. Mig Boyle, Report to the Board of Directors, January 1968, 11/NCCW/CUA.

27. "Of Human Life: A Conversation," *Word* 6, no. 2 (November 1968): 5–11, 1968(2)/66/NCCW/CUA.

28. Arlene Swidler, "Make Theology Your Business," Word 7, no. 3 (December 1969): 4–11, 66/NCCW/CUA; Arlene Swidler, "Feminist Liturgies," Catholic Woman 1, no. 1 (January 1975): 3–5, 1975/66/NCCW/CUA. In the previous year, Swidler published a book on feminist liturgy titled SisterCelebrations: Nine Worship Experiences (Philadelphia: Fortress Press, 1974).

29. Theodora Briggs Sweeney, "Children, Church,—and Lib," Word 8, no. 1 (January 1971): 18–19, 1971/66/NCCW/CUA.

30. Paddenburg, 57.

31. Mrs. Louis H. Sweterlitsch, "NCCW: People and Structures," 1968 Conference Proceedings, 1968/24/NCCW/CUA, 74.

32. Lillian O'Connor, "Women: Their Own Worst Enemies," Word 5, no. 3 (December 1967):6, 1967(2)/66/NCCW/CUA; Sweterlitsch, 8; Joanne M. Moran, editorial, Word 7, no. 1 (October 1969):2, 1969(2)/66/NCCW/CUA.

33. Joanne M. Moran, editorial, Word 7, no. 9 (June–July 1970): 2, 1970(2)/66/ NCCW/CUA.

34. Mary Perkins Ryan, quoted in Swidler, "Make Theology your Business," 9; Dan W. Dodson, "Why Women's Organizations?" 1968 Conference Proceedings, 1968/24/NCCW/CUA, 41, 46.

35. Statements Adopted by Board of Directors at Annual Meeting, January 22–25, 1968, Statements of Board of Directors/26/NCCW/CUA, 2; Kelly, "Cooperation," 4.

36. NCCW was not alone in linking Vatican II and feminism; self-identified Catholic feminists made the same connection. See Henold, Catholic and Feminist.

37. See Margaret Mealey, Executive Director's Report to the Board, February 1970, 12/NCCW/CUA, 1.

38. For the details on the brief merger of NCCW and NCCM, see O'Halloran, chapter 5.

39. Mealey, "50th Executive Director's Report," 5–6.

40. It is worth noting that such a position is not unprecedented. For instance, it was not uncommon for suffragists to argue using both the rhetoric of female essentialism and the rhetoric of equality and rights in the last twenty years of the suffrage movement in the United States. See Nancy Cott, The Grounding of Modern Feminism (New Haven, Conn.: Yale University Press, 1987), 19.

41. Margaret O'Connell, editorial, Word 2, no. 11 (October 1965):3, 1965/66/ NCCW.

42. Letters to the editor, Word 7, no. 8 (May 1970): 21, 1970(1)/66/NCCW/CUA; Rita M. Burke, letter to Catherine Schaefer, March 18, 1969, NCCW General Correspondence 64–70/161/NCWC-USCC/CUA (emphases in the original).

43. Mrs. Ralph LeBlanc, letter to the editor, Word 6, no. 5 (August–September 1969): 16, 1969(1)/66/NCCW/CUA; Mrs. Richard Spiering, letter to the editor, Word

7, no. 3 (December 1969): 15, 1969(1)/66/NCCW/CUA; Catherine M. Cullimore, letter to the editor, *Word* 6, no. 4 (June–July 1969): 17, 1969(1)/66/NCCW/CUA.

44. 1968 National Convention Program Evaluation, NCCW/CUA.

45. Report from the 1972 General Assembly, 26/NCCW/CUA, 27.

46. NCCW National Board Meeting Minutes, January 1969, 12/NCCW/CUA.

47. General Assembly minutes, 5–7 (September 1974), NCCW minutes, vol, 1 (58–79)/10/NCCW/CUA, 14.

48. For two sources that discuss the rise of women's organizations on the religious right, see Donald T. Critchlow, *Phyllis Schlafly and Grassroots Conservatism: A Woman's Crusade* (Princeton, N.J.: Princeton University Press, 2005), and Ronnie Schreiber, *Righting Feminism: Conservative Women and American Politics* (New York: Oxford University Press, 2008).

49. Resolutions, 1975 NCCW Convention, 25/NCCW/CUA, 1.

9. Who Will Guard the Guardians? Church Government and the Ecclesiology of the People of God, 1965–1969

JEREMY BONNER

1. The contemporary debate over closing parishes with falling membership is illustrative of this point. See John C. Seitz, *No Closure: Catholic Practice and Boston's Parish Shutdowns* (Cambridge, Mass.: Harvard: Harvard University Press, 2011).

2. Diocese of Pittsburgh: Council for Consultation on Pastoral Problems and Policies, transcript, March 23, 1968, 201, RG12, box 876, folder 16, Archives of the Catholic Diocese of Pittsburgh (hereafter ADP).

3. See, for example, *Apostolicam Actuositatem*, chapter 5, par. 26, at the Vatican website, http://www.vatican.va.

4. Revd. William F. Nerin to Victor Reed, March 5, 1964, St. John the Baptist Church, Edmond File, Victor Reed Papers, Archives of the Catholic Archdiocese of Oklahoma City, Oklahoma City (hereafter AAOC). Father Nerin declared the majority of his parishioners to be lacking a developed social conscience, a spirit of poverty, and the theological background necessary to read and comprehend the work of such contemporary theologians as Karl Rahner, John Courtney Murray, and Hans Küng.

5. James Hennesey, *American Catholics: A History of the Roman Catholic Community in the United States* (New York: Oxford University Press, 1981), 55–88, at 85.

6. On England, see Patrick W. Carey, *An Immigrant Bishop: John England's Adaptation of Irish Catholicism to American Republicanism* (Yonkers, N.Y.: U.S. Catholic Historical Society, 1982). Note the words of praise for England's initiative in Daniel Callahan, *The Mind of the Catholic Layman* (New York: Charles Scribners, 1963), 25–27.

7. See Patrick W. Carey, *People, Priests and Prelates: Ecclesiastical Democracy and the Tensions of Trusteeship* (Notre Dame, Ind.: University of Notre Dame Press, 1987).

8. See John T. McGreevy, *Catholics and American Freedom.* (New York: Norton, 2003), 43–126.

9. On the New Deal and American Catholicism, see Francis L. Broderick, *Right Reverend New Dealer, John A. Ryan* (New York: Macmillan, 1963); David J. O'Brien, *American Catholics and Social Reform: The New Deal Years* (New York: Oxford University Press, 1968); Thomas E. Blantz, *A Priest in Public Service: Francis J. Haas and the New Deal* (Notre Dame, Ind.: University of Notre Dame Press, 1982); Kenneth J. Heineman, *A Catholic New Deal: Religion and Reform in Depression Pittsburgh* (University Park: Pennsylvania State University Press, 1999).

10. On the Catholic Club of the City of New York and secular politics, see, in this volume, Patrick J. Hayes, "Catholic Action in the Archdiocese of New York: The Case of the Catholic Club of New York City"; on San Francisco labor activism, see above, Issel chapter.

11. See David J. O'Brien, *Public Catholicism* (New York: Macmillan, 1989), 158–229; James M. O'Toole, *The Faithful: A History of Catholics in America.* (Cambridge, Mass.: Harvard University Press, 2008), 145–98.

12. "Sometimes people talk as if suburbanites are an entirely different race or breed of cat, from those who live in the inner-city. For the love of God, what has become of your memories? The people of the suburbs of Pittsburgh were born in the inner-city, and if they were not, their parents were. . . . Most of them are living in the suburbs in mortgaged property, having moved out of the inner-city." Diocese of Pittsburgh: Council for Consultation on Pastoral Problems and Policies, transcript, June 14, 1968, 46.

13. See, in this volume, Katharine E. Harmon, "The Liturgical Movement and Catholic Action: Women Living the Liturgical Life in the Lay Apostolate."

14. John A. Ryan, *The State and the Church* (New York: Macmillan, 1922), 38. Ryan did concede that such an eventuality was highly unlikely.

15. *Oklahoma Courier*, November 1, 1963.

16. Vincent A. Yzermans, *American Participation in the Second Vatican Council* (New York: Sheed and Ward, 1967), 311–12.

17. *Pittsburgh Catholic*, October 24, 1963, 1.

18. Bishop Wright's speech to opening session of Diocesan Pastoral Council, June 17, 1967, 1, RG 12, box 876, folder 11, ADP (emphasis in the original).

19. Leslie Tentler, *Catholics and Contraception: An American History* (Ithaca, N.Y.: Cornell University Press, 2004), 257. For more on Dearden's Damscene conversion, see, in this chapter, Samuel J. Thomas, "Empowering the People of God: Cardinal John Dearden's Church of Tomorrow."

20. See *Time*, April 11, 1969; *National Catholic Reporter*, April 13, 1966, 1. See also, in this volume, Thomas, "Empowering the People of God."

21. See Frank V. Manning, *A Call to Action* (Notre Dame, Ind.: Fides/Claretian, 1977), and David O'Brien, "On Detroit," at American Catholic Council, http://americancatholiccouncil.org.

22. Wright speech, June 17, 1967, 10, RG 12, box 876, folder 11, ADP.

23. See David J. O'Brien, "When It All Came Together: Bishop John J. Wright and the Diocese of Worcester, 1950–1959," *Catholic Historical Review* 85, no. 2 (April 1999): 175–94.

24. In the foreword to his study of the lay apostolate, Tavard, a professor at Assumption College in Worcester until 1959, thanked Wright for his "personal interest, advice, and encouragement." See his *The Church, the Layman, and the Modern World* (New York: Macmillan, 1959), viii. That year, Tavard transferred to Pittsburgh's Mount Mercy College (remaining there until 1966) and was later named by John XXIII as a *peritus conciliaris* to the Second Vatican Council. Timothy Kelly concludes that Wright resented direct challenges to his authority. See his discussion of Wright's reaction to the threat from the Catholic Interracial Council to picket the bishop's Labor Day Mass if he persisted in his refusal to embrace Project Equality—a civil-rights initiative that committed churches to work with contractors who refused to discriminate in their hiring practices— unless other Christian churches agreed to make it an ecumenical undertaking. See Timothy Kelly, *The Transformation of American Catholicism: the Pittsburgh Laity and the Second Vatican Council, 1950–1972* (Notre Dame, Ind.: University of Notre Dame Press, 2009), 208–12.

25. Yzermans, *American Participation in the Second Vatican Council* (New York: Sheed and Ward, 1967), 20–21, 37, 194 (quotation at 37).

26. On Reed's formative years as a priest, see Jeremy Bonner, *The Road to Renewal: Victor Joseph Reed and Oklahoma Catholicism, 1905–1971* (Washington D.C.: Catholic University of America Press, 2008), chapter 2.

27. The most recent biography of Archbishop O'Boyle is Morris J. MacGregor, *Steadfast in the Faith: The Life of Patrick Cardinal O'Boyle* (Washington D.C.: Catholic University of America Press, 2006). For Archbishop McIntyre, see Francis J. Weber, *His Eminence of Los Angeles: James Francis Cardinal McIntyre*, 2 vols. (Mission Hills, Calif.: Saint Francis Historical Society, 1997), and Mark Massa, " 'To Be Beautiful, Human, and Christian': The IHM Nuns and the Routinization of Charisma," in *Catholics and American Culture: Fulton Sheen, Dorothy Day, and the Notre Dame Football Team* (New York: Crossroad Publishing Company, 1999), 172–94. Charles Dahm provides a less than sympathetic discussion of the situation in Chicago in *Power and Authority in the Catholic Church: Cardinal Cody in Chicago* (Notre Dame, Ind.: University of Notre Dame Press, 1981), while a more nuanced account appears in Edward R. Kantowicz, "The Beginning and End of an Era: George William

Mundelein and John Patrick Cody in Chicago," in Gerald P. Fogarty, ed., *Patterns of Episcopal Leadership* (New York: Macmillan, 1989), 202–15. On Archbishop Lucey, see Saul Bronder, *Social Justice and Church Authority: The Public Life of Archbishop Robert E. Lucey* (Philadelphia: Temple University Press, 1982).

28. Kelly draws a stark contrast between Wright's commitment to the process of lay consultation and the disengagement of his successor. See Kelly, *The Transformation of American Catholicism*, 266–71.

29. Callahan, *The Mind of the Catholic Layman*, 152–53.

30. On the Kennedy election, see Mark Massa, "A Catholic for President? JFK, Peter Berger, and the 'Secular' Theology of the Houston Speech, 1960," in Massa, *Catholics and American Culture*, 128–47. For a more personal account of the intersection of Catholic Action and politics, see Abigail McCarthy, *Private Faces / Public Places* (Garden City, N.Y.: Doubleday, 1972). On the new phenomenon of suburban Catholicism, see Andrew M. Greeley, *The Church and the Suburbs* (New York: Sheed and Ward, 1959).

31. Bonner, *Road to Renewal*, 151–52. One of Timothy Kelly's case-study parishes, St. Thomas More, has a similar profile. See Kelly, *The Transformation of American Catholicism*, 274–82.

32. On the national political activities of CFM, see Jeffrey M. Burns, *Disturbing the Peace: A History of the Christian Family Movement, 1949–1974* (Notre Dame, Ind.: Notre Dame University Press, 1999).

33. *Pittsburgh Catholic*, March 14, 1963, 11.

34. See Bonner, *Road to Renewal*, 247–48, 273–75, 356–61.

35. Victor Reed to Governor-Elect and Mrs. Dewey F. Bartlett, November 9, 1966, Reed Papers, AAOC.

36. Leo Ward, *The Living Parish* (Notre Dame, Ind.: Fides, 1959), 27.

37. Bernard Lyons, "Parish Councils," in John McCudden, ed., *The Parish in Crisis* (Techny, Ill.: Divine Word Publications, 1967), 159.

38. *National Catholic Reporter*, June 21, 1967, 1, 8.

39. See Bonner, *Road to Renewal*, 160.

40. See Ibid., 169–70.

41. Ibid., 163–64.

42. *National Catholic Reporter*, December 21, 1966, 5. See also, Bonner, *Road to Renewal*, 91.

43. *Pittsburgh Catholic*, September 16, 1965, 1–2.

44. The National Council of Catholic Women was among those lay organizations to encourage its members to become involved in parish government. See, in this volume, Mary Henold, "'This Is Our Challenge! We Will Pursue It': The National Council of Catholic Women, the Feminist Movement, and the Second Vatican Council II, 1960–1975."

45. Diocese of Pittsburgh: Council for Consultation on Pastoral Problems and Policies, transcript, March 23, 1968, 112–17, RG12, box 876, folder 14, ADP. See also Kelly, *The Transformation of American Catholicism*, 200–1.

46. *Pittsburgh Catholic*, February 10, 1966, 3.

47. *National Catholic Reporter*, June 21, 1967, 1, 8.

48. See *National Catholic Reporter*, June 28, 1967, 5.

49. Diocese of Pittsburgh: Council for Consultation on Pastoral Problems and Policies, transcript, March 23, 1968, 151, RG12, box 876, folder 15, ADP.

50. Diocese of Pittsburgh: Council for Consultation on Pastoral Problems and Policies, transcript, March 23, 1968, 117–119, 122, 125, RG12, box 876, Folder 15, ADP.

51. See *National Catholic Reporter*, October 22, 1968, 5.

52. See Diocese of Pittsburgh: Council for Consultation on Pastoral Problems and Policies, Transcript, March 23, 1968, 164, RG12, box 876, folder 15, ADP.

53. Albert S. Rutkowski to members of finance board, St. Mary's Church, February 1, 1967, St. Mary's Church, Tulsa file, box 14.1, ADT.

54. A complete account of the conflict at St. Mary's is found in Bonner, *The Road to Renewal*, 162–63.

55. See Bonner, *Road to Renewal*, 164–65.

56. Diocese of Pittsburgh: Council for Consultation on Pastoral Problems and Policies, transcript of Proceedings, March 23, 1968, 175–76 (quotation at 175).

57. See Bonner, *Road to Renewal*, 165–66.

58. Ibid., 166–69.

59. Monsignor Gregory Gier, interviewed by Jeremy Bonner, May 10, 2004, Tulsa, Oklahoma.

60. See *National Catholic Reporter*, April 3, 1968, 10. On Ireland, see Marvin R. O'Connell, *John Ireland and the American Catholic Church* (St. Paul: Minnesota Historical Society Press, 1988).

61. See *National Catholic Reporter*, March 13, 1968, 3.

62. See, in this chapter, Andrew S. Moore, "Christian Unity, Lay Authority, and the People of God: The Community of Christ Our Brother in the Archdiocese of Atlanta, 1967–1969."

63. See *National Catholic Reporter*, April 24, 1968.

64. See *National Catholic Reporter*, January 11, 1968, 5; August 9, 1967, 8.

65. See Thomas J. Reese, *Episcopal Conferences: Historical, Canonical, and Theological Studies* (Washington, D.C.: Georgetown University Press, 1989). See also, Thomas chapter.

66. On the lay congress, see, in this volume, Moore, "Christian Unity, Lay Authority, and the People of God."

67. See Bonner, *The Road to Renewal*, 121–22. The Pittsburgh diocesan newspaper drew attention to the shift in Oklahoma from advisory to regulatory school board. See *Pittsburgh Catholic*, April 4, 1963, 9.

68. See Diocesan Schools Office—Statement to the Diocesan Council, June 17–18, 1967, 3, 5–6, 8, RG12, box 876, folder 11, ADP; *Pittsburgh Catholic*, January 11, 1965, 1, 3. The first lay deputy superintendent of schools in the United States was appointed in the Diocese of Pittsburgh.

69. *Pittsburgh Catholic*, September 5, 1963, 2; *National Catholic Reporter*, September 21, 1966, 12. The paper made much of the fact that Wright had not ruled out the possibility that other tribunal positions, including that of judge, would be held by laymen in the future.

70. See *National Catholic Reporter*, April 12, 1967, 2.

71. *National Catholic Reporter*, May 24, 1967, 3.

72. See Bonner, *The Road to Renewal*, 92.

73. *National Catholic Reporter*, April 12, 1967, 1, 10.

74. See *National Catholic Reporter*, March 22, 1967, 7; April 19, 1967, 1, 4; July 5, 1967, 1, 8.

75. See *National Catholic Reporter*, October 27, 1965, 1, 3.

76. By November 1966, thirty dioceses had established senates, seventy more in development, and fifty-three still in consultation mode. See *National Catholic Reporter*, November 23, 1966, 9.

77. See *National Catholic Reporter*, December 21, 1966, 5.

78. *National Catholic Reporter*, October 27, 1965, 8–9. It is not clear from the newspaper account whether the document referenced is Vatican II's *Lumen Gentium* (Dogmatic Constitution on the Church), formally ratified by the Council in 1964.

79. See *National Catholic Reporter*, January 26, 1966, 1, 10; July 20, 1966, 1, 6; William B. Faherty, *Dream by the River: Two Centuries of St. Louis Catholicism* (St. Louis: Piraeus, 1973), 208–10.

80. *Oklahoma Courier*, February 12, 1965.

81. See Bonner, *Road to Renewal*, 108–9.

82. Ibid., 110–11.

83. Nominating papers for candidates for board of presidents, 1967, Ecumenical Council and Council of Churches Papers, AAOC.

84. Revd. John T. Jackson to Little Council, April 24, 1968, Ecumenical Council and Council of Churches Papers, AAOC.

85. *Oklahoma Courier*, April 26, 1968.

86. See Bonner, *Road to Renewal*, 112, 308.

87. See Bonner, *Road to Renewal*, 113.

88. Jack M. Bickham, "An Interview with Bishop Reed," *Decade of Change: A Supplement to the Oklahoma Courier* (March 1, 1968), 6.

89. Wright speech, June 17, 1967, 2, RG 12, box 876, folder 11, ADP.

90. Questionnaire on Diocesan Pastoral Council, analysis, October, 1968, RG12, box 876, folder 4, ADP (emphases in the original).

91. The forms preserved in the archives were designed to be anonymous, although some respondents did identify themselves. For the most part, the only identifying marker is the date of receipt in September and October 1968.

92. Questionnaire of Diocesan Pastoral Council, Responses, 9/21, 9/13, 9/17, RG12, box 876, folder 6, ADP.

93. Ibid., 9/30, RG12, box 876, folder 7, ADP.

94. Ibid., 9/24, RG12, box 876, folder 7, ADP.

95. Ibid., 10/1, 9/24, RG12, box 876, folder 8, ADP.

96. Ibid., 9/16, RG12, box 876, folder 6, ADP.

97. Ibid., 9/17, RG12, box 876, folder 6, ADP.

98. Ibid., 9/27, RG12, box 876, folder 7, ADP.

99. Ibid., 9/19, RG12, box 876, folder 6, ADP.

100. Ibid., 10/24, RG12, box 876, folder 8, ADP.

101. Ibid., 9/27, RG12, box 876, folder 7, ADP (emphasis in the original). Not every member of the diocese felt this way: "There would be more value to the members if they could be reminded again and again that they are not a legislative body—they only represent the feelings of the Catholic population. Some seem to think they are making the laws." Questionnaire of Diocesan Pastoral Council, Responses, 9/30, RG12, box 876, folder 7, ADP.

102. Ibid., 9/18, RG12, box 876, folder 6, ADP.

103. Ibid., 10/23, RG12, box 876, folder 8, ADP. This correspondent also urged that committees spending funds thoroughly investigate all contractors and make inquiries of business associations and the district attorney.

104. Ibid., 9/25, RG12, box 876, folder 7, ADP; 10/2, RG12, box 876, folder 7, ADP.

105. Ibid., 10/2, RG12, box 876, folder 6, ADP (emphasis in the original).

106. Diocese of Pittsburgh: Council for Consultation on Pastoral Problems and Policies, Transcript, March 23, 1968, 221, RG12, box 876, folder 15, ADP.

107. Diocese of Pittsburgh: Council for Consultation on Pastoral Problems and Policies, transcript, June 17–18, 1967, 46–47, RG12, box 876, folder 10, ADP.

108. Diocese of Pittsburgh: Council for Consultation on Pastoral Problems and Policies, transcript, June 15, 1968, 8–9, RG12, box 876, folder 17, ADP.

109. Ibid., 73–75 (quotation at 75).

110. See, in this chapter, Thomas, "Empowering the People of God."

111. Patrick K. McCarren to the Reverend Vanyo, 15 May 1969, quoted in Kelly, *The Transformation of American Catholicism*, 246.

112. See *National Catholic Reporter*, December 11, 1968, 5.

113. See *National Catholic Reporter*, March 27, 1968, 3.

114. The conference wrote to the bishops of the ten neighboring dioceses and to Archbishop John Dearden (as president of the National Conference of Catholic Bishops). Dearden and three other bishops replied, with responses that ranged from "curt to encouraging." See *National Catholic Reporter*, March 19, 1969, 9.

115. See *National Catholic Reporter*, February 12, 1969, 9.

116. See *National Catholic Reporter*, March 5, 1969, 5.

117. See Kelly, *The Transformation of American Catholicism*, 242–71.

118. Kiernon Stenson to Father Vanyo and members of the General Coordinating Board of the Synod, 5 March 1971 in Kelly, *The Transformation of American Catholicism*, 267–68.

119. Roseanne Reiser to Bp. Wright, April 2, 1967, RG12, box 876, folder 2, ADP.

120. Wright speech, June 17, 1967, 12, RG 12, box 876, folder 11, ADP.

121. Diocese of Pittsburgh: Council for Consultation on Pastoral Problems and Policies, transcript, June 17–18, 1967, 82, RG12, box 876, folder 10, ADP.

10. Empowering the People of God: John Cardinal Dearden's Church of Tomorrow

SAMUEL J. THOMAS

This essay is a revision of a previously published article, "Immanence and Transcendence: John Cardinal Dearden's Church of Tomorrow," *American Catholic Studies* 54 (Winter 2010): 1–30. It is used here with the kind permission of the editors.

1. Ronald B. Flowers, *Religion in Strange Times: The 1960s and 1970s* (Macon, Ga.: Mercer University Press, 1984), 1.

2. William Chafe, *The Unfinished Journey: America Since World War II* (New York: Oxford University Press, 2007), 362.

3. See theologian Luke Timothy Johnson, quoted in Bradford Wilcox, "The Facts of Life and Marriage: Social Science and the Vindication of Christian Moral Teaching," *Touchstone: A Journal of Mere Christianity* (January–February, 2005), reprinted at *Natural Family Planning Outreach*, http://www.nfpoutreach .org/library/facts_life-marriage.htm (accessed December 1, 2012).

4. The conciliar *Dogmatic Constitution of the Church*, paragraphs 15–16, adopts and explains "People of God." See also the conciliar *Decree on the Apostolate of Lay People*.

5. The definitions of "liberal" and "conservative" used in this essay interchangeably with "progressive" and "traditional," originate in meanings suggested by Scott Appleby and George Weigel. Appleby argues that "liberals and conservatives, despite their important differences and vehement disagreements, share a basic orientation and set of assumptions about the United States and its worthiness as a model for the Roman Catholic Church. The conservatives . . .

tend to apply the lessons learned in two hundred–plus years of U.S. political and economic history to Roman Catholic social doctrine, while the liberals tend to apply Americanist insights to the ecclesiology, or internal governance, of the church itself." R. Scott Appleby, "The Triumph of Americanism: Common Ground for U.S. Catholics in the Twentieth Century," chapter 2 in *Being Right: Conservative Catholics in America*, ed. Mary Jo Weaver and R. Scott Appleby (Bloomington: Indiana University Press, 1995), 41–42. Weigel offers another useful perspective: A self-described "neo-conservative," he understands the crisis in the Church today as one of faith, not, as liberals and conservatives contend, as one of authority. His understanding of liberalism and conservatism in the Church of the 1960s is useful for understanding those terms in the context of the Council and its commentators. For Weigel, the writings of Xavier Rynne (the Redemptorist moral theologian Francis X. Murphy) were most influential. In the latter's articles and books on the Council, liberals were those who, inspired by Pope John XXIII, were open to modernity and opposed to "clericalism, legalism, and triumphalism." Conservatives feared modernity and reacted to any who opposed the essential immutability of Church doctrine and practice. George Weigel, "The Neo-Conservative Difference: A Proposal for the Renewal of Church and Society," chapter 6 in *Being Right*, ed. Weaver and Appleby, 141–42.

6. Born in Rhode Island and raised in Cleveland, Dearden (1907–88) served as bishop of Pittsburgh from 1950 to 1958 and as archbishop of Detroit from 1959 to 1980. An early postconciliar source of criticism of Dearden and his supporters is in George A. Kelly, *The Battle for the American Church* (Garden City, N.Y.: Doubleday, 1979). An even stauncher defense of the conservative position is in Ralph M. McInerny, *What Went Wrong with Vatican II* (Manchester, N.H.: Sophia Institute, 1998). For the opposing view, see, for example, Eugene C. Kennedy's laudatory profile of Dearden in "The Dearden Inheritance," *The Now and Future Church: The Psychology of Being an American Catholic* (Garden City, N.Y.: Doubleday, 1984), 20–39. A timely papal inclusion on the theology of the Mystical Body and the People of God is in Pope Paul VI, "The Credo of the People of God," June 30, 1968, http://www.newadvent.org/library/docs_pa06cr.htm (accessed June 9, 2010). "Mystical Body of Christ" derives its context from a similarly titled preconciliar encyclical (1943) by Pope Pius XII. The usage and value of both phrases continues to be a point of contention between liberals and conservatives. See "Mystical Body of the Church," *Catholic Encyclopedia* (1911), and Joseph Ratzinger, "The Ecclesiology of Vatican II," *L'Osservatore Romano* (January 23, 2002): 7, http://www.ewtn.com/library/curia/cdfeccv2.htm (accessed October 19, 2009).

7. "Ecclesiology," as used here, is "the branch of theology concerned with the nature and the constitution and the functions of a church." *WordNet: A Lexical Database for English*, http://wordnetweb.princeton.edu/perl/webwn (accessed June 10, 2010).

8. On the eve of his retirement, Dearden reaffirmed that "the optimism comes from my own religious faith." "Retirement Dinner, Civic Salute, October 30, 1980," in funeral-Mass booklet *I Serve in the Gospel* (August 5, 1988), 5.

9. The quote from Dearden is in Harold Schachern, "Dearden Welcomes Changes in the Church," *Detroit News*, January 1, 1969, 1f. To appreciate the extensive and labor-intensive responsibilities of the NCCB, see the report prepared by a committee of bishops and approved in February 1971, which included a job description for the second election of a president in November 1971. Its report reflected the arduousness of the job that engaged Dearden during his five-year tenure. After Dearden, presidential terms were limited to three years, with no opportunity to run again. A copy of the job description is among the papers of now-retired Detroit auxiliary bishop Thomas Gumbleton (GUM) in the Archives of the University of Notre Dame (AUND): See the "Ad hoc Committee on the Role of the NCCB President," GUM, box 11, folder 05, "NCCB Synod 1969 and 1971" (AUND). In 2001, the bishops reorganized as the United States Conference of Catholic Bishops (USCCB).

10. David O'Brien, "American Reform Catholicism," address to the Call to Action Conference, November 2005, published on the website of the Association for the Rights of Catholics in the Church, http://arcc-catholic-rights.net/ameri can_reform_catholicism.htm (accessed January 20, 2010). Another such call, the gathering of several reform organizations in a movement known as the American Catholic Council, took place on Pentecost weekend, June 10–12, 2011, at Cobo Hall in Detroit, Michigan, site of the first Call to Action, NCCB-commissioned and Dearden-led, in 1976.

11. Use of the terms "transcendence" and "immanence" as central to my thesis owes a debt to several scholars: Joseph P. Chinnici, O.F.M., "An Historian's Creed and the Emergence of Postconciliar Culture Wars," *Catholic Historical Review* 94 (April 2008): 239; David Tracy, *The Analogical Imagination: Christian Theology and the Culture of Pluralism* (New York: Crossroad, 1981), chapter 9; and Andrew Greeley, *The Catholic Myth: The Behavior and Beliefs of American Catholics* (New York: Scribner's, 1990), chapters 3 and 9. A similar appreciation of the terms "immanence" and "transcendence" may be found in the posthumous publication of Richard Schoenherr, *Goodbye Father: The Celibate Male Priesthood and the Future of the Catholic Church* (New York: Oxford University Press, 2002), 126–29. For in-depth analyses of the identities that constitute the American Catholic, see the *Pew Forum on Religion*, http://religions.pewforum.org/reports; and the latest of four studies by sociologist William D'Antonio, "Catholics in America: Persistence and Change in the Catholic Landscape," *National Catholic Reporter* (October 28–November 10, 2011): 1–28.

12. An early and still very useful study of how various national conferences responded to *Humanae Vitae* is John Hogan, ed., *Humanae Vitae and the Bishops:*

The Encyclical and the Statements of the National Hierarchies (Shannon, Ireland: Irish University Press, 1972). See too Samuel J. Thomas, "Episcopal Authority and Clerical Dissent: Walter J. Burghardt, S.J., and *Humanae Vitae,*" *American Catholic Studies* 119 (Summer 2008): 35–69, and "A 'Final Disposition' . . . One Way or Another: The Real End of the First Curran Affair," *Catholic Historical Review* 91 (October 2005): 714–42.

13. Correspondent, "American Self-Scrutiny," *The Tablet* (January 18, 1969): 55–56, copy in Dearden Papers (CDRD), box 35, folder 28, AUND.

14. "Dearden bishops" is a phrase used by Rembert Weakland, O.S.B., former archbishop of Milwaukee, to distinguish them from American ultramontanists who, at their "worst . . . evolved . . . a closed mentality where loyalty was prized above honesty and where American Catholics remained second-class citizens." Rembert Weakland, *A Pilgrim in a Pilgrim Church: Memoirs of a Catholic Archbishop* (Grand Rapids, Mich.: Eerdmans, 2009), 295–96. Among the progressives, other Dearden supporters were Ritter of St. Louis, Cushing of Boston, Sheehan of Baltimore, Hallinan of Atlanta, Shannon of St. Paul, Primeau of Manchester, Buswell of Pueblo, Tracy of Baton Rouge, Dozier of Memphis, Gerety of Portland, Hunthausen of Helena and later Seattle, and Sullivan of Richmond. David O'Brien, e-mail to author, April 12, 2010. Other bishops sometimes included in this category are arguable, especially as conflicts and dissent mounted. They included Wright of Pittsburgh, Cody of Chicago, Lucey of San Antonio, and Helmsing of Kansas City. See Barrett McGurn, *A Reporter Looks at American Catholicism* (New York: Sheed and Ward, 1967), 108. In 1968, Thomas Gumbleton and Walter Schoenherr became auxiliaries of Detroit and two more Dearden bishops. See http://www.nytimes.com/1988/08/02/obituaries/john-car dinal-dearden-80-dies-leading-liberal-voice-in-church.html (accessed September 4, 2009). The general makeup of the NCCB, as late as the early 1980s, was still a source of hope for reformers such as psychologist and former priest Eugene Kennedy, though he also expressed serious concern over future appointments under Pope John Paul II. See Eugene C. Kennedy, *Re-Imagining American Catholicism: The American Bishops and Their Pastoral Letters* (New York: Vintage, 1985), chapters 1 and 2.

15. Harold Schachern, "The Unobtrusive Liberal Made Cardinal," *Detroit News,* April 29, 1969, reprinted in Jane Wolford Hughes, ed., *Golden Jubilee Mass of Priestly Ordination of John F. Dearden* (Detroit, 1982): "John Cardinal Dearden . . . won for himself the sobriquet, unobtrusive liberal, during the four sessions of the Second Vatican Council. Of all the labels ever applied to him, this is his favorite." Jane Wolford Hughes, "In Memoriam, Cardinal John F. Dearden: Teacher," *Living Light* 25 (June 1989): 308. Also by Hughes, "I Remember John Cardinal Dearden," *Parish Ministry Today* (November 6, 2003). She served as executive director from 1966 to 1985.

16. Bishop Ken Untener, *The Practical Prophet: Pastoral Writings* (New York: Paulist Press, 2007), 272–73 (Untener's words), 275–76 (Dearden's words). The issue of divorced and remarried Catholics engaged Dearden's pastoral skills. See Thomas, "Dissent and Due Process after Vatican II: An Early Case Study in American Catholic Leadership," *U.S. Catholic Historian* 17 (Fall 1999): 1–22.

17. Dearden defeated John Krol, the conservative archbishop of Philadelphia, on the third ballot; Krol became Dearden's vice president by plurality vote. In 1971, Krol succeeded Dearden as president and served what thereafter would be a standard three-year term. During that time, Dearden's status was such that Krol did little to vary the progressive direction in which Dearden had led the conference during its first five years. The third president, from 1974 to 1977, Joseph Bernardin, then archbishop of Cincinnati, proved to be a moderate who "displeased conservatives and disappointed . . . progressives" but also a consensus builder in the style of his mentor, Dearden. The fourth president, from 1977 to 1980, was San Francisco archbishop and progressive John Quinn, whose views were similar to Dearden's. The aforementioned each served with a theologically conservative vice president: Krol with St. Paul archbishop Leo Byrne; Bernardin with St. Louis archbishop Cardinal John Carberry; and Quinn with St. Paul archbishop John Roach. See Thomas J. Reese, S.J., *A Flock of Shepherds: The National Conference of Catholic Bishops* (Kansas City, Mo.: Sheed and Ward, 1992), chapter 3.

18. Dearden, quoted in John T. McGreevy, *Catholicism and American Freedom: A History* (New York: Norton, 2003), 284.

19. Bishop James Malone, quoted in Lawrence J. Engel, "The Influence of Saul Alinsky on the Campaign for Human Development," *Theological Studies* 59, no. 4 (December 1998): 636–37.

20. Dearden has yet to receive his biographical due in large part because of lack of access to his papers in the archives of the Archdiocese of Detroit. Both the archivist of the archdiocese and the chancellor concur that the cardinal's papers are neither catalogued nor completely inventoried. They expected them to be accessible by summer 2012, but at this writing there has been no change. Heidi Christein, e-mail to author, January 10, 2010; Judy Holmes, e-mail to author, July 20, 2010, and August 29, 2012. In the interim, scholars have mined other repositories such as the valuable and chiefly, though not exclusively, Vatican II Dearden papers in the archives of the University of Notre Dame, numerous letters and reports among the Alexander Zaleski papers in the archives of the Diocese of Lansing, scattered documents in the archives of the Catholic University of America, and the extensive press coverage of Dearden's career after Vatican II. For a detailed explanation of NCCB consensus techniques and results, see Thomas J. Reese, S.J., "Conflict and Consensus in the NCCB/USCC," in *Episcopal Conferences: Historical, Canonical, and Theological Studies*, ed. Thomas J. Reese, S.J. (Washington, D.C.: Georgetown University Press, 1989).

21. See Thomas, "After Vatican II: The American Catholic Bishops and the 'Syllabus' from Rome, 1966–68," *Catholic Historical Review* 83 (April 1997): 249–51; and "A 'Final Disposition,'" 719.

22. In 1959, Pope John XXIII mentioned the need to revise canon law when he called for the Second Vatican Council. After the Council, it took two years to formulate the general principles that would guide the revision. Late in 1965, Pope Paul VI announced plans to reform the curia. He began with the Holy Office, which he renamed the Sacred Congregation for the Doctrine of the Faith (CDF), stating it would no longer rule by fear and fiat. See *Integrae Servandae* (December 7, 1965), translated by Austin Vaughn in *The Pope Speaks* 11 (1966): 13–16. He also promised that local jurisdictions and due process would precede any final judgments by the Congregation. See too "Paul VI Apostolic Letter Reforming the Holy Office" and "Pope Paul Spells Out Duties, Scope of Congregation for Doctrine of the Faith," *Catholic Weekly*, January 14, 1966, 12. In 1967, at the first Ordinary Synod in Rome, there was near consensus among the two hundred bishops present when the pope formally commissioned the revision of the Church's canon law. John Beal et al., eds., *New Commentary on the Code of Canon Law* (New York: Paulist Press, 2002), 122. For more detail on the issue of due process within the NCCB, see Thomas, "In No Sense an Inquisition: Alexander Zaleski and the Bishops' Committee on Doctrine, 1966–1970," *Polish American Studies* 57 (Spring 2000): 63–67.

23. "Human Life in Our Day," 1968, in Hugh J. Nolan, ed. *Pastoral Letters of the United States Catholic Bishops*, vol. 3, *1962–1974* (Washington, D. C.: United States Catholic Conference, 1975), 172–73. For a vivid description of the way in which the bishops reached consensus on their pastoral, see Reese, *Flock of Shepherds*, 157. For the Coriden quotation, see James A. Coriden, ed., *The Case for Freedom: Human Rights in the Church* (Washington: Corpus, 1969), 1. This volume on freedom and rights in the Church was the first edited collection of the explanation by the Canon Law Society of America (CLSA) for the necessity of due process and recourse for all Catholics. Among the "Principles to Direct the Revision of the Code" were the following: "[The] Code must define and protect the rights and obligations of each person, it is expedient that the rights of persons be appropriately defined and safeguarded, it is necessary to develop procedures for the protections of subjective rights." James Coriden, *The Rights of Catholics in the Church* (New York: Paulist Press, 2007), 7. During his pontificate, John Paul II rejected the bill of rights before he promulgated the revised Code in January 1983; he later amended the Code further to reflect his conservative ecclesiology. See, for example, his motu proprio of 1998, *Ad Tuendam Fidam,* "by which certain norms are inserted into the Code of Canon Law," http://www.vatican.va/holy_father/john_paul_ii/motu_proprio/documents/hf_jp-ii_motu-proprio_30061998_ad-tuendam-fidem_en.html (accessed June 28, 2010); James A.

Coriden, "What Became of the Bill of Rights?" *CLSA, Proceedings of the Fifty-Second Annual Convention, 1990* (Washington, D. C.: Canon Law Society of America, 1991), 47–60. For examples of the contentiousness surrounding the quest for due process, see Thomas, "In No Sense an Inquisition," 62–67; and Thomas, "Walter Burghardt, S.J., and *Humanae Vitae*," *American Catholic Studies* 119 (Summer 2008): 53–56.

24. See Leslie Woodcock Tentler, *Catholics and Contraception: An American History* (Ithaca, N.Y.: Cornell University Press, 2004), 269, 273; Thomas, "Dissent and Due Process after Vatican II," 14–15. A notable example of the prudence and caution Dearden used in press statements on marriage and marital intimacy is in Floyd Anderson, ed., *Council Daybook, Vatican II, Session 3* (Washington, D.C.: National Catholic Welfare Conference, 1965), 203–5.

25. In 1967, the newly constituted NCCB issued its first pastoral, "The Church in Our Day," a cautiously optimistic document that acknowledged the controversies plaguing the Church. It counseled all Catholics to become a "community of charity" in their dealings with one another. It also reminded them of their obligation "to write, speak out and act against indignity, injustice, and inhumanity at any time, in any place, toward any man." Nolan, *Pastoral Letters of the United States Catholic Bishops*, 69, 74, 84. See also Timothy A. Byrnes, *Catholic Bishops in American Politics* (Princeton, N.J.: Princeton University Press, 1991), 52, for a quote from an early Dearden speech on the importance of episcopal collegiality.

26. Victoria Beck, "Jane Wolford Hughes," Talbot School of Theology, http://www2.talbot.edu/ce20/educators/view.cfm?n=jane_hughes (accessed February 12, 2010). Between the end of Vatican II and 1983, when Pope John Paul II promulgated the revised Code of Canon Law, there were fifteen diocesan synods, eight in the late 1960s and four in the 1970s. At this writing, only a third of U.S. dioceses have held postconciliar synods. See Bradford Hinze, *Practices of Dialogue in the Roman Catholic Church: Aims and Obstacles, Lessons and Laments* (New York: Continuum, 2006), 44. Jane Wolford Hughes, executive director of the Detroit archdiocese's Institute for Continuing Education, spearheaded the drive to engage Catholics in the archdiocese in the process that led to Synod/69. Others who assisted Wolford Hughes included Judy M. Holmes, the center coordinator of adult education and currently director of the John Cardinal Dearden Legacy Project. "1969 Synod—Archdiocese of Detroit" (March 30, 1969). A copy of the entire booklet, *1969 Synod of Detroit; celebrated by the Most Reverend John F. Dearden, together with the Church of Detroit* (Detroit: The Archdiocese, 1969), is among the papers of Lansing bishop Alexander Zaleski (ZP) in a folder labeled "Provincial Activities, Metropolitan, Cardinal John Dearden" in the archives of the Diocese of Lansing (ADL).

27. "1969 Synod, Archdiocese of Detroit" (March 30, 1969) in "Provincial Activities, Metropolitan, Cardinal John Dearden," ZP, ADL. There is a very brief

NOTES TO PAGES 258-259 369

description of the 1969 synod in Leslie Tentler, *Seasons of Grace: A History of the Archdiocese of Detroit* (Detroit: Wayne State University Press, 1990), 523 (epilogue). Her entire epilogue is well worth reading and does an excellent job of placing the synod in the broader context of the changing city and the changing Church of the 1960s. See too Harold Schachern, "Dearden Welcomes Changes in the Church," *Detroit News*, January 1, 1969, 1, and "How Detroit's Archdiocese Is Being Remade—At a Price," *Detroit News*, January 26, 1969, 19–21. The latter report shows how new, more collaborative approaches to Church governance were already in place before the synod's official promulgation. On February 15, 1969, six weeks before its promulgation, the final draft of the synod document received approval by the vast majority of delegates. See Hinze, *Practices of Dialogue*, 48.

28. *Herder Correspondence*, August 1969, reprinted in "Democracy in Detroit," (Archdiocesan) Institute for Continuing Education, Detroit, Michigan, 2. John C. Haughey, "Evolution of a Revolution," *America* (April 19, 1969): 475–78, is a sympathetic but insightful analysis of the synod-inspired restructuring of the archdiocese.

29. "1969 Synod," 5, 9, 12–13, 15–17. At the Vatican and in conservative circles generally, Teilhard's wisdom was still suspect. His words in the synod booklet may have been among the first attempts to rehabilitate his reputation, a process that has also made progress under Pope Benedict XVI. See "An Evolutionary Leap for Teilhard?" *National Catholic Reporter*, August 7, 2009, 15. Judy M. Holmes, Coordinator of Adult Education for the archdiocese, helped select these and other quotes used throughout the entire synod booklet, while Jane Wolford, Executive Director of the institute, served as editor of the synod publication. Judy Holmes, e-mail to author, February 10, 2010.

30. Archdiocese of Detroit, "Synod," 8, 16.

31. "Synod," 17. In 1968 and 1969, Father Walter Burghardt, S.J., the outgoing president of the Catholic Theological Society of America (CTSA), echoed Dearden's public and some of his private sentiments on inclusiveness, less hierarchical or more decentralized control, and greater community or concentricity. "Presidential Address: Towards an American Theology," *Catholic Theological Society of America: Proceedings of the Twenty-Third Annual Convention on June 17–20, 1968* (Yonkers, NY: St. Joseph's Seminary), 22–27; and Walter J. Burghardt, "The Authority–Freedom Issue: Destructive or Creative?" *Spiritual Life*, 15 (Spring 1969): 228–40. See too the address by incoming CTSA president Richard McCormick, S.J., "The Teaching Role of the Magisterium and of the Theologians," *Catholic Theological Society of America: Proceedings of the Twenty-Fourth Annual Convention, June 16–19, 1969* (Yonkers, NY: St. Joseph Seminary): 239–54.

32. John Cardinal Dearden, from "'Covenant', Cardinal Dearden, Marriage and Family, *Gaudium et Spes*," his presentation on marriage at St. John Provincial

Seminary, November 4, 1986. Judy Holmes, Director, Cardinal Dearden Legacy Project, e-mail to author, February 10, 2010. Readily apparent in this address is the influence of Dearden's role in drafting parts of Vatican II's 1965 "Pastoral Constitution on the Church and the Modern World" and specifically part 2, chapter 1, sections 47–52. The nature and extent of his role may be assessed from his Vatican II papers housed at the archives of the University of Notre Dame. Very helpful is Msgr. Vincent A. Yzermans, ed., *American Participation in the Second Vatican Council* (New York: Sheed and Ward, 1967), 191–94, who quotes Dearden's highly nuanced statements in support of Church teaching on marriage and intimacy as a sine qua non to an informed conscience even as he demonstrated his debt to the advice of John T. Noonan Jr., whose study *Contraception: A History of its Treatment by the Catholic Theologians and Canonists* (Cambridge, Mass.: Belknap Press, Harvard University Press, 1965) is still the best treatment of the topic.

33. "Synod," 17.

34. See David O'Brien, *Public Catholicism*, 2nd ed. (New York: Maryknoll, 1996), 236–52. O'Brien was closely involved with Detroit's Call to Action conference in 1976 and wrote his NCCB-commissioned volume on the American Church to coincide with the nation's bicentennial. In it, he also describes how "Many [of the American bishops] were . . . transformed by" Vatican II, "returning different men, determined to build a more community-oriented, open and mission-centered church" (235). Dearden's friend, Lansing bishop Alexander Zaleski, implemented his own plan for diocesan renewal two years before the synod. Dearden incorporated small parts of Zaleski's plan during the restructuring of the Detroit archdiocese outlined in Synod/69. For a brief summary of Zaleski's program, see Clarence E. Rhodes, "The Lansing Program," *America* 117 (August 26, 1967): 202–3. On pages 18–34 of the Synod/69 booklet, immediately following the archbishop's introduction, documents detail the rights and responsibilities of the laity and religious in the archdiocese. Nationally, fewer than a third of American dioceses implemented a formal plan of renewal during the 1960s and 1970s, about the same number that held synods between 1965 and 2000. See Hinze, *Practices of Dialogue*, 44.

35. For Vatican II's support of *Gemeinschaft* over *Gesellschaft*, see Charles Meyer, "Christian Freedom," in Coriden, ed., *Case for Freedom*, 86–88; Reese, *Archbishop: Inside the Power Structure of the American Catholic Church* (San Francisco: Harper and Row, 1989), 77. The irony in the reorganization is that Dearden pursued *Gemeinschaft* ends with *Gesellschaft* means. His plan considerably raised the number of lay and religious Catholics employed in the archdiocese but did so by bureaucratizing and professionalizing its administration. In the twentieth century, subsidiarity, the principle that a matter should be resolved by the lowest authority competent to do so, appears in Pope Pius XI's social encyclical *Quadragesimo Anno*, paragraphs 79–80.

36. Bradford E. Hinze, *Practices of Dialogue*, 44–50; see David R. Maines and Michael J. McCallion, *Transforming Catholicism: Liturgical Change in the Vatican II Church* (Lanham, Md.: Lexington Books, 2007), 22–23.

37. Dearden, quoted in *Emmanuel Magazine* (November 1979), cited in Jane Wolford Hughes, "In Memoriam—Cardinal John F. Dearden: Teacher," *Living Light* 25 (June 1989): 313. Two documents from post-synod Detroit show in detail how Dearden's emphasis on a collaborative approach to church governance continued until his retirement in 1980. See John Cardinal Dearden, "Archdiocesan Goals—for Year 1973–1974: Preamble," *Michigan Catholic*, March 14, 1973, 5; and Margaret Cronyn, "Announce Archdiocesan Goal for 1979–1982," *Michigan Catholic*, March 9, 1979, 1–2. There has not been another Detroit synod since 1969. To understand why, one need only look at the succession of conservative archbishops, beginning with Edmund Szoka (1980–89), who shifted authority back to the chancery from the vicariates.

38. *Time*, April 4, 1969, www.time.com/time/magazine/article/0,9171,840025 ,00.html (accessed September 21, 2009). Detroit auxiliary bishop emeritus Thomas J. Gumbleton, e-mail to author, August 3, 2010.

39. John Dearden, "Church of Tomorrow," *Catholic Mind* (June 1969): 1–2.

40. Dearden, "Church of Tomorrow," 1–2; Martin Luther King Jr. "Letter From Birmingham Jail," in King, *Why We Can't Wait* (New York: Mentor, 1964), 79–80. My inference from Dearden's address derives in part from a study of many of his other written and public pronouncements, and in part on the recollection of one of Dearden's longtime (1959–71) personal secretaries, who recalled that the archbishop was meticulous about his choice of words in his writing and speeches (Bishop Joseph L. Imesch, then ordinary of Joliet, Illinois, letter to author, July 12, 1997). In a more recent letter, Bishop Imesch could not recall Dearden's meeting King and could not say with certainty that he had read King's "Letter from Birmingham Jail," although "I would imagine that he did read it" (Bishop Emeritus Joseph L. Imesch, letter to author, June 24, 2010). A further basis for my inference comes from the fact of Dearden's precedent-setting embrace of the black civil-rights movement. See John McGreevy, *Parish Boundaries: The Catholic Encounter with Race in the Twentieth Century Urban North* (Chicago: University of Chicago Press, 1996), 137–38, 209–15. See also the transcript of Dearden's remarks in a press release dated April 15, 1968, shortly after the assassination of King, in which Dearden describes a "Huge Drive on White Racism," particularly in the suburbs of the archdiocese. "Press Release, Launch of Drive on Racism" (April 15, 1968), GUM, box 30, folder 9, AUND (copy).

41. Dearden, "Church of Tomorrow," 2–3. Dearden's strongly stated forecast is strikingly similar in tone to King's prediction that violence would be the inevitable outcome of not successfully resolving segregation and racism through nonviolent direct action. Dearden's message also anticipates the either–or thesis of

books such as Peter Steinfels' *A People Adrift: The Crisis of the Roman Catholic Church in America* (New York: Simon and Schuster, 2004).

42. Dearden, "Church of Tomorrow," 2–3.

43. Dearden, "Church of Tomorrow," 3. An explanation of authority as "a ministry of service" is also in Cardinal John Dearden, "Toward a Working Relationship among Clergy, Laity, and Bishops," *Homiletic and Pastoral Review* 70 (October 1970): 741–42.

44. Dearden voted in June 1966 against the proposition that contraception was inherently evil. See Robert McClory, *Turning Point: The Inside Story of the Papal Birth Control Commission* (New York: Crossroad, 1995), 188–90; Dearden, "Church of Tomorrow," 4–5. In the summer of 1969, his confidence in the soundness of the vision he had outlined to his brother bishops seems to have peaked when he sent to Rome his friend and confidante, Bishop Alexander Zaleski, who chaired the NCCB's Committee on Doctrine. Zaleski, with other doctrinal committee chairs, traveled to Rome in response to a summons by Cardinal Josef Seper, prefect of the Sacred Congregation for the Doctrine of the Faith (CDF). There Zaleski tactfully and incisively admonished, with apparent impunity, the theoretically reformed but still hidebound CDF to drop its inquisitorial modus operandi and publicly adopt due process. See Thomas, "In No Way an Inquisition," 64–68. Bishop emeritus Thomas J. Gumbleton, e-mail to author, August 3, 2010, comments on the address's reception in the NCCB as well as on one of Dearden's motives for giving it. He also suggests that given the "spirit of the times . . . this talk probably did not cause any great concern in the Curia" in 1969.

45. Meyer, "Freedom," in *The Case for Freedom*, ed. Coriden, 88.

46. Examples of internal issues that had national import included the continuing breach of trust between bishops and priests, a growing and vocal support by priests for a reconsideration of mandatory celibacy, specific issues related to due process, and a controversial NCCB-commissioned study of the priesthood. For information on other internal issues that demanded Dearden's attention and that of the NCCB between 1969 and 1971, see the following at the archives of the University of Notre Dame: the Dearden Papers (CDRD), box 34, folder 12; box 35, folder 13; and box 35, folder 28 (AUND). See also GUM, box 09, folder 05; and box 12, folder 03 (AUND); and James P. Shannon, *Reluctant Dissenter: An Autobiography* (New York: Crossroad, 1998), 142–62. For an overview of the theologians' dissent and its aftermath, see C. Joseph Nuesse, *The Catholic University of America: A Centennial History* (Washington, D.C.: Catholic University of America, 1990), 401–22.

47. "Presidential Report by His Eminence John Cardinal Dearden, President, NCCB/USCC," GUM, box 11 folder 05; "NCCB Cardinal Dearden," 1, AUND (copy).

48. Dearden, "Presidential Report," GUM, box 11, folder 5, AUND (copy), 1.

49. Ibid., 2–6.

50. Ibid.

51. Ibid., 7. The key words noted above appear throughout the address.

52. Dearden, "Presidential Report," GUM box 11, folder 05, AUND (copy), 8.

53. See David O'Brien's 1977 and 2009 detailed recollections and assessments of the CTA in 1976: "On Detroit," http://www.americancatholiccouncil.org/re sources/Obrien-on-detroit (accessed December 19, 2009). See too O'Brien's "Marking the 10th Anniversary: A Call to Action, An Unfinished Experiment," *Commonweal* (special supplement) 113 (December 26, 1986): 698–702. Cardinal John Dearden, "Opening Address: Call to Action Conference," October 1976, 1 in http://www.justpeace.org/NCCB101976.htm (accessed August 8, 2010).

54. "Report to the NCCB by the Ad Hoc Committee for the Bicentennial, John Cardinal Dearden, Chairman," November 1, 1976, at http://www.cta-usa .org/whobishconference/A_reporttoNCCB.html (accessed August 8, 2010).

55. Under Bernardin, the NCCB refused to consider the consensus that delegates to the CTA had reached on issues related to Church teaching or discipline: e.g., homosexuality, contraception, women's ordination, optional celibacy, and admission to the sacraments of divorced and remarried Catholics. See NCCB, "To Do the Work of Justice: A Plan of Action for the Catholic Community in the U. S. (May 4, 1978). Hinze, *Practices of Dialogue*, 77–88; 281–83, annotated footnotes 25–40.

56. It is noteworthy that the second Call to Action, at first a local organization, runs a banner on its website that goes beyond the call for justice that characterized the 1976 event. It reads: "Catholics Working Together for Justice and Equality." http://cta-usa.org/about/history/ (accessed September 28, 2012).

57. Chicago archbishop Cardinal Joseph Bernardin endorsed the initiative's mission statement, "Called to Be Catholic: Church in a Time of Peril," in late August 1996. A forecast of the opposition facing Bernardin from the very start of his initiative may be found in the response to his address on the same day by Boston's Bernard Cardinal Law, "Response to 'Called to be Catholic.' " Both statements are at http://www.ewtn.com/library/bishops/comgroun.htm (accessed January 10, 2010). Cardinal Anthony Bevilacqua, of Philadelphia, Cardinal James Hickey of Washington, D.C., and Cardinal Adam Maida of Detroit also wrote in opposition. See Gustav Niebuhr, "Cardinal Opposed in Effort to Find 'Common Ground,'" *New York Times*, August 24, 1996, https://www.nytimes.com/1996/08 /24/us/cardinal-opposed-in-effort-to-find-common-ground.html (accessed July 21, 2010). In 2009 the headquarters of Bernardin's initiative moved to the Catholic Theological Union in Chicago; see http://www.catholiccommonground.org (accessed December 1, 2012). For one of many posthumous examples of supporters and opponents praising Bernardin's accomplishments, see Julie Irwin, "Cardinal Bernardin Was a Leader," *Cincinnati Enquirer*, November 14, 1996, 1. See

Steinfels, *A People Adrift*, 24–29, for a plausible explanation of the opposition to Bernardin.

58. For example, O'Brien, "American Reform Catholicism." In June 2011, the consortium of reform groups known as the American Catholic Council held its meeting at Detroit's Cobo Hall largely to celebrate Cardinal Dearden's ecclesiology and his efforts that culminated in Call to Action 1976.

59. See David Gibson, *The Coming Catholic Church: How the Faithful Are Shaping a New American Catholicism*, rev. ed. (New York: HarperCollins, 2004); John Allen, *The Future Church: How Ten Trends Are Revolutionizing the Catholic Church* (New York: Random House, 2009).

60. See John O'Malley's essay, "Vatican II: Did Anything Happen?" in *Vatican II: Did Anything Happen?* ed. David G. Schultenover (New York: Continuum, 2008), 68–79; and Joseph Chinnici, "An Historian's Creed," 242. See also Jay P. Dolan, *In Search of An American Catholicism: A History of Religion and Culture in Tension* (New York: Oxford University Press, 2002); McGreevy, *Catholicism and American Freedom*; Andrew Greeley, *The Catholic Revolution: New Wine, Old Wineskins and the Second Vatican Council* (Berkeley: University of California Press, 2004); James A. Coriden, *Rights of Catholics*; and George B. Wilson, S.J., *Clericalism: The Death of Priesthood* (Collegeville, Minn.: Liturgical Press, 2008). The leading progressive Catholic newspaper is the *National Catholic Reporter*, established in 1965.

61. See James Hitchcock, *The Decline and Fall of Catholic Radicalism* (Garden City, N.Y.: Image, 1972); Weigel, *The Courage to Be Catholic: Crisis, Reform, and the Future of the Church* (New York: Basic, 2002).

62. These titles, of course, are but examples of a much longer list. Important conservative Catholic newspapers include the *National Catholic Register*, now run by the Eternal Word Television Network, and *Our Sunday Visitor*. Much farther to the right is the *Wanderer*.

63. For a persuasive analysis of the unique literary genre and language used in the documents of Vatican II, see Schultenover, ed., *Vatican II: Did Anything Happen?* and especially the essay by John O'Malley, S.J., 51–91. For a staunchly conservative argument, see McInerny, *What Went Wrong?*

64. Massimo Faggioli, *Vatican II: The Battle for Meaning* (New York: Paulist, 2012). An incisive analysis of the compromises struck at Vatican II is in Giuseppe Alberigo, *A Brief History of Vatican II* (Maryknoll, N.Y.: Orbis, 2006), 68–69, 74. For an excellent recent essay on the battle over collegiality, see John Wilkins, "Bishops or Branch Managers: Collegiality after the Council," *Commonweal* (October 12, 2012): http://commonwealmagazine.org/bishops-or -branch-managers (accessed October 18, 2012). *A People Adrift* (Steinfels) and *What Went Wrong* (McInerny) are examples of the sense of urgency that progressives and conservatives have expressed in their arguments for further re-

form or restoration. Both raise the probability of dire consequences unless changes occur.

65. John Cardinal Dearden, "Talk to Milwaukee Diocesan Parish Councils, 1974," reprinted in a supplement to the *Michigan Catholic*, October 24, 1980, 14.

66. See Kennedy, *Now and Future Church*, 26; Chinnici, "An Historian's Creed," 239.

11. Christian Unity, Lay Authority, and the People of God: The Community of Christ Our Brother in the Archdiocese of Atlanta, 1967–1969

ANDREW S. MOORE

1. An earlier version of this chapter appeared in the Fall 2006 issue of *U.S. Catholic Historian*.

2. *Gaudium et Spes*, par. 4, at the Vatican website, http://www.vatican.va.

3. "First Synod: Lay Congress Will Provide Prior Views," *Georgia Bulletin*, September 9, 1965; see also, "Callison Elected to Head Lay Congress Meet Here," *Georgia Bulletin*, February 17, 1966.

4. "59 Laymen, 7 Priests, 7 Nuns Serve on Archdiocesan Boards," *Georgia Bulletin*, February 16, 1967.

5. On Foust and the civil rights movement, see "Atlanta Negroes Demand Civil Rights Speed-Up," *Georgia Bulletin*, December 19, 1963; on the "folk mass," Hugh F. Fenlon Jr., e-mail to Andrew S. Moore, June 7, 2011.

6. See Mary J. Henold, "Breaking the Boundaries of Renewal: The American Catholic Underground, 1966–1970," *U.S. Catholic Historian* 19, no. 33 (Summer 2001): 97–118; for more on "seeker" spirituality, see Robert Wuthnow, *After Heaven: Spirituality in America since the 1950s* (Berkeley: University of California Press, 1998).

7. On the relationship between Catholics, the South's Protestant culture, and the civil rights movement, see Andrew S. Moore, *The South's Tolerable Alien: Roman Catholics in Alabama and Georgia, 1945–1970* (Baton Rouge: Louisiana State University Press, 2007).

8. King, quoted in Charles Marsh, *The Beloved Community: How Faith Shapes Social Justice from the Civil Rights Movement to Today* (New York: Basic Books, 2005), 45.

9. Hallinan, pastoral letter, January 10, 1966, box 011/4, folder 1, Archives of the Catholic Archdiocese of Atlanta (hereafter ACAA).

10. On Hallinan, see Thomas J. Shelley, *Paul J. Hallinan: First Archbishop of Atlanta* (Wilmington, Del.: Michael Glazier, 1989).

11. See Ronald H. Bayor, *Race and the Shaping of Twentieth-Century Atlanta* (Chapel Hill: University of North Carolina Press, 1996); and Gary Pomerantz,

Where Peachtree Meets Sweet Auburn: The Saga of Two Families and the Making of Atlanta (New York: Scribner, 1996).

12. On the behind-the-scenes negotiations necessary to insure an interracial banquet, see Pomerantz, *Where Peachtree Meets Sweet Auburn*, 334–40; and Taylor Branch, *Pillar of Fire: America in the King Years, 1963–1965* (New York: Simon and Schuster, 1998), 568–70.

13. "Remarks of Archbishop Paul J. Hallinan at Civic Dinner Honoring Dr. Martin Luther King, Jr., Atlanta, January 27, 1965," box 001/6, folder 42, ACAA.

14. Quoted in Shelley, *Paul J. Hallinan*, 230.

15. Martin Luther King, Jr. to Hallinan, March 8, 1965, box 001/2, folder 7, ACAA.

16. John J. Mulroy, "St. Joseph's Athens—A Parish of Liturgical Progress," *Georgia Bulletin*, October 24, 1963, 3.

17. Conald Foust to Lou Erbs, Liturgy Commission, Archdiocese of Atlanta, May 25, 1967, box 011/4, folder 2, ACAA.

18. Foust, "What About Experimentation in Atlanta?" box 043/3, folder 2, ACAA. See also Foust, "The Laymen's Share in the Authority of the Church Related to the Atlanta Lay Congress," box 006/6, folder 8, ACAA.

19. New Parish Experiment, Minutes of Meeting 1, February 7, 1967, box 043/3, folder 2, ACAA.

20. Conald Foust to Archbishop Paul J. Hallinan, January 30, 1967, box 043/3, folder 2, ACAA.

21. Ibid.

22. Foust, "The Laymen's Share In the Authority of the Church."

23. New Parish Experiment, Minutes of Meeting 1, February 7, 1967.

24. New Parish Experiment, Minutes of Meeting 5, March 7, 1967, box 043/3, folder 2, ACAA; New Parish Experiment, Minutes of Meeting 2, February 14, 1967, box 043/3, folder 2, ACAA.

25. New Parish Experiment, Minutes of Meeting 2, February 14, 1967.

26. Ibid.

27. Ibid.

28. New Parish Experiment, Minutes of Meeting 1, February 7, 1967.

29. Conald Foust to Auxiliary Bishop Joseph Bernardin, February 11, 1967, box 043/3, folder 2, ACAA.

30. Bernardin to Foust, February 15, 1967, box 043/3, folder 2, ACAA.

31. For *Unitas Redintegratio* (Decree on Ecumenism), see the Vatican website, http://www.vatican.va.

32. Hallinan to Foust, March 14, 1967, box 043/3, folder 2, ACAA.

33. Foust to Hallinan, March 17, 1967, box 043/3, folder 2, ACAA.

34. Foust to Bernardin, March 17, 1967, box 043/3, folder 2, ACAA.

35. New Parish Experiment, Minutes of Meeting 2, February 14, 1967.

36. New Parish Experiment, Minutes of Meeting 1, February 7, 1967.

37. "Some Reasons for the Establishment of a Non-Territorial Parish and Some Problems Concerning Its Establishment," box 043/3, folder 2, ACAA.

38. See Moore, *South's Tolerable Alien*; and John T. McGreevy, *Parish Boundaries: The Catholic Encounter with Race in the Twentieth-Century Urban North* (Chicago: University of Chicago Press, 1996).

39. See Wuthnow, *After Heaven*.

40. New Parish Experiment, Minutes of Meeting 4, February 28, 1967, box 043/3, folder 2, ACAA.

41. Foust to Hallinan, March 2, 1967, box 043/3, folder 2, ACAA.

42. On the Community of John XXIII, see Jeremy Bonner, *Road to Renewal: Victor Joseph Reed and Oklahoma Catholicism, 1905–1971* (Washington, D.C.: Catholic University of America Press, 2008), 154–57 (quotation at 156).

43. Mary Lackie, "They Help Poor Help Themselves," *Georgia Bulletin*, March 16, 1967.

44. "Faith and Credit Union Solve Financial Problem," *Georgia Bulletin*, March 16, 1967.

45. "Some Reasons For the Establishment of a Non-Territorial Parish and Some Problems Concerning Its Establishment," box 043/3, folder 2, ACAA; "Some General Principles for Discussion Regarding a Parish Community Without Boundaries," box 043/3, folder 2, ACAA.

46. Foust to Hallinan, March 2, 1967.

47. Bernardin to Foust, March 14, 1967, box 008/6, folder 1, ACAA.

48. New Parish Experiment, Minutes of Meeting 6, March 14, 1967, box 043/3, folder 2, ACAA.

49. Herb Farnsworth [and Michael A Doyle] to Hallinan, March 22, 1967, box 008/6, folder 1, ACAA.

50. New Parish Experiment, Minutes of Meeting 7, March 28, 1967, box 043/3, folder 2, ACAA.

51. Bernardin to James Callison, chairman, Archdiocesan Pastoral Council, April 8, 1967, box 008/6, folder 1, ACAA.

52. Ibid.

53. F. R. Rauton to Hallinan, May 29, 1967, box 043/3, folder 2; Hallinan to Rauton, June 5, 1967, box 043/3, folder 1, ACAA (emphasis in the original).

54. Hallinan to Rauton, June 5, 1967.

55. " 'Parish Without Boundaries' Established in Atlanta," June 30, 1967, press release, Religious News Service, box 043/3, folder 1, ACAA.

56. See Conald Foust, "Parish without Bounds," *Commonweal* (August 25, 1967): 514–15.

57. "2 Faiths Set Up Joint Community," *Atlanta Constitution*, July 22, 1967, box 043/3, folder 2, ACAA.

58. Foust, "Parish without Bounds."

59. Foust, "December, 1967 Report of Community of Christ Our Brother," box 043/3, folder 2, ACAA. See also Bishop Bernardin to Luigi Raimondi, apostolic delegate to the United States, Washington, D. C., April 19, 1968, box 043/3, folder 2, ACAA.

60. Bernardin to Raimondi, April 19, 1968.

61. Hallinan to Foust, July 25, 1967, box 043/3, folder 2, ACAA. For the newspaper story in question, see "2 Faiths Set Up Joint Community," Atlanta *Constitution*, July 22, 1967, box 043/3, folder 2, ACAA.

62. Foust to Hallinan, August 27, 1967, box 043/3, folder 2, ACAA.

63. Bernardin to Raimondi, April 19, 1968.

64. Memo from Bernardin, archdiocesan administrator, April 19, 1968, box 043/3, folder 2, ACAA.

65. Ibid.

66. See Memo from Noel C. Burtenshaw, chancellor, May 24, 1968, box 043/3, folder 2, ACAA.

67. Bernardin to Foust, May 26, 1968, box 043/3, folder 2, ACAA.

68. Donnellan to Raimondi, December 18, 1968, box 043/3, folder 2, ACAA.

69. See Jay P. Dolan, *The American Catholic Experience: A History from the Colonial Times to the Present* (Notre Dame, Ind.: University of Notre Dame Press, 1992), 435–36; Charles R. Morris, *American Catholic: The Saints and Sinners Who Built America's Most Powerful Church* (New York: Times Books, 1997), 361–62.

70. "Archbishop Donnellan Supports Encyclical," *Georgia Bulletin*, August 1, 1968, 1, 4.

71. "Fr. Foust Opposes Pope's Encyclical," *Georgia Bulletin*, August 8, 1968, 1.

72. Foust, "Some Observations on the Papal Encyclical on Birth Control," box 043/3, folder 2; Foust to Donnellan, August 10, 1968, box 043/3, folder 2, ACAA.

73. Foust, "Some Observations on the Papal Encyclical on Birth Control."

74. "Community's Statement Supports Fr. Foust," *Georgia Bulletin*, August 15, 1968.

75. See Dolan, *American Catholic Experience*, 435.

76. See Donnellan to Kathleen K. Goedecke, secretary, Community of Christ Our Brother, December 18, 1968, Donnellan to Raimondi, December 18, 1968, box 043/3, folder 2, ACAA.

77. Foust's statement on the Community of Christ Our Brother, prepared for the apostolic delegate, at Donnellan's request, December 18, 1968, box 043/3, folder 2, ACAA.

78. Hugh F. Fenlon to Donnellan, January 5, 1969, box 043/3, folder 2, ACAA.

79. Noel C. Burtenshaw, chancellor, memorandum re Community of Christ Our Brother, January 30, 1969, box 043/3, folder 2, ACAA.

80. Fenlon to Andrew S. Moore, June 7, 2011; see Dolan, *American Catholic Experience*, 436–37.

81. See Moore, *South's Tolerable Alien*, chapter 6.

Contributors

JEREMY BONNER is an independent scholar currently based in Sheffield, England. He is the author of *Called Out of Darkness into Marvelous Light: A History of the Episcopal Diocese of Pittsburgh, 1750–2006* (Wipf and Stock, 2009) and *The Road to Renewal: Victor Joseph Reed and Oklahoma Catholicism, 1905–1971* (Catholic University of America Press, 2008) and the editor of a forthcoming retrospective on the impact of the Kikuyu Crisis of 1913 on the Church of England. He has published scholarly articles on Mormon and Anglican history and taught American history at Robert Morris University, Duquesne University, and the University of Sheffield.

MARY ELIZABETH BROWN received her PhD from Columbia University in 1987, partly on the strength of a dissertation on Italian immigrants in the Archdiocese of New York. She is currently the archivist at Marymount Manhattan College and at the Center for Migration Studies, from which she drew the material for her chapter on Catholic Action among Italian immigrants.

JEFFREY M. BURNS has been an archivist for the Archdiocese of San Francisco since 1983, and director of the Academy of American Franciscan History since 2002. He serves on the faculty at the Franciscan School of Theology and St. Patrick's Seminary and is the author of *Disturbing the Peace: A History of the Christian Family Movement, 1949–1974* (University of Notre Dame Press, 1999).

MARY BETH FRASER CONNOLLY, currently the assistant director of the Lilly Fellows Program in Humanities and the Arts, is an adjunct in history at Valparaiso University. She has taught American, women's, and religious history at universities in New Hampshire and Indiana. She has also worked as the historian for the Sisters of Mercy Chicago Regional Community, writing their community's history.

CHRISTOPHER D. DENNY is an associate professor in the Department of Theology and Religious Studies at St. John's University in New York City, teaching courses in Church history and Christian historical theology from the patristic era to the contemporary period. He is the coeditor, with Christopher McMahon, of *Finding Salvation in Christ: Essays on Christology and Soteriology in Honor of*

William P. Loewe (Pickwick, 2011). Other recent publications include an essay on John Courtney Murray in *Vatican II: Forty Years Later* (Orbis, 2006) and articles in the *Journal of Ecumenical Studies, Logos, Communio,* and *Horizons.* The recipient of best-article awards from the Catholic Press Association and the College Theology Society, Denny is a former regional director and board member of the American Academy of Religion.

ELIZABETH DUCLOS-ORSELLO is a publicly engaged scholar wedding social-justice concerns with and to humanistic and social-scientific inquiry, much of it connected to the complex concept of "community" in the United States. She is an associate professor of interdisciplinary studies and coordinator of American studies and faculty fellow for service learning at Salem State University, where she teaches and conducts research on a range of topics that link history, literature, cultural studies, and social theory to public-policy discourse. She holds a bachelor's degree in history and sociology from Connecticut College and a PhD in American studies from Boston University. She has taught at Harvard University, was a Fulbright Faculty Scholar at the University of Luxembourg, has worked as a museum educator and social worker, has directed federal K–12 grants, and has consulted for numerous museums and cultural public-sector collaborations. Her interest in the links between gender and Catholic identity began when she was a child and was solidified by her service in the Jesuit Volunteer Corps.

KATHARINE E. HARMON is a Lecturer in liturgical studies at the Catholic University of America in Washington, D.C., where she enjoys teaching the history, theology, and ritual dimensions of Christian worship. Her current research and writing centers on the retrieval of lay Roman Catholic initiatives for liturgical participation and renewal in the modern American context, particularly with respect to the intersection of worship and social action. Her first book, *There Were Also Many Women There* (Liturgical Press, 2013), examines the involvement of lay nonreligious women in the liturgical movement during the preconciliar era in the United States. She completed her PhD in liturgical studies at the University of Notre Dame and is a native of southern Indiana.

PATRICK J. HAYES is the archivist for the Baltimore Province of the Redemptorists, based in Brooklyn, New York. He has taught in theology and religious-studies departments in colleges in the United States and in Sierra Leone, West Africa. The author of a number of articles on American Church history and *A Catholic Brain Trust: The History of the Catholic Commission on Intellectual and Cultural Affairs, 1945–1965* (University of Notre Dame Press, 2011), Hayes is editor of *The Making of Modern Immigration: An Encyclopedia of People and Ideas* (ABC-CLIO, 2012).

MARY J. HENOLD is the author of *Catholic and Feminist: The Surprising History of the American Catholic Feminist Movement* (UNC Press, 2008). She received her PhD in American History from the University of Rochester in 2003 and taught for two years at Valparaiso University as a Lilly Post-Doctoral Fellow in the Humanities and Arts. Henold is currently an associate professor of history at Roanoke College.

WILLIAM ISSEL is a professor emeritus of history at San Francisco State University and visiting professor of history at Mills College. His books include *Social Change in the United States, 1945–1983* (Schoken, 1985); *"For Both Cross and Flag": Catholic Action, Anti-Catholicism, and National Security Politics in World War II San Francisco* (Temple University Press, 2009); and *Church and State in the City: Catholics and Politics in 20th-Century San Francisco* (Temple University Press, 2013). He was coeditor of the book series The Contemporary USA for Palgrave Macmillan. His articles concerning religion, ethnicity, and politics in the American West have appeared in the periodicals *Journal of Urban History, Journal of Church and State, U.S. Catholic Historian*, and *American Catholic Studies* and in three anthologies, *A Rosary of Hidden Voices: Catholicism in the American West, California Jews*, and *American Labor and the Cold War*.

ANDREW S. MOORE is associate professor of history at Saint Anselm College in Manchester, New Hampshire. He earned a bachelor's degree from the University of the South and a PhD from the University of Florida, Gainesville. He is the author of *The South's Tolerable Alien: Roman Catholics in Alabama and Georgia, 1945–1970* (Baton Rouge: Louisiana State University Press, 2007), as well as articles in the *Journal of Church and State*, the *Journal of Southern Religion*, and the *Georgia Historical Quarterly*, among others. He is currently at work on a biography of former President Jimmy Carter.

SAMUEL J. THOMAS is professor emeritus in the Department of History at Michigan State University in East Lansing, Michigan, where he was on the faculty from 1966 to 2011. He taught courses in Western European and American intellectual, cultural, political, and religious history. The recipient of several competitive research grants, he has presented numerous conference papers and authored many scholarly essays, chiefly in nineteenth- and twentieth-century American Catholic history. His articles have appeared in journals such as *The Catholic Historical Review, American Catholic Studies, Journal of Church and State, International Journal of Women's Studies*, the *U.S. Catholic Historian*, and *Religion and American Culture: A Journal of Interpretation*.

Index

CATHOLIC PRACTICE IN NORTH AMERICA

James T. Fisher and Margaret M. McGuinness (eds.), *The Catholic Studies Reader*

Jeremy Bonner, Christopher D. Denny, and Mary Beth Fraser Connolly (eds.), *Empowering the People of God: Catholic Action before and after Vatican II*